KALI ARTOGRAPHER

INTRODUCTION BY MATT TYRNAUER

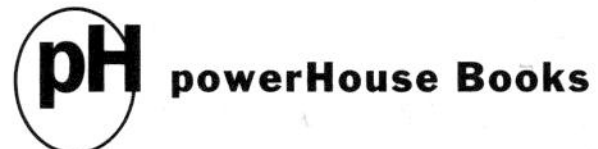

pH powerHouse Books

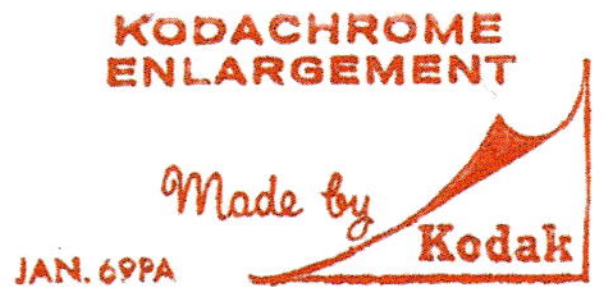

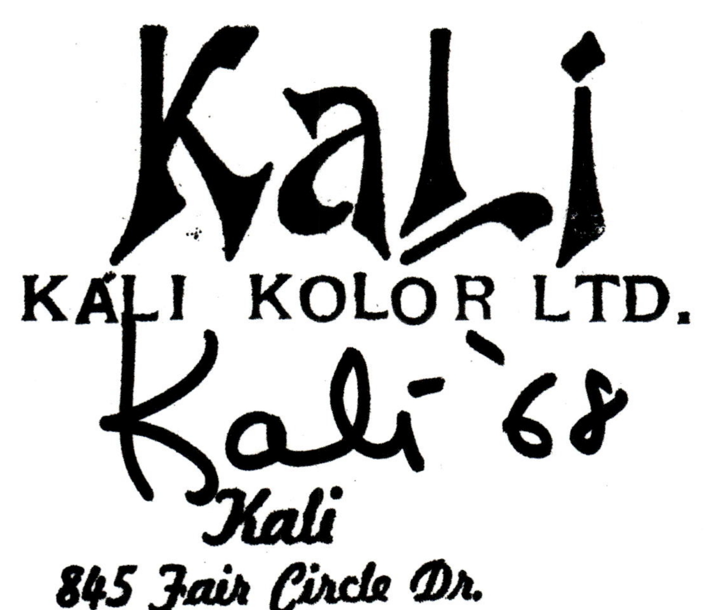

KALI KOLOR LTD.
TRADEMARK ∞ ARTOGRAPHY
NO REPRODUCTION WITHOUT
WRITTEN PERMISSION

The 8 black and white jumbo 3¼ x 4¼ cost me under $2.70 (kind
of expensive) but produced fast results. However, my slides were
still in color. I decided to sleep on it--meditate about it, but
not before having some fun shooting from the T V screen, while
watching the all night movies. This is quite easy to do, sitting
approximately 39 inches from the set, and doing double exposures
is quite easy also. My T V is black and white, with an 18"
screen. The important thing is to have your picture as sharp and
contrast as possible.

The next evening, I thought I had figured out the way to print
my color slides, instead of photographing them by projection.
Here are the results of those experiments:

1.   The first thing I did was to read the directions <u>two</u> times
     on both camera and film, to understand clearly the nature
     of the materials I would be using. I would use the BIG SHOT,
     not as a camera, but as my processor, or printing box. I
     used my Bessler enlarger to expose the paper (or Polaroid film)
     as in any printing method, except I used color slides instead
     of negatives, as the no. 7 principal of Polaroid is positive
     image to positive image.

2.   The second step is to take a white mounting card from the box,
     3¼ x 4¼--remove the brown paper and place it on your enlarger
     board, exactly where you will, in total darkness, place your
     film box on top of.

3.   Then take an empty film box and place a white card on top of
     it for focusing.

4.   Next, place your color slide (I used a 35 mm, after trying
     an inner negative) (You could use any size positive in theory)
     into your film holder and focus on the white card that is on
     the top of the empty film box.

5.   Then place your 108 color film into the BIG SHOT camera, as
     per directions. Turn out the room lights, and pull out the
     black paper, as per film directions. Open camera again, and
     finally...

6.   Remove film box, with negative material up towards enlarger
     lens. Place the box over the white card on the enlarger board,
     (You get to the point where you can do this quite easily) and
     do your exposing. My first exposures were as follows: (The
     <u>first nine</u> were done with an inter negative of the slide)

Experiment 1. F16 - ½ sec. exposure, no filter - dev. 60 sec.
     what you do next, after exposing, is this...While still in the
     dark, you open your camera and reinsert the film box into its
     groove, the same position that it is always in. <u>Close the
     camera</u>, being sure the <u>white tabs</u> are on the <u>outside</u>. This
     is quite easy to do with the BIG SHOT, as it is a very simple
     camera to operate, and to get the feel of in the dark.

7   **AN INTRODUCTION** BY MATT TYRNAUER

24   **PORTRAITS AND LANDSCAPES**

134   **KALI'S SECRET ARCHIVE** BY BRIAN WALLIS

142   **POLAROIDS**

190   **OUTER SPACE**

217   **AFTERWORD** BY LEN PRINCE

218   **KALI ARTOGRAPHER** BY NANNETTE MACIEJUNES

222   **IMAGE INDEX**

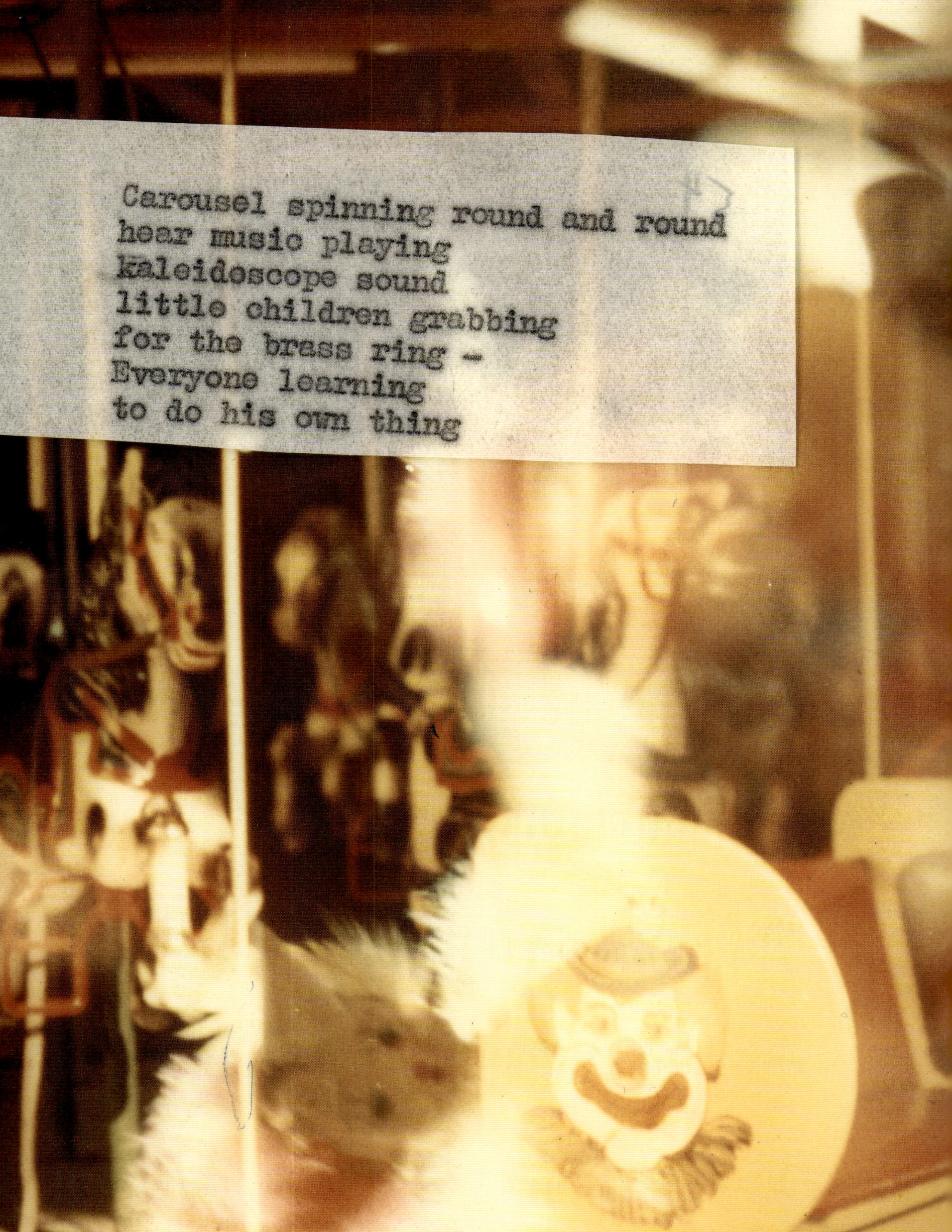

Carousel spinning round and round
hear music playing
kaleidoscope sound
little children grabbing
for the brass ring -
Everyone learning
to do his own thing

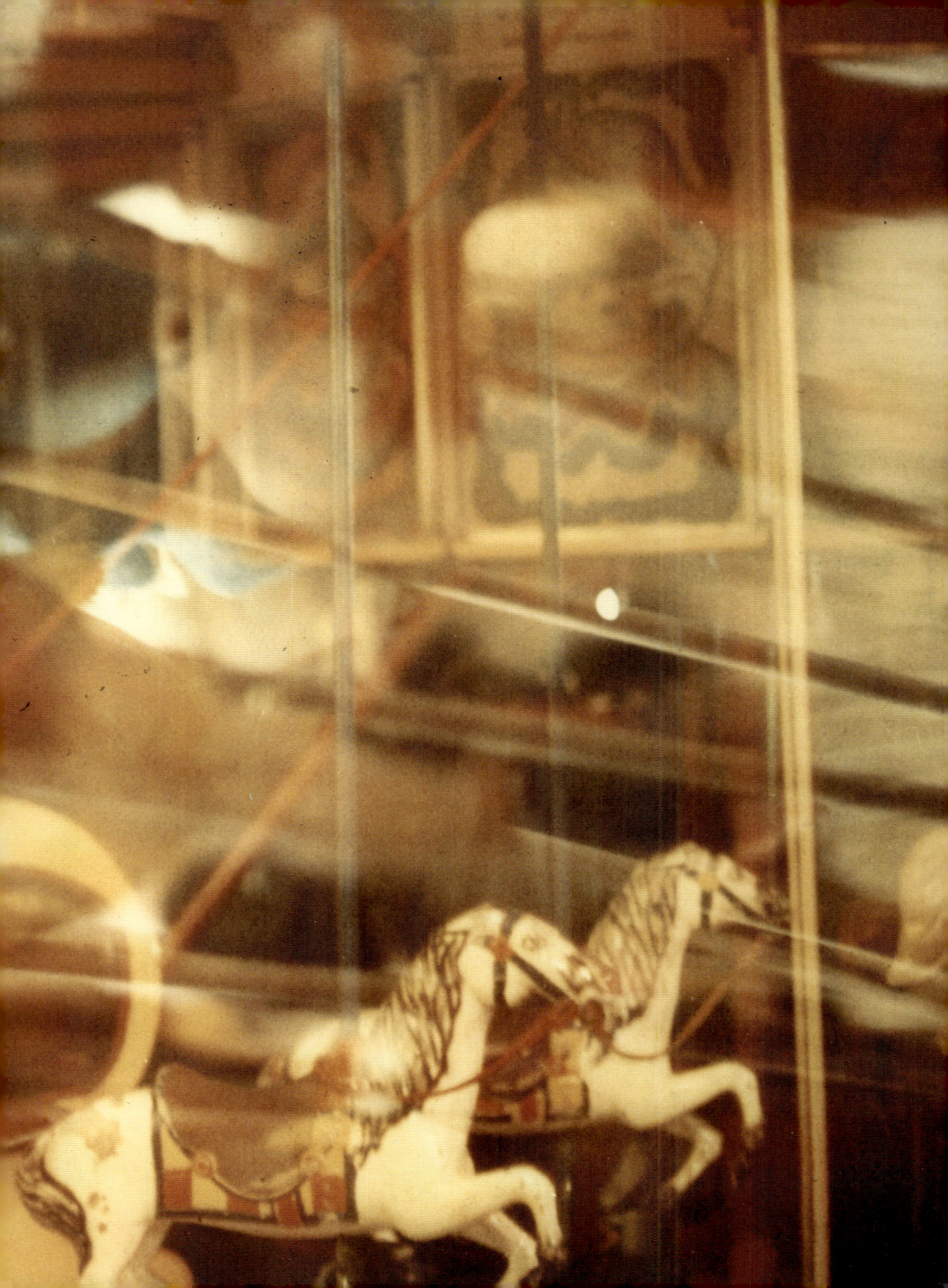

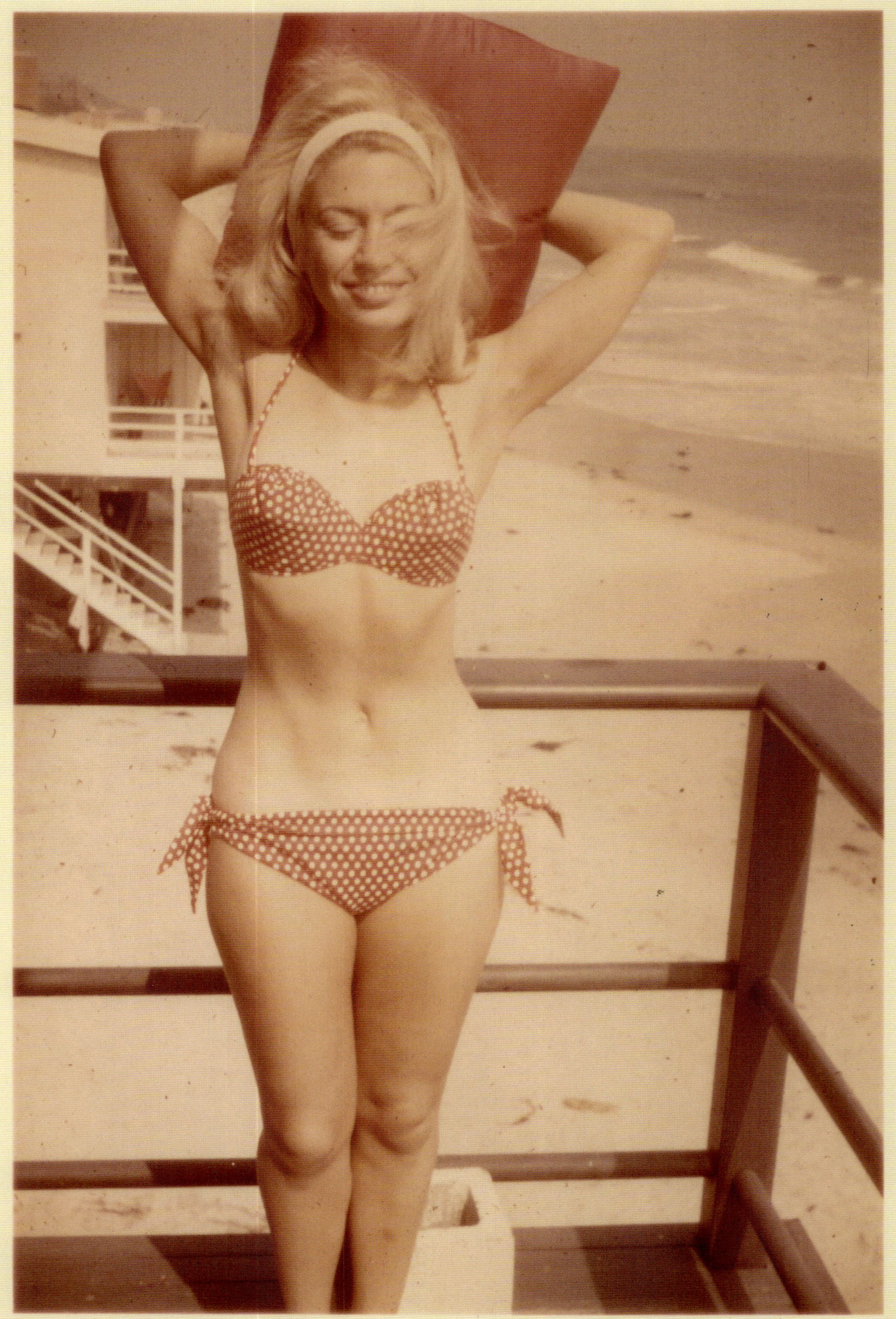

AN INTRODUCTION BY MATT TYRNAUER

A few years back I received an email from Len Prince about a lost trove of photographs. Len and I had met when I was a writer at *Vanity Fair*, and he was one of the magazine's top photographers, a master of light whose work, in its glamour and rigorous classicism, was at times reminiscent of George Hurrell or Cecil Beaton. Len had even taken a few portraits of me, and included some in a monograph of his work. There was backstory I needed to know, Len told me. He'd once been married to Susan Archibald, and while they were divorced in 1987, they were still close, and it had come to pass that Susan's mother, Joan, was an avid and—according to Len—shockingly original photographer. Joan Archibald, who signed her photographs "Kali," had died in January of 2019, and when Susan was cleaning out the house in Pacific Palisades, she'd stumbled upon hundreds upon hundreds of prints, negatives, and Polaroids. The work was so powerful that Len said he went down a curatorial rabbit hole from which he was just emerging.

Susan had shipped him the whole trove to his farm house in upstate New York. And then for two full years, Len commenced sorting, conserving and obsessing. There was, he told me, a book in this lost archive, and he wanted me to see the draft of the layout, which had been done by the venerable graphic designer Sam Shahid. A few days later, the very heavy printout of the preliminary layout arrived in a large box from Shahid's Manhattan studio. I remember cutting open the box, and thinking to myself, "These guys have really gone overboard. *Three volumes?* On a photographer in the Pacific Palisades no one ever heard of? Sam Shahid has gone down the rabbit hole, too!"

I started to turn pages.

I was soon in the rabbit hole.

The purpose of Len's getting in touch was to ask me to write an introduction to the book that would bring Kali's work to the world. When I began paging through Sam's drafts of the volumes, skepticism fell away. I soon became enveloped by the world of Kali—effectively peering into an eerie lost era of Los Angeles, Malibu, and greater California of the 1960s and '70s—the period right before my own Los Angeles youth. I was a convert.

Sam had divided Kali's work into three separate volumes, designed to fit into an elegant cloth slipcase. This was the perfect conceit, as Kali's work falls very neatly into three genres: "Portraits and Landscapes," which can be thought of as the High Kali period, where she was, as you will read below, innovating with developing processes, colorization, and formatting "Polaroids," largely from the same period, but for Kali, another experimental medium in which she augmented the developing process to create unique effects; and "Outer Space," which can be thought of as Late Kali, photos made when she was older, and a shut-in at her Pacific Palisades house, obsessed by other-worldly objects viewed and photographed through closed circuit security monitors. A fourth volume, containing my original introduction, (reprised here in shorter form), and photos of the artist and ephemera from her salad days was added, after I went a bit hog wild with my assessment of Joan Archibald's work as Kali.

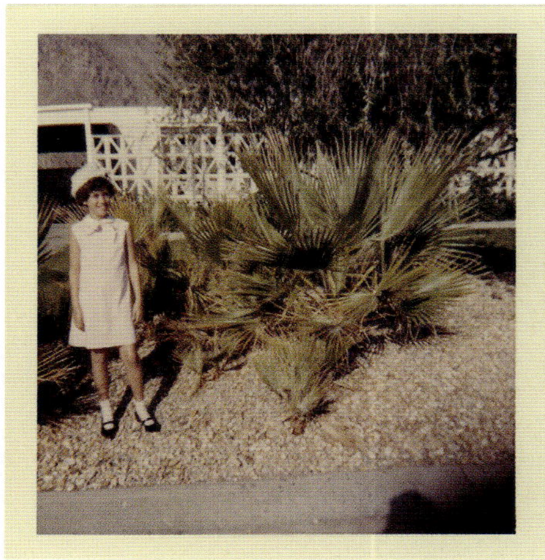 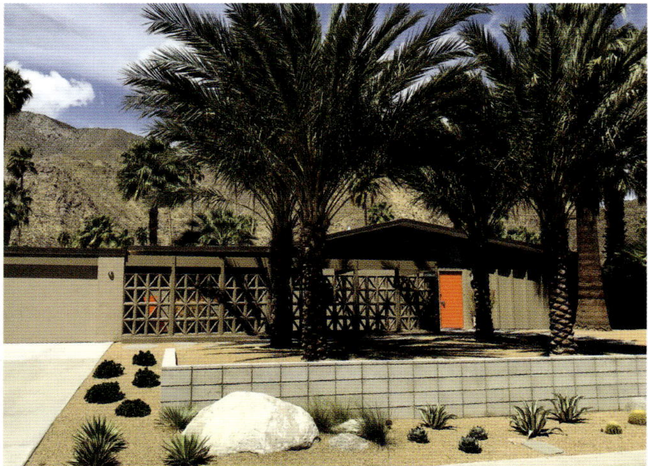

By the time I arrived at the final page of the original layouts, I felt as if I had taken a Proustian journey back to the slightly frightening Elysium of late-mid-century in the place that, at about that time, came to be called Cali: the province marked in everyone's minds by the Manson murders, Janice Joplin's death, and the contrasting governorships of Ronald Reagan and Jerry Brown. (To what extent, whole or partial, Archibald meant to pay homage to the nickname of her adopted state and or the Hindu goddess of time, doomsday, and death, will never be known.) It was actually a trip, as they used to say in that period, without a trace of irony. And what a gift and great good luck to have had Susan Archibald discover these photos and to have delivered them to the loving, curatorial hands of Len Prince, who entrusted the gifted Sam Shahid to enshrine them so perfectly in book form. As you will read here, this is how Kali affected me. What you will learn over subsequent pages is how she will affect you.

I moved recently to a house in a canyon in Los Angeles, which is similar in its situation to the house in which I grew up in a neighboring foothill section of the city. Like the house my parents had, this property has views onto nearby canyon ridges. It is all quite picturesque in these canyons—as well as voyeuristic—because of views overlooking the backs of other canyon homes, framed by tall, non-indigenous trees. In the distance—after dusk—there are city lights; in the foreground, coyotes. Overhead, in the L.A. canyons, with surprising frequency, there is the thunder of police helicopters. As I have not lived in an L.A. canyon for some years, the effect of returning is Proustian; being back above the city I live in, where I am from, now half-remembering, half experiencing anew the microclimate of these hills. The marine layer, the same botanical perfumes wafting seasonally—orange blossom; then night-blooming jasmine; then frangipani; then sage—over the driveway, or the pool decks, which retain, to the touch of bare feet, the afternoon heat.

This ridge, with this view and attendant memories, is an especially good perch to be on as I peruse the photos in this book you are about to explore. The photos of Joan Archibald—or Kali, as she styled herself in about 1964— evoke a deep feeling, or better yet, realization of Los Angeles, or Greater Los Angeles, or the Southland, as local TV news talent for some reason have long insisted on calling it. The photos in these volumes, for the most part, came from a similar, timelessly picturesque canyon; they were developed in makeshift darkrooms. Those that didn't come from the garage darkroom in the nearby canyon came from the companion terrain of the L.A. canyon-dweller: The Desert, developed in a master bath darkroom in Palm Springs, to be specific. Canyon and desert were the main environments of Kali, who, for the explosively productive years of her life—from the mid 1960s to the mid 2000s—was a secretive and therefore obscure master of the visual arts, hidden among the mostly conventional West L.A. housewives of her generation; the woody station wagon-driving carpool moms and the occasional white Mercedes-driving grande dames, indigenous to the Southland canyons and the stylish desert cities of the 1960s and 1970s. Joan Archibald—or Kali, in the darkroom—turns out to have been one the great chroniclers, and interpreters, of the waning 20th century years of her adopted hometown; a secret historian of the era we now know mostly from the heavily marketed triumphs of The Beach Boys, The Doors, Joni Mitchell, Joan Didion, and *Shampoo.*

What you have in front of you is, in effect, a discovered memoir; an interior monologue in visual form. And, while thoroughly personal, the images—for the most part never-before-seen, and maybe never intended to be seen—will stir up memories and emotions for anyone who got even a peek at those hazy, dazed years of psychedelic, hippie, haywire L.A.—a place virtually indescribable to anyone who turned up here any time after the dawn of the '80s, when the city simultaneously cleaned up its air, got good restaurants, and the freeways were no longer commonly referred to by their more romantic, given names: the Santa Ana, the Ventura, the Hollywood.

———————————

Kali was born Joan Marie Yarusso in 1932, in Islip, New York. She married Bob Archibald, a trumpet player. He was apparently on the road a lot. Joan Archibald was divorced by the age of 30, and, according to her daughter, Susan, got in a car and headed across the country. She ended up in the Malibu of 1962. With her good looks and some allure, she became a fixture at the beach parties of the era, which extended from house to house, and rolled from orange-tinted sunset into the gray Malibu dawn.

From an unedited transcript of a conversation with Susan Archibald, regarding her recollections from this period:

Well, my mom had two children and she needed to get away, and my brother and me, we went to boarding school; my mom needed to expand herself, whatever she was searching for, and she landed in Malibu…She was hobnobbing with Richard Chamberlain, and I have a couple snapshots of him with my mom; she fit right in because she was a stunner. So my mom rented a place, and then she was in real estate for a minute, and then she needed to find a place, through my grandmother's guidance (because my grandmother was the matriarch of the family), and she told my mother that Malibu was not a place for her kids. After that, my mother went to Palm Springs and she bought Sandra Dee and Bobby Darin's house, and you know, you can already feel my mom is starting to break free. Frank Sinatra wanted to date my mom, but my mom wanted nothing to do with him.

———————————

845 FAIR CIRCLE DRIVE, IN PALM SPRINGS—FORMER HOME OF SANDRA DEE AND BOBBY DARIN, reads the listing on a Pinterest page from a Google search. No more information. No mention of its more recent occupant: Kali.

The swimming pool in the back was probably what mattered most to Kali when she lived there, as she used it as a giant wash for photographic prints.

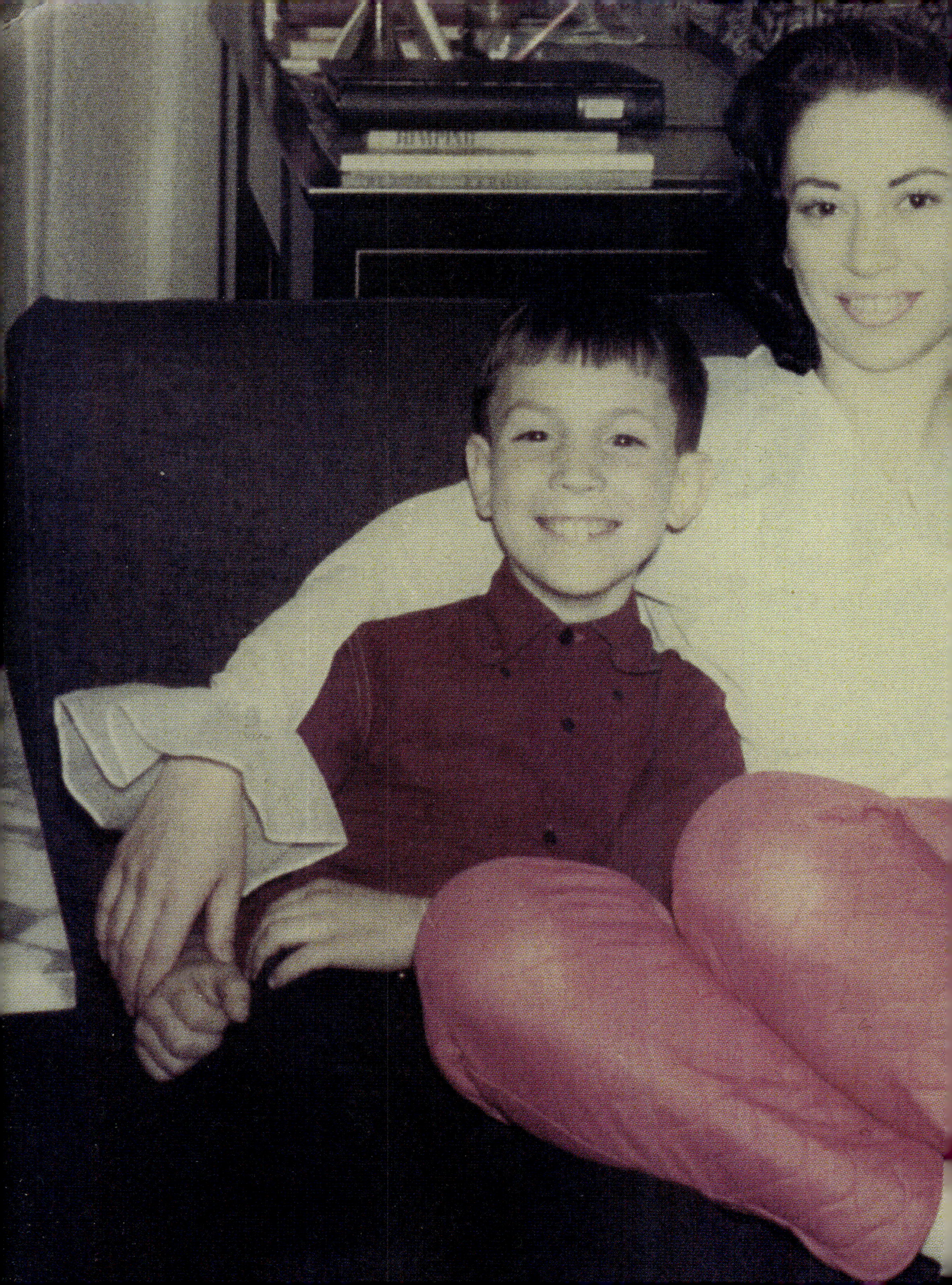

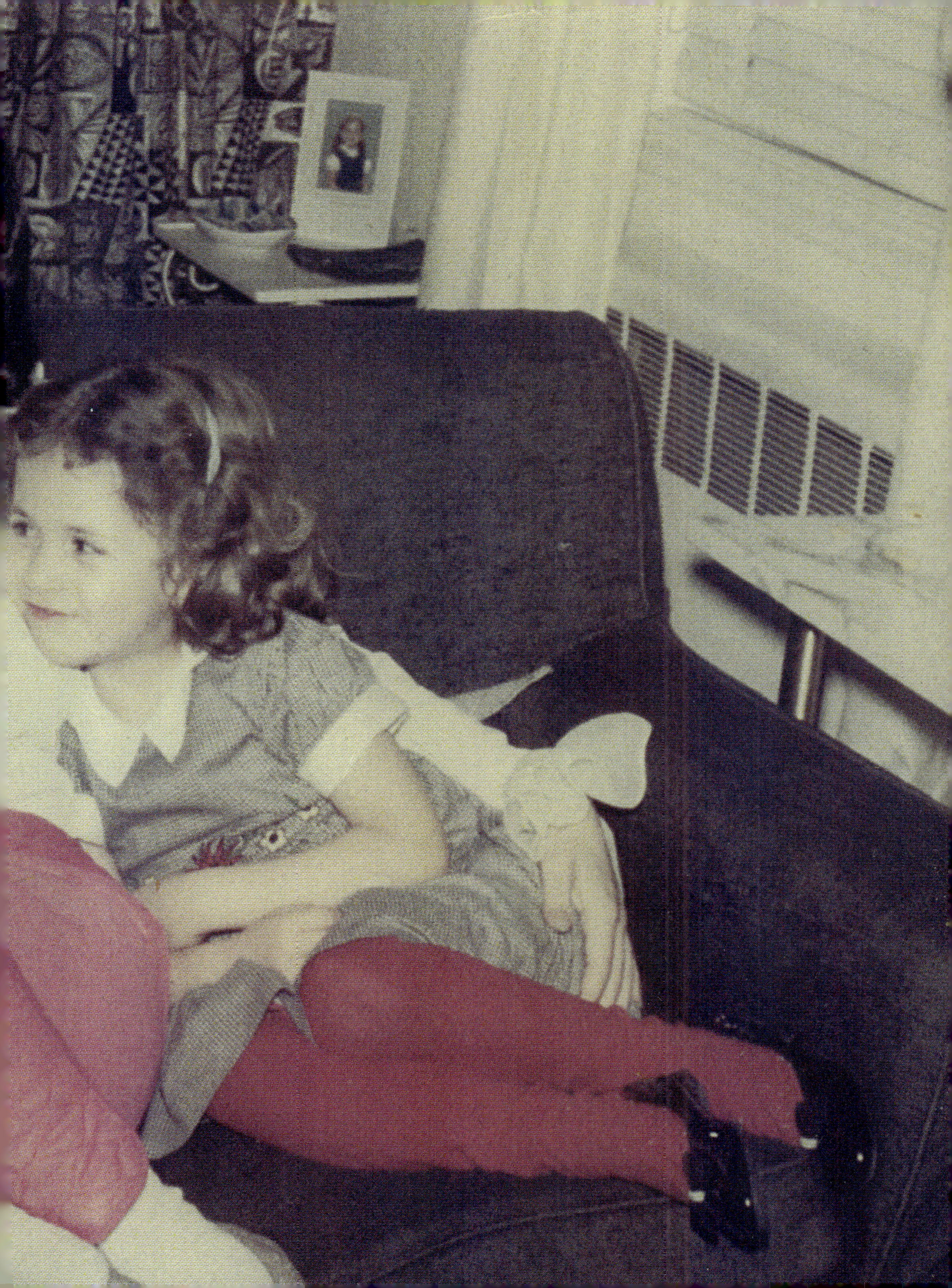

From the Susan Archibald transcript:

She would let the chlorine go down to ground zero. I would know that I wasn't going to be swimming that day in the pool. There would be a ton of prints floating around in the pool when I woke up and she would be heaving these massive prints, some of them on rolls, and she'd be rinsing them and drying them in the sun, I mean like the old fashioned way in the '60s and '70s; she was washing the prints and doing her printing in her master bathroom on Fair Circle Drive and then she would get them dry and then start to paint them with Krylon spray paint, she would use sand, she would use everything unconventional known to man.

Kali took photography classes at The College of the Desert, in Palm Desert, down Fred Warring Drive from Palm Springs. But no one knows exactly when and how her style developed. She had, at one time, been interested in painting. She painted wine bottles. Only one of those wine bottles survived a flood and break-ins at the house on Fair Circle Drive. The urge to paint was never sublimated by the consuming, seemingly manic, foray into photography. An improvised dark room in the master bath in the Palm Springs house—where Sandra Dee put on her face and Bobby Darin greased his pompadour—started churning out sixteen-by-twenty-inch black-and-white prints on silver Portriga paper, semi-gloss or canvas-textured, all with rough edges. Many of them multiple exposures. Then, after a stop bath in Sandra Dee's Roman tub, the prints were floated in the pool; the water of the pool would become colored with Dr. Ph. Martin inks, for tints; spray developer may be applied, which could create abstraction; swirling prints in the uncleaned pool caught bugs and desert sand on the surface for texture. The prints were sun dried on the pool deck, where more sand or bugs may have stuck to them.

After this process, the prints ceased to be simply photography. They were impressionistic or expressionistic works. They seemed to have no category, which prompted Kali to trademark her work "Artography" (unrecorded at this point). This went along with the name change to Kali (probably in 1964), and a recorded copyright, Kali Kolor Ltd. The back of the works were stamped with a wood cut-style "Kali" logo. Its design shrieks "psychedelic era." The name Kali, for Joan Archibald of Islip, Long Island, is a kind of rebranding inspiration rivaling Rock Hudson for Roy Harold Scherer, Jr., or, for that matter, Sandra Dee for Alexandra Zuck.

Her portrait and landscape subjects, and her treatment of these images, depict a serial acid trip—one she may or may not, in fact, have been on—articulated as well as anyone who ever made the attempt. Certain characters recur: Debbie, classic beauty; Susan, model, daughter; Mary, Renaissance visage; Kali, artist on the edge; Paul in the Speedo, satellite of love.

Later on, when Polaroid film became the rage, she added a new step to her process. She would copy the swimming pool-processed prints in slide form, then project them with her Bessler enlarger and shoot the projected images with a Polaroid camera. On occasion she would layer little pieces of transparencies over the slide, adding bridges, water, flowers, arabesques, etc.

A few days into looking at the images in the Portraits and Landscapes volume, I thought I should re-read Joan Didion's *Play It As It Lays*, as I could not get what I remembered from it out of my head. As I was reading it, and,

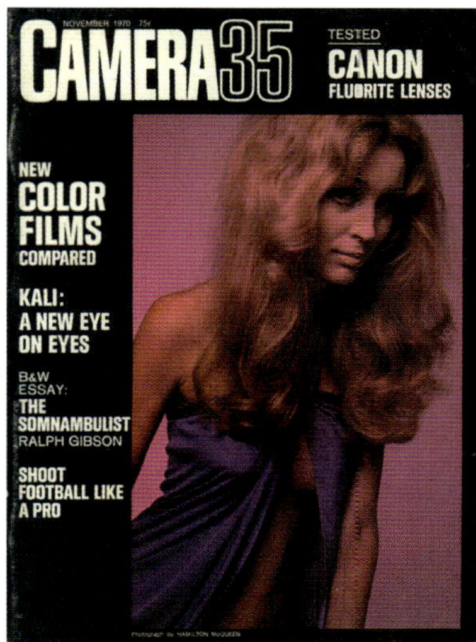

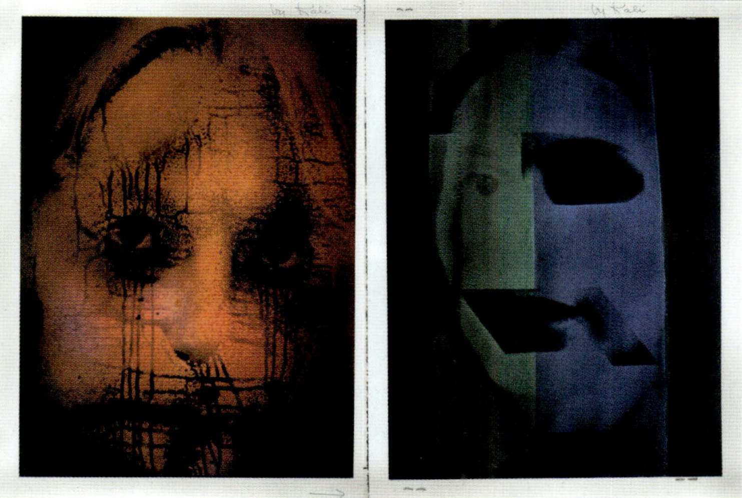

alternately, staring at the b ack-and-white photo of the stacked freeway overpasses, and, a few pages later, the attractive couple not quite connecting, with an overlaid exposure of a menacing, atomic age motherboard of some sort, it seemed to me that the text of *Play It As It Lays* could be poured in next to these images and somehow match up perfectly. Both of the wor‹s capture the disquieting potential for the devastating mood which relentlessly fair-skied Southern California can breed—a creeping ennui verging into madness, which both Joan Didion and Joan Archibald's work captures. They each evoke looming cataclysm; alienation underneath facades of beauty; potential loss of control in the form of Santa Ana wind, earthquake, fire, or, just possibly, in these canyons and the desert, rattlesnake.

In the November 1970 edition of *Camera 35* magazine, there was the only article ever published on the work of Kali. The article is called "Eyes By Kali," and it ran with some of her photos focusing on young people's eyes, the magazine's editors clearly at pains to pick a theme from her voluminous portfolio. "Kali is…a young woman who lives in Palm Springs, California, and creates painterly pictures for a living," reads the text. "Her subjects range from her teenage daughter to the family cat to anything and everything that she might encounter with her camera…Kali feels her Artography (a word she coined and has since copyrighted) is a category of visual communication complete unto itself…No argument there. They offer physical texture and surface modulations that are beyond the capabilities of mere machines. In fact, there is not a way to reproduce one of her images; as a resu t each of them is an original. Which, of course, enables her to sell them in galleries, not as photographs that can be run off in multiples, but as unique works of art."

There might have been, as *Camera 35* suggests, some Artography sold. Susan suggests that Kali sometimes sent her work to the Transworld Feature Syndicate, a now-defunct photo agency. There are no records of any sales. There was only one known gallery show of Kali's work, which was, according to Susan, in Monterey in the early '70s. "Ansel Adams stopped by and he saw my mother's work and was like, 'Wow, who is this persor?' Ansel thought something of my mother's work in the day; I believe he lived in Monterey at the time." Mostly, the hundreds of prints were tossed into storage cabinets and large, white, hard-shell American Tourister suitcases, never to be seen until now.

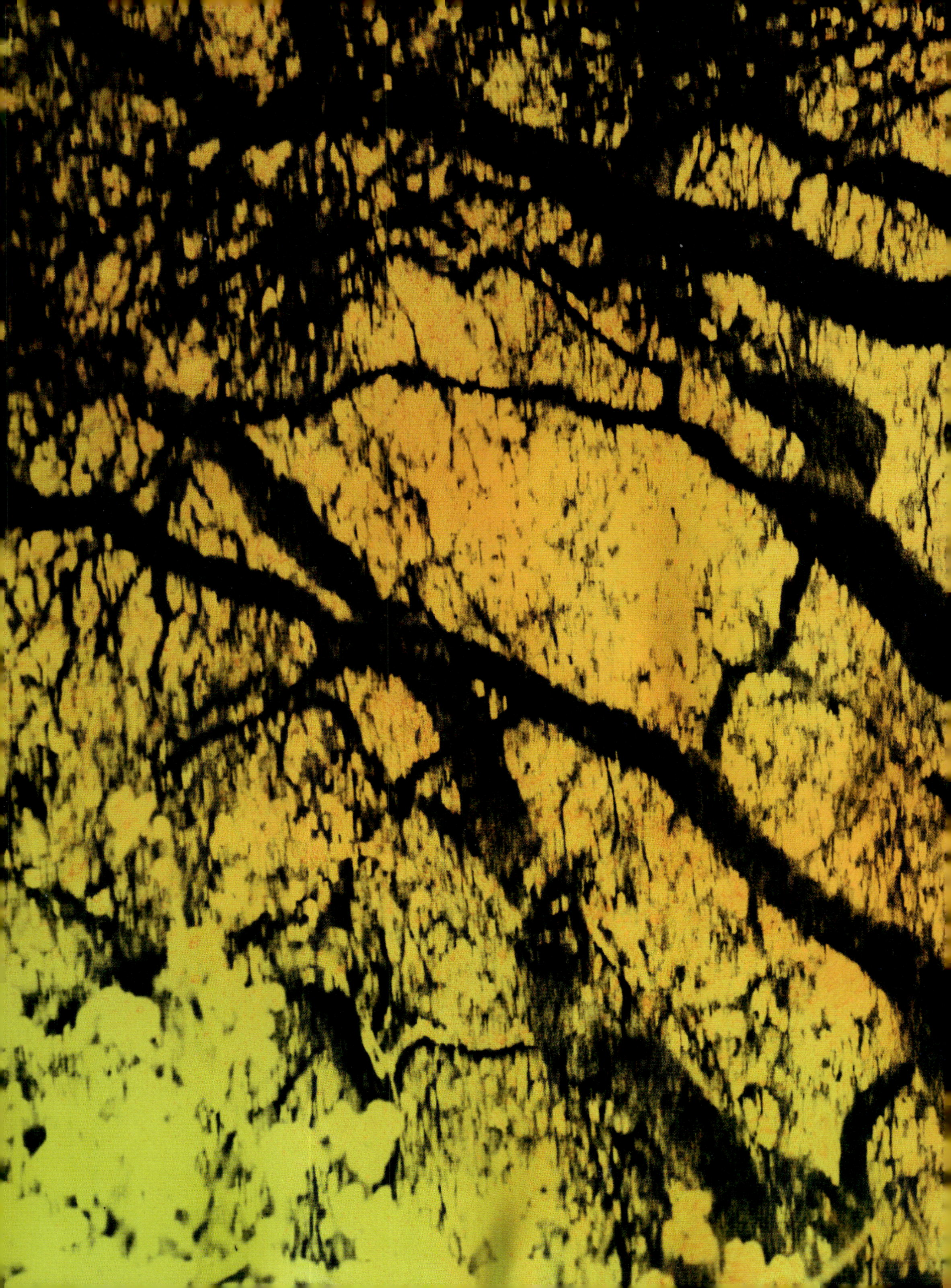

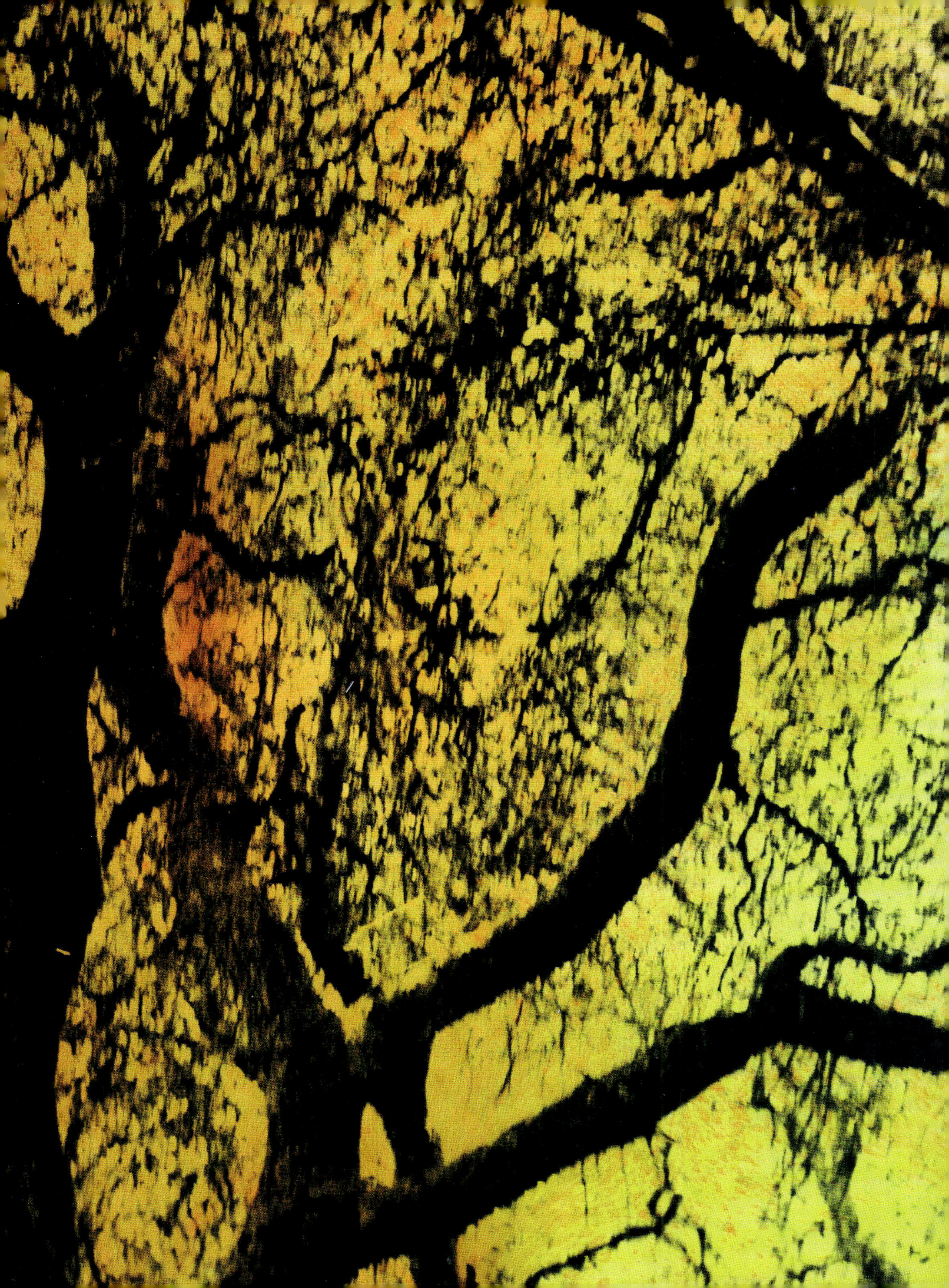

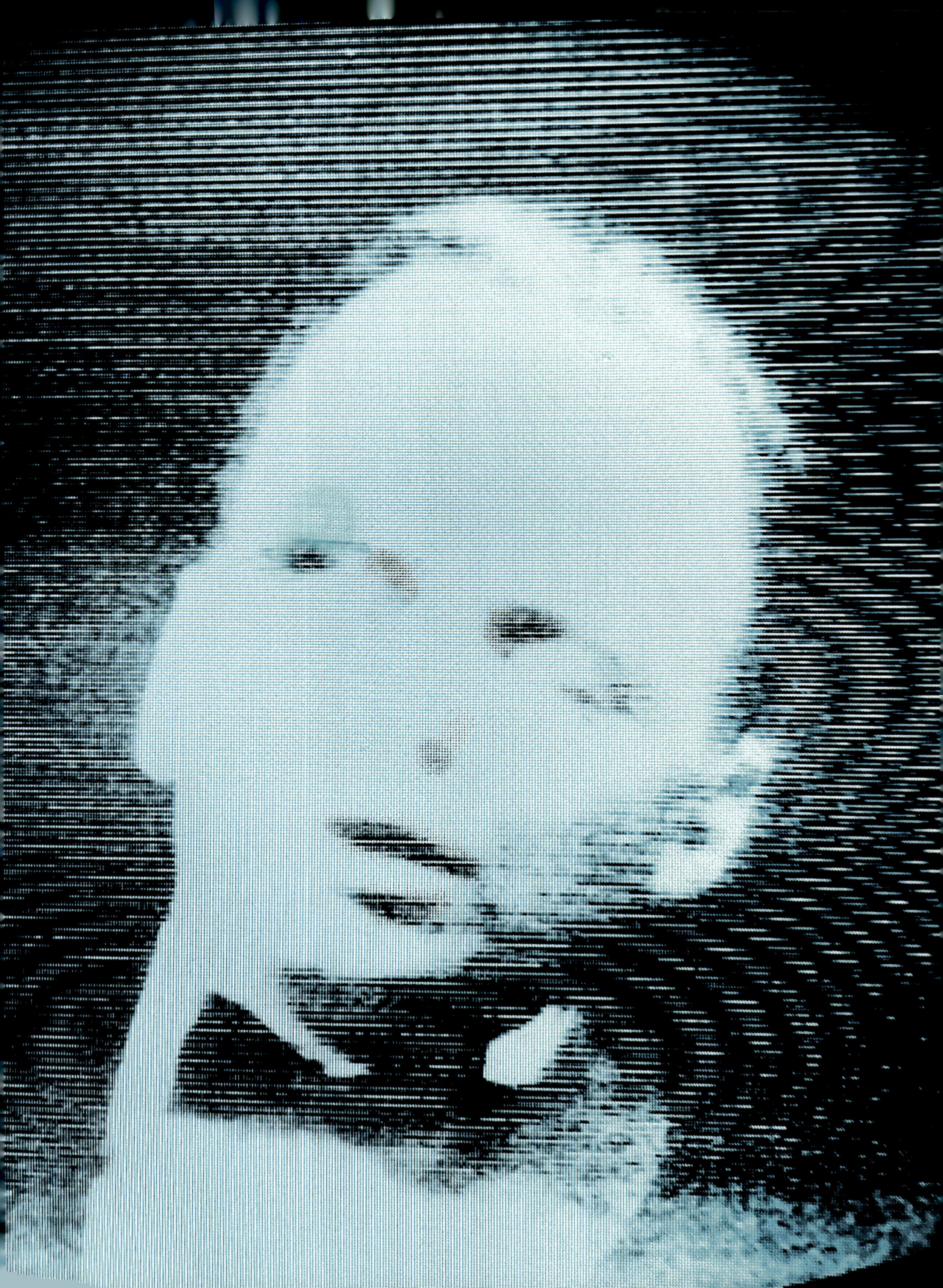

From the Susan Archibald transcript:

It started in Palm Springs which is pretty weird. In the late '60s, my mom would take my brother and me out in her '62 Studebaker and all of a sudden she would see something like going over a power line, and at that time from Palm Springs to Indio, California wasn't that built up, so it was very dark going to Indio, and my mother would see these sightings and then she'd go home and call whomever. The airport, whoever would listen to her. And they basically shunned her out: they were trying to shut her up. But my mother, I remember her drawing these crazy drawings. Circular and really weird. And they never believed my mom and they shut her up.

In 1973, Kali married Karl Davis, Jr., a lawyer. They met in Palm Springs and lived together at his house at 16900 Enchanted Place, in the canyons of the Pacific Palisades, just south of Malibu. Kali set up a second darkroom in the garage, and the oval swimming pool in the backyard became the wash tray. Kali continued to take the meticulously kept 1962 Studebaker Gran Turismo Hawk out to Palm Springs, though she no longer frequented the fading nightclubs of the affluent desert colony. It was at Jilly Rizzo's in Palm Springs that Kali snapped her photo of Sinatra performing over a closed circuit monitor, in the safety of the green room. Sinatra used to tell her to slip in the side door of Jilly's, and to watch his show from the green room.

Kali did not stop taking photos, and developing them. As Karl had money, there was no imperative to sell Artography, but the dark rooms were still active—especially in the Pacific Palisades, where, after Karl died in 2000, Kali became a quasi-shut in. "She always loved animals," says Susan. "When Karl died she started feeding raccoons and pumas in her yard. She had six or eight infrared cameras in the back of the Palisades house."

———————————

The UFOs, Susan believes, had been following her mother for years in both barren Indio County and in the Palisades canyon. There was an uptick in the sightings after Karl died.

From the Susan Archibald transcript:

Orbs or orbies, she called them, and my mother started documenting them with the film she was shooting on the infrared feeds in the Pacific Palisades house. She was doing Polaroids of these images which were outstanding. She would call me up and say, "Susan you need to get up here right now!" I lived eight hours away.

Most of the film of the orbs was never processed. Kali recorded, obsessively, the appearance of the flashes and unidentified images in her closed circuit monitors, sketched them, and made notes, logging the time codes in her journal and on the bottom of Polaroids. The unprocessed film was discovered in a flight bag by Susan in 16900 Enchanted Circle. It was recently processed, and selections appear here in Outer Space. Approximately 500 more unprocessed rolls were mistakenly thrown out by a cleaner. The time codes in the journals, matched with the time codes from the infrared monitors on the processed film, give an immediacy, and insight into Kali's late nights in the canyon house, in blue lit rooms: a Polaroid of the infrared screen for camera 4 is labeled in pen: "01.11.14 4/23/2004 ET-LANDED-POOL CAM 4": its corresponding journal page is a sketch of what Kali saw on camera 4: "A SOLID WHITE GLOWING WINGED FLYING CREATURE THIS ONE LOOKS LIKE ALL WINGS AND NO LEGS AS ON [PAGE] 153 BUT LEGS OR EXTENSIONS COULD BE PULLED IN FOR FLIGHT. DRAWING CAN'T DO IT JUSTICE."

The journals are extensive. Kali frequently contacted the FBI and the Air Force to report sightings. They paid no attention. She continued to make detailed records for years.

In 2017, suffering from Parkinson's and memory loss, Kali was found wandering in the canyon near her house, 16900 Enchanted Place. She was picked up by authorities, and placed in a public assisted living facility. Eventually, Susan was contacted, and she was moved to a private nursing home.

As the house was being cleared of her belongings, all of the photos in these volumes were discovered, amounting to a major discovery of an almost-lost oeuvre from a genre-defining artist.

On January 14, 2019, Kali died from complications of Parkinson's disease. She was 87.

Since the discovery of the photographs of Vivian Maier, and the posthumous publication and celebration of her work, the thrilling prospect of finding other unknown or forgotten masters of the art form has more than ever been in the back of many an aesthetes' mind. The particular excitement derives from the utter improbability that there could be complete archives of unsung masters out there, either in attics or the cupboards of hoarder houses or, as was the case with Maier, in a neglected storage unit whose contents were put up for auction. Maier, after her work was posted on a Flickr account, became a viral web sensation, and was quickly appraised to be the equal of Diane Arbus and Robert Frank, her rough contemporaries, both celebrated in their lifetimes; Maier, in the wake of her posthumous fame (boosted by a documentary film, books, galley exhibitions, and a raft of press coverage).

Kali herself seems to be a different kind of rare breed. The record shows that she started to get some recognition for her work, but then retreated. Was she insecure? Distracted? Thrown by a tragic event? Suffering a mental break? Comfortable in her identity as the wife of a prosperous lawyer, who lived in close proximity to Ronald and Nancy Reagan in the Pacific Palisades and in Sandra Dee and Bobby Darin's house in Palm Springs? Or was it the sexism of the times, combined with the lack of seriousness attached to the art of photography? We will never know for sure. But one of the key standards of artistic judgment is the so-called test of time. In that regard, the delayed discovery of Kali's complete works, long shuttered in her scattershot archive, may have been a favor to everyone—and to Kali most of all. Her '60s and '70s work is evocative of its time. Much of it looks like the Age of Aquarius, and if it had been widely known at that time, it may have been judged as dated by the time the go-go '80s had set in. Tie-dye shirts and VW buses were something to snicker at when I was in middle school. Leg warmers, Dolphin shorts and Vuarnets had taken hold. *Hair* seemed to us what *Yankee Doodle Dandy* must have seemed like to our parents. But, by hiding her work, Kali, intentionally or not, avoids any charge that her skill—I'd venture genius—can have been diluted by having the "fashion of the day injected into it to gain wider acceptance," as a critic once defined the main demerit of the test of time standard. We can, as this book proves, better appreciate, and, yes, judge the work of Joan Archibald aka Kali at a distance, and, in what amounts to a catalogue raisonné, better appraise the depth and breadth of her work: the architectural and landscape photography, the portrait work, the high Artography of the hippie era, and, finally what herein is grouped as Outer Space. Viewed all together, it's an astonishing, coherent oeuvre, with marked stylistic shifts and distinct periods. Most of all, it's an utter joy, and the rarest kind of visual feast, not to mention a journey of discovery in multiple dimensions. Kali vs. the test of time. If you are ready, turn the page!

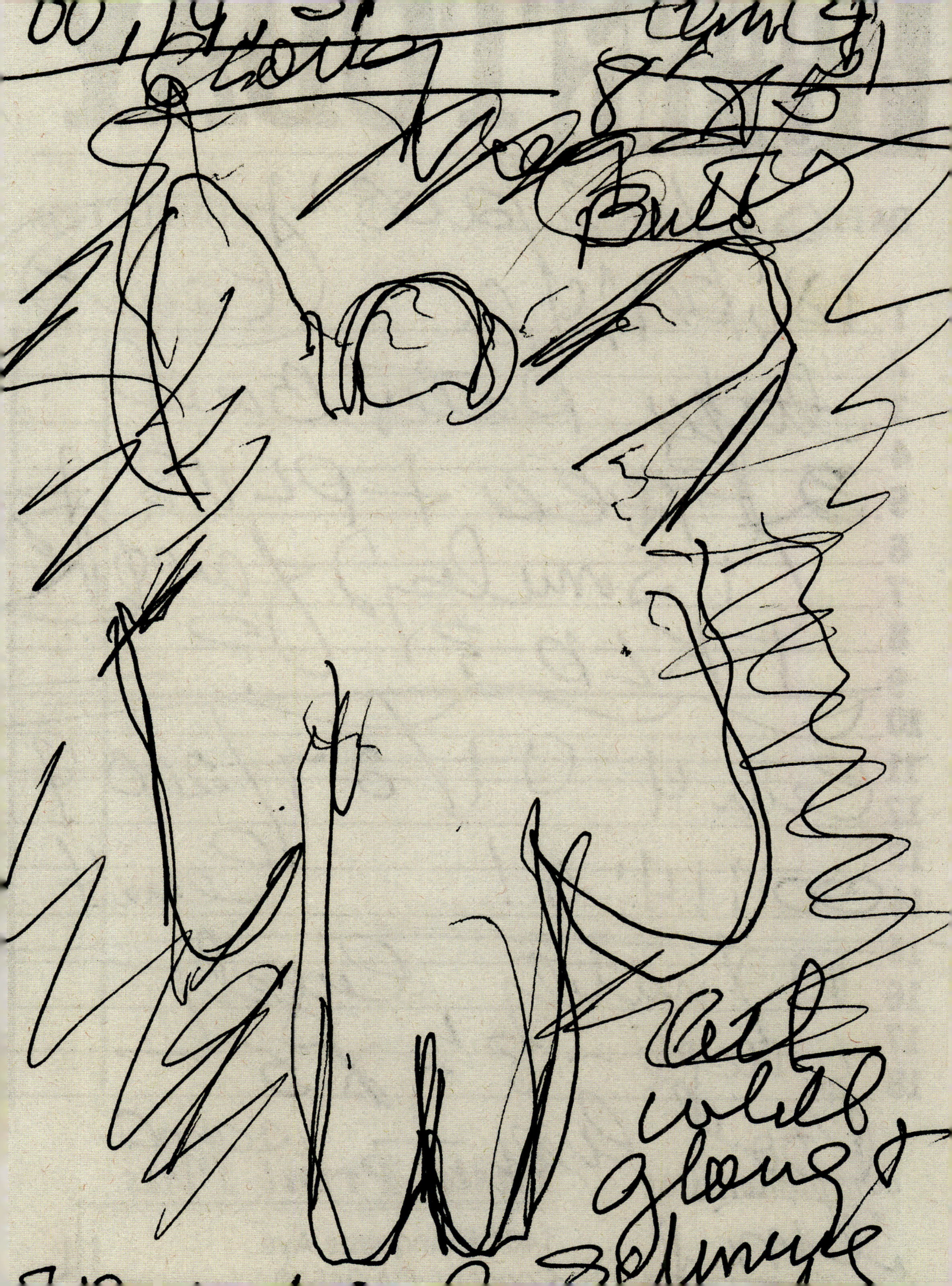

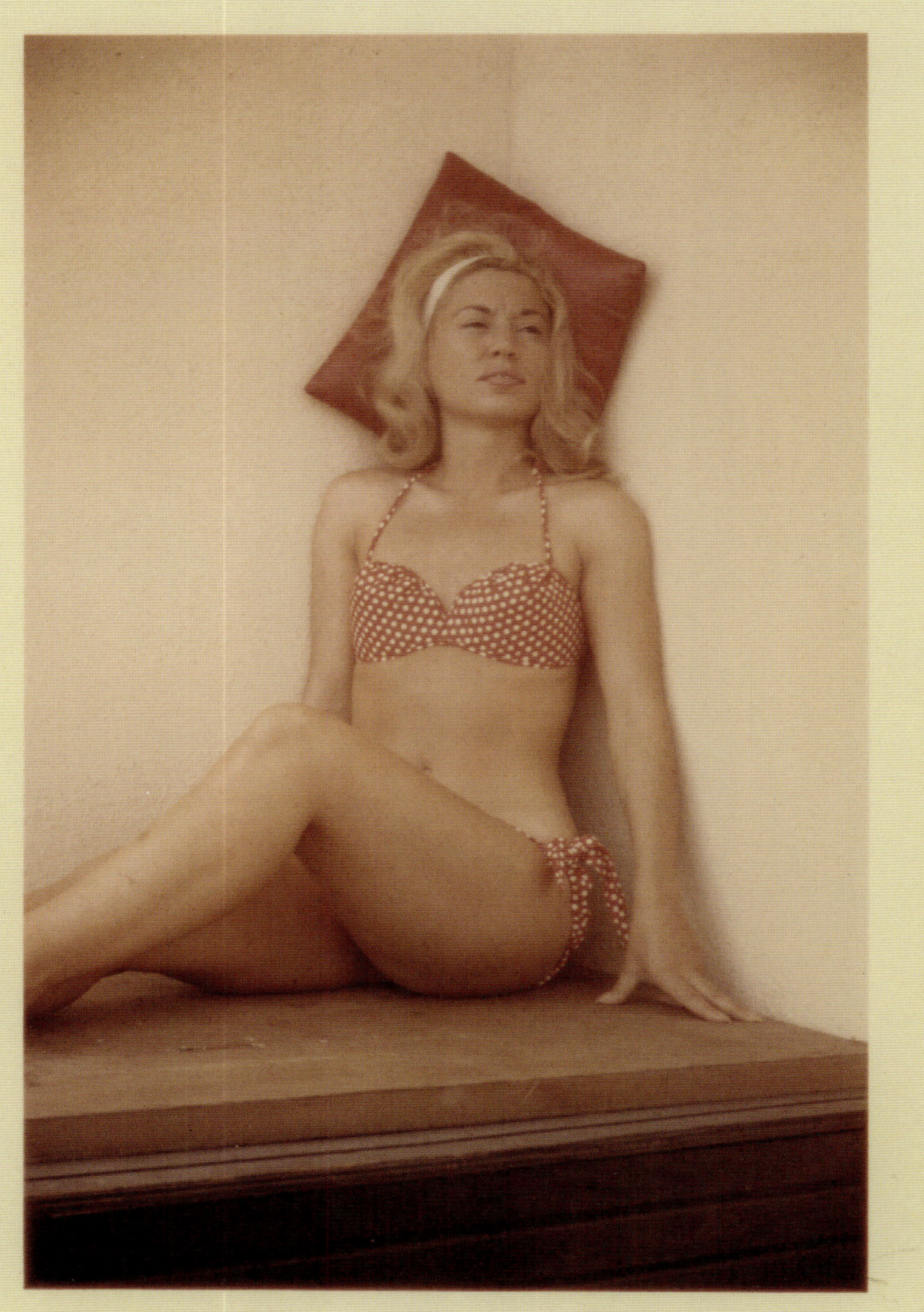

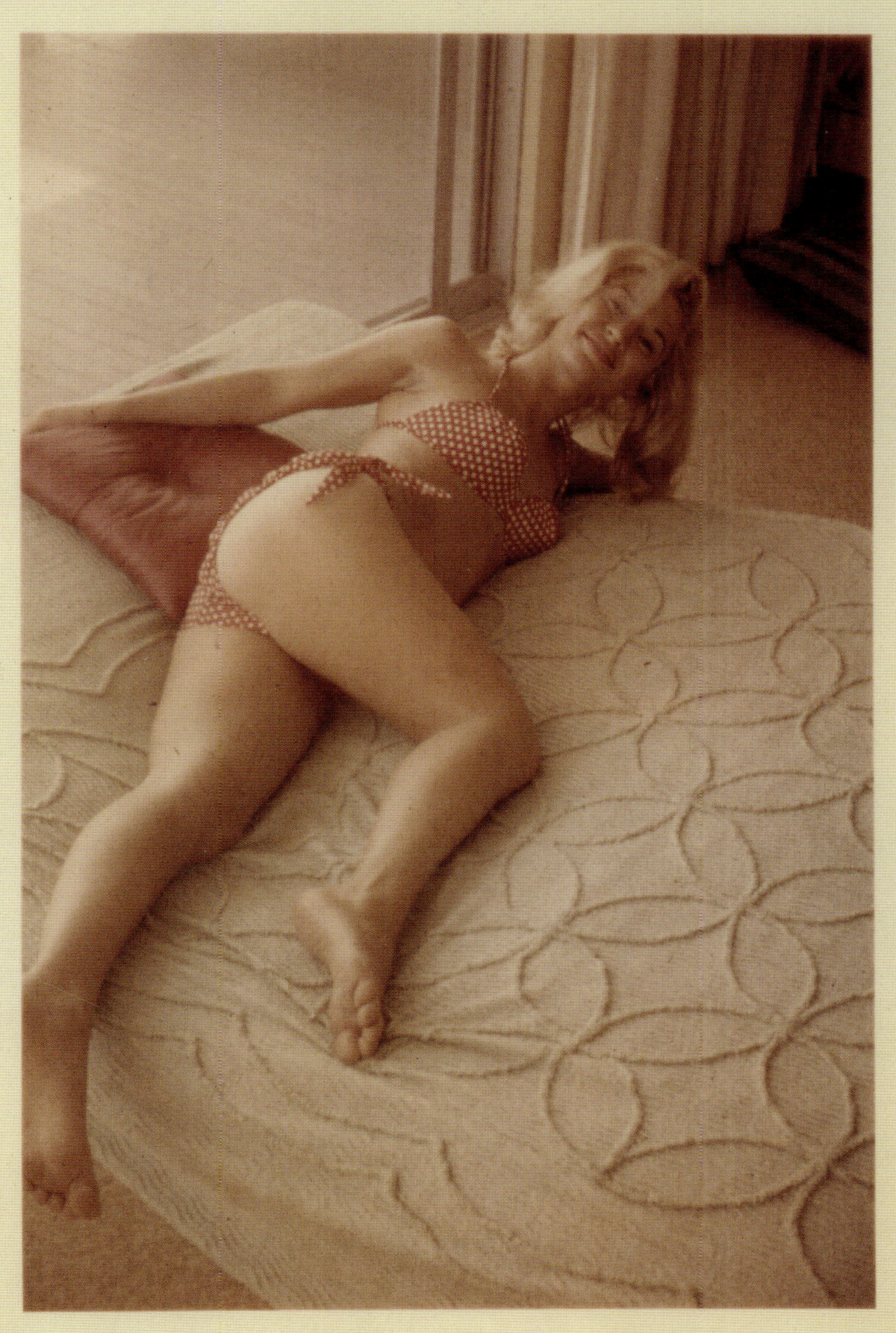

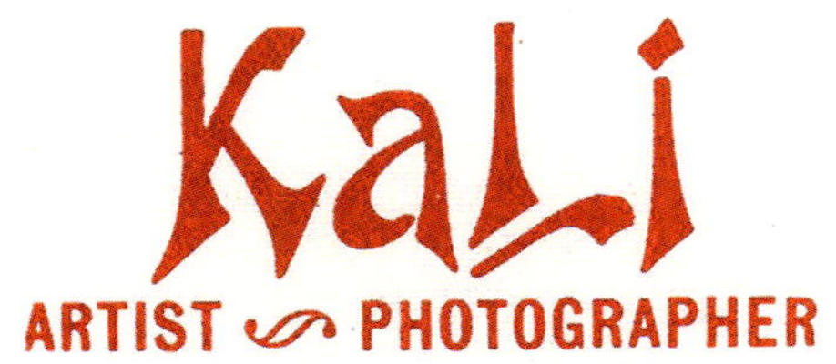

845 fair circle dr.   palm springs, calif. 92262   (714) 325-5265

Page 2. Mr. Ed Meyers

I believe there are no limits in the future for photography
and photographers, and that many new fields will open up. For
me, it is a progressive art form; fast, satisfying and complete.

The Kali Experiment of "Mary, 100 Ways" was based on one, black
and white Tri-x film, 35 mm, shot. It was taken with a Mamiya
Sekor, with a 50 mm lens. It was the last frame on a roll of
36, shot in the park in Carmel, California, very late in the
day. It was taken at about 1/30 of a second, or less, with
the lens wide open.

I did not know the girl, but her face had a haunting, captivating
quality.

I later printed the black and white in 8 x 10s, 11 x 14s and
16 x 20s, and did art work on about ten of these. These original
creations were later re-shot on color slide film (35 mm).

The basic techniques involved were shooting the re-shot artography
slides, when projected, onto Polaroid film, and then double or
triple exposing them with another slide or two.

They were all done at the same time, and rather compulsively,
as once I start a job, or an experiment, I usually work until
I am finished with it, no matter how much time is involved.
Most of the finished versions were in my mind before attempting
to expose the film, as film waste of this type is costly. Also,
for the most part, they are one of a kind originals, and no
copies exist.

My art techniques vary a great deal. I have evolved forty-five
art techniques that were applied to the black and white prints.
I also use most of the creative technical photographic techniques
that are available to photographers everywhere.

I work with a great deal of emphasis on double and triple exposing,

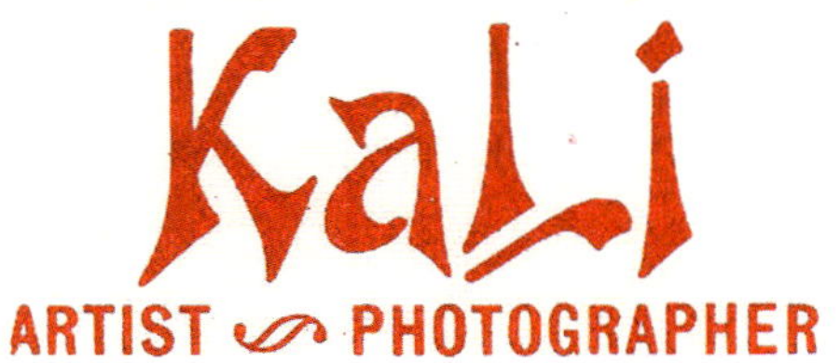

845 fair circle dr.   palm springs, calif. 92262   (714) 325-5265

Page 3. Mr. Ed Meyers

sandwiching, double printing, and use refracted light,
prisms and glass, and multi-image combinations. I also
make my own texture screens.

I work quite fast in every medium, but to me the Polaroid
is the fastest and easiest method that I have ever employed,
and I have enjoyed it immensly!

Please advise me if I can further assist you.

Cordially yours,

(Signed) Kali

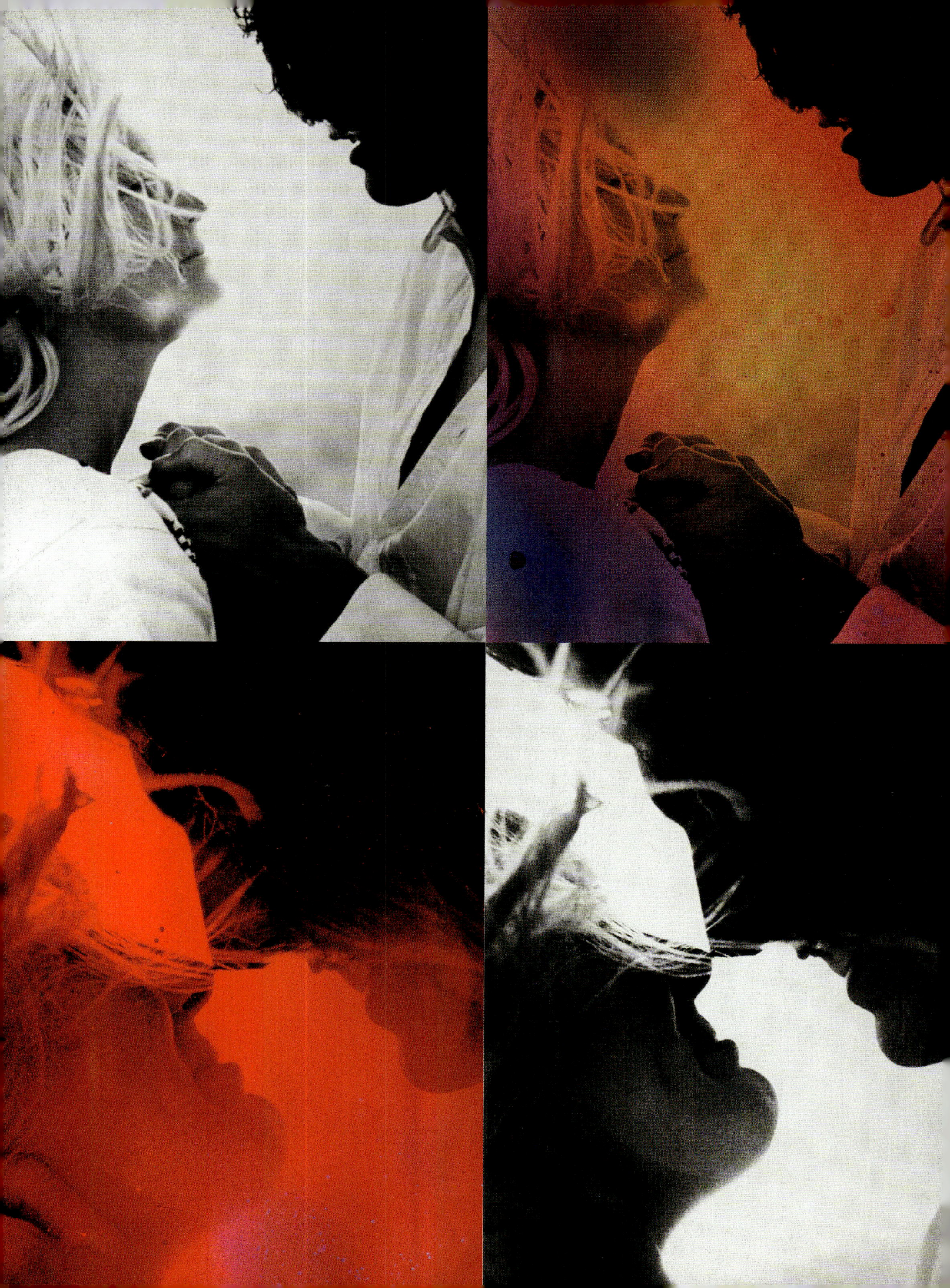

PORTRAITS AND LANDSCAPES

Kali was a pioneer of alternative photography. She coined the term *Artography* to describe her painterly photographs, trademarking the name around 1967.

The artistic process of Artography started with a black-and-white landscape or portrait taken by Kali with her Nikon F camera. In the 1960s, she was living in Palm Springs, California; the house's master bathroom included a Roman bathtub fitted with a Beseler enlarger. Kali would place chosen parts of other photographs she had taken on top of the first photograph, layering them into a unique print. The resulting images were original and arresting.

Kali would bring the wet silver-gelatin prints out to her swimming pool in the morning. Susan and Archie, her two children, knew swimming that day would be off-limits when finding their mother in the dechlorinated water agitating her prints, physically bringing them to life with the movements of her body. Kali sprayed the prints with paint, developer, eye drops of Dr. Ph. Martin's liquid colors, and whatever other materials she thought to add or happenstance landed on the prints; a bit of desert sand here, an errant insect landing there. The prints would then be laid to dry on the pool deck under the desert sun.

To see a Kali original is an experience. They are thick, textured, layered, collaged, and alluringly composed. A true example of the portrait-landscape image as envisioned by Kali is *Blue Cypress*, a print that also happens to have been one of her personal favorites. A landscape of a cypress tree, washed in blue, with a layering of youthful eyes—previously unchartered innovations in the photography world. A *Camera 35* magazine article from 1970 proclaimed of Kali's Artography prints, "They offer physical texture and surface modulations that are beyond the capabilities of mere machines," and noted of her process, "She experiments on the print to take it out of the realm of photography and *almost* into the world of painting."

This was a time in art history during which photography had not achieved the standing it has now. It was uncommon for galleries to exhibit photographs, let alone recognize alternative visions in photography. As the social movements of the '60s swept the California coast, Kali blazed a trail ahead of its time, pushing the limits of photography.

—ALEXANDRA JARRELL

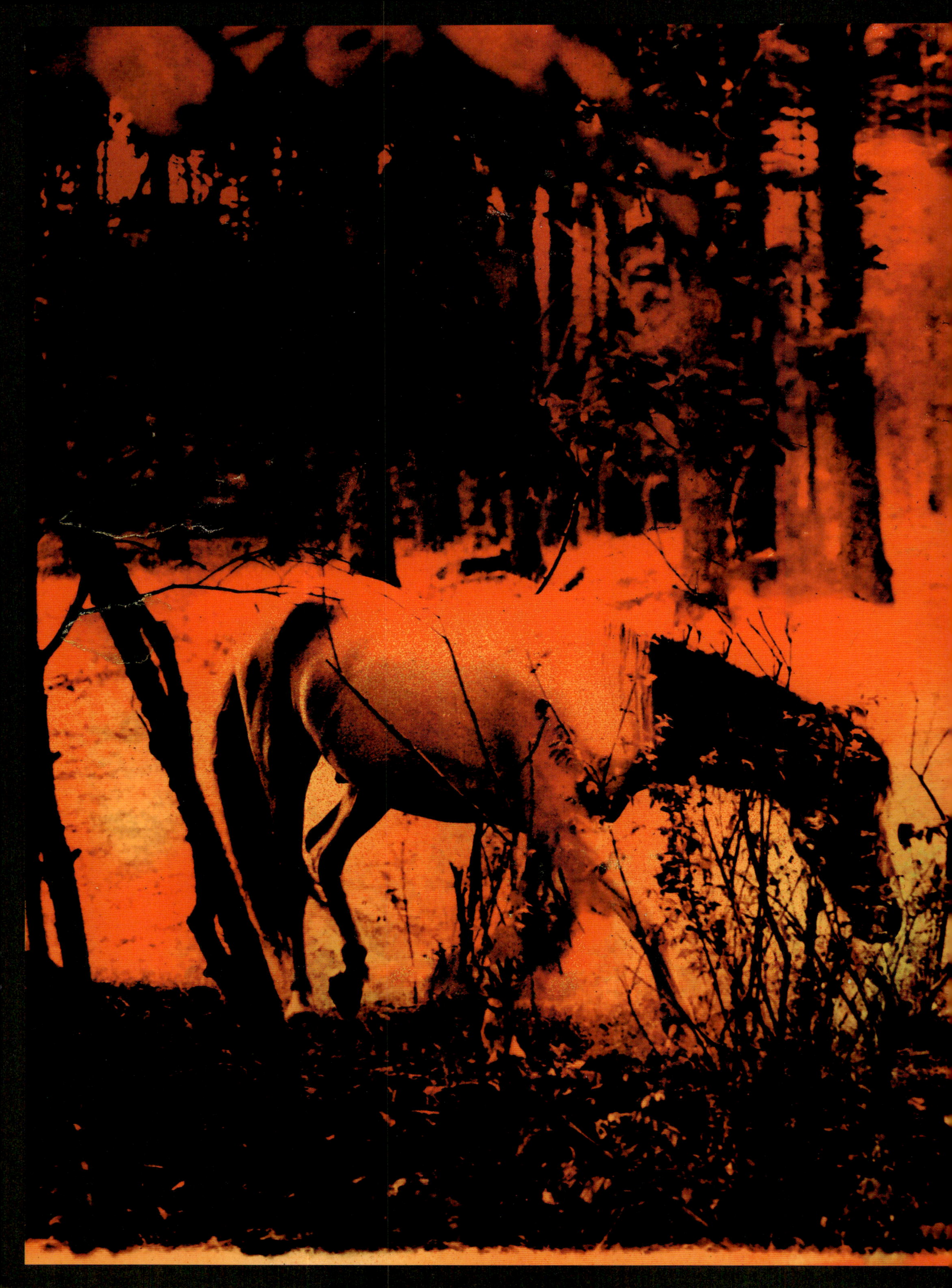

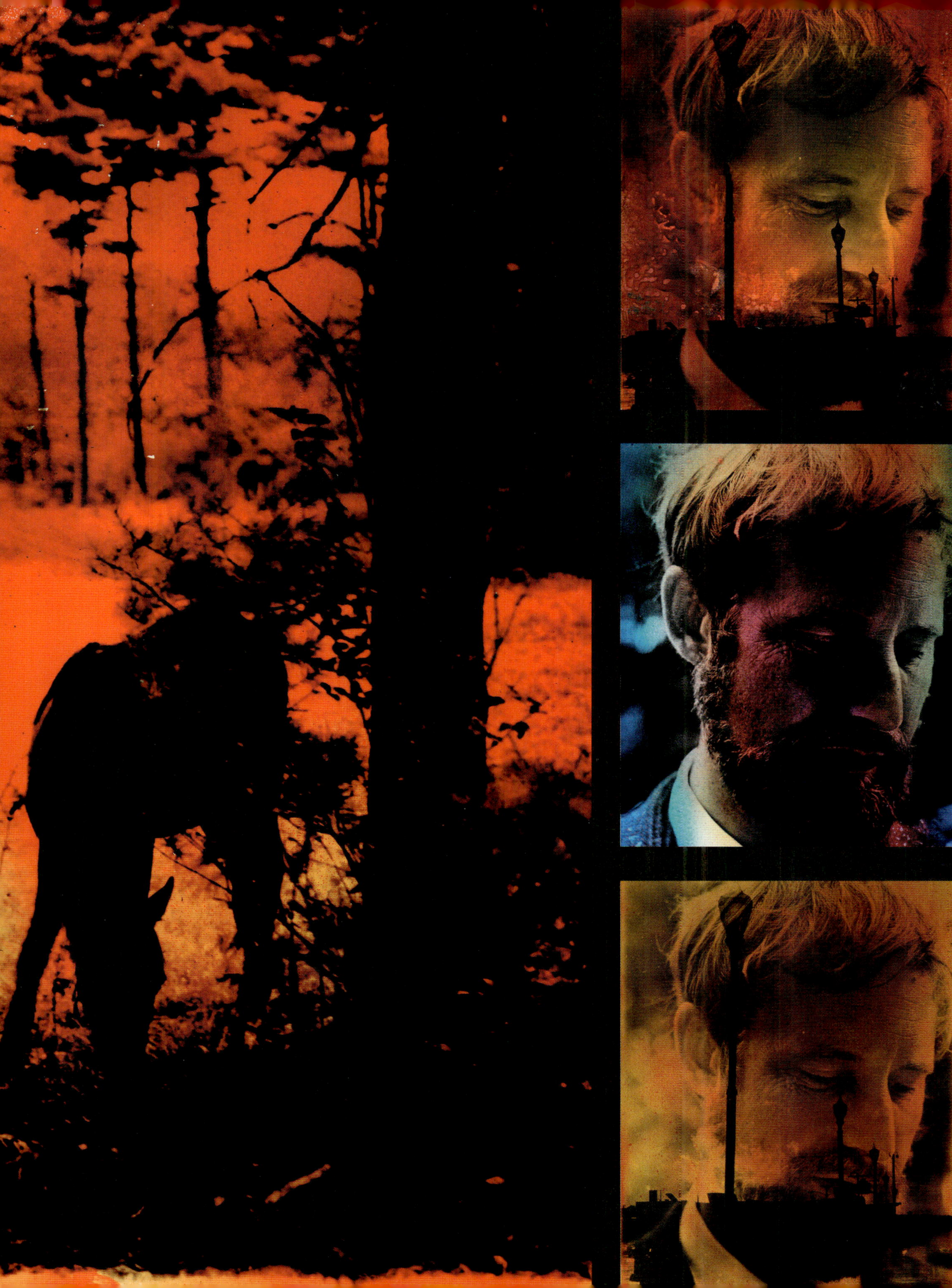

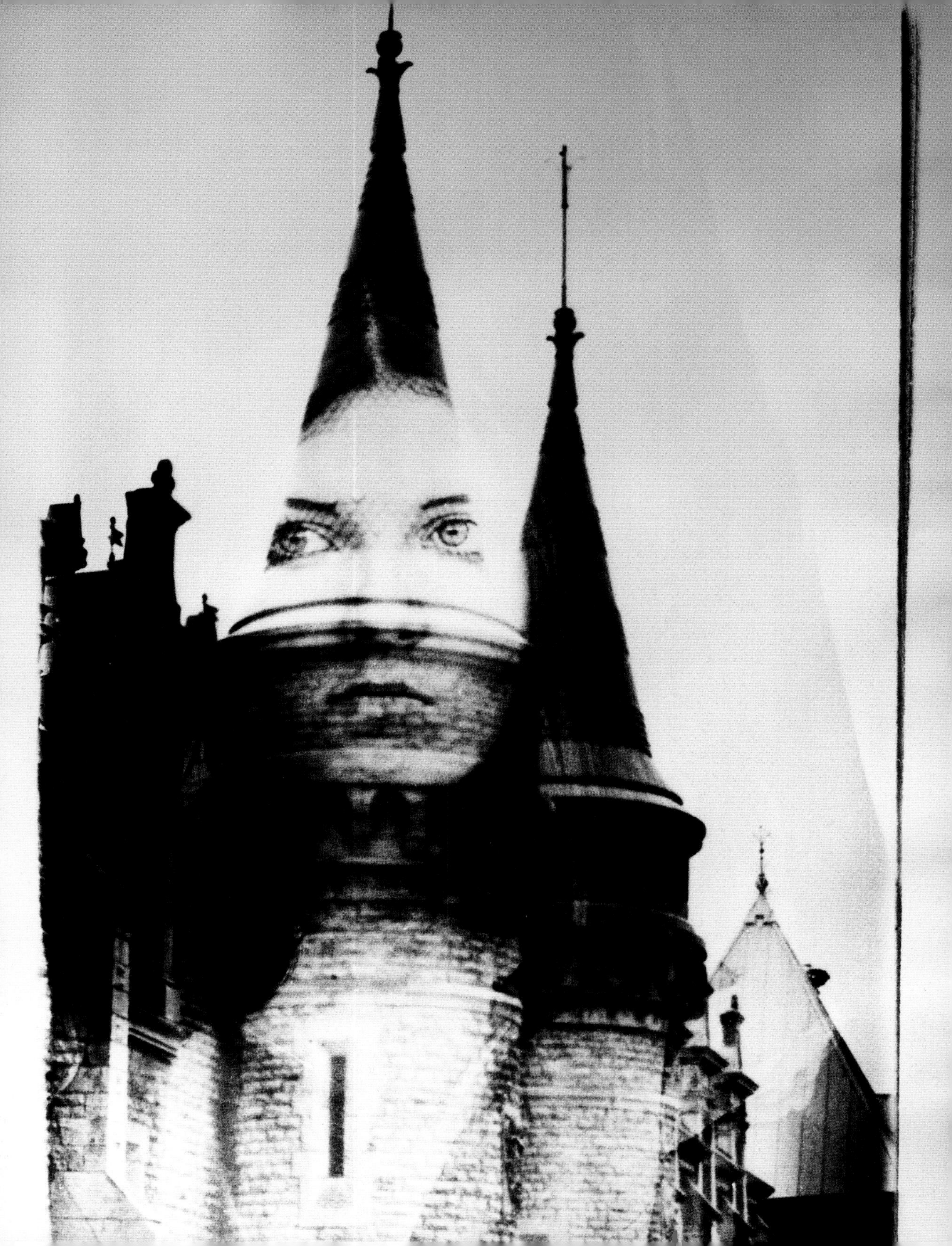

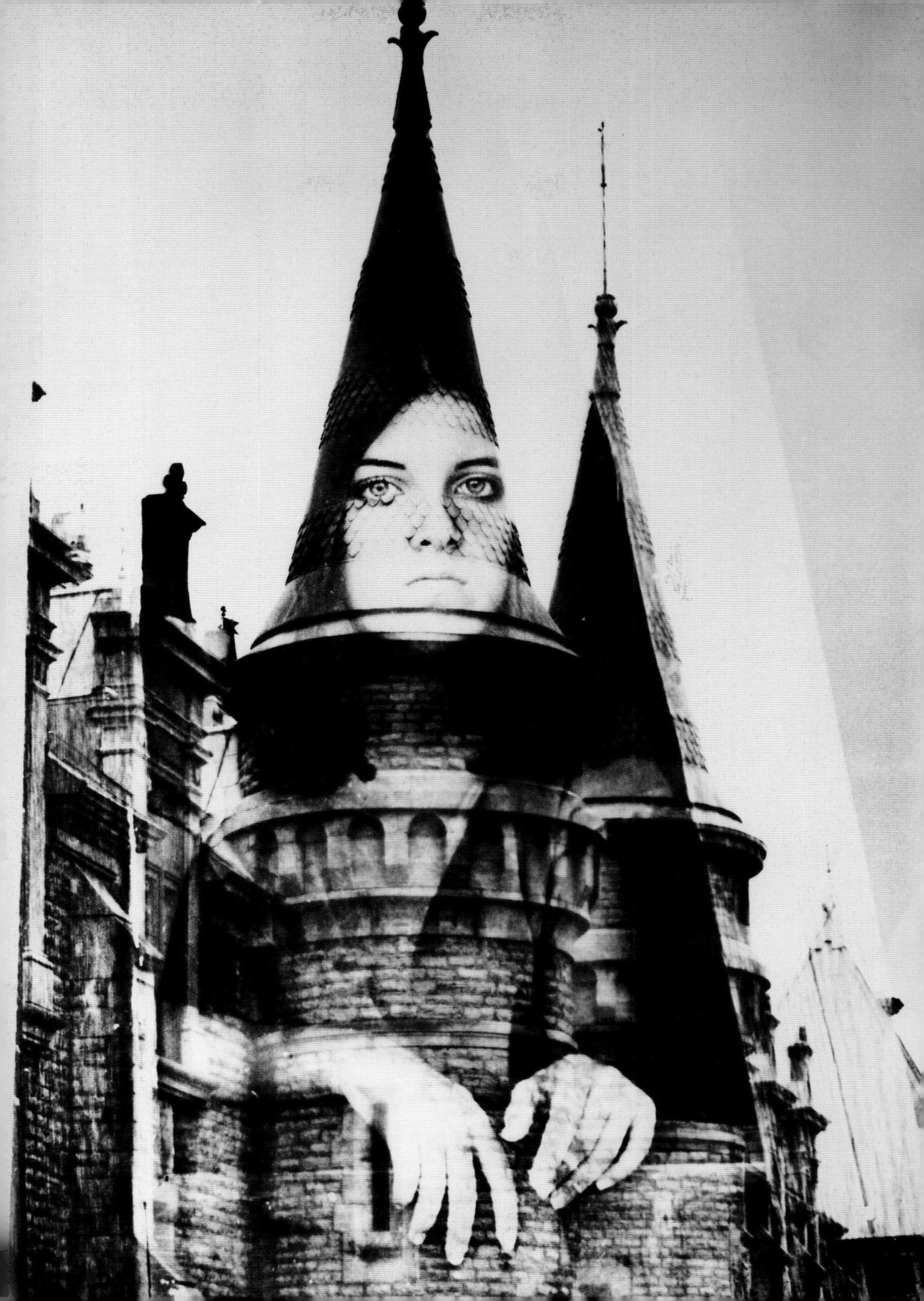

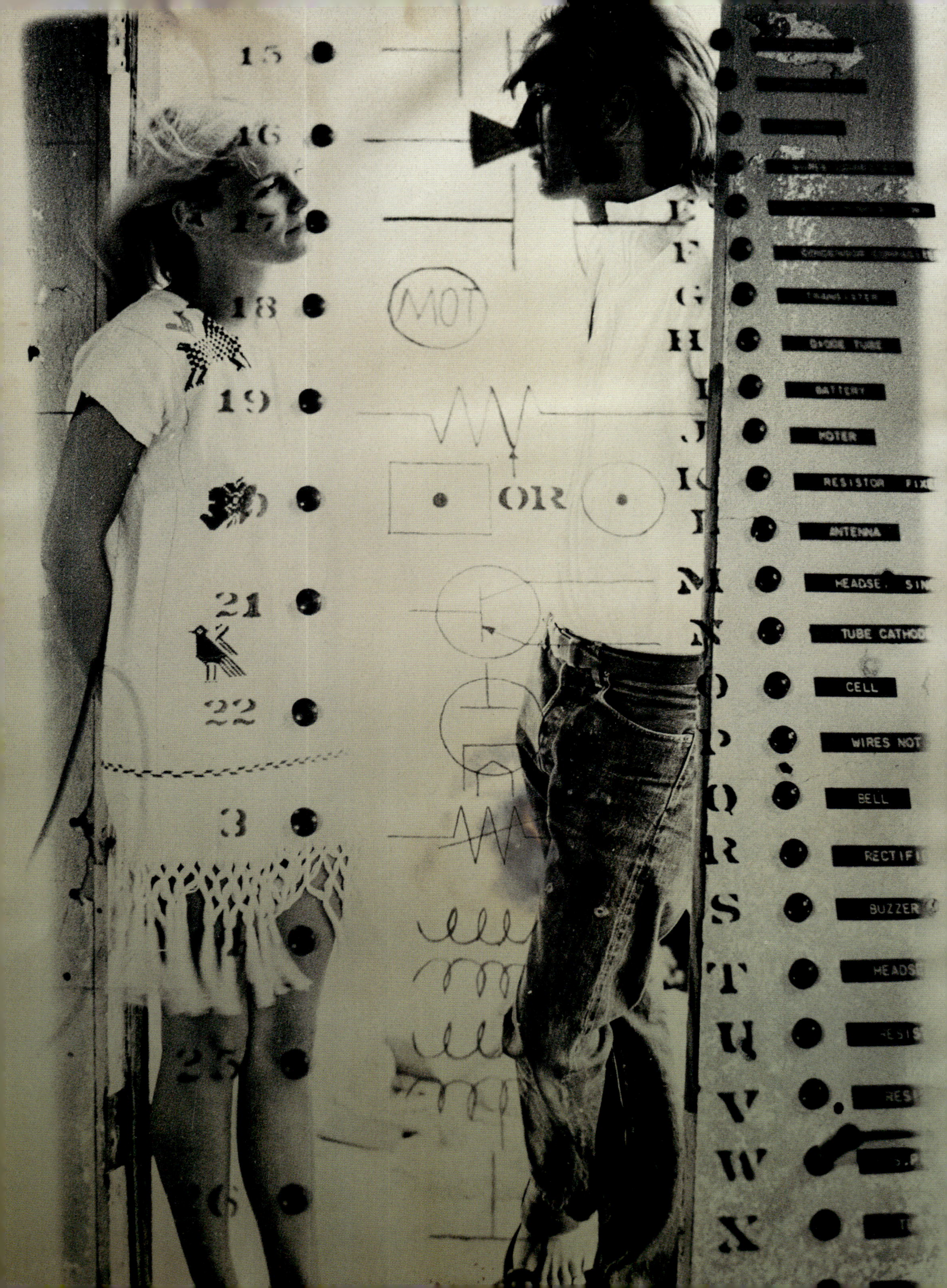

15
16
17
18
MOT
19
20
OR
21
22
3
25
6
E
F
G
H
I
J
K
L
M
N
O
P
Q
R
S
T
U
V
W
X
CONDENSER
TRANSISTOR
DIODE TUBE
BATTERY
MOTOR
RESISTOR FIXED
ANTENNA
HEADSET SIN
TUBE CATHODE
CELL
WIRES NOT
BELL
RECTIFI
BUZZER
HEADSE
RESIS
RESIS
TE

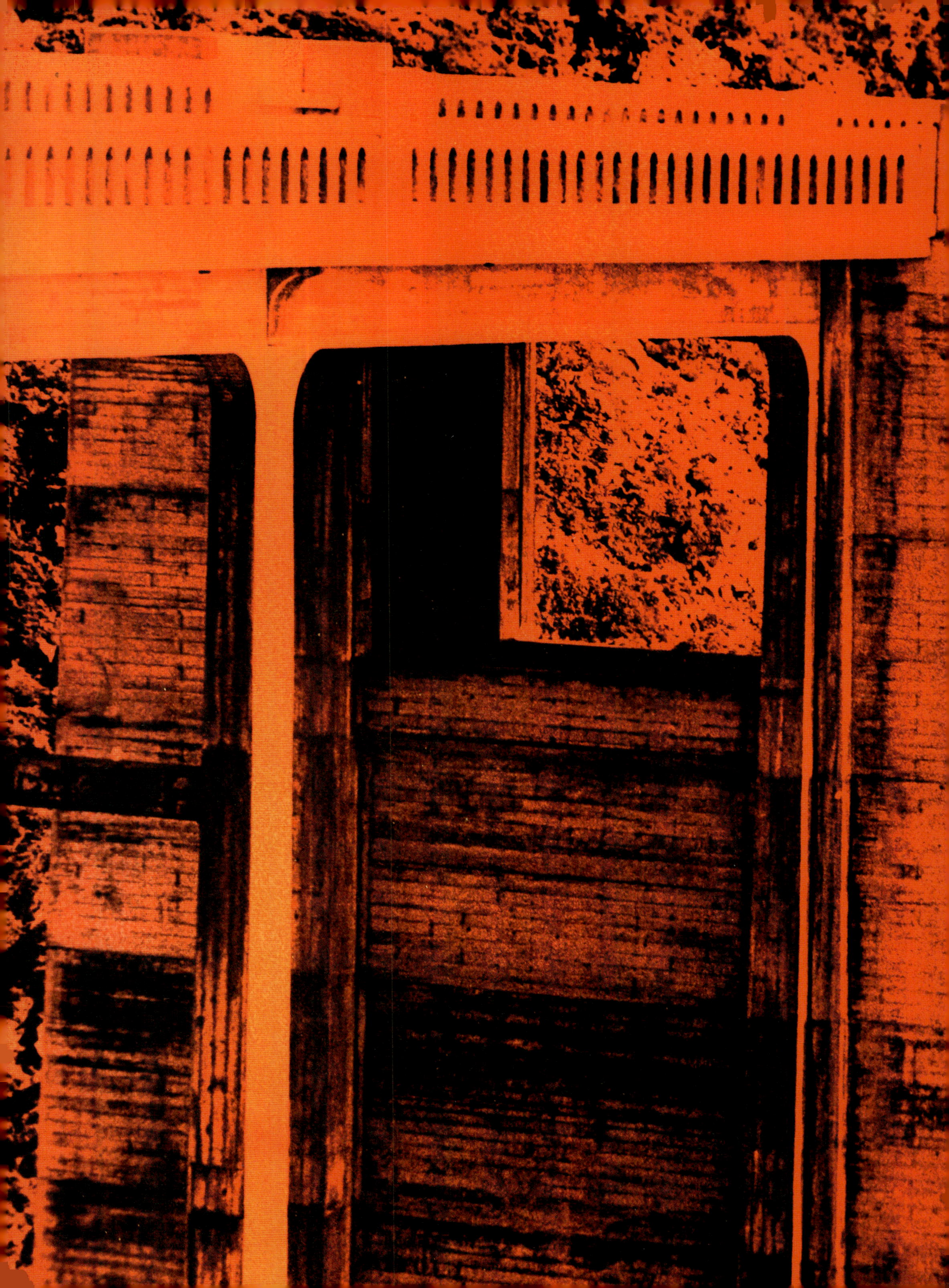

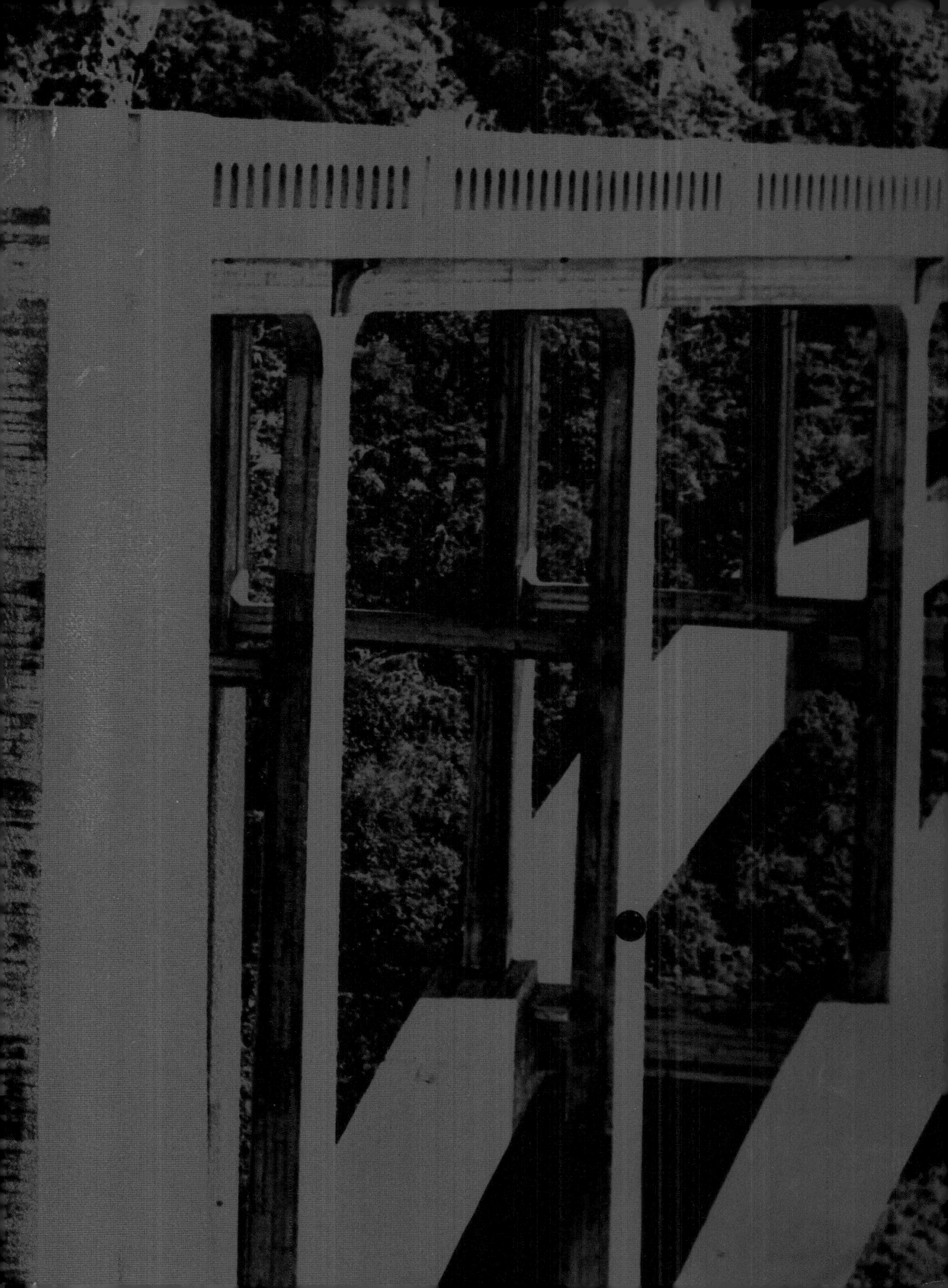

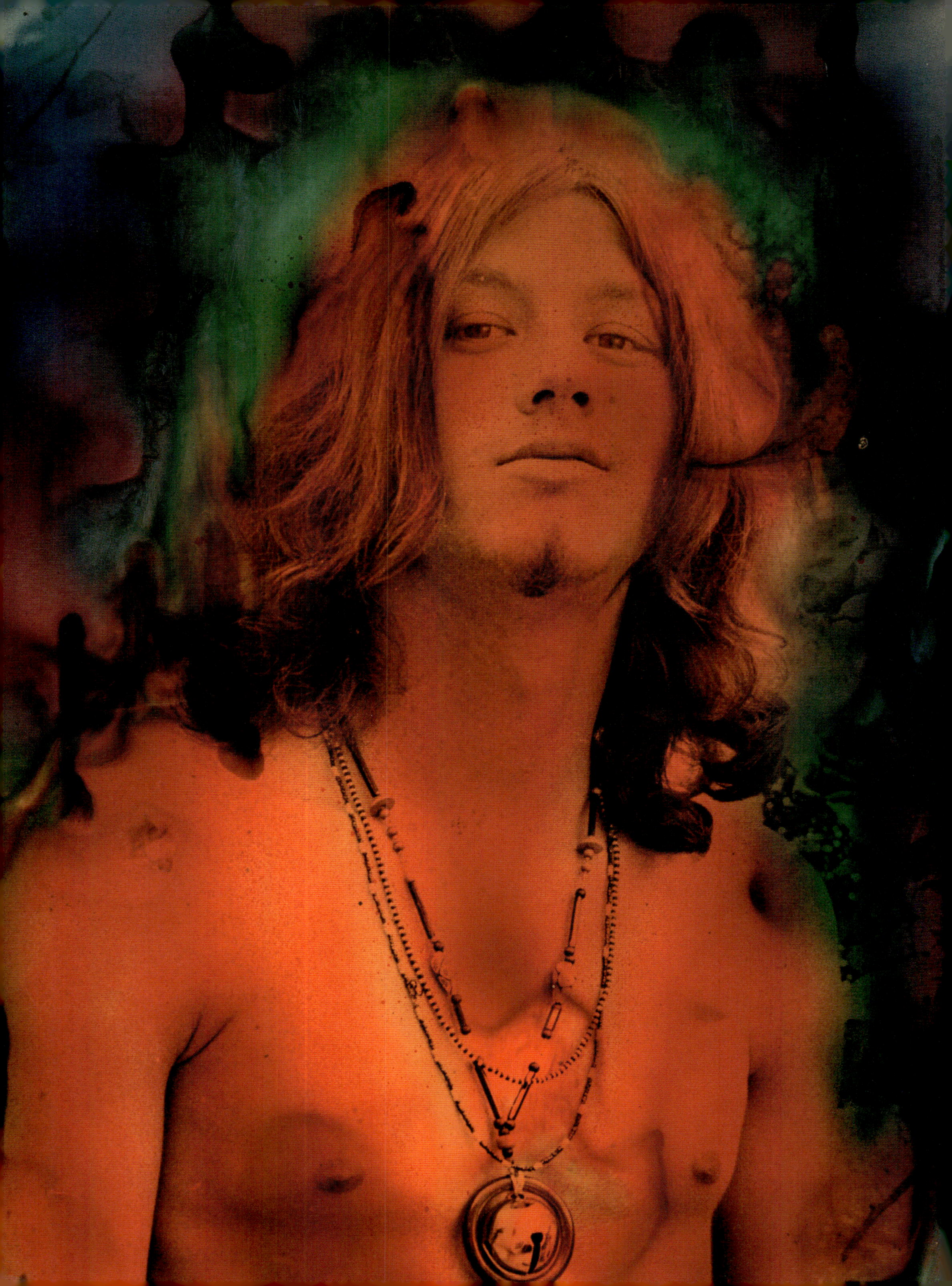

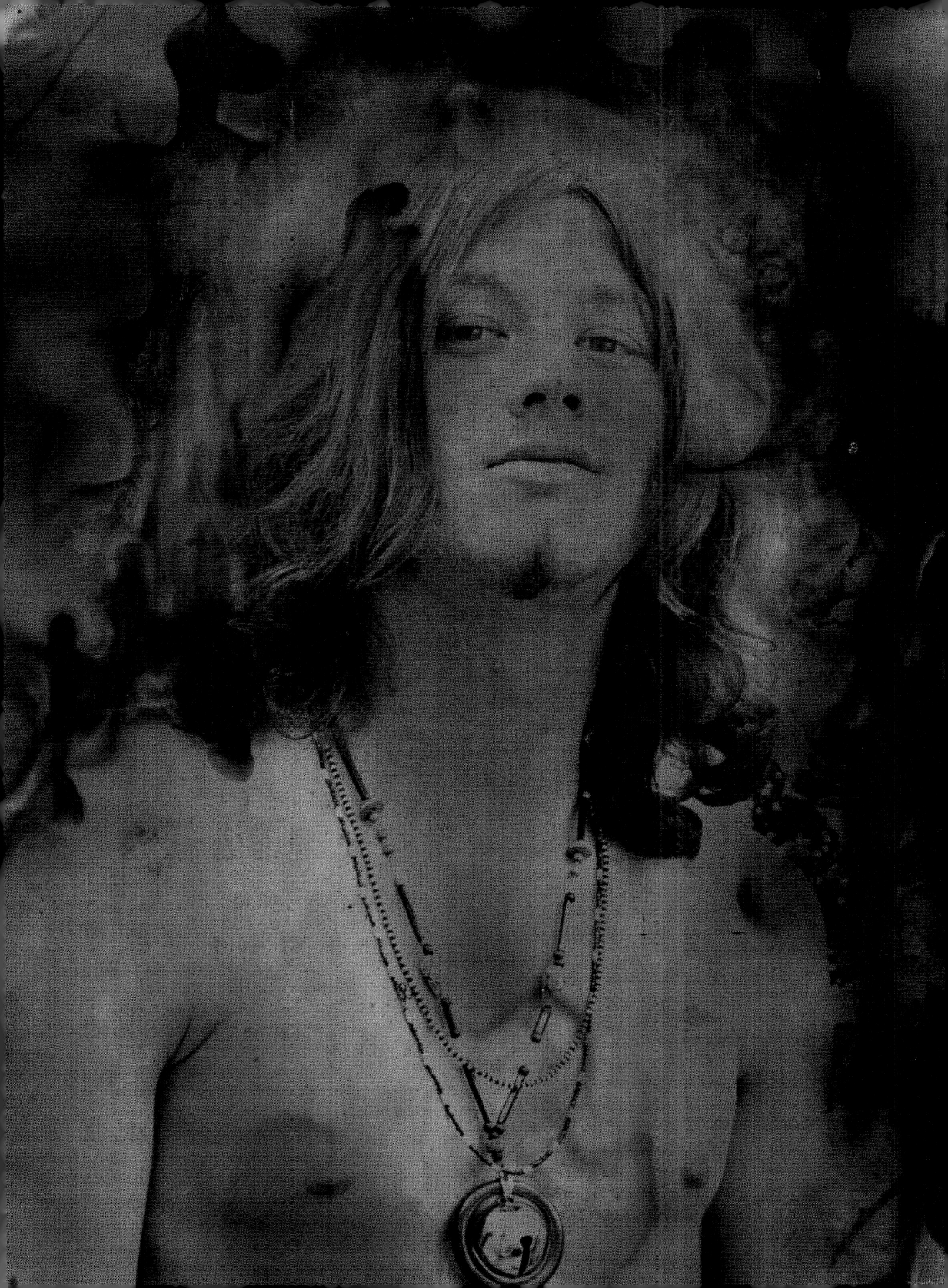

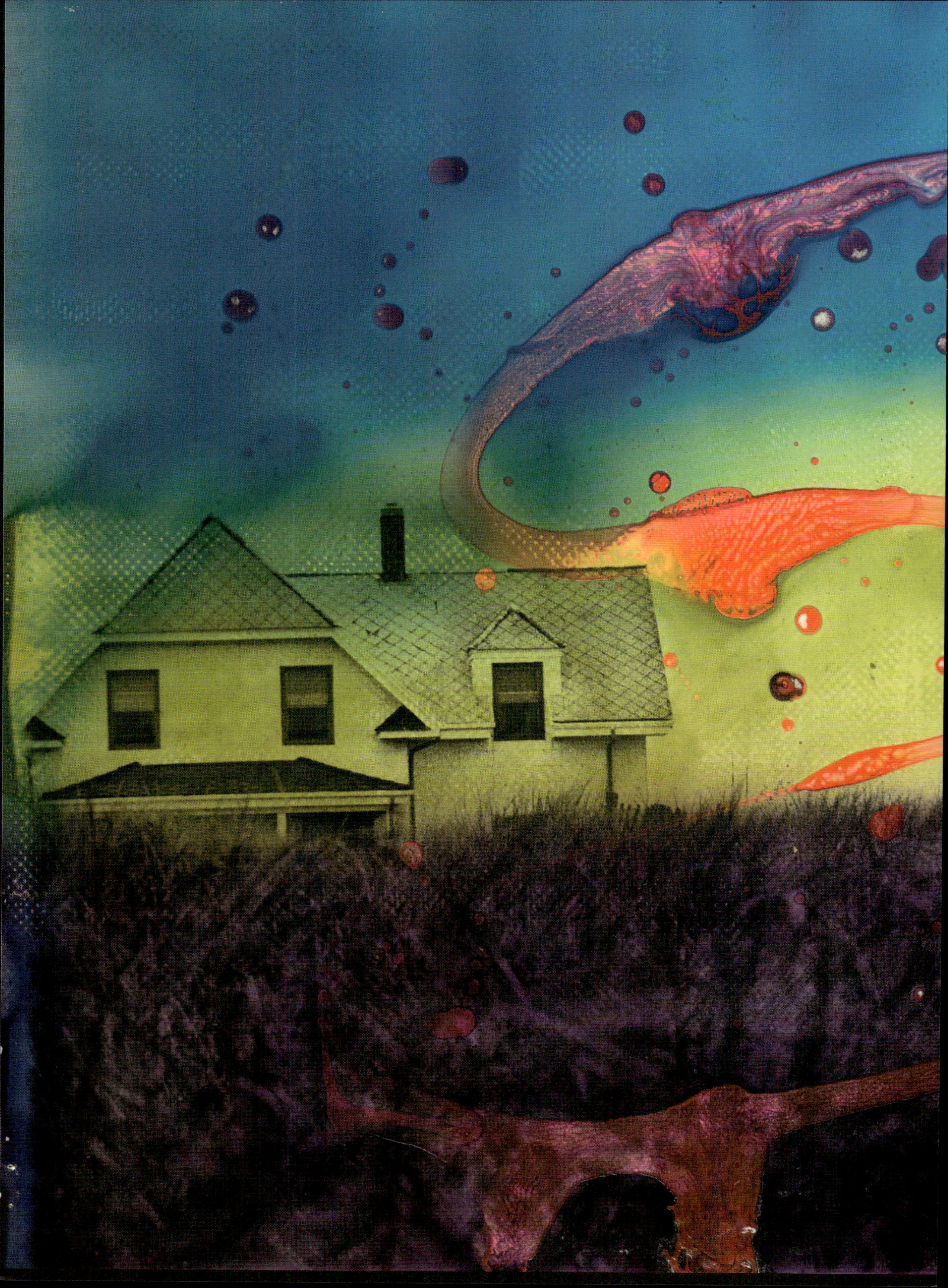

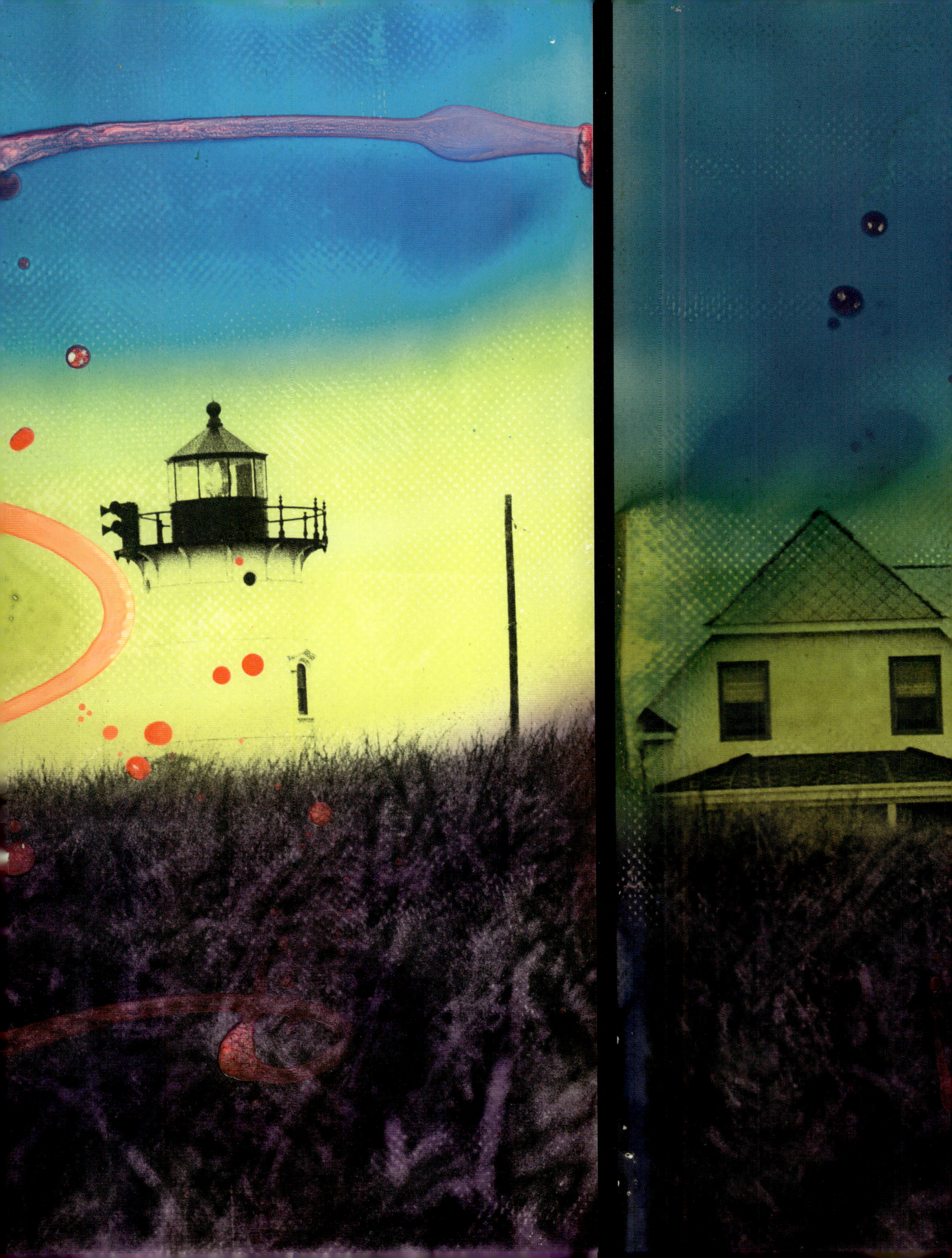

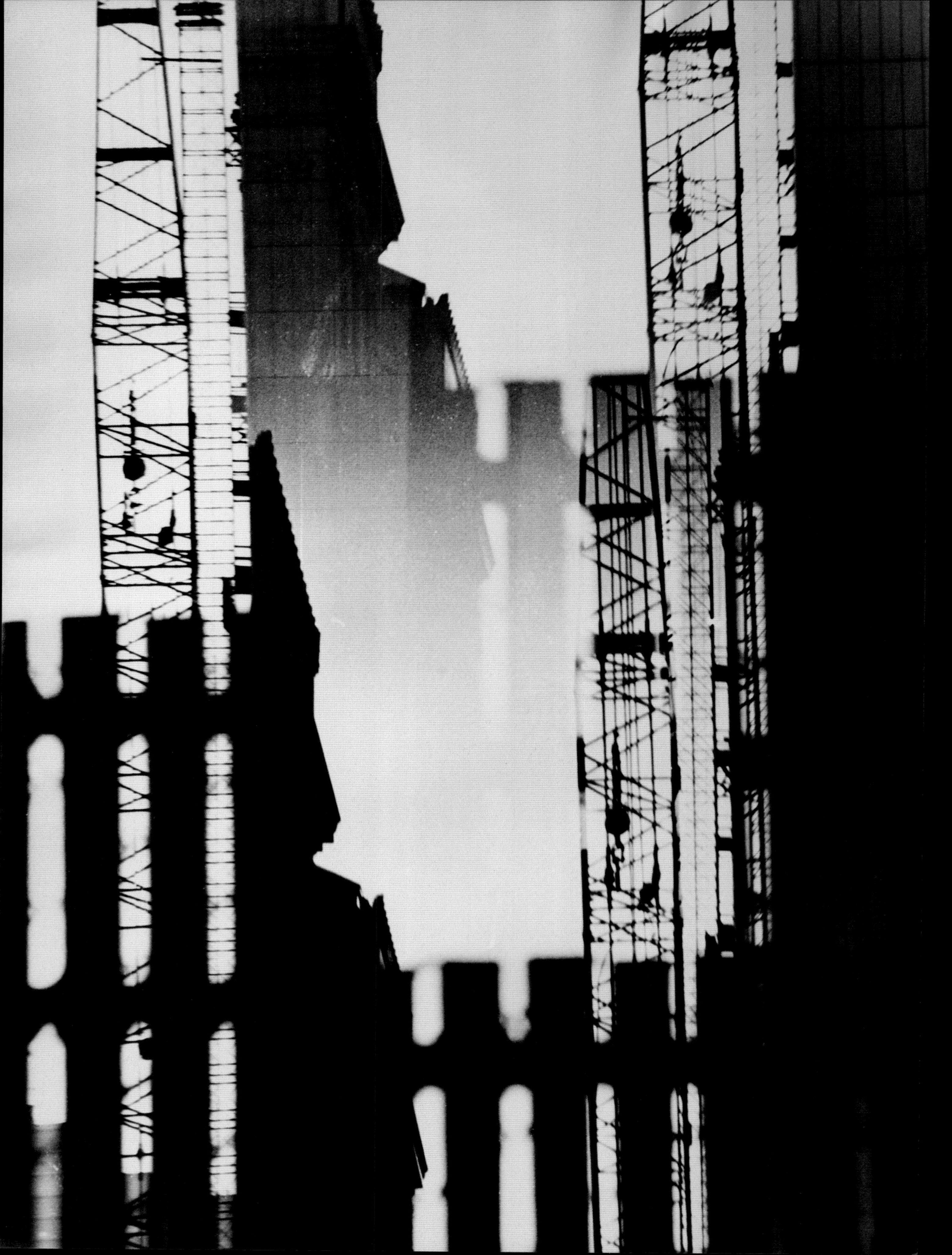

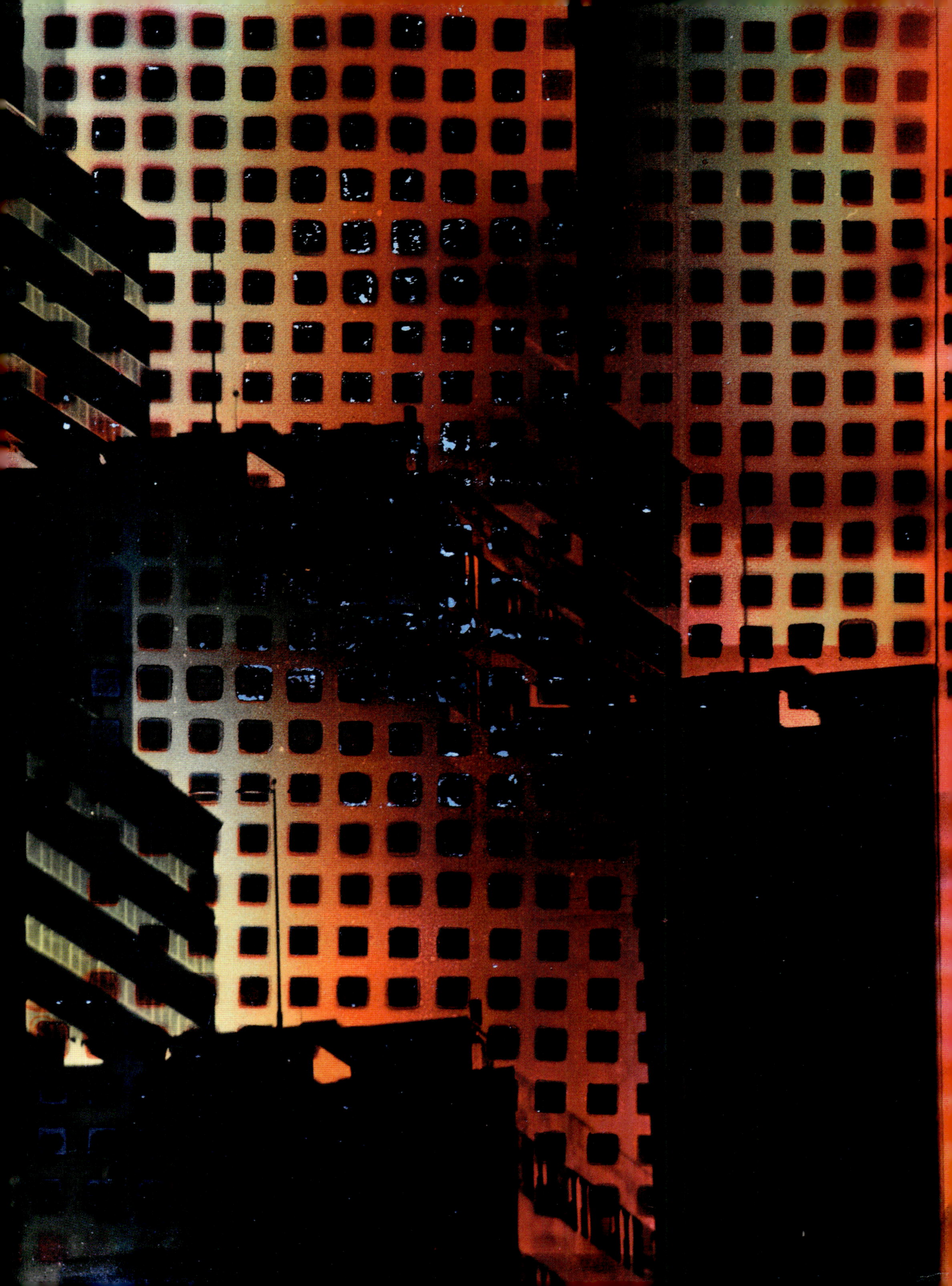

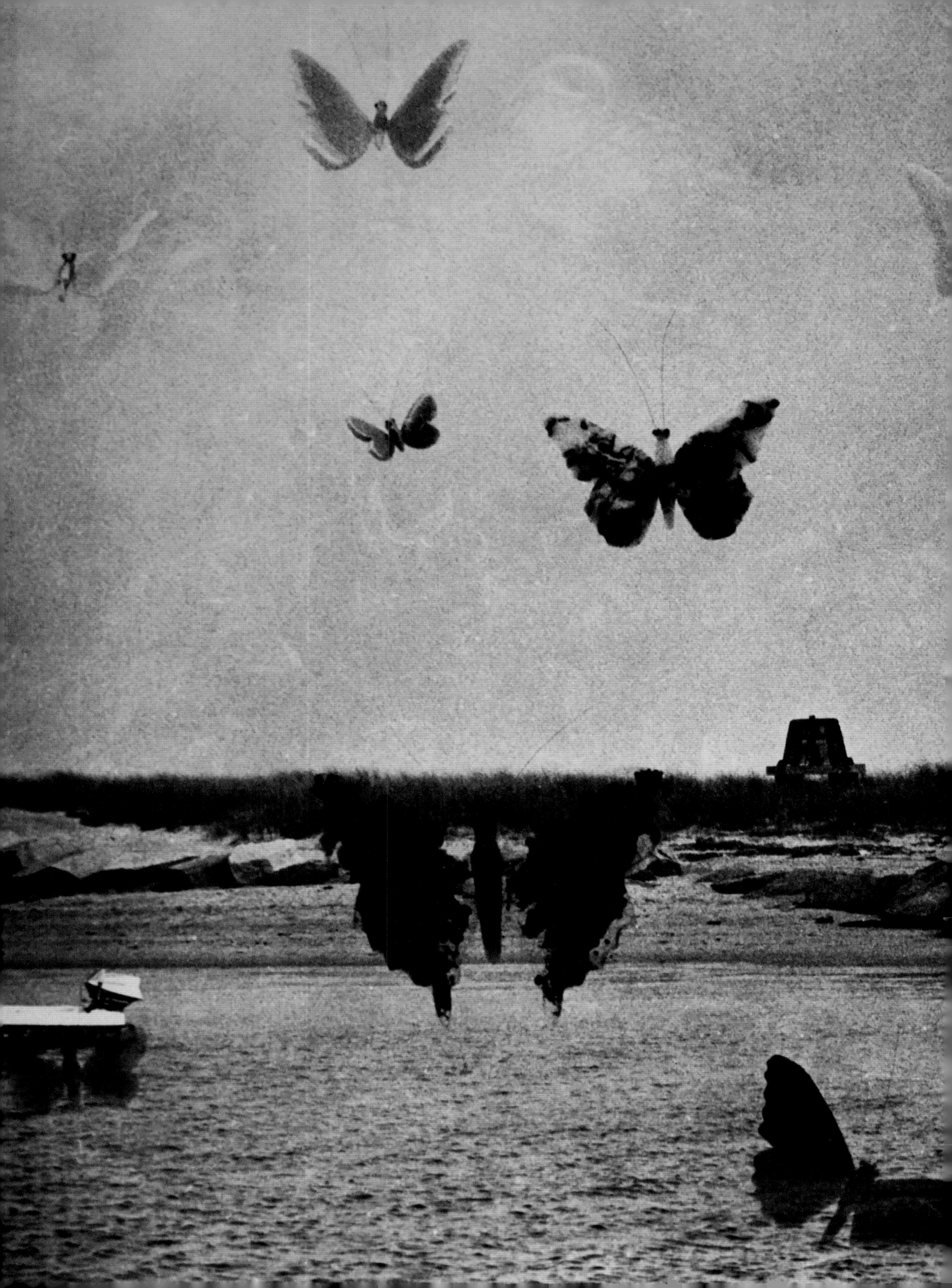

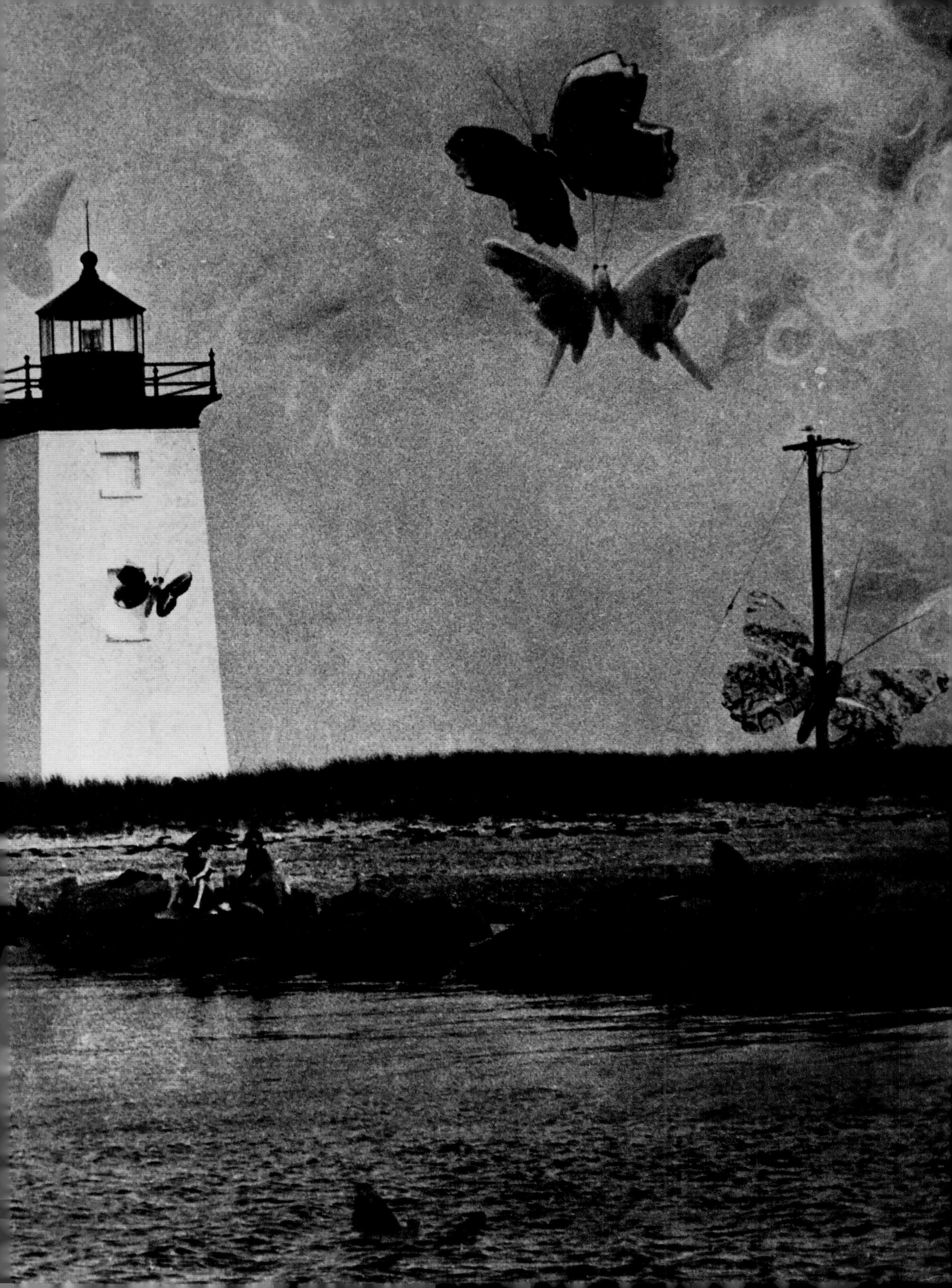

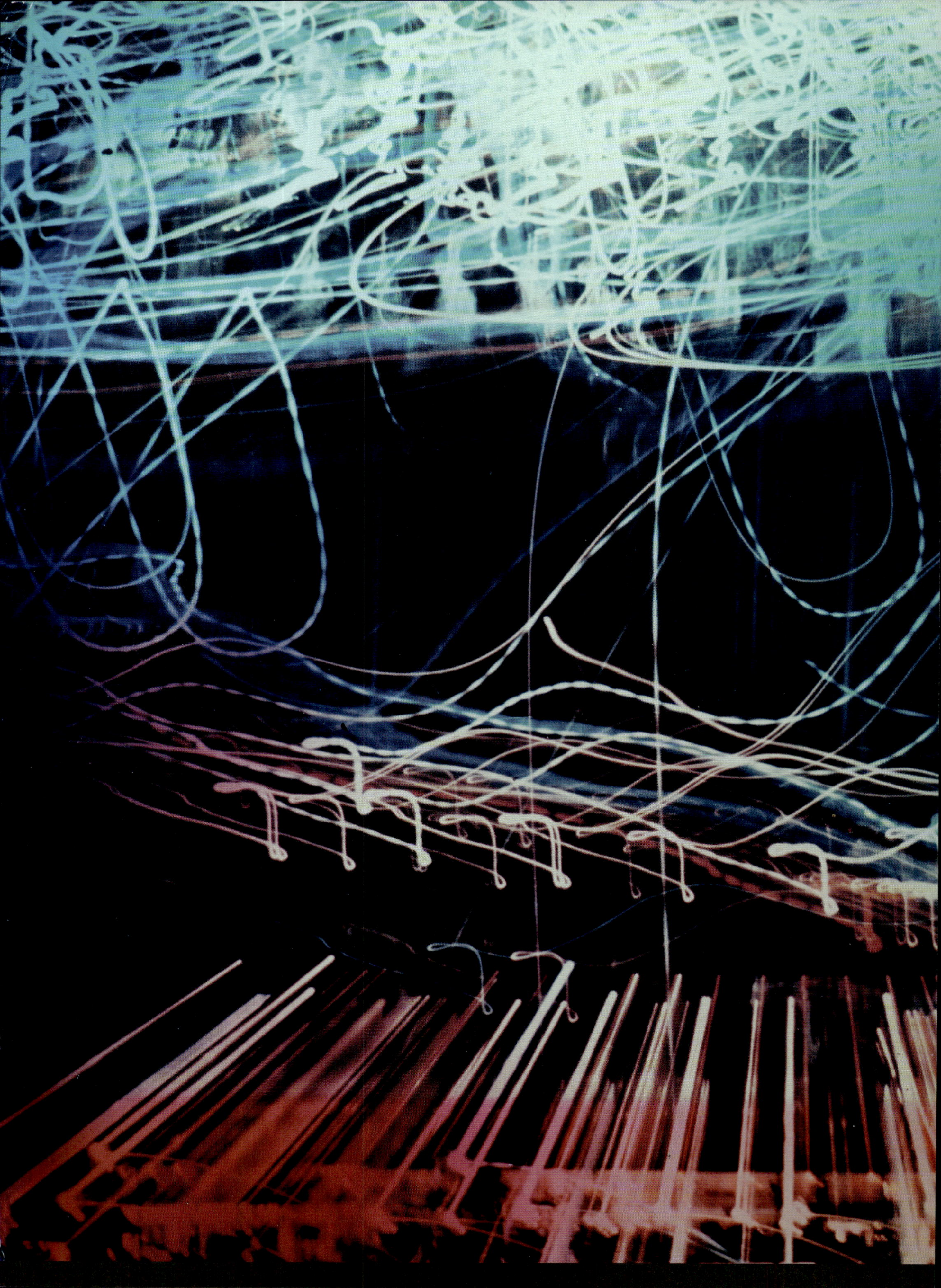

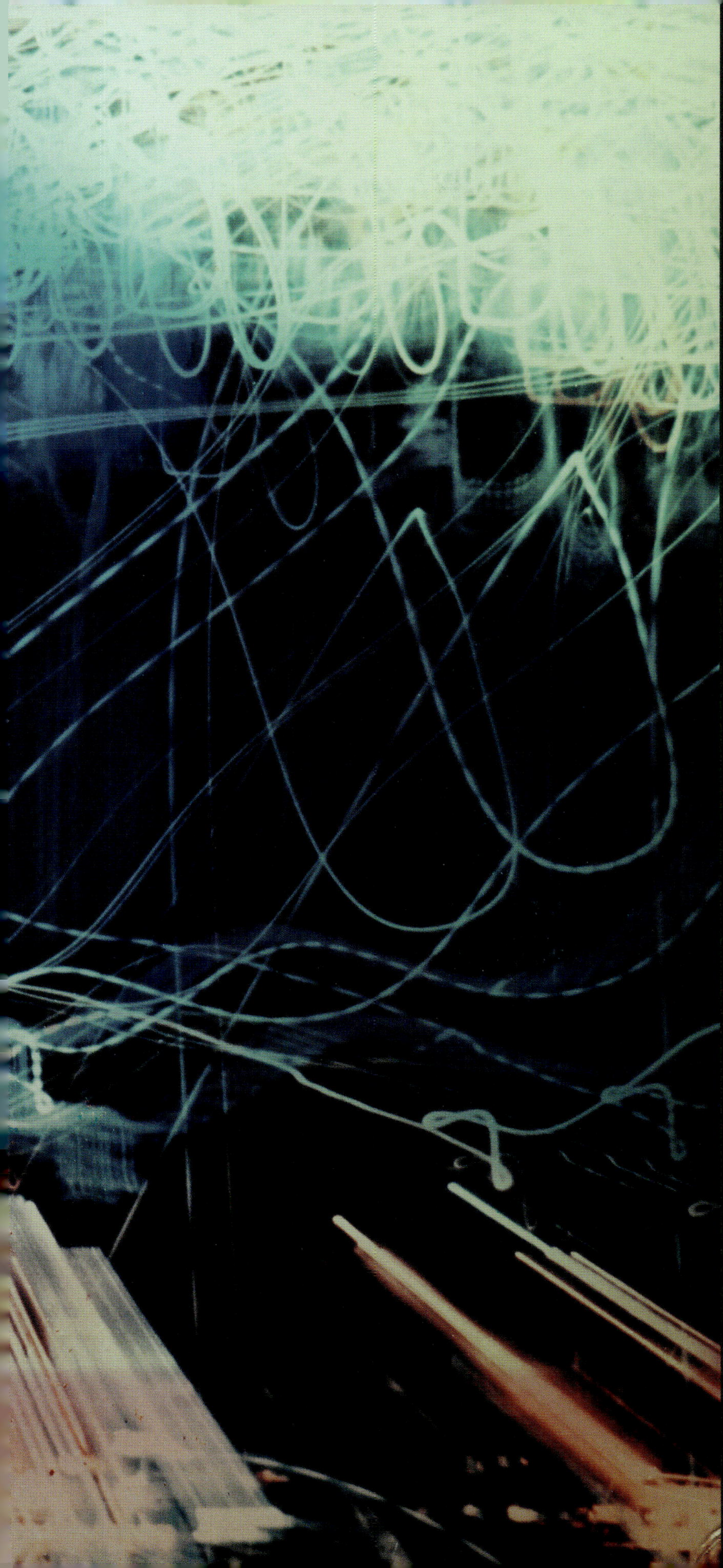

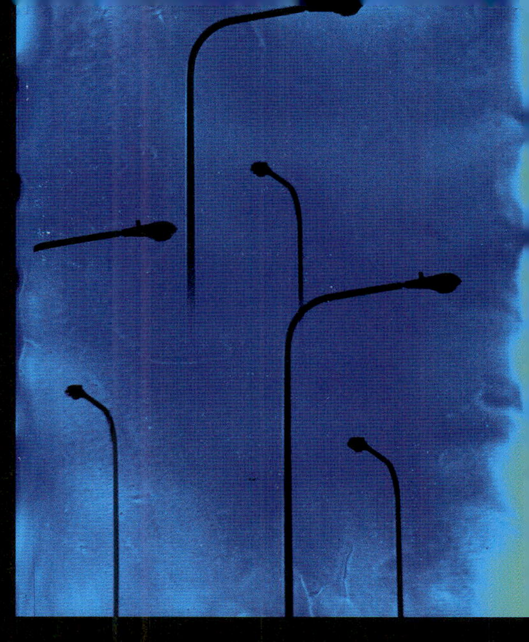

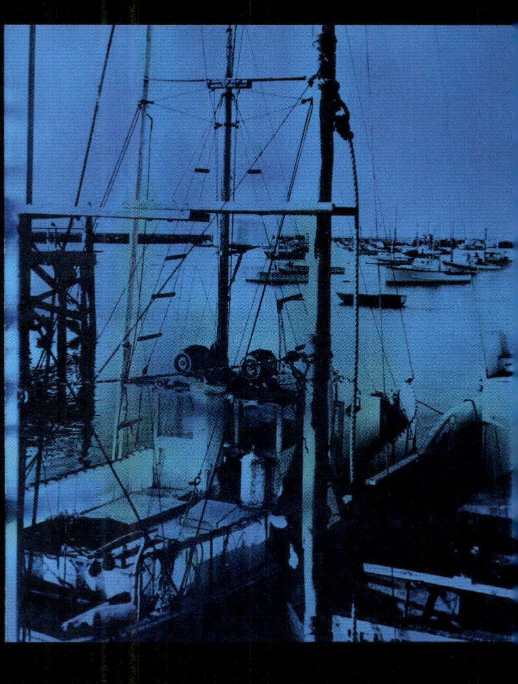

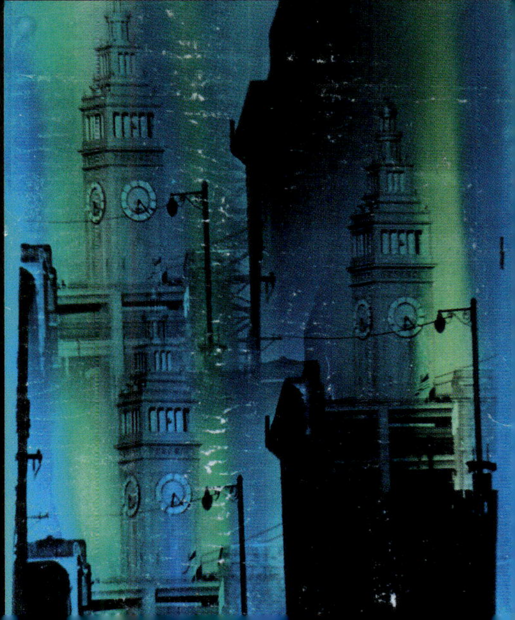

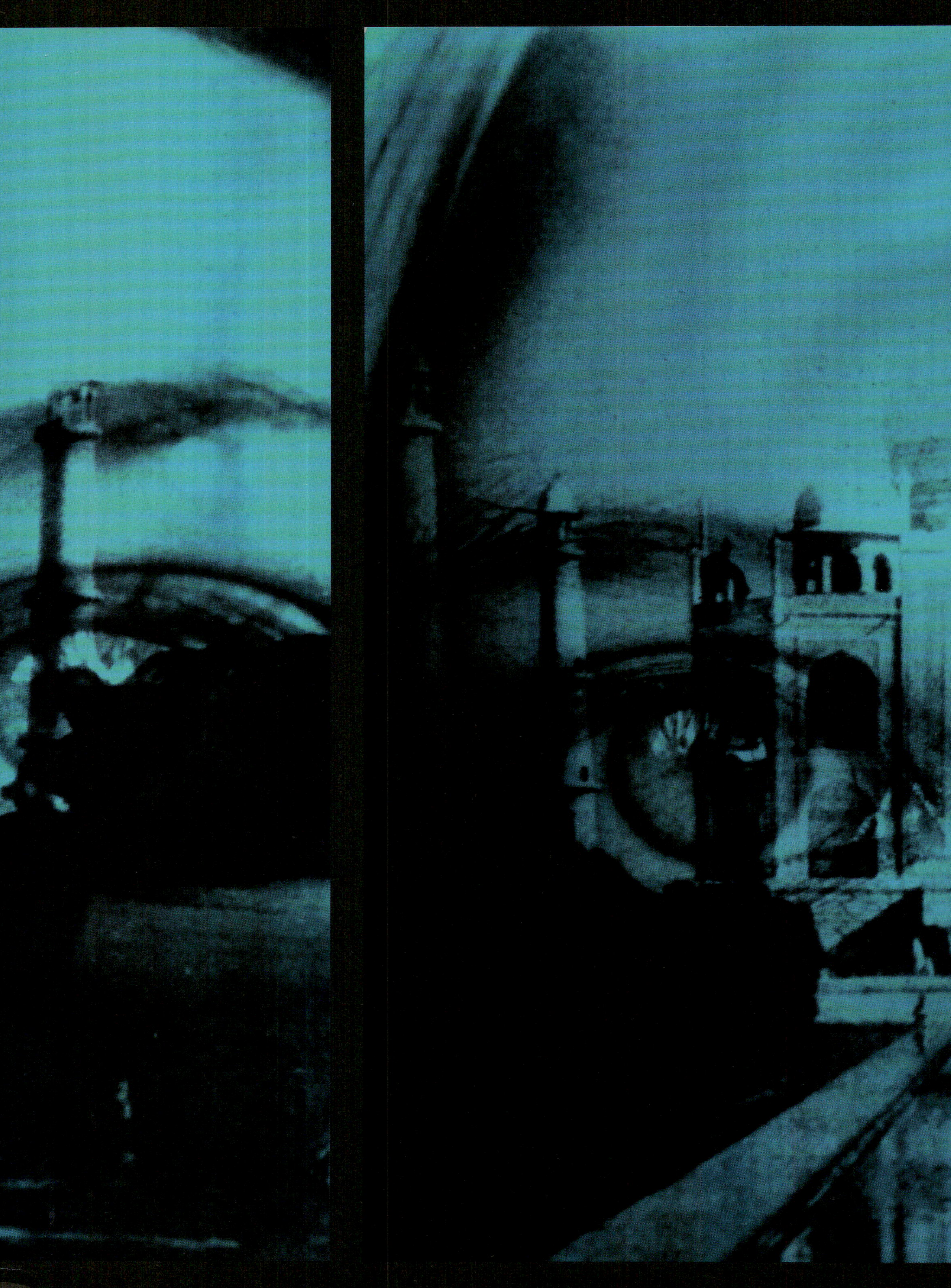

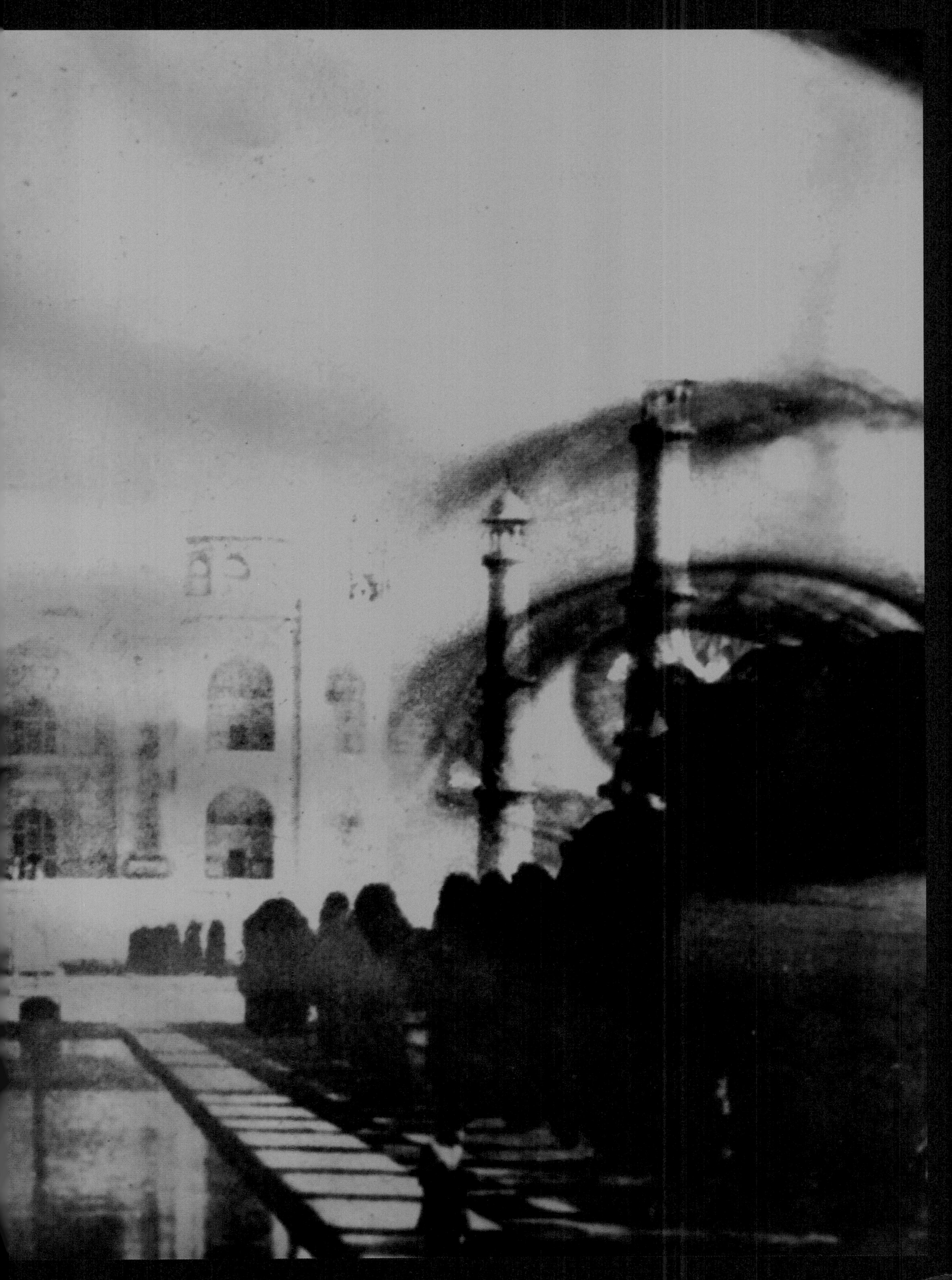

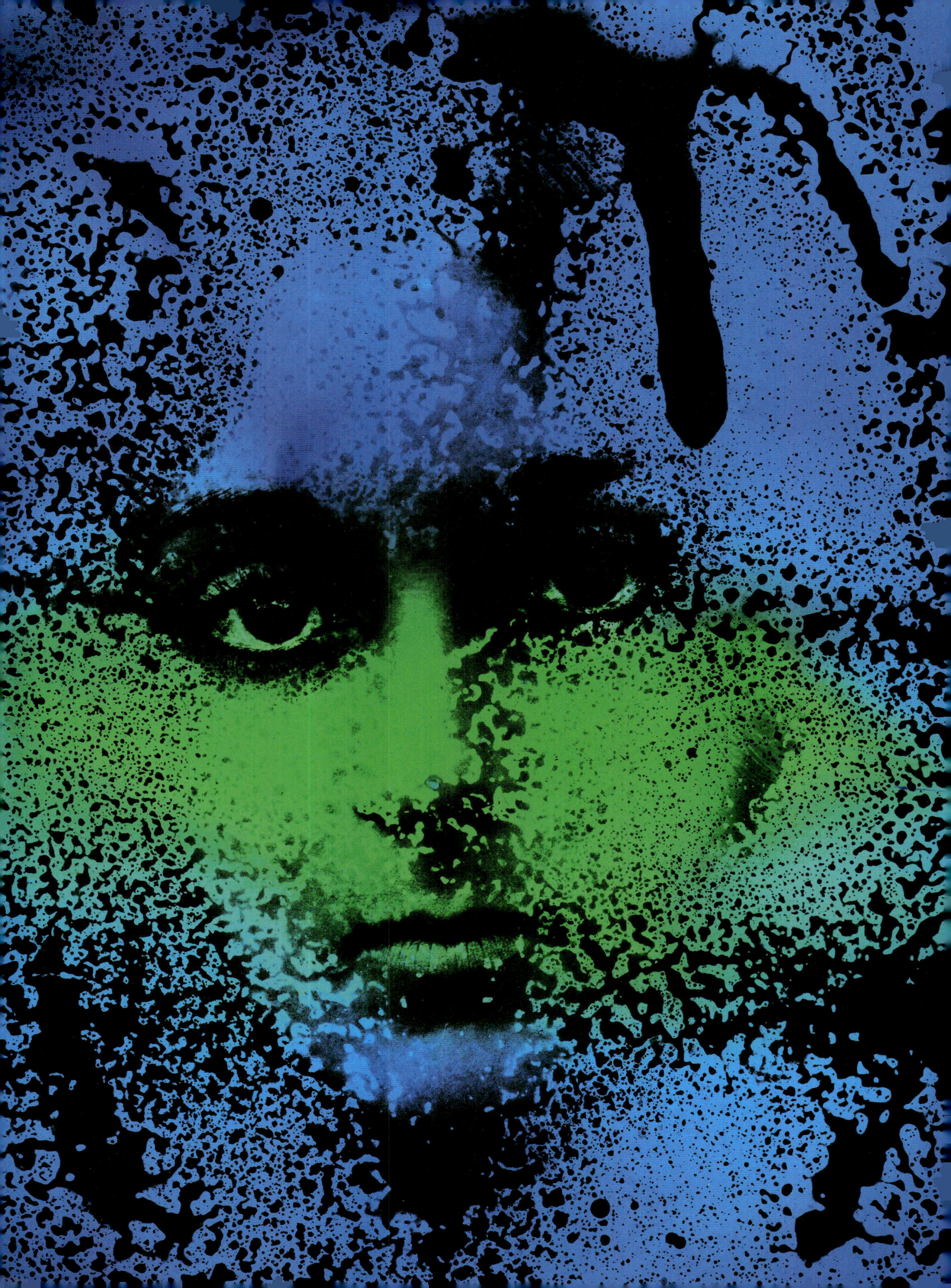

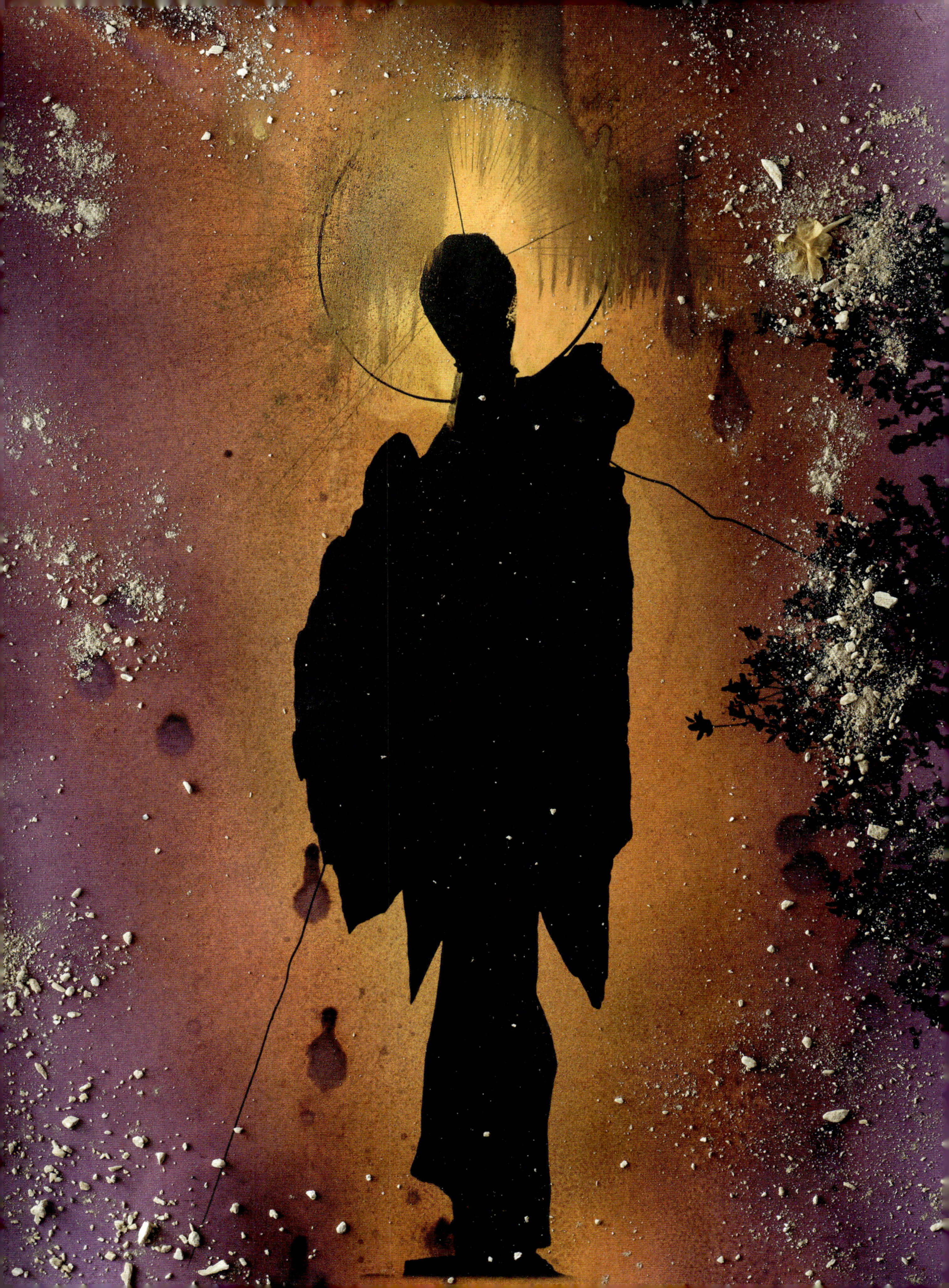

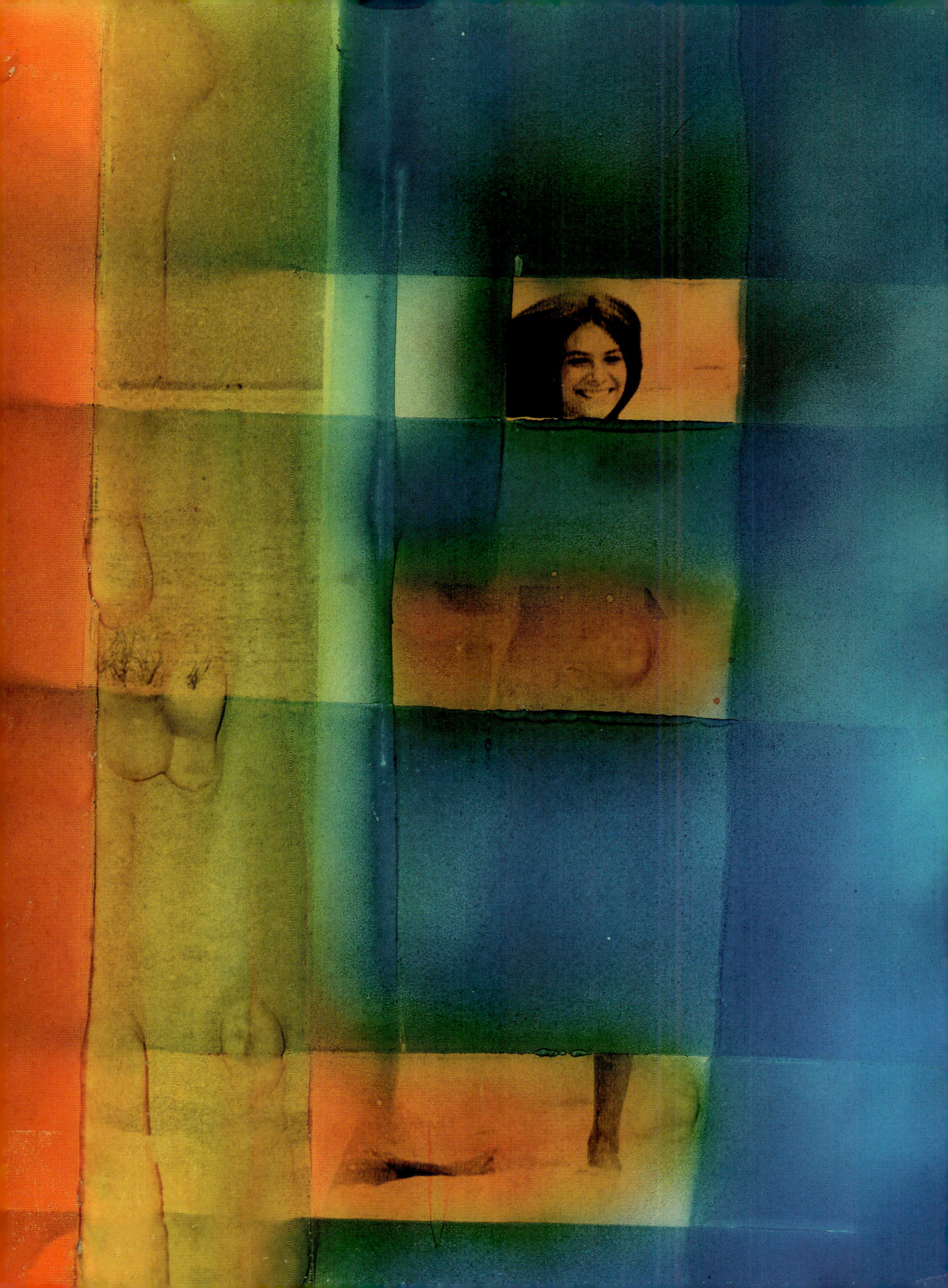

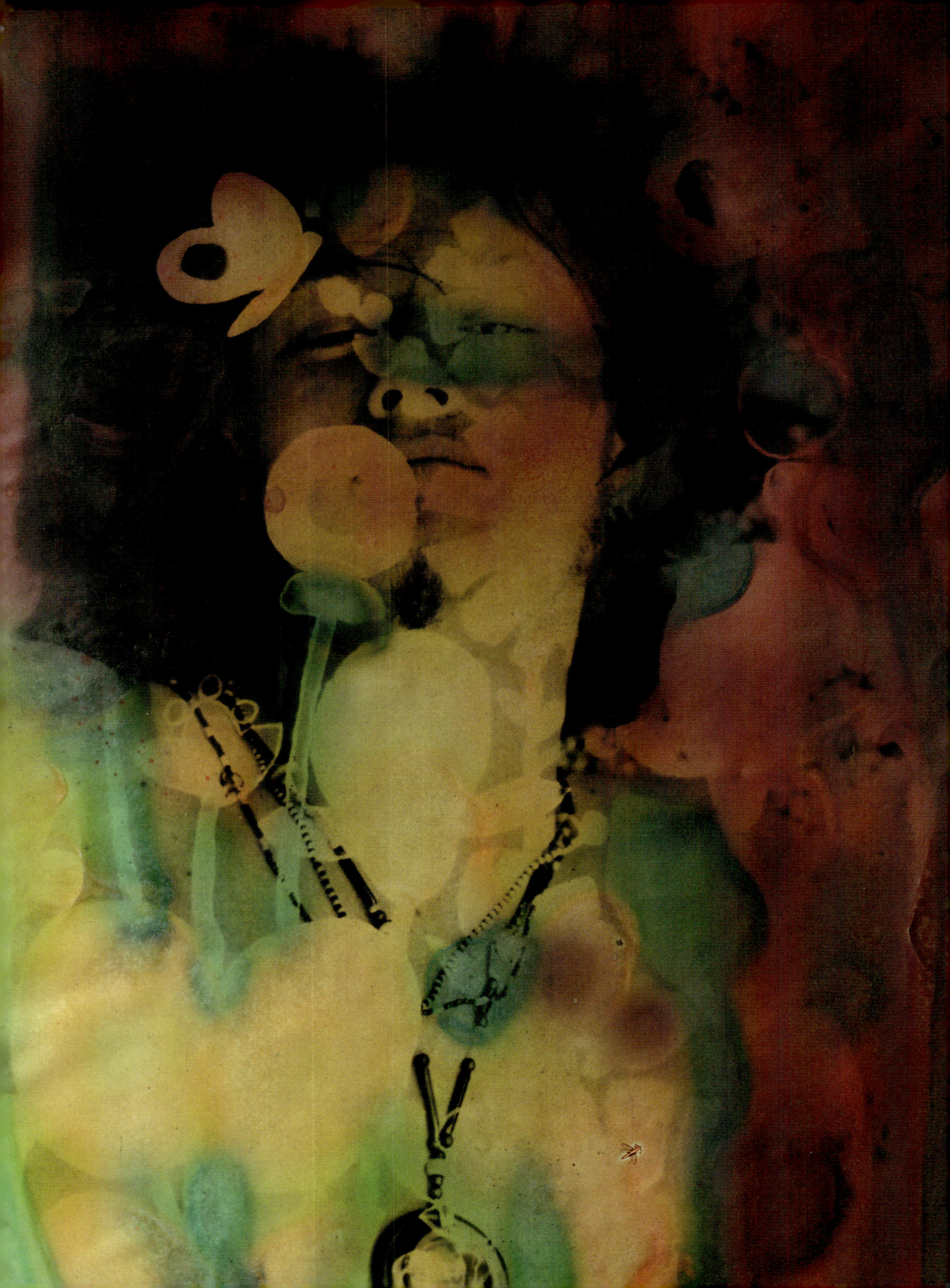

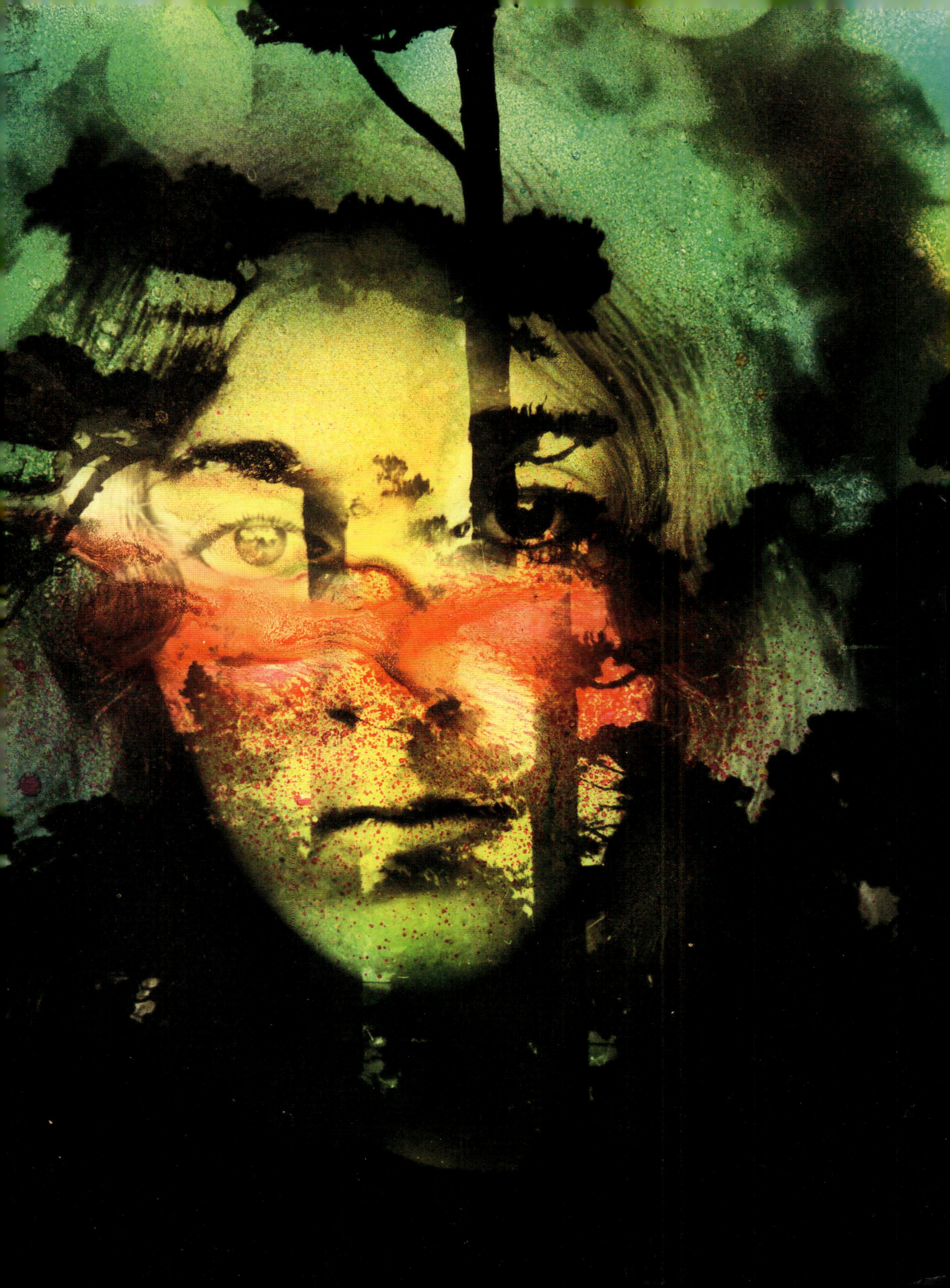

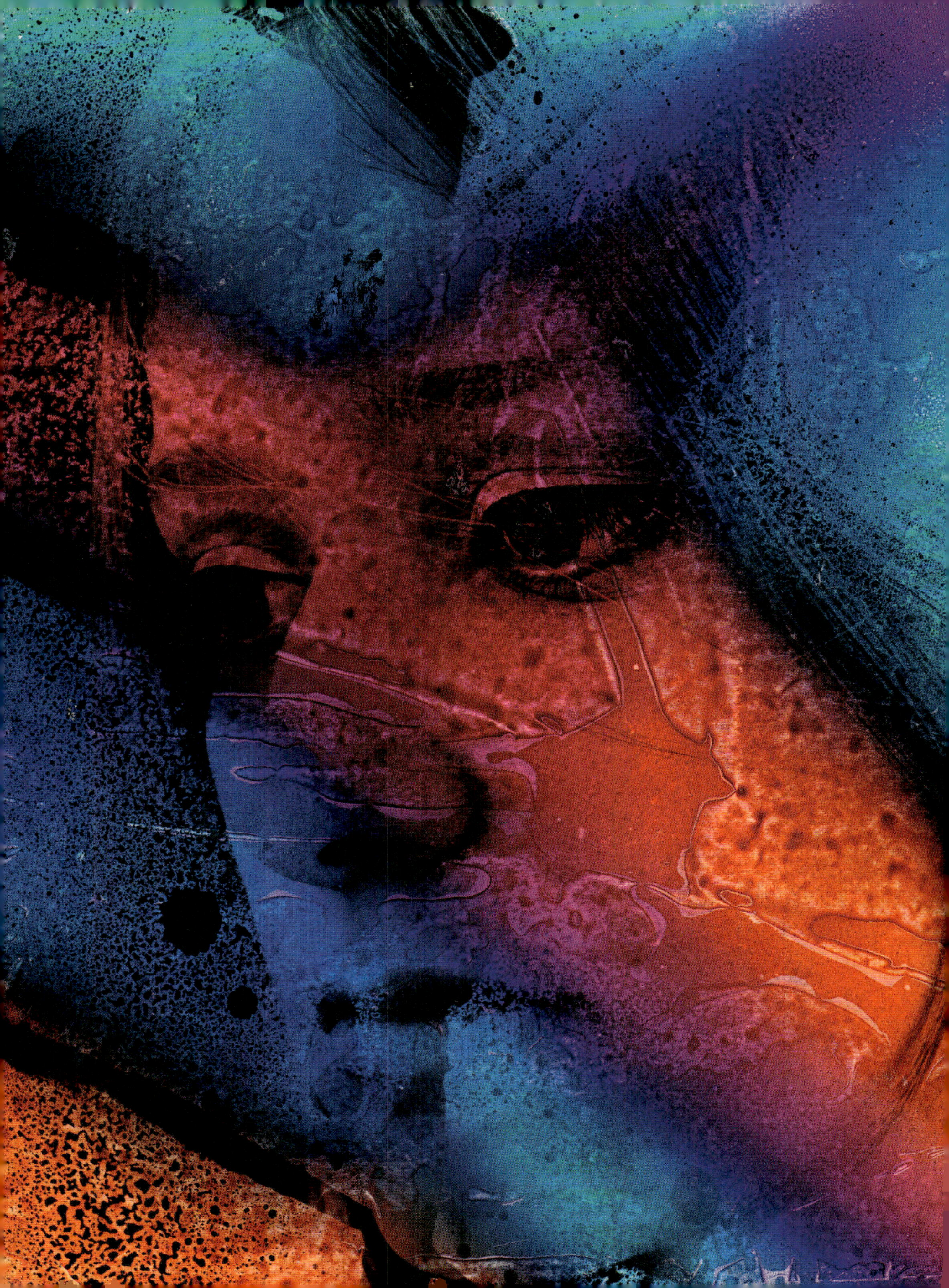

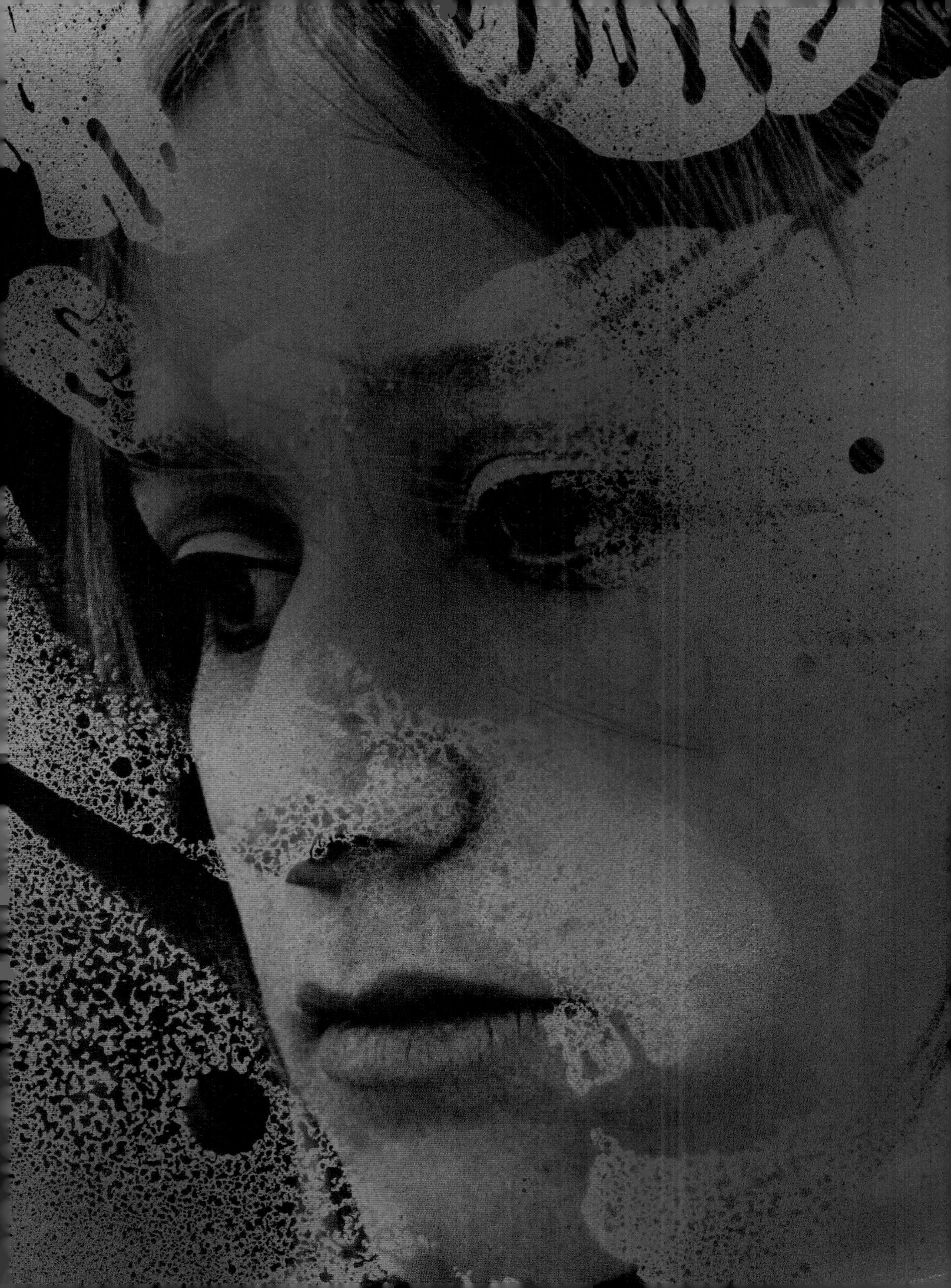

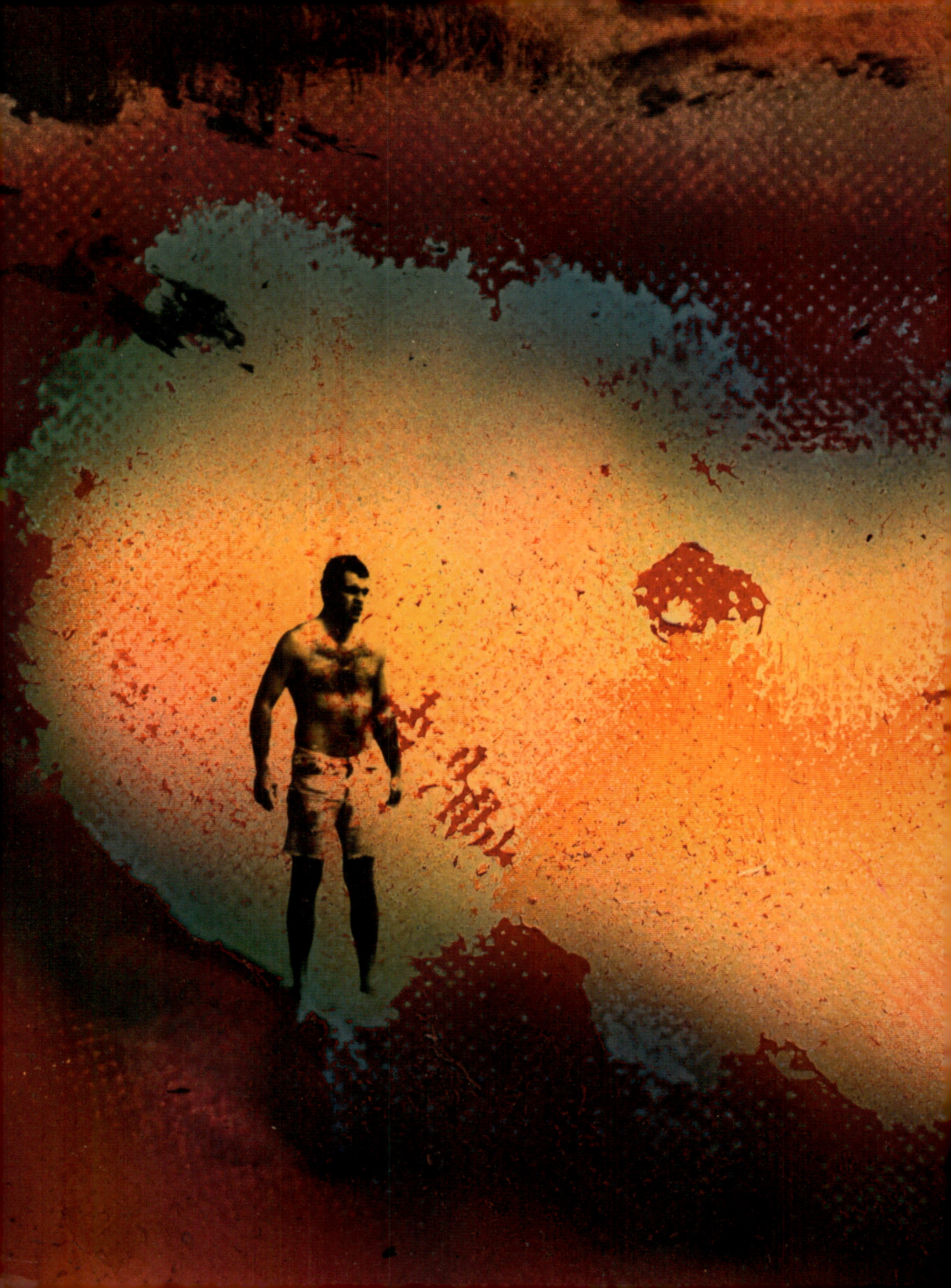

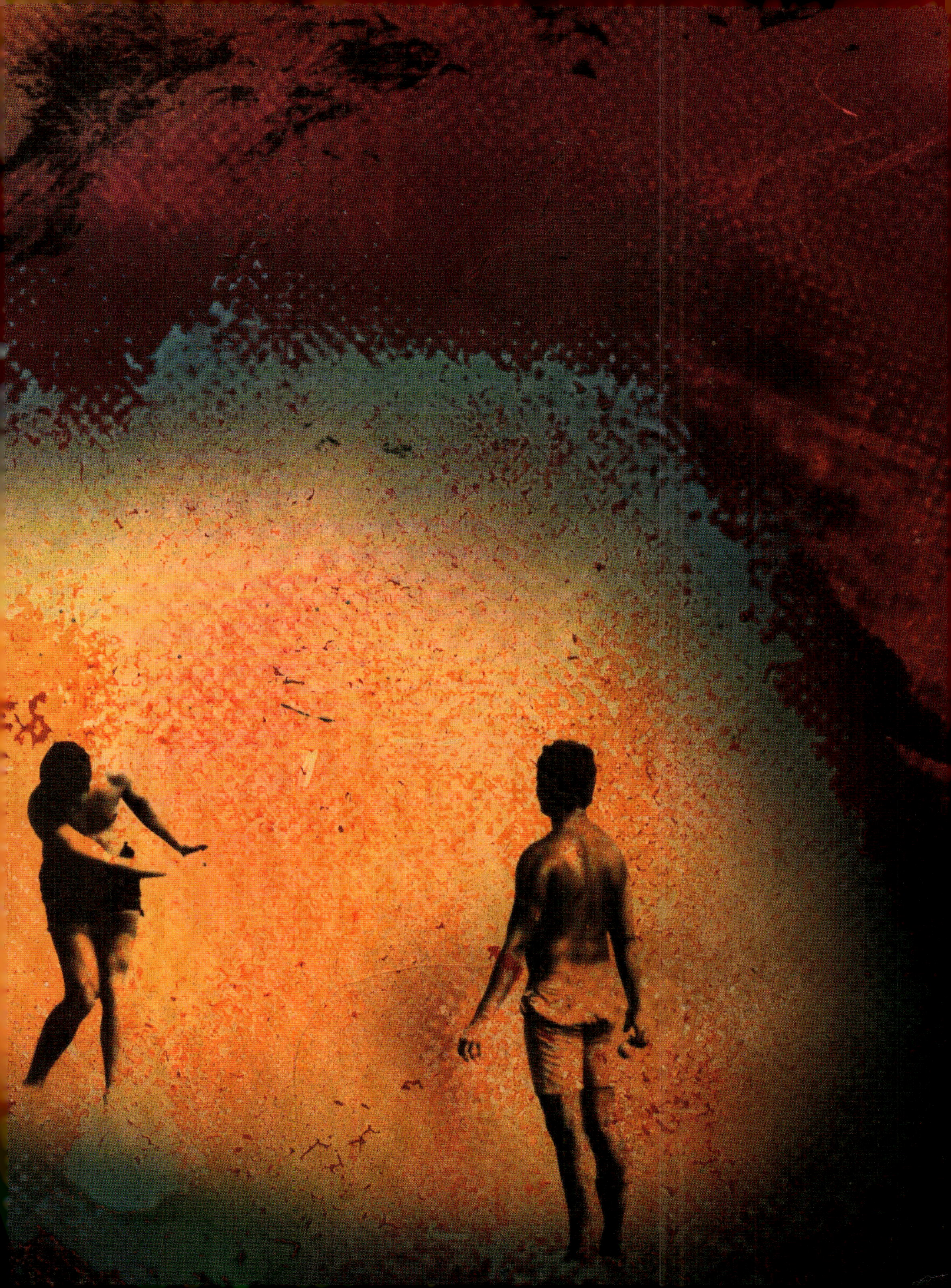

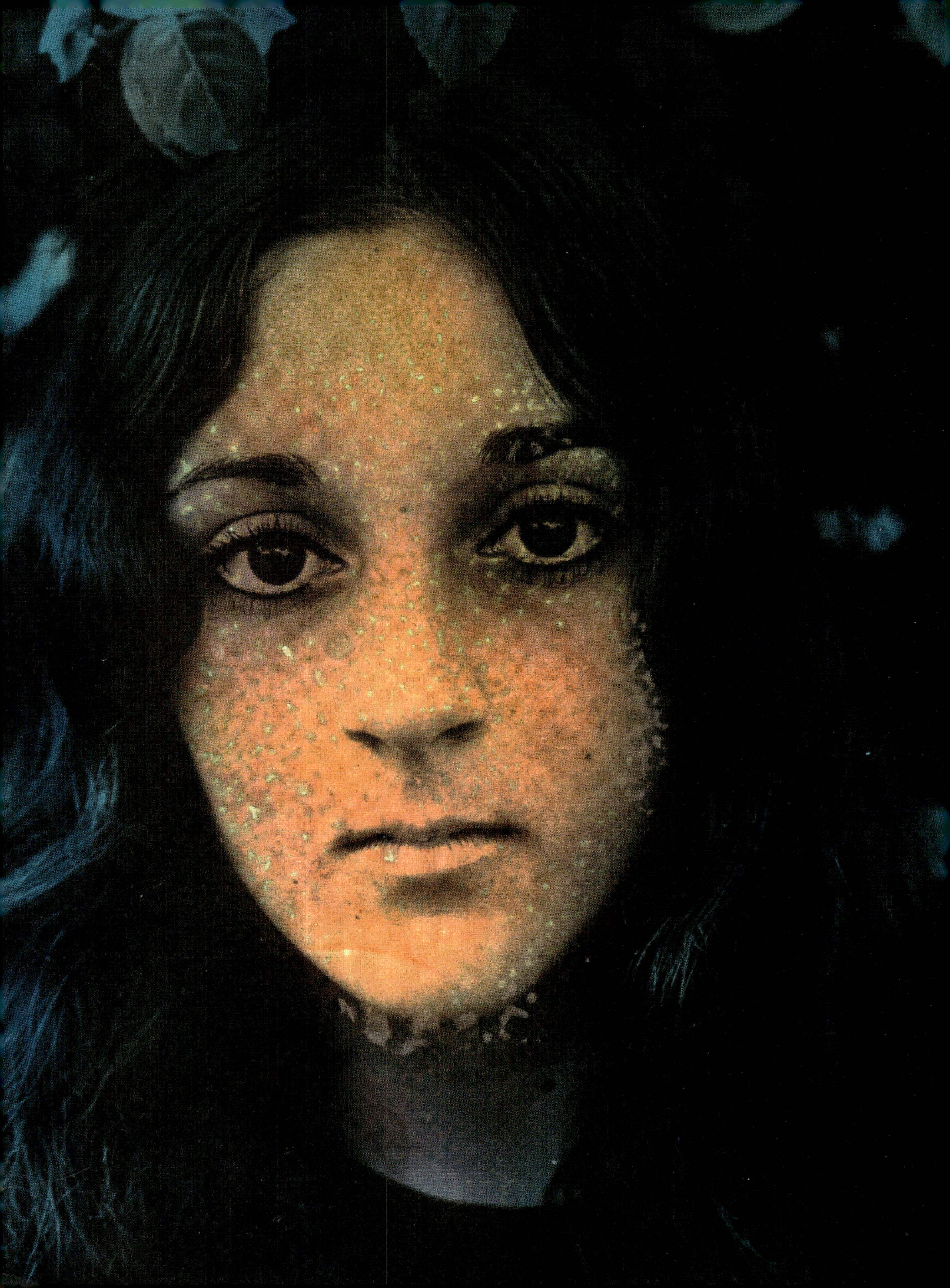

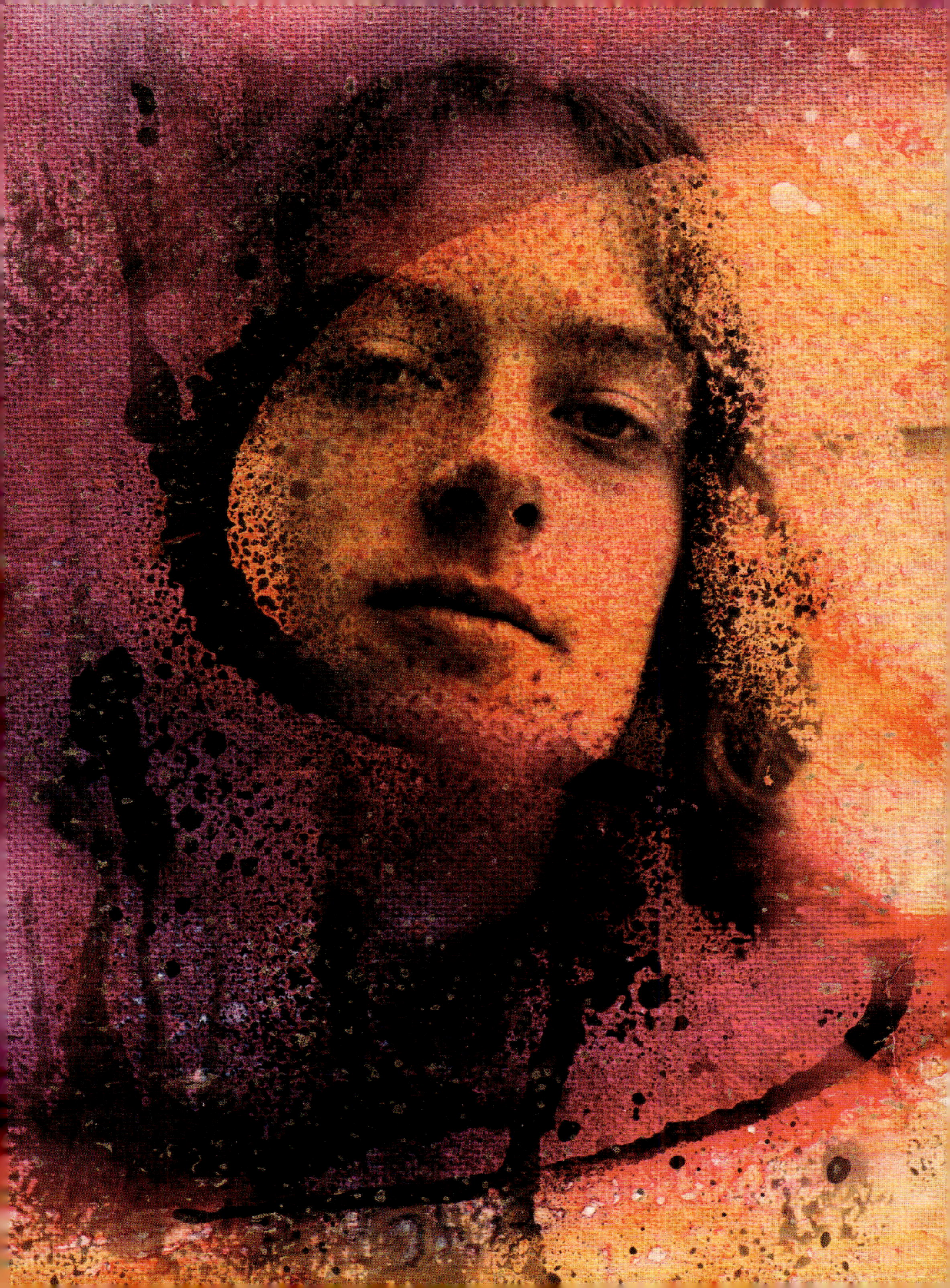

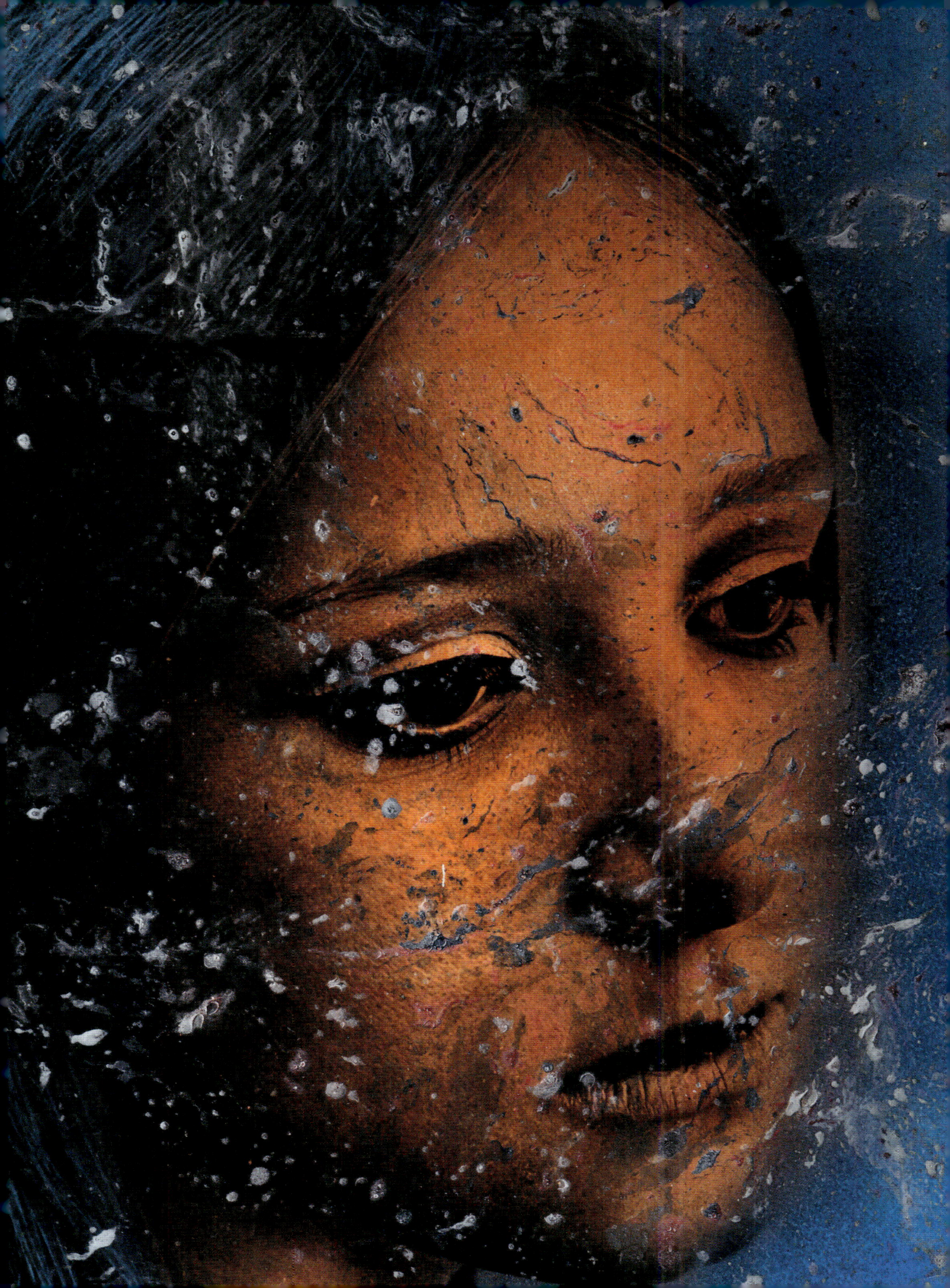

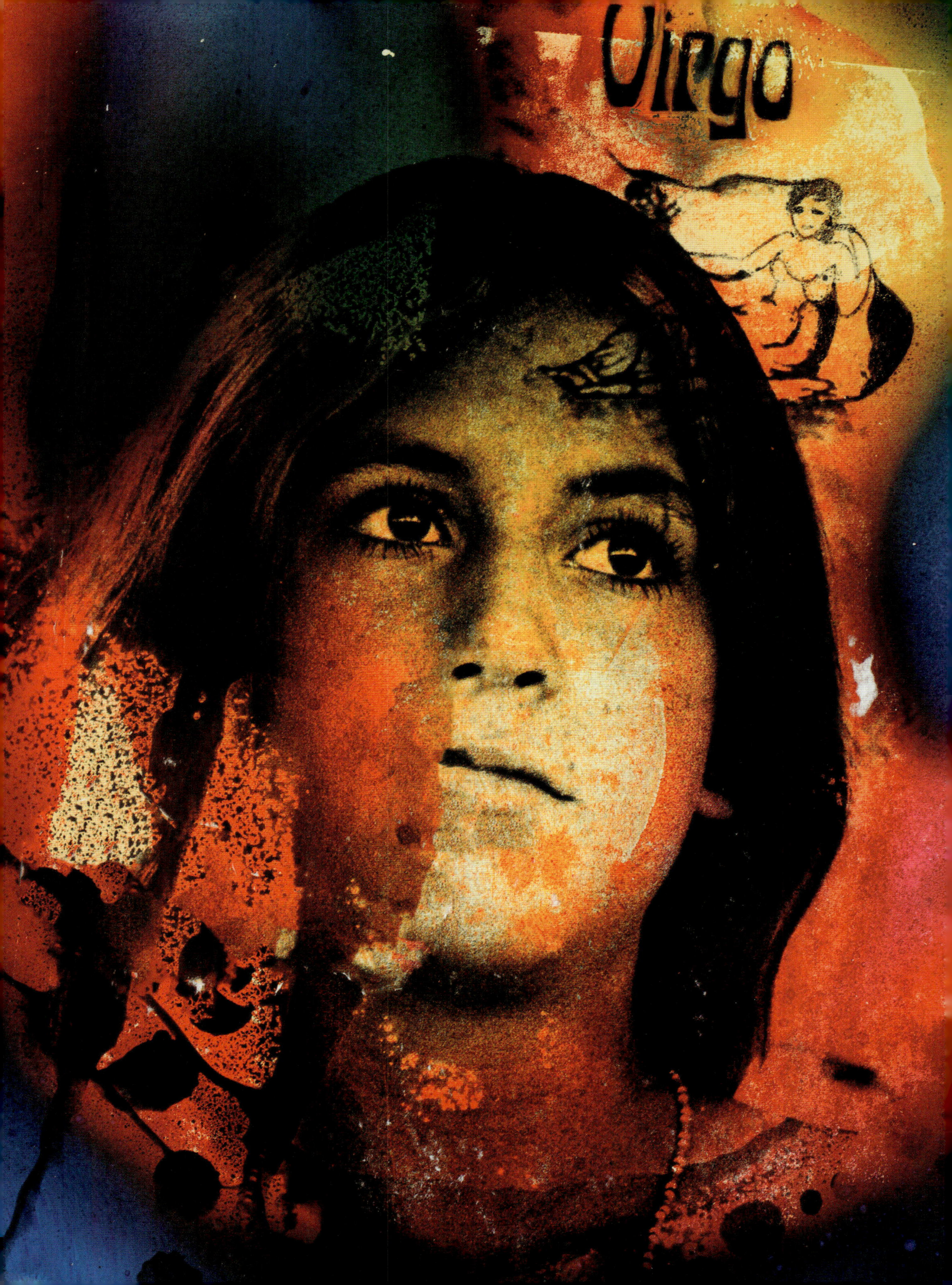
Virgo

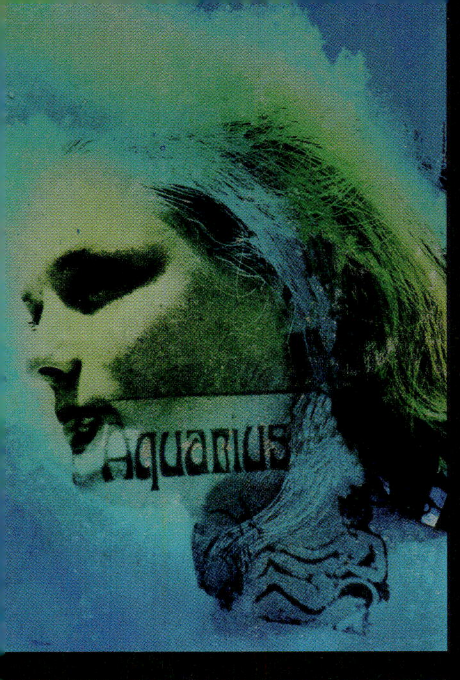
Aquarius

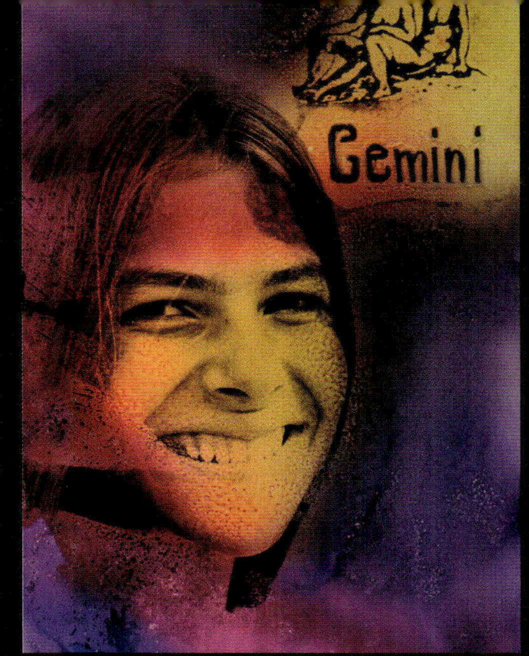
Gemini

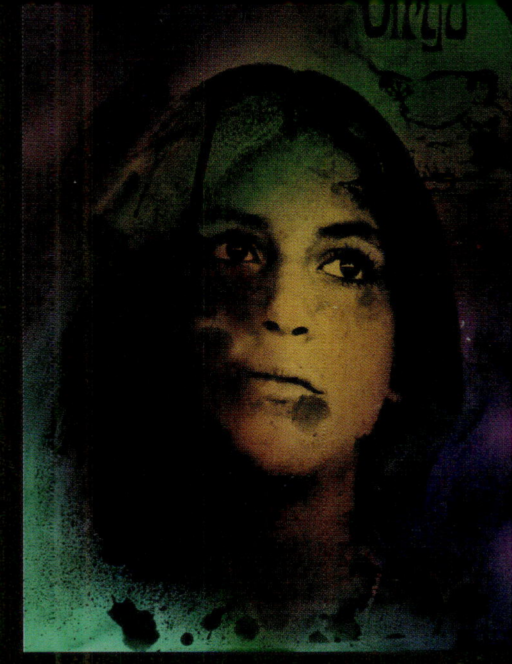
Virgo

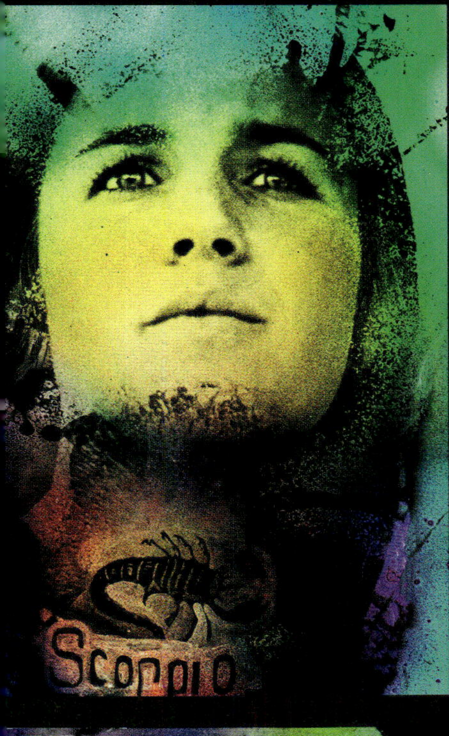
Scorpio

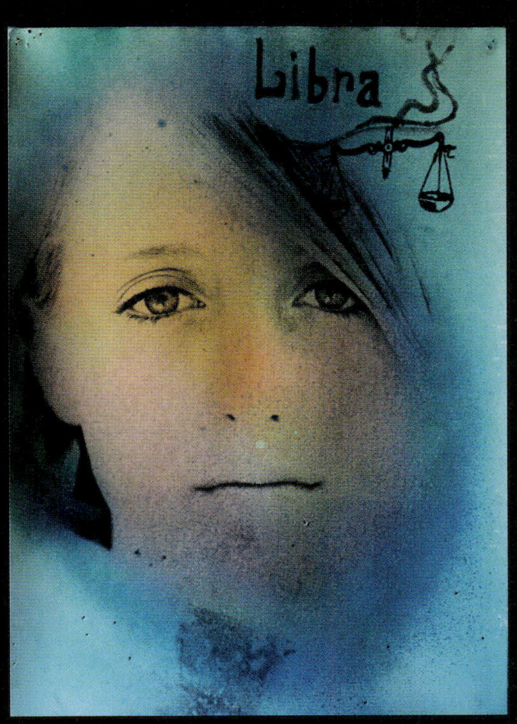
Libra

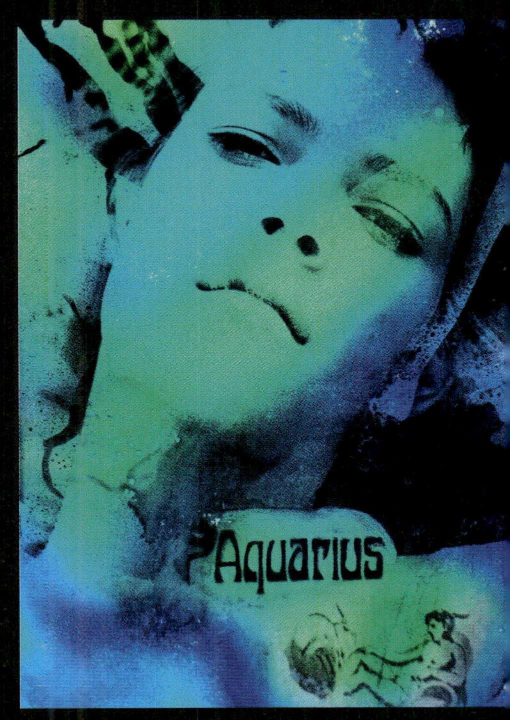
Aquarius

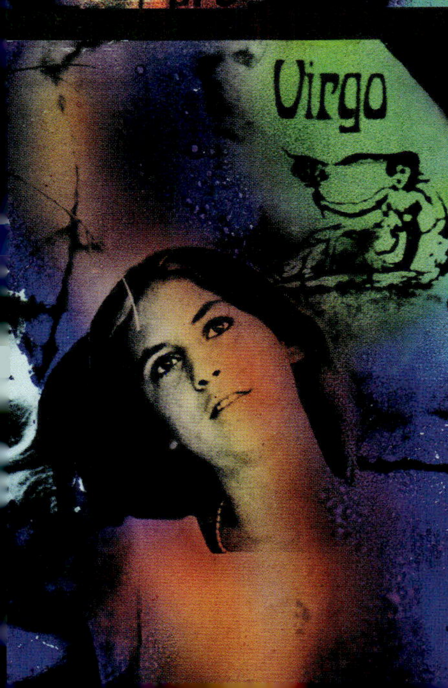
Virgo

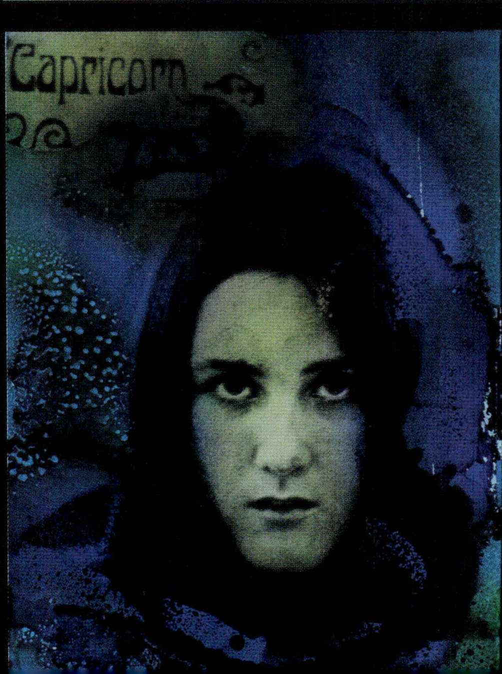
Capricorn

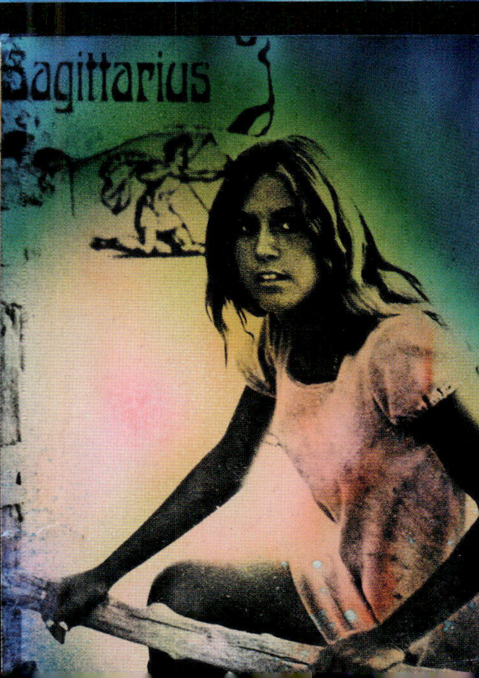
Sagittarius

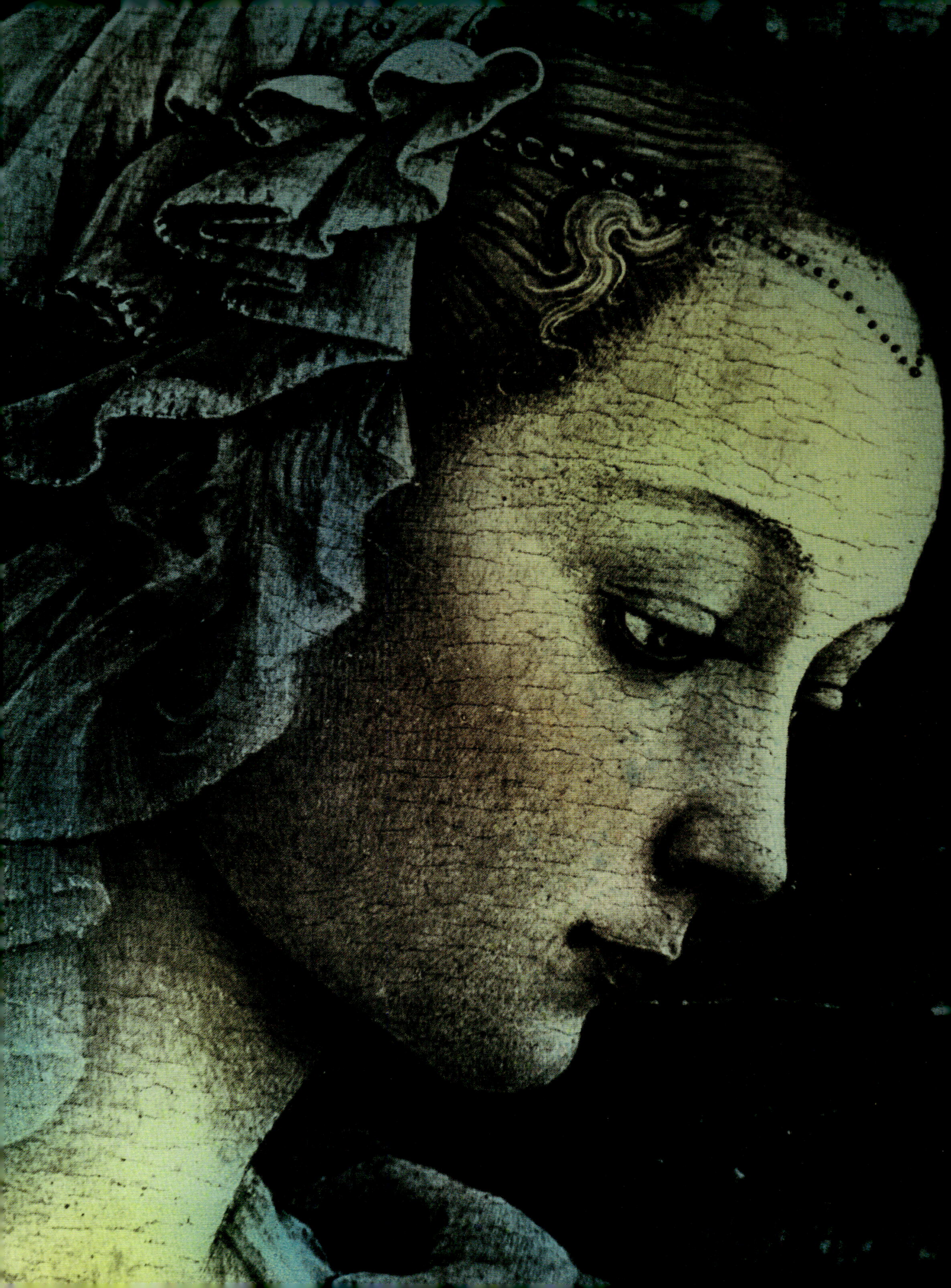

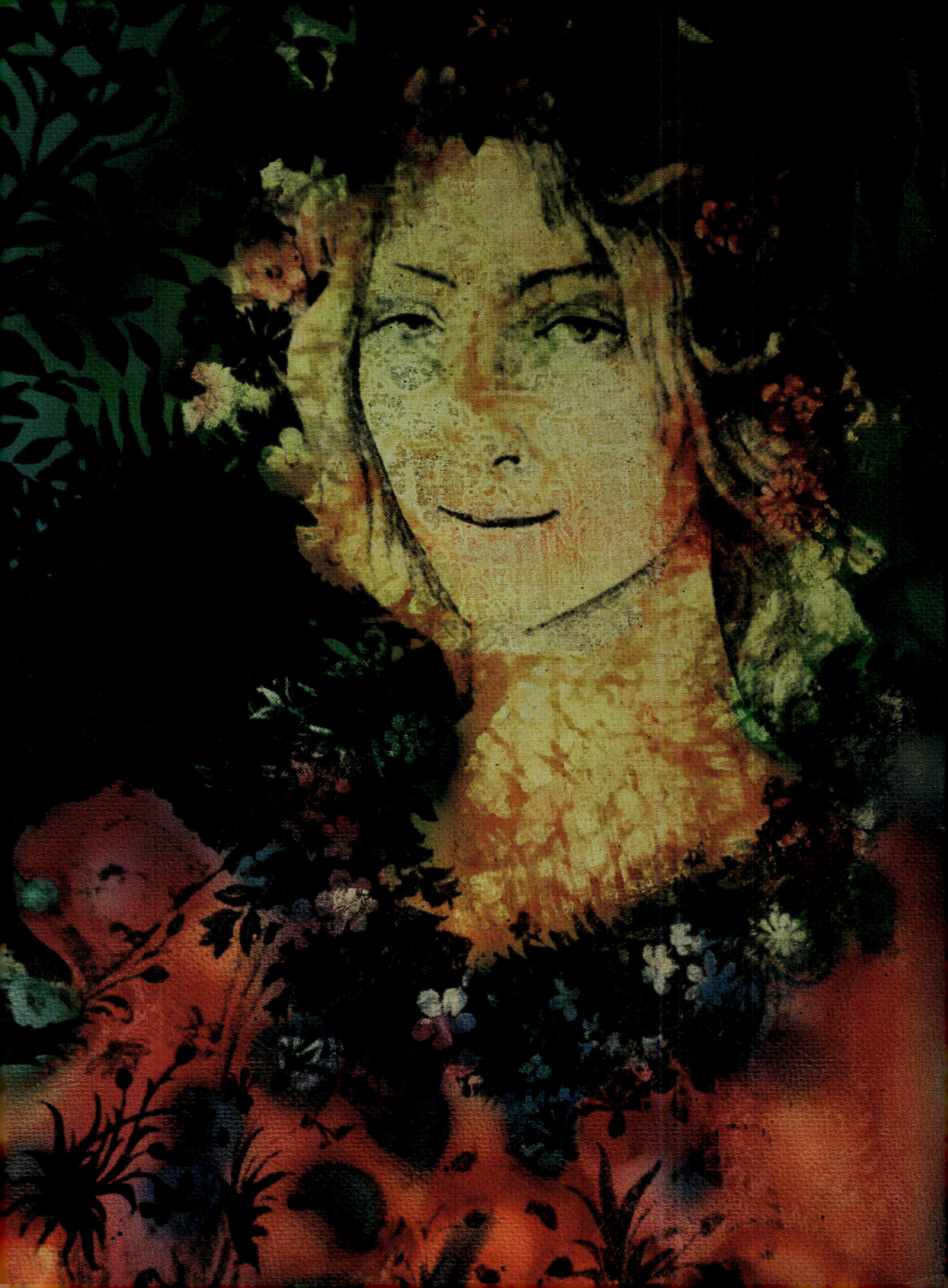

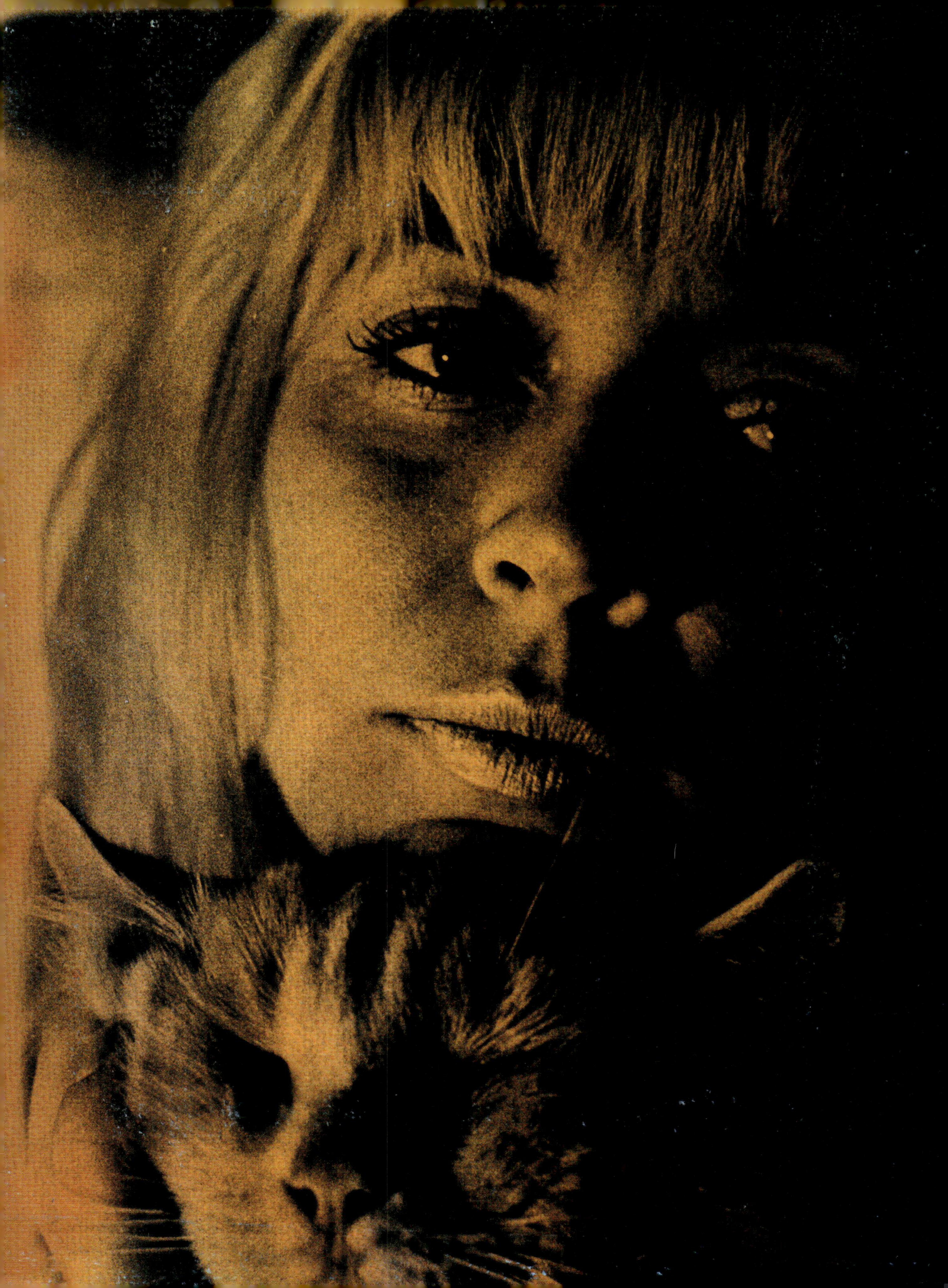

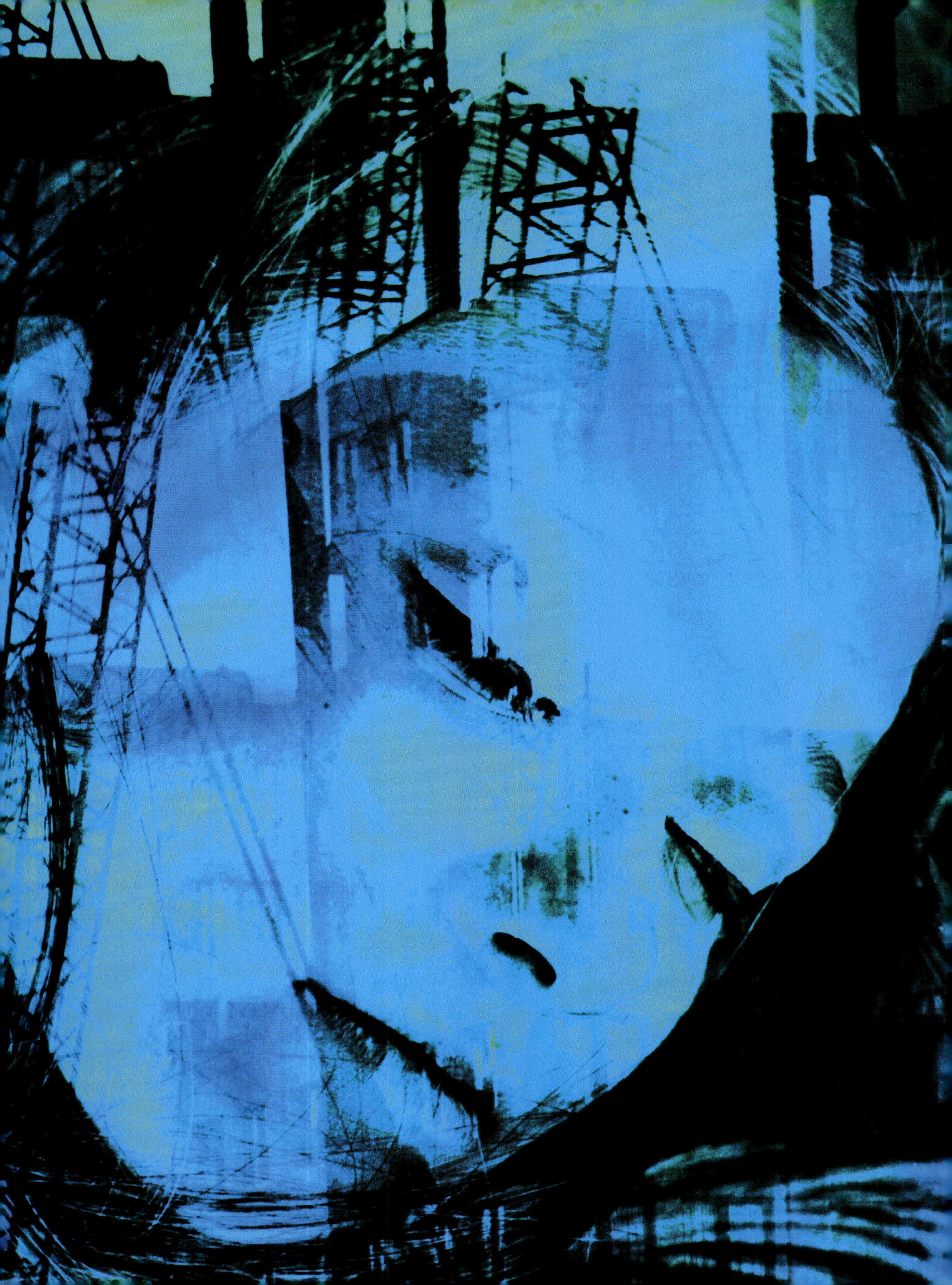

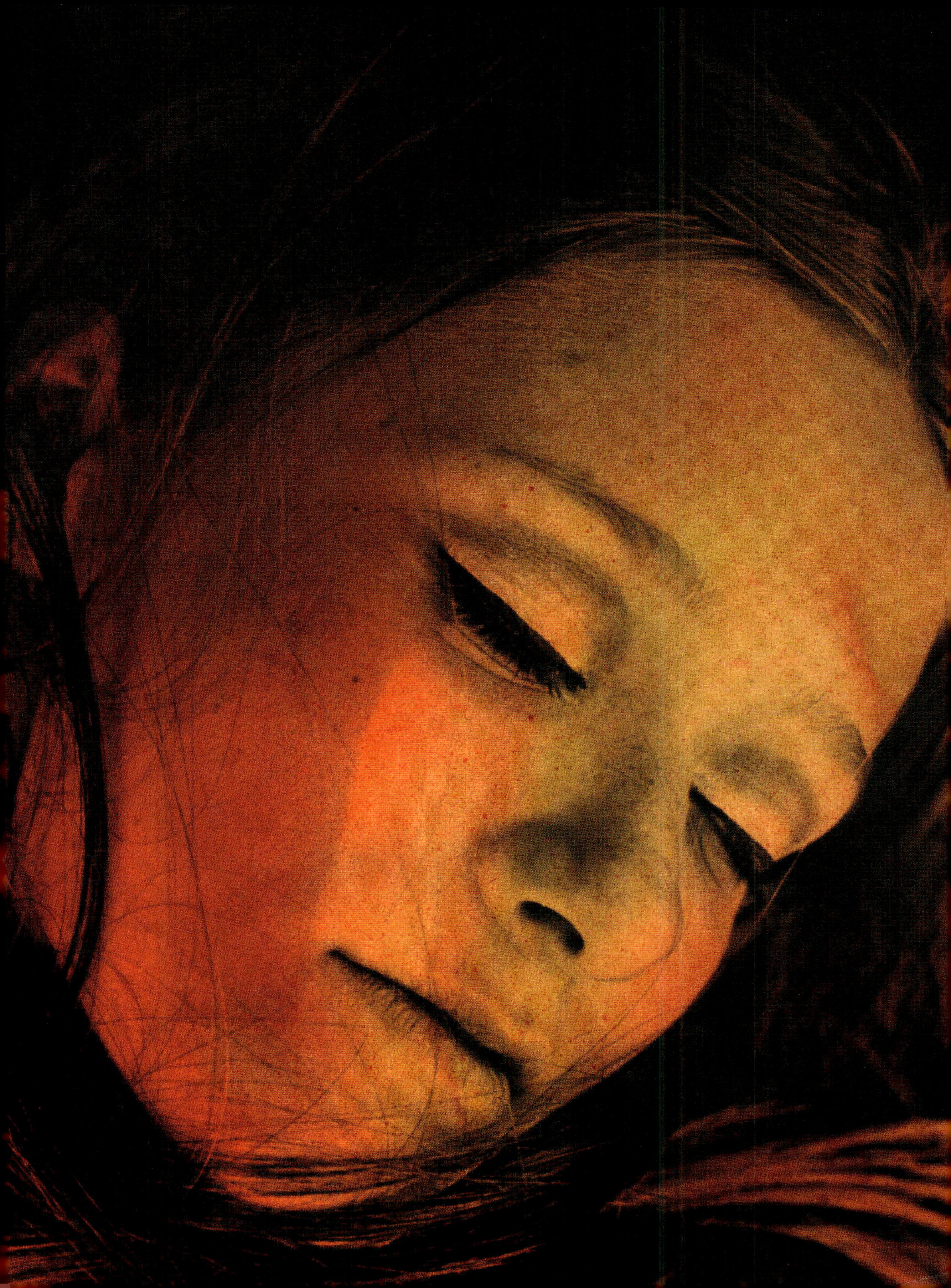

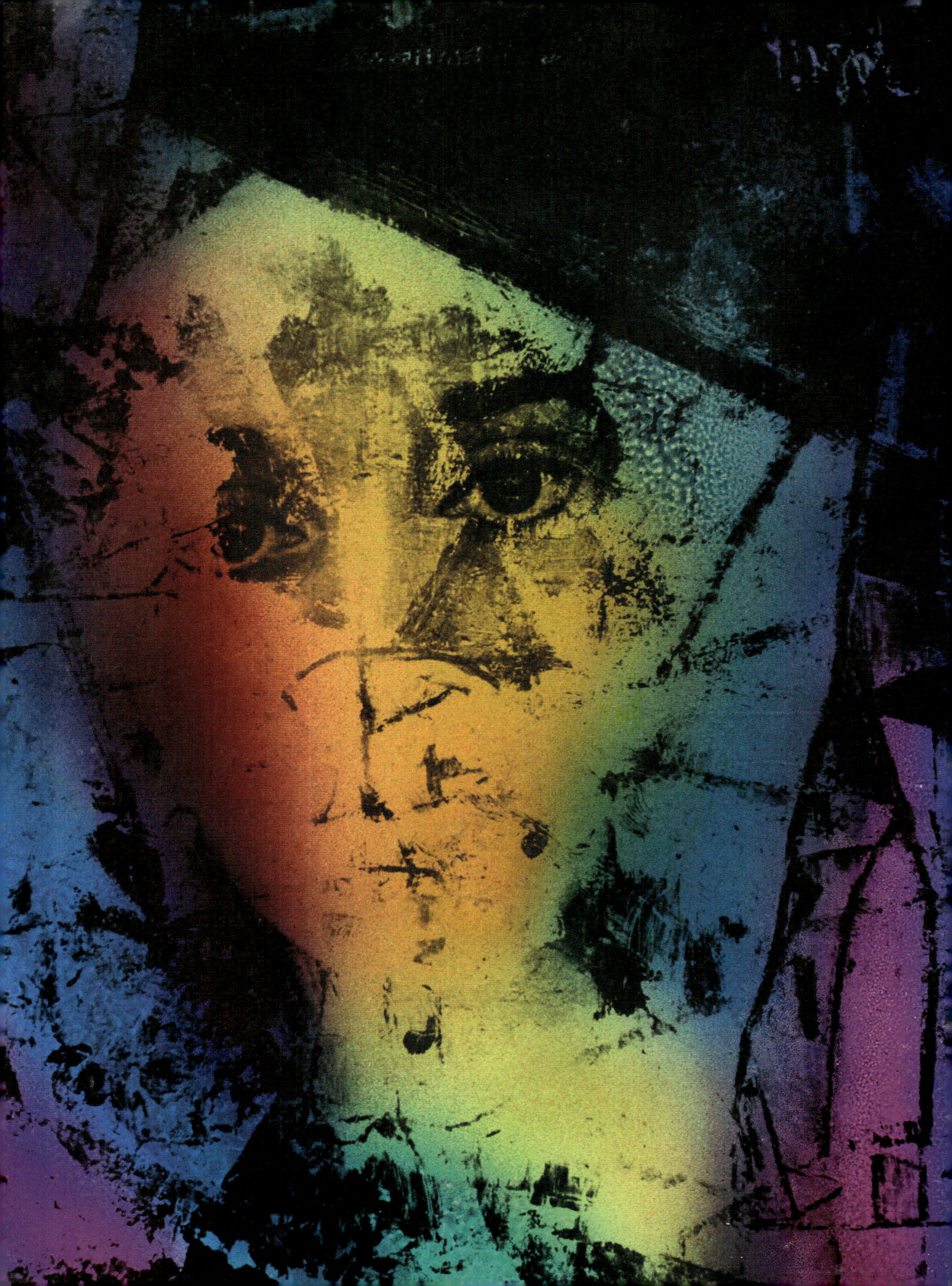

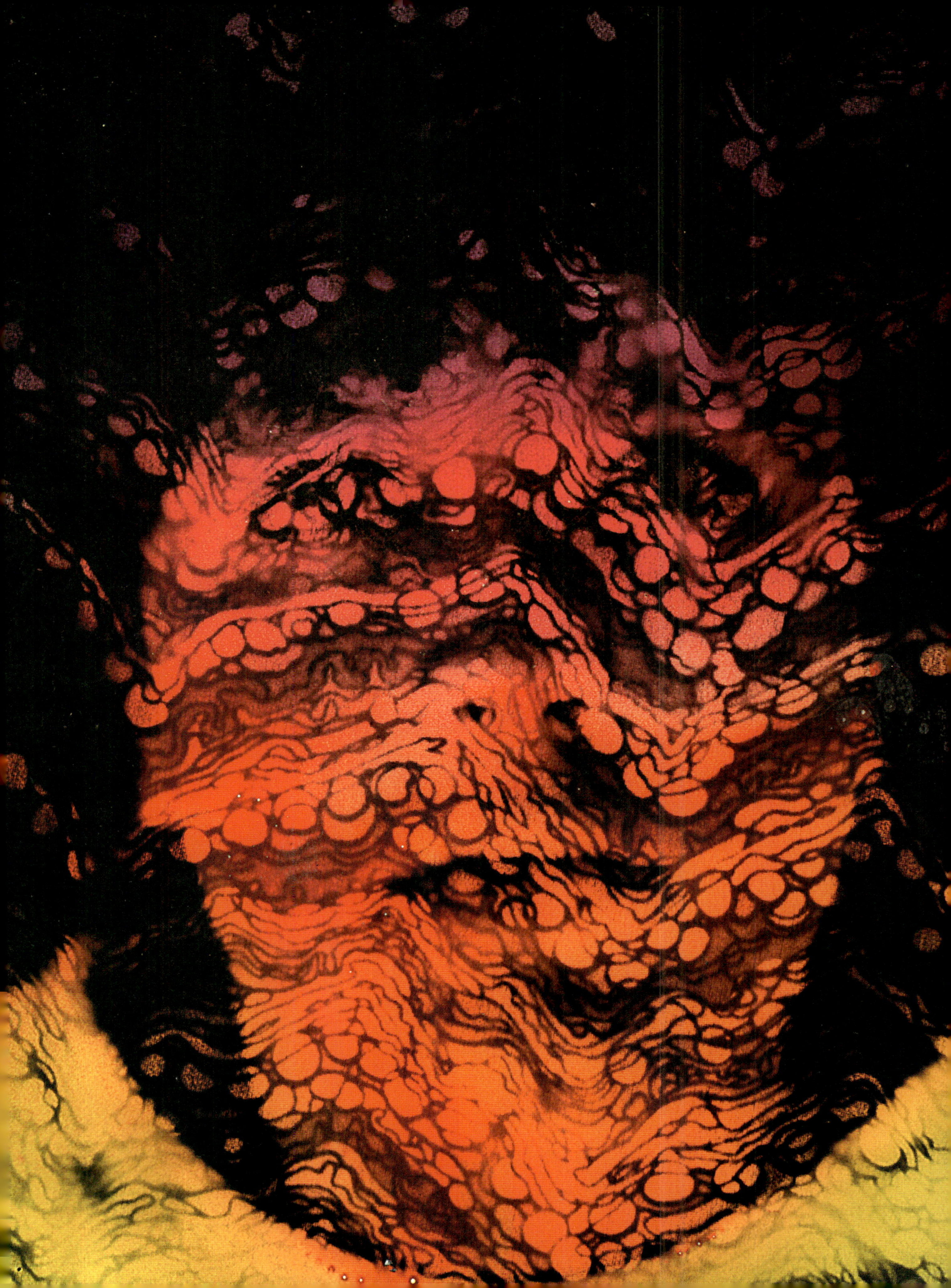

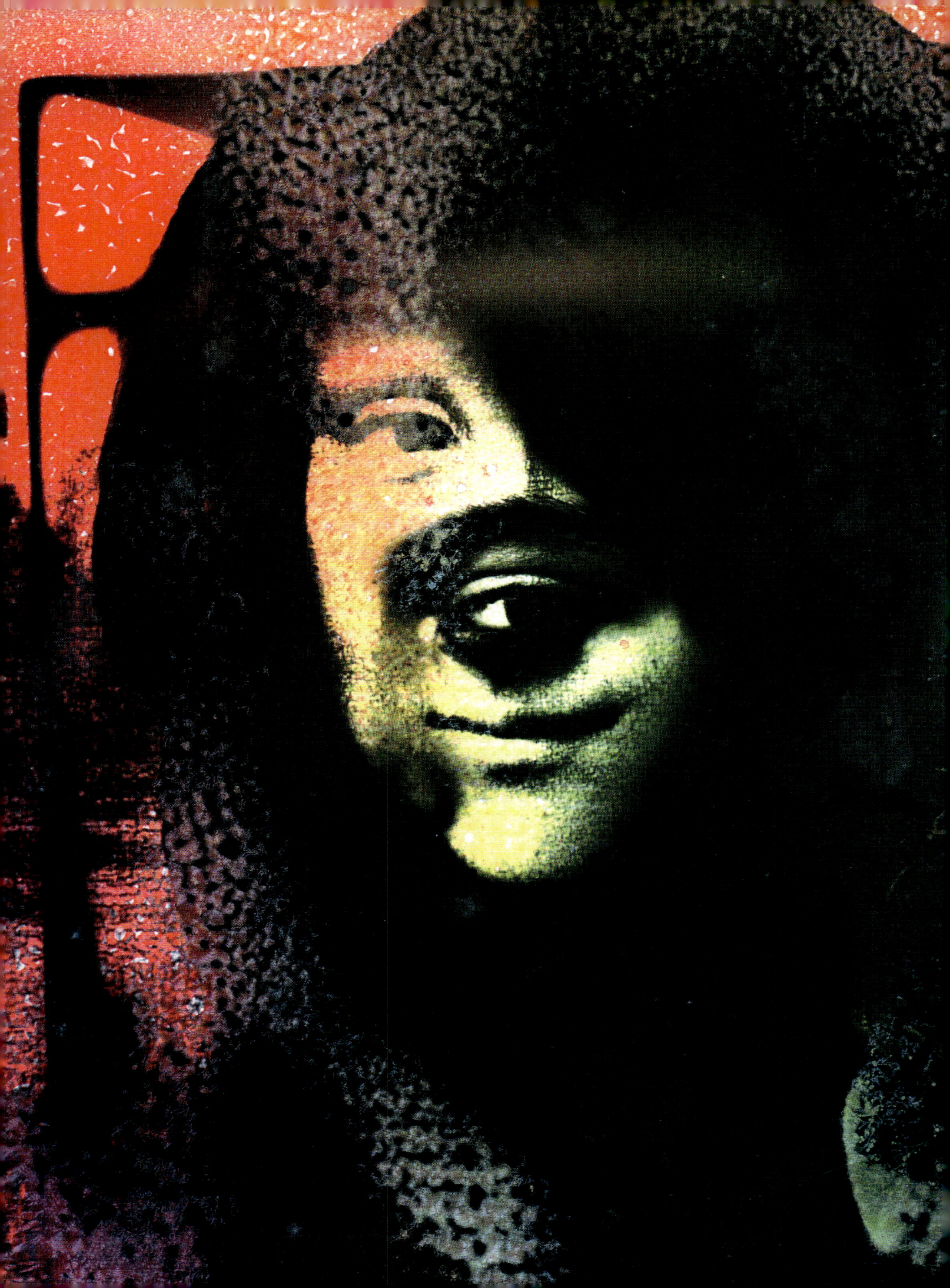

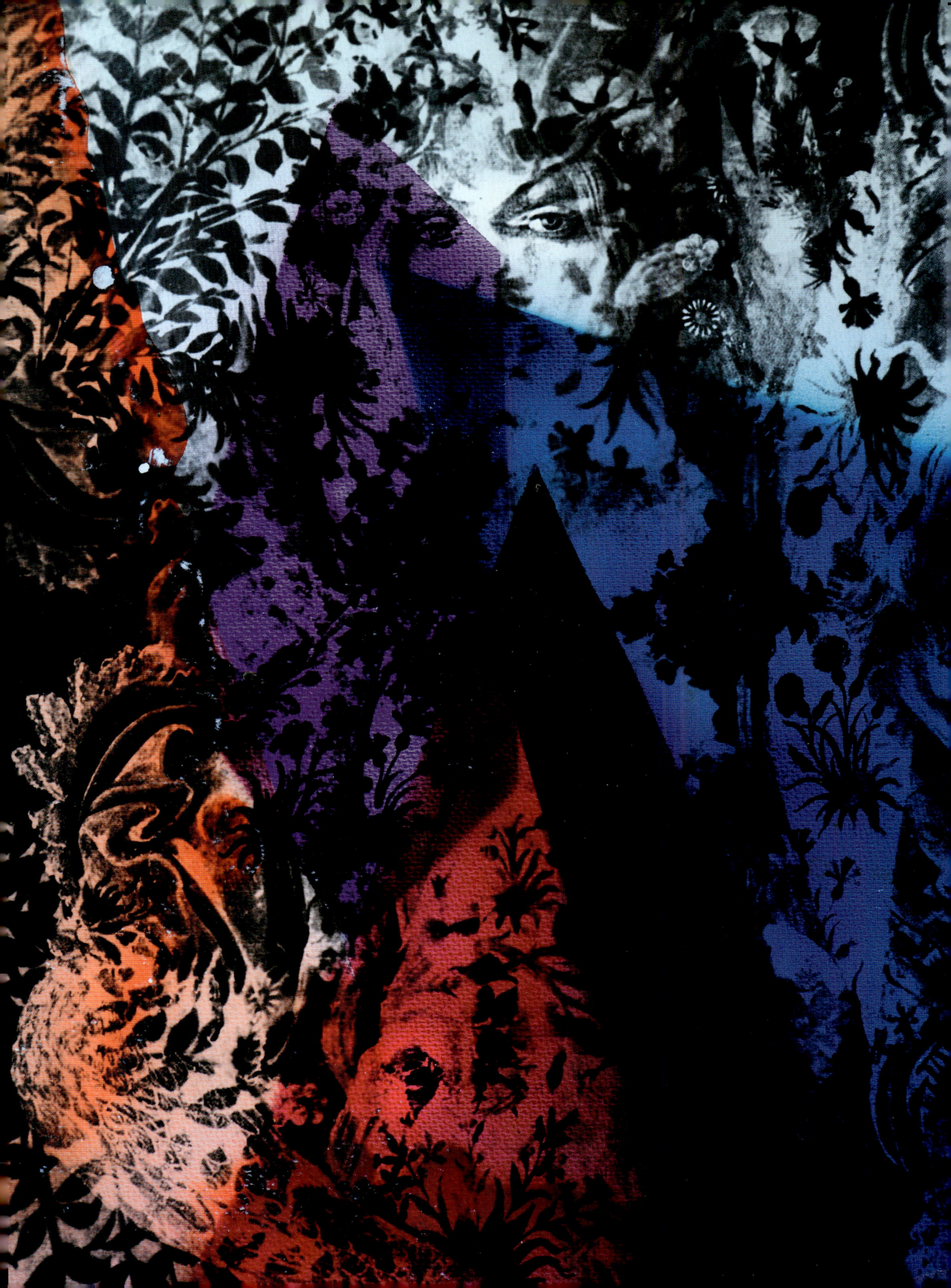

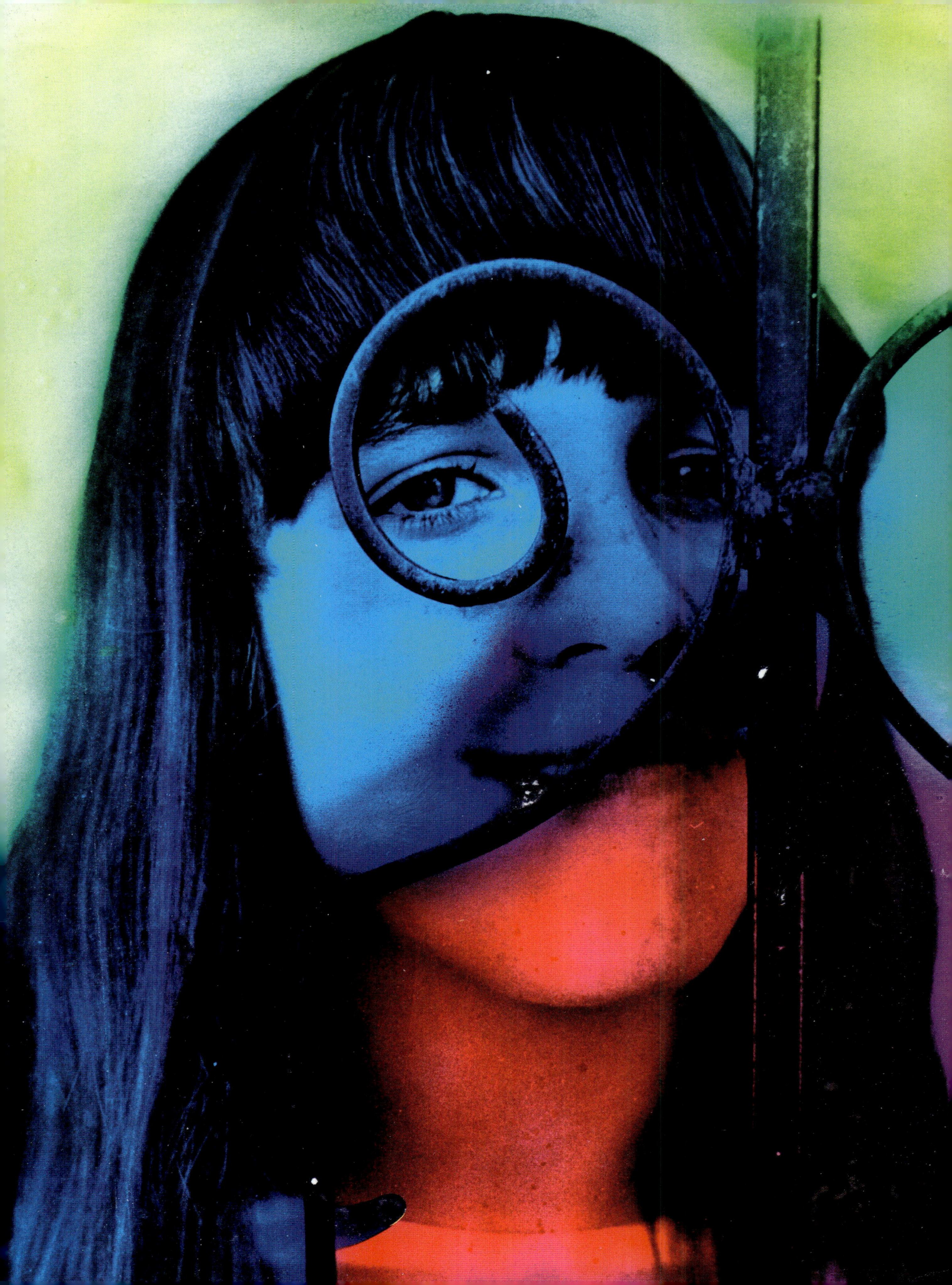

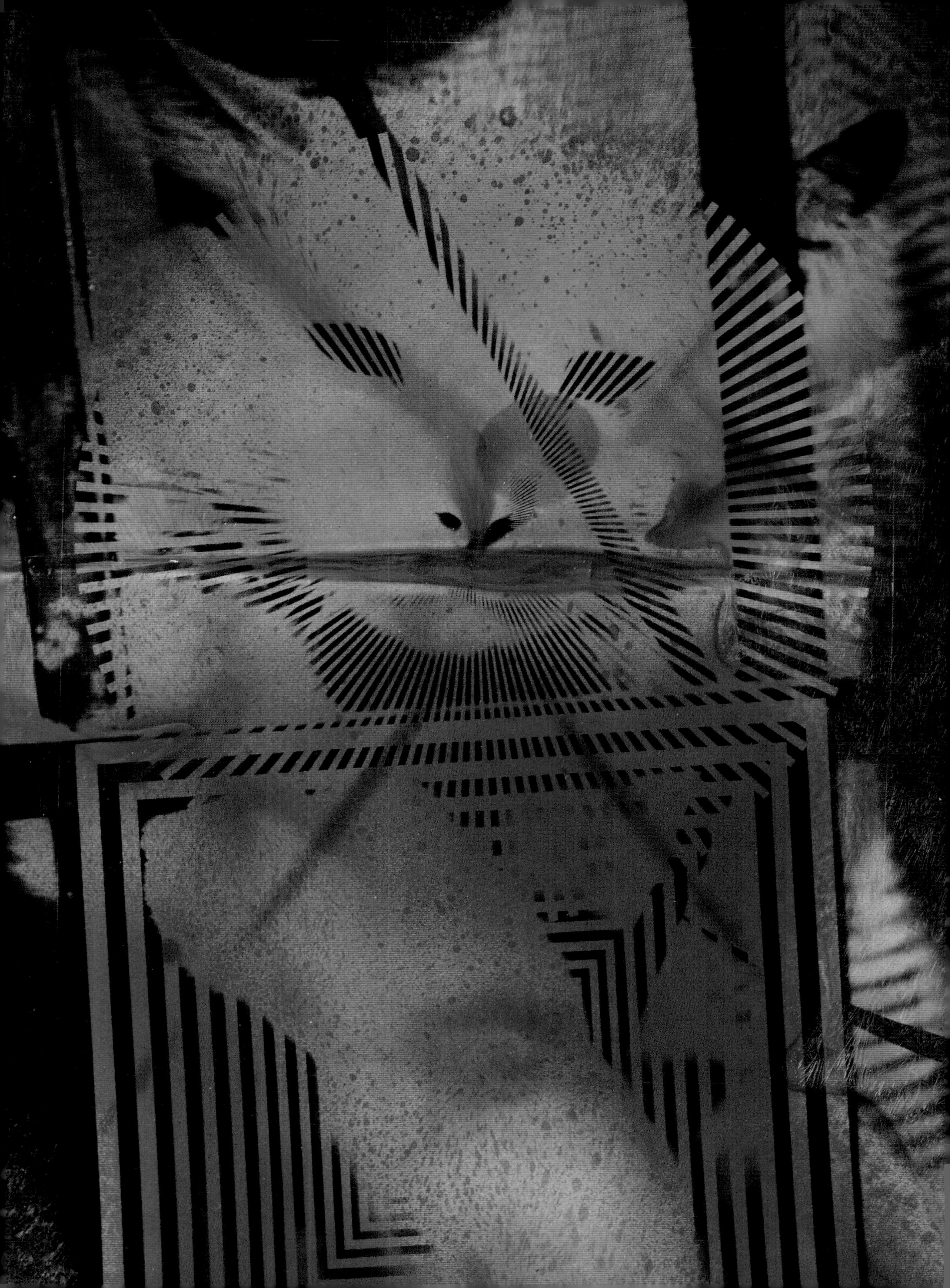

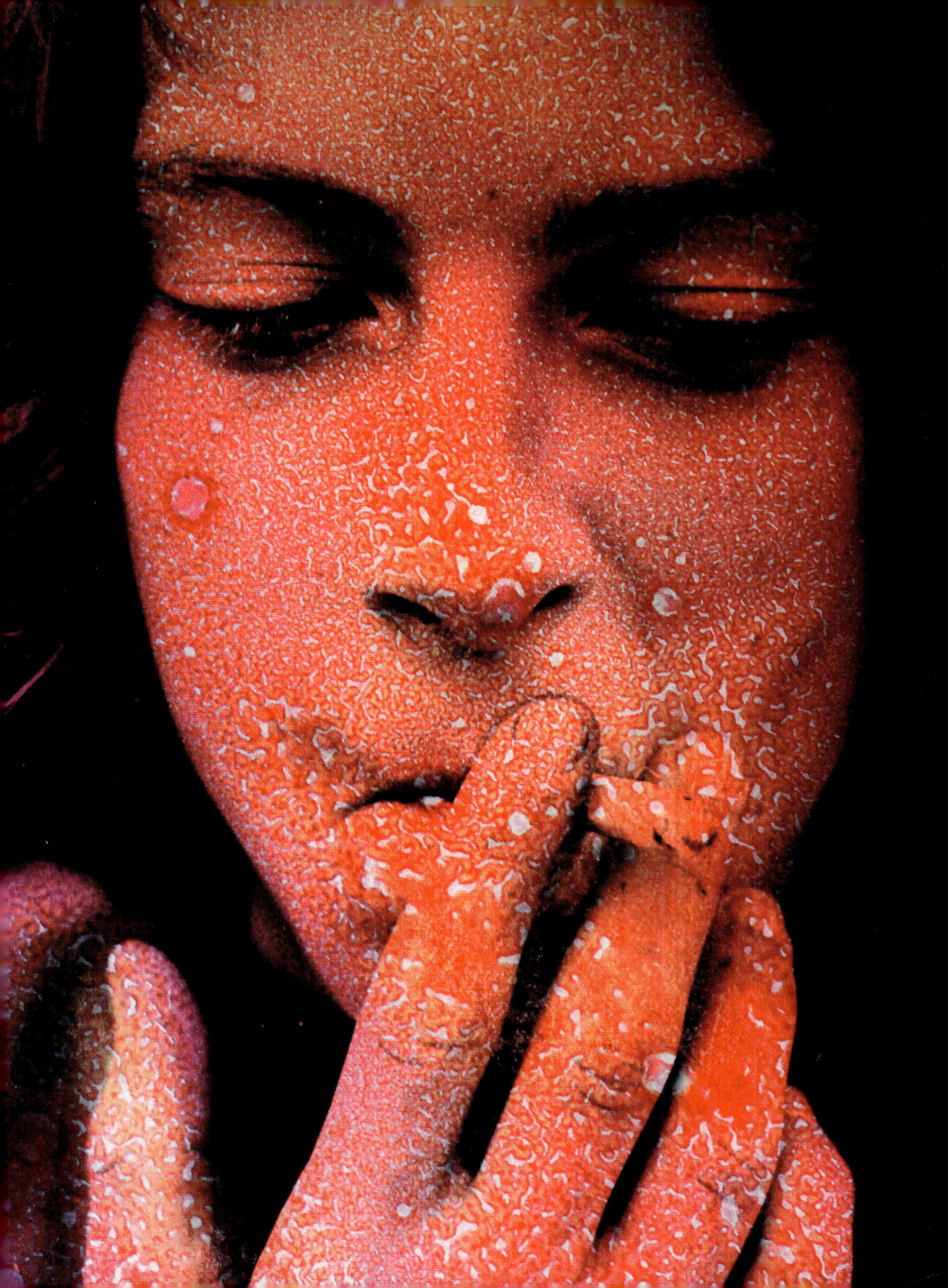

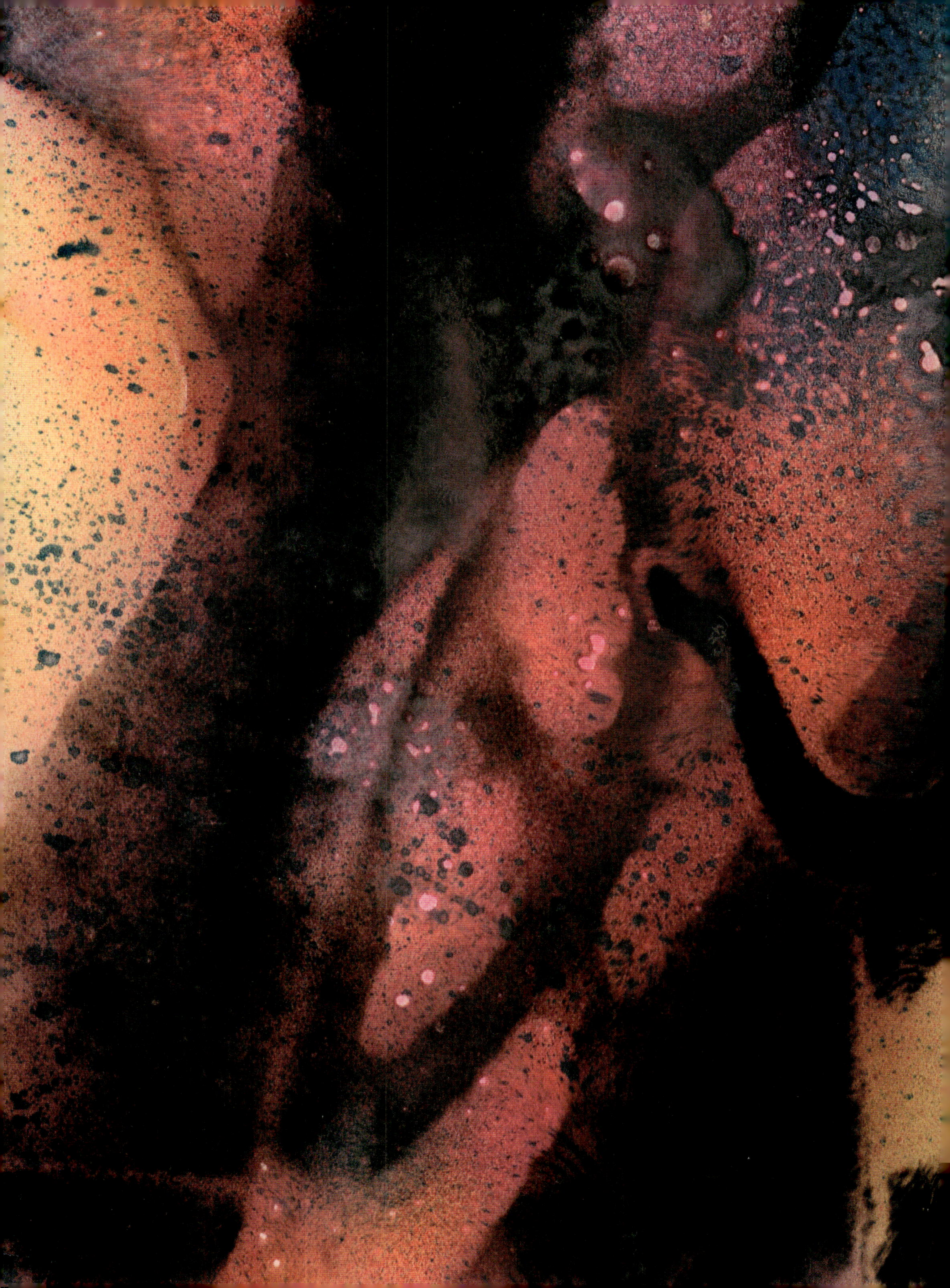

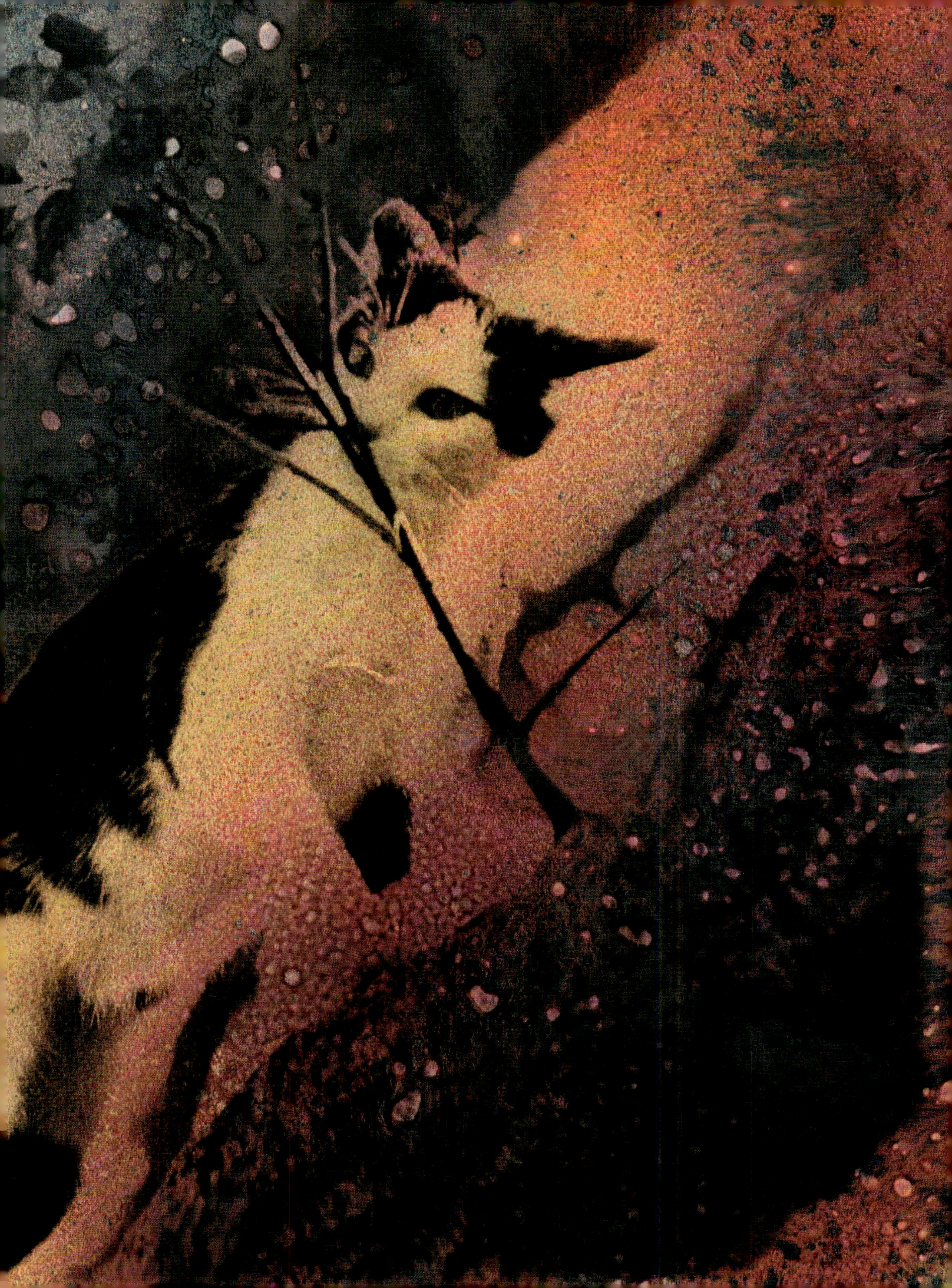

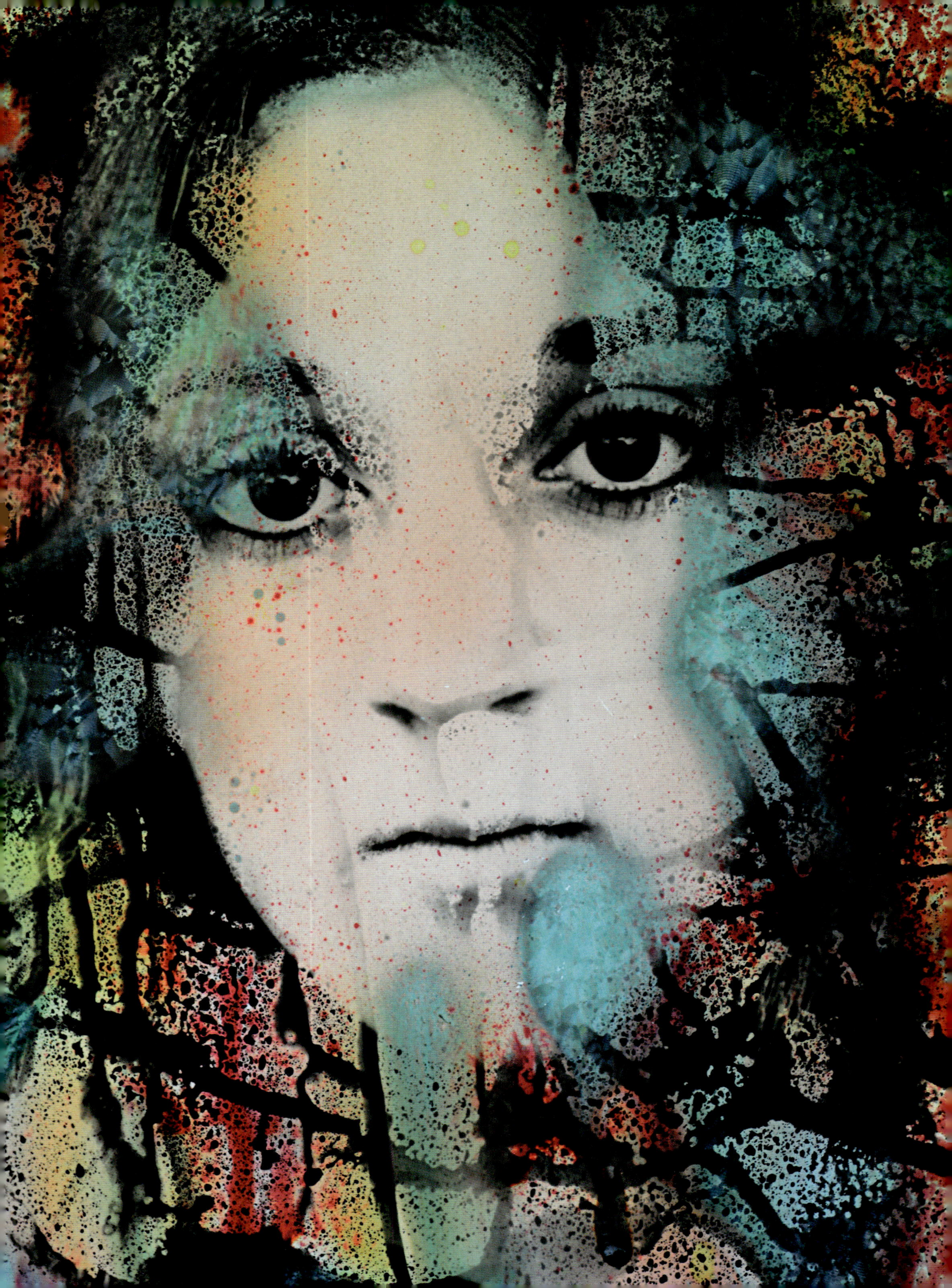

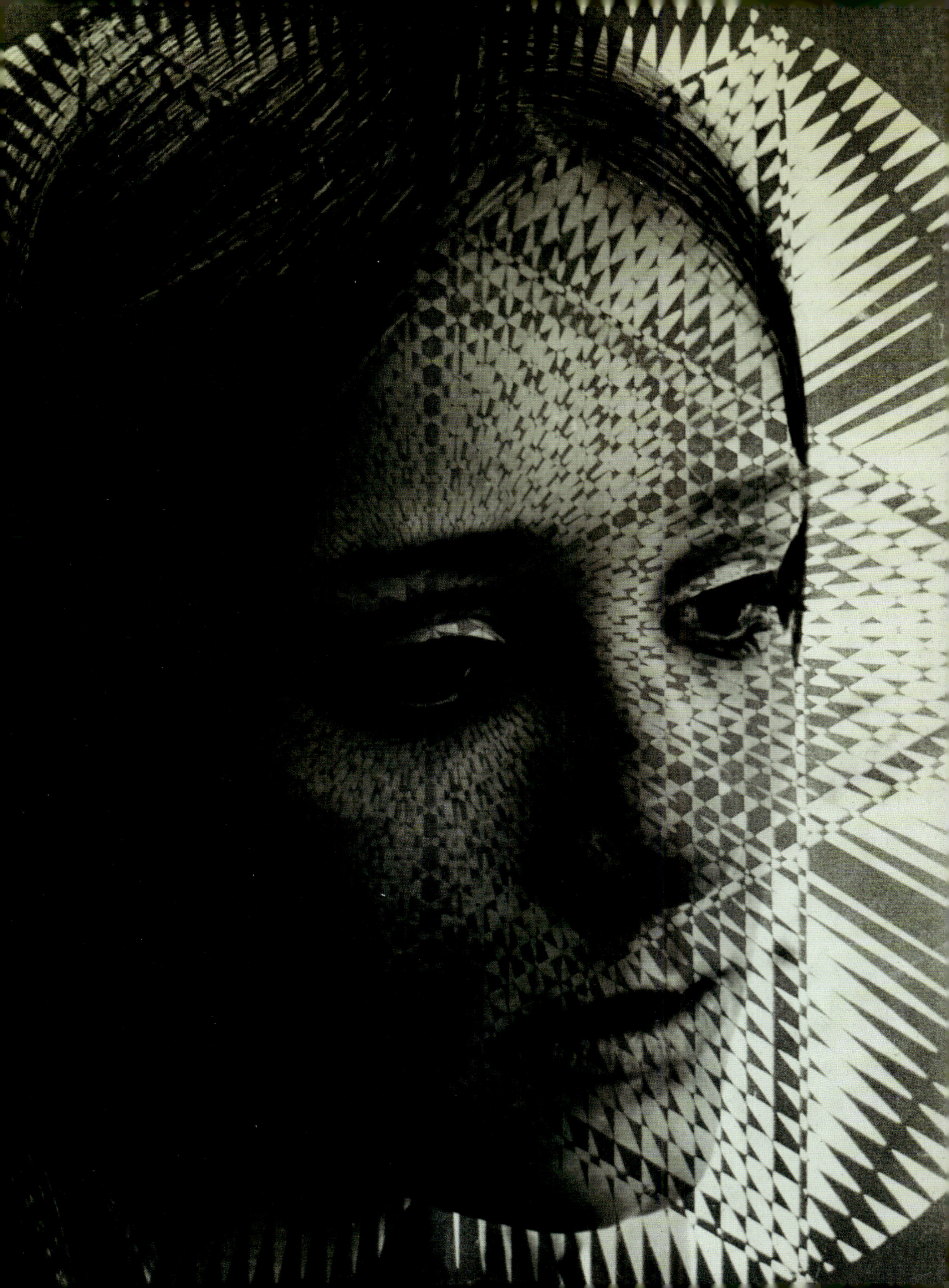

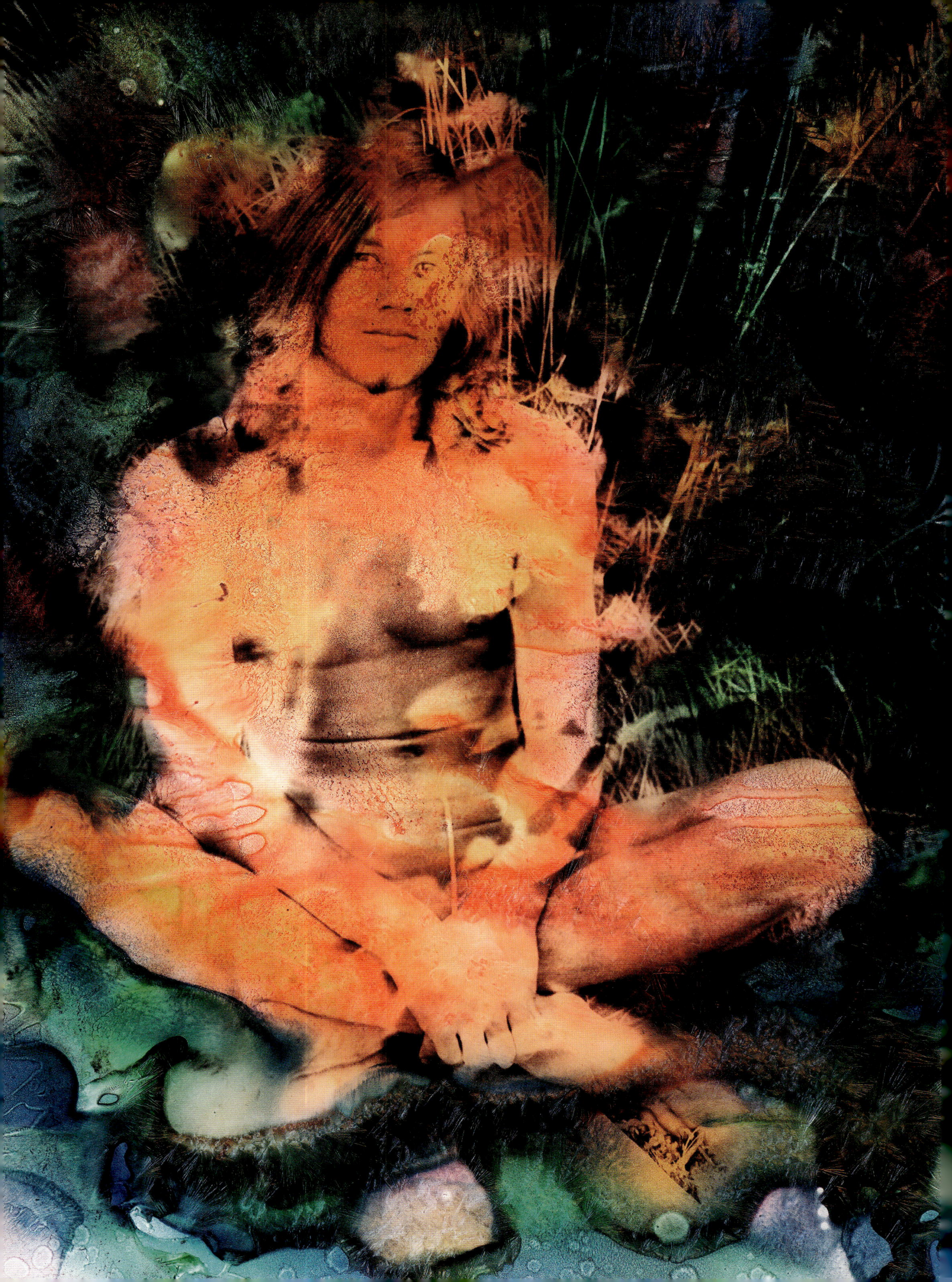

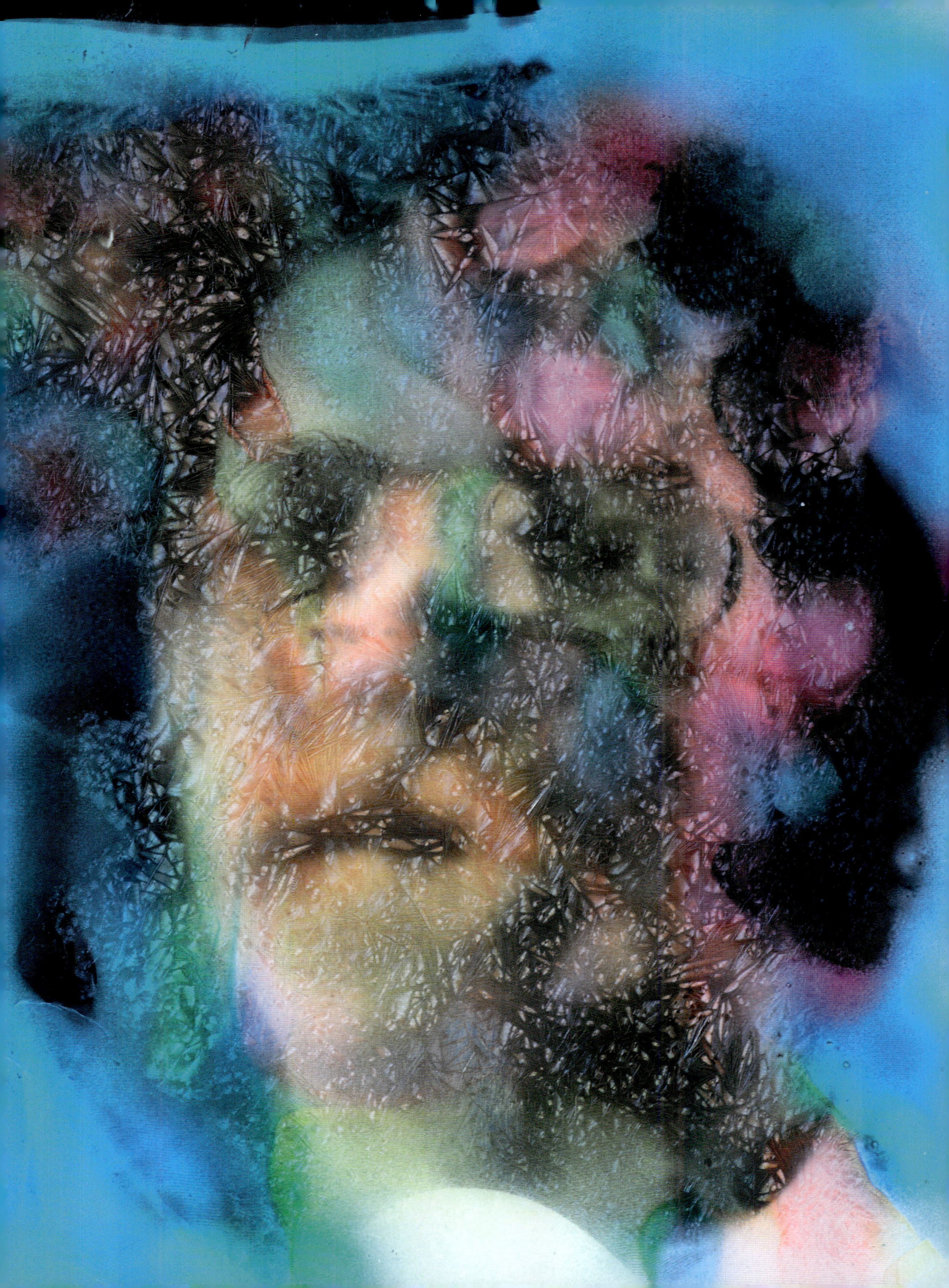

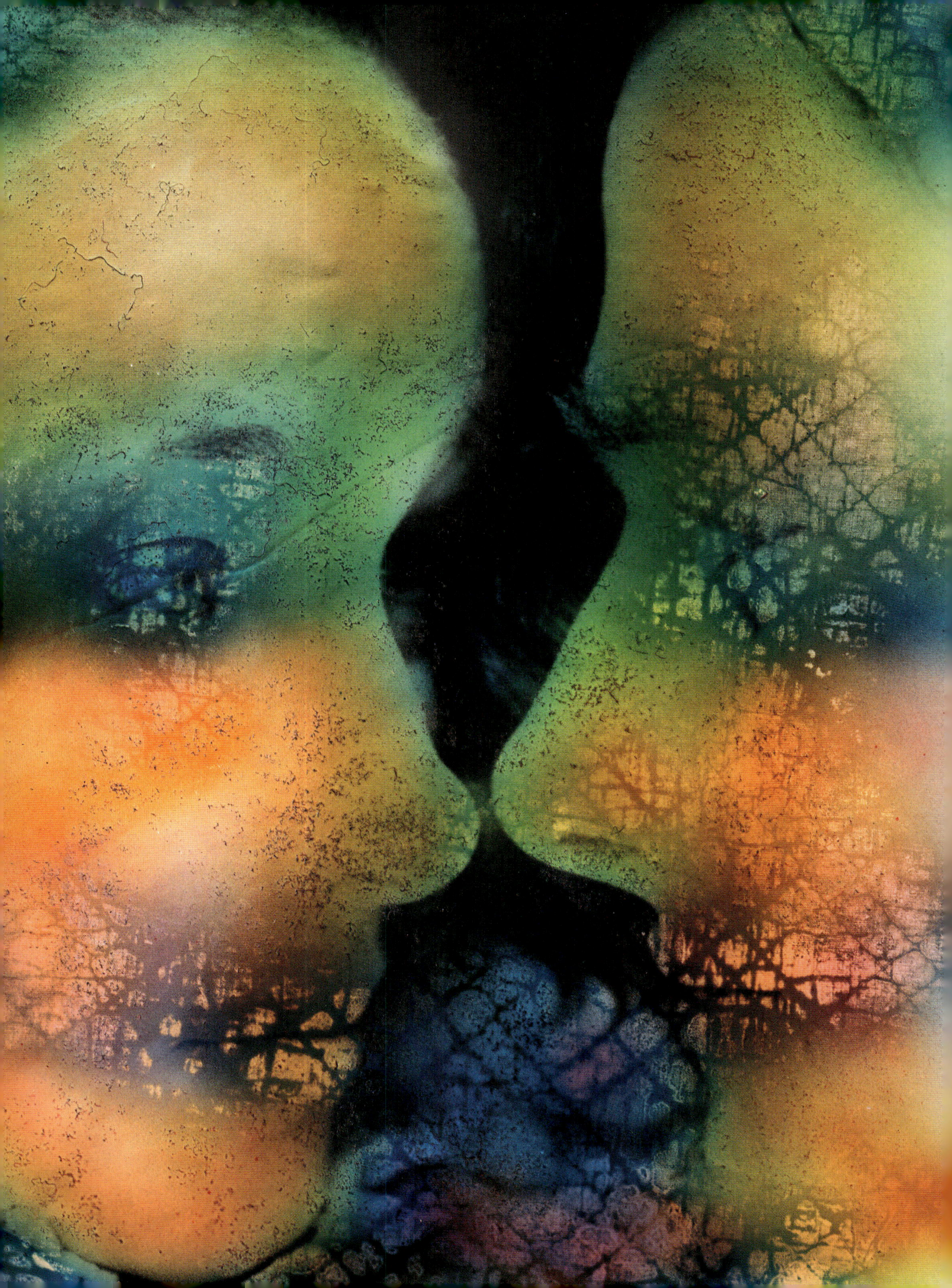

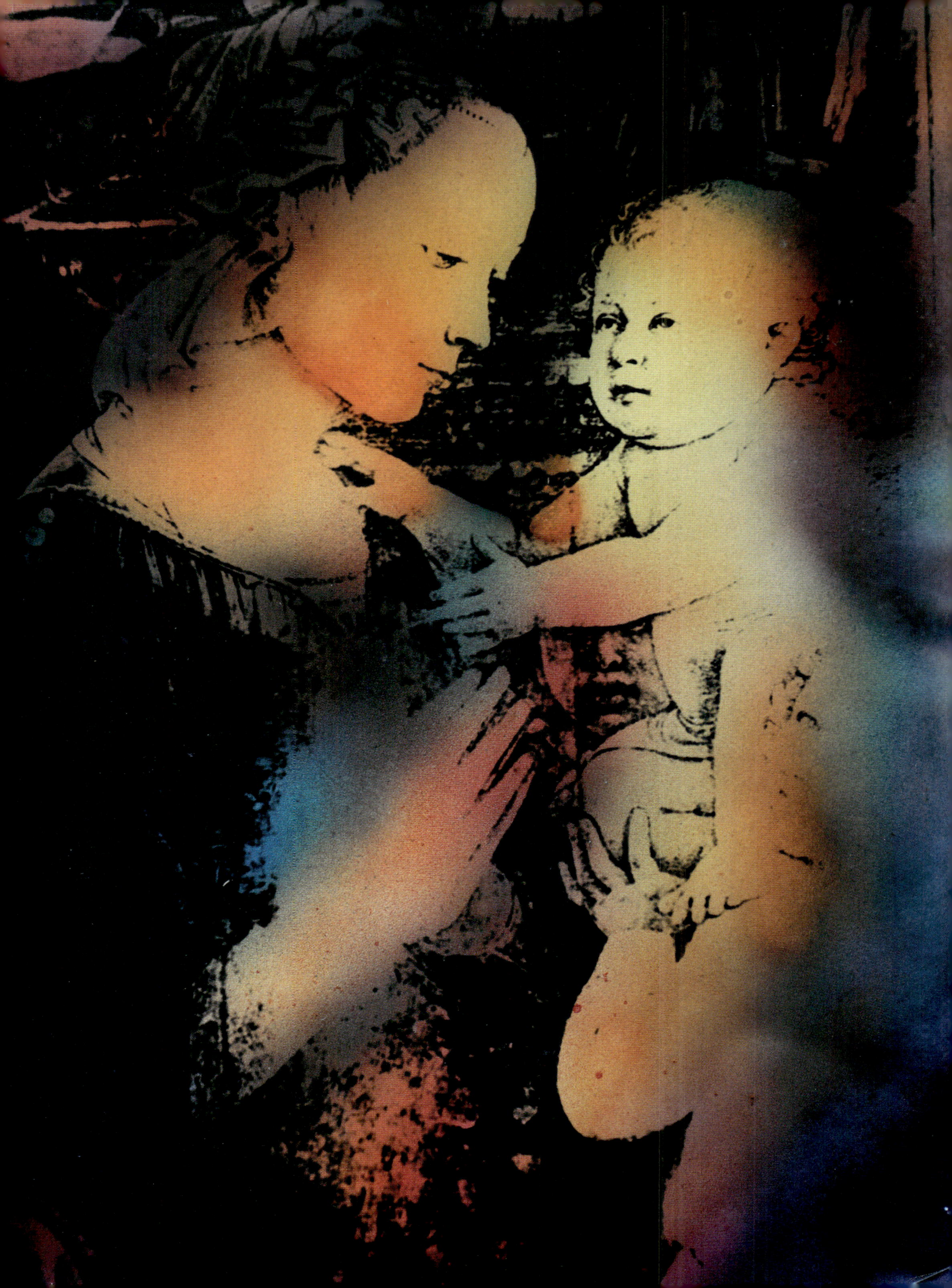

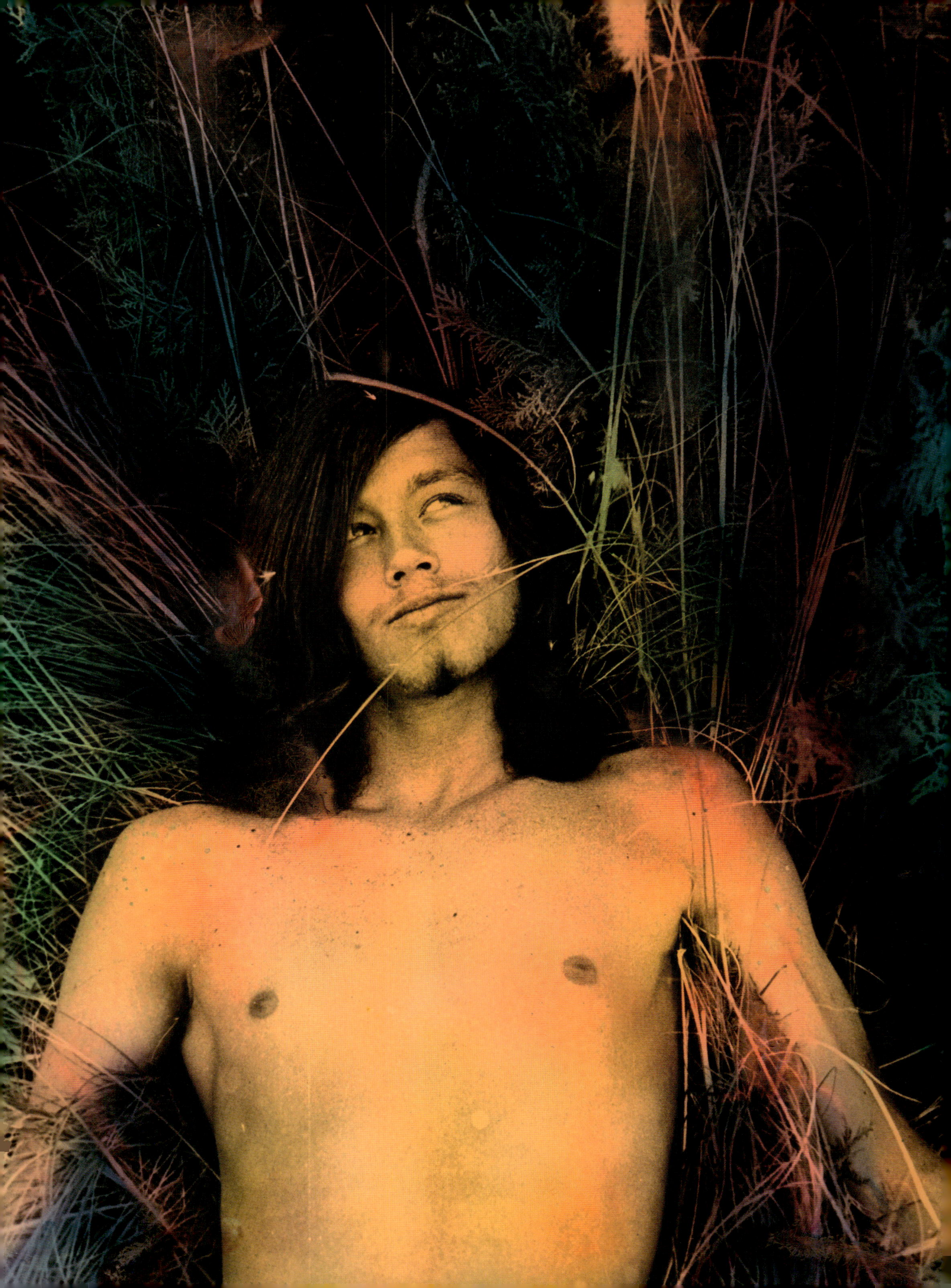

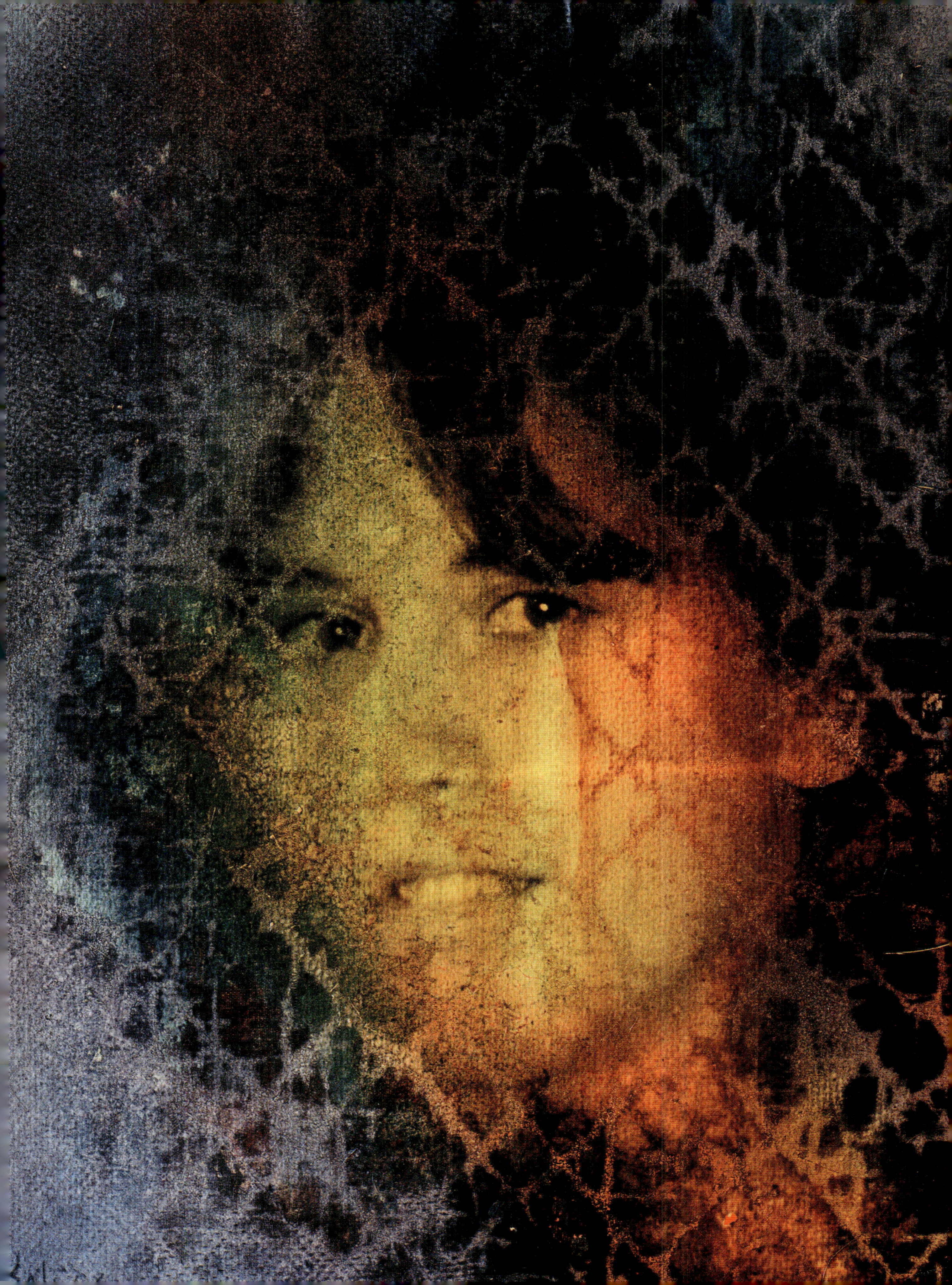

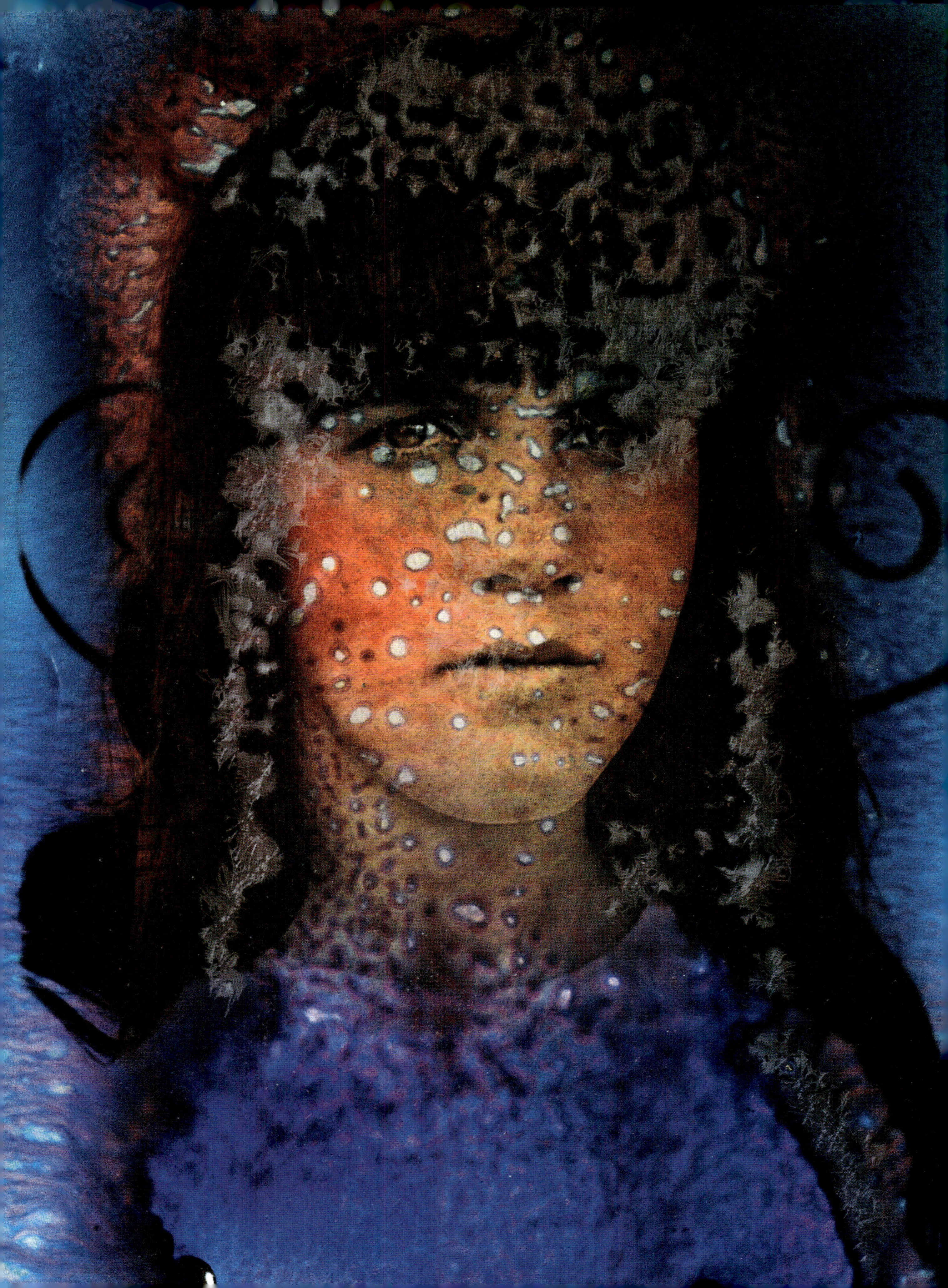

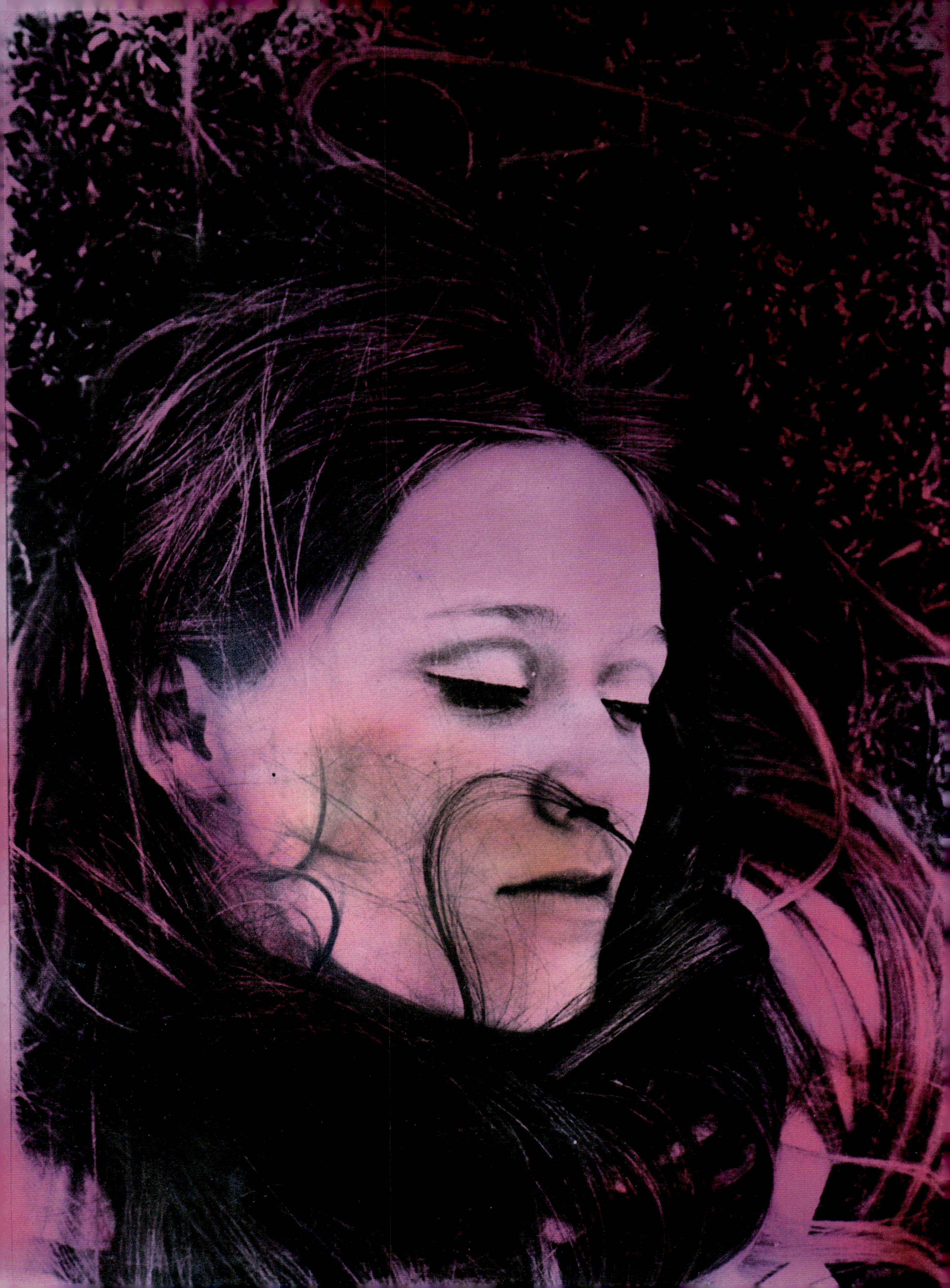

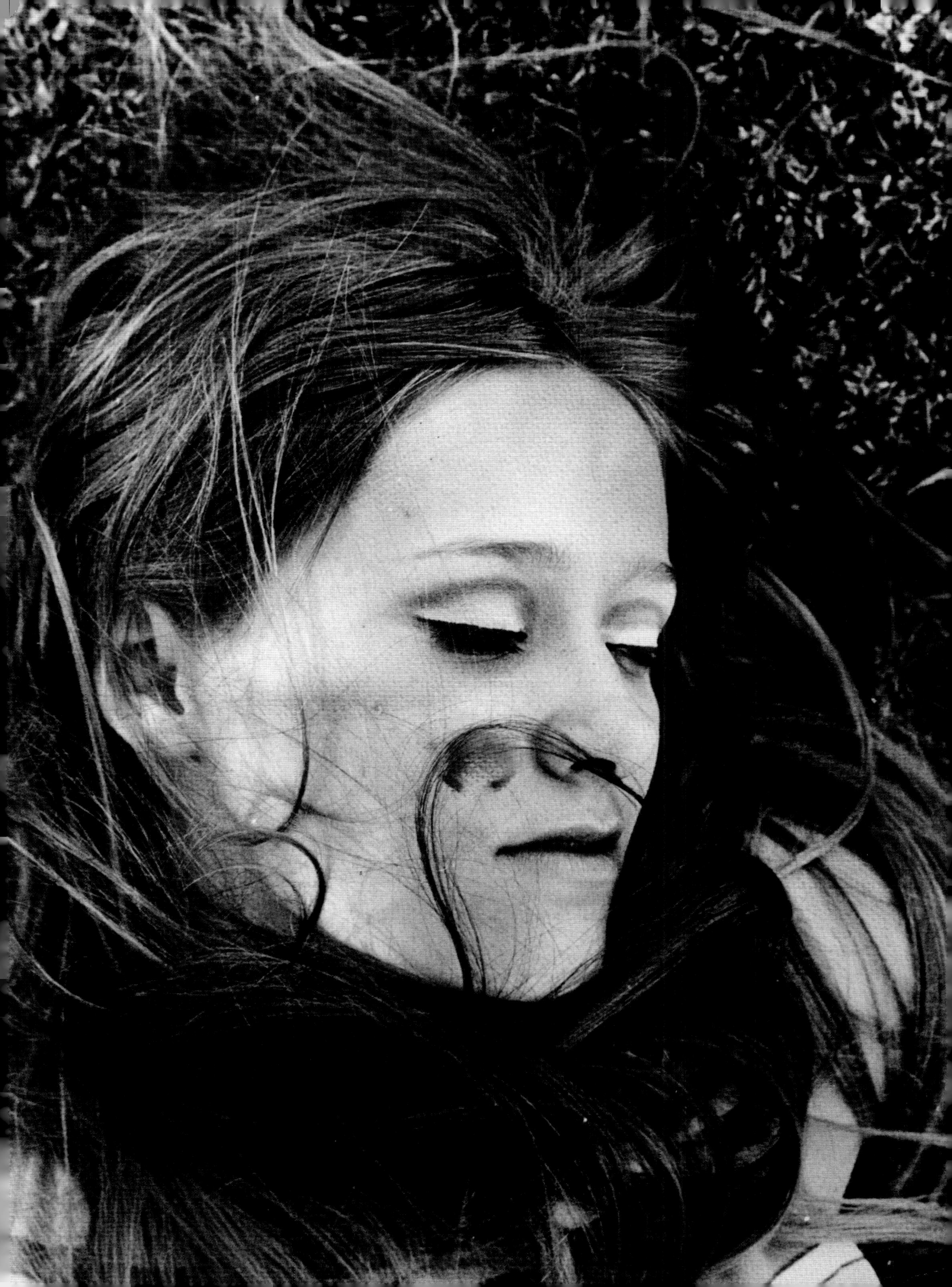

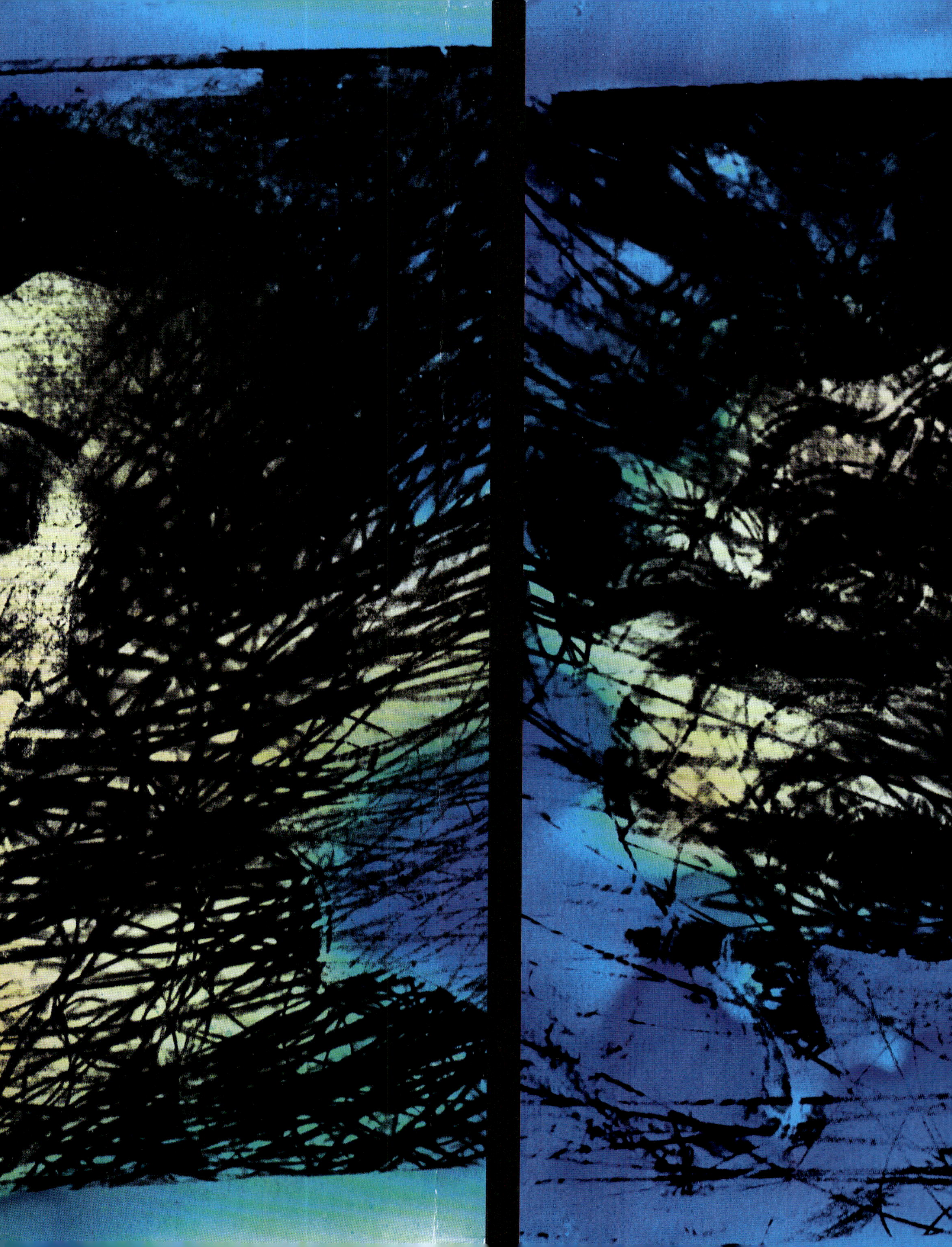

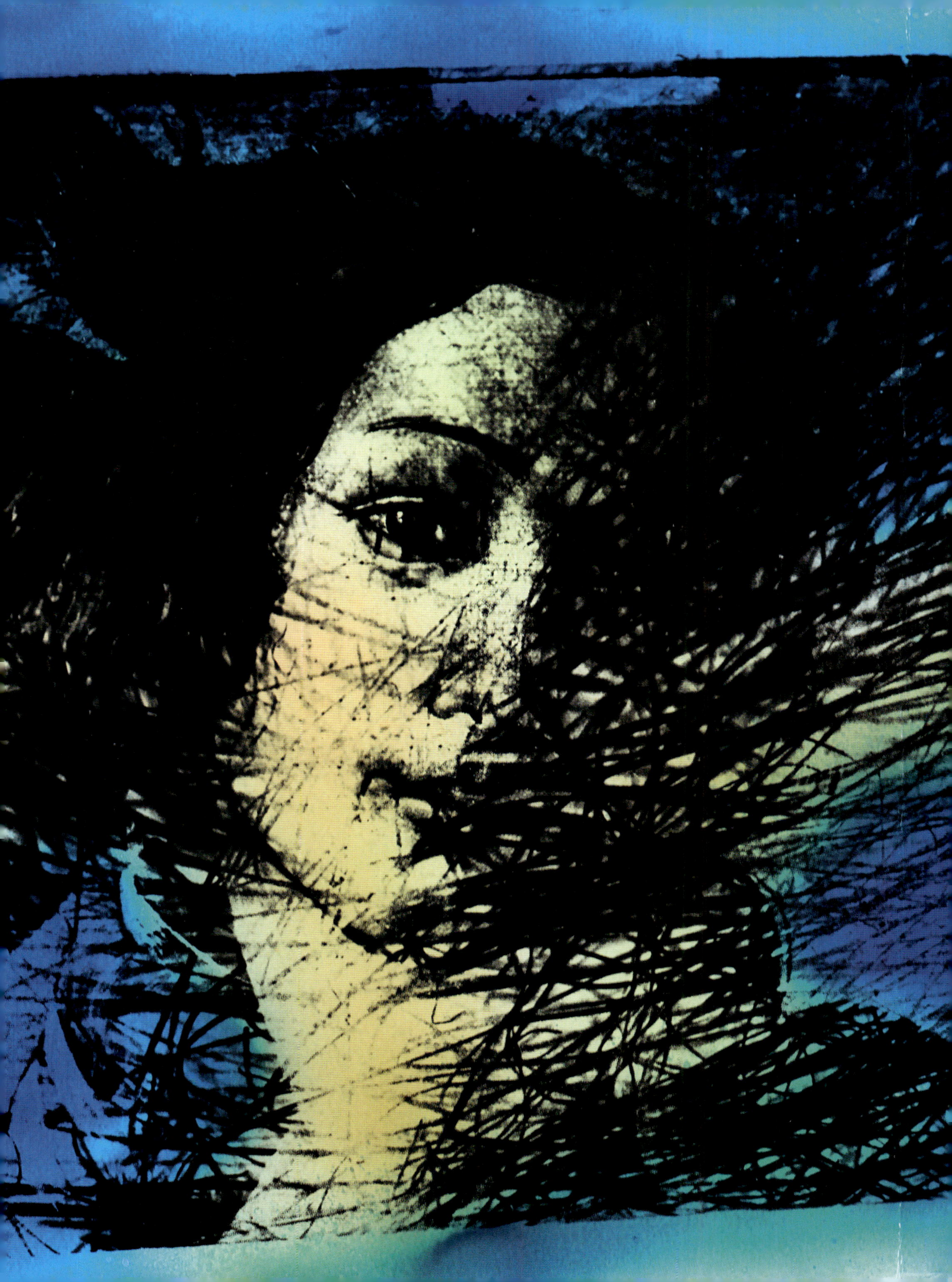

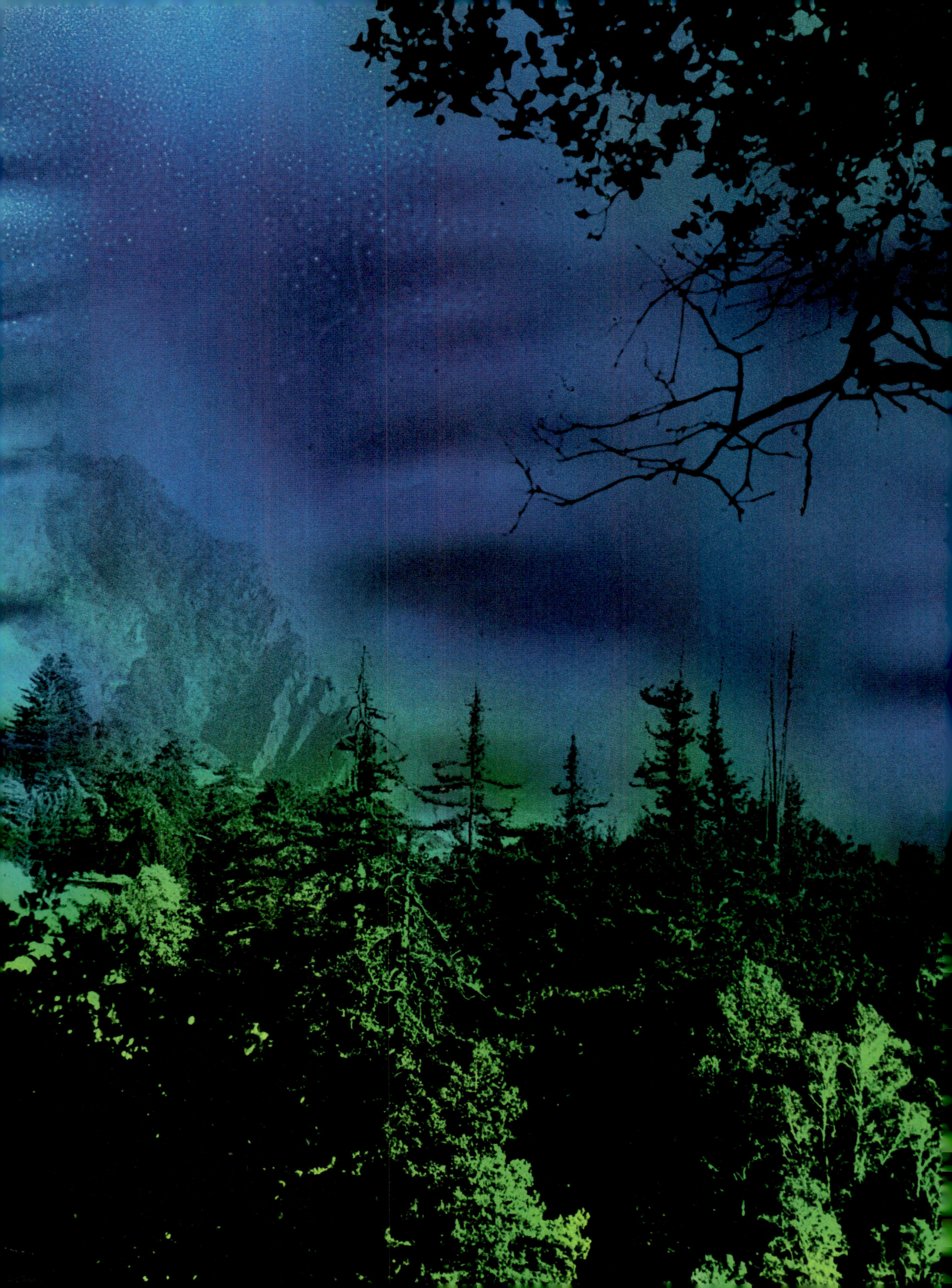

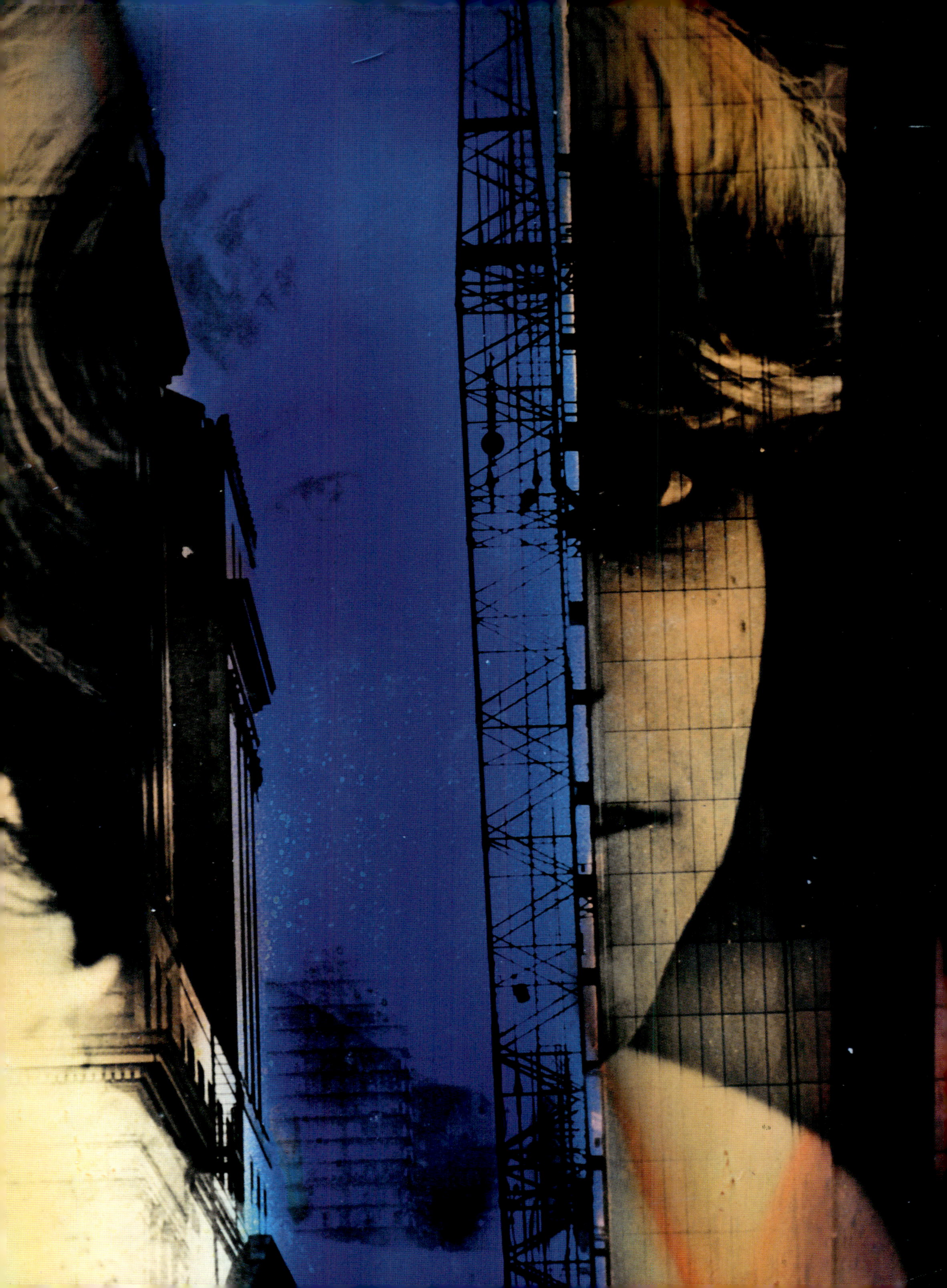

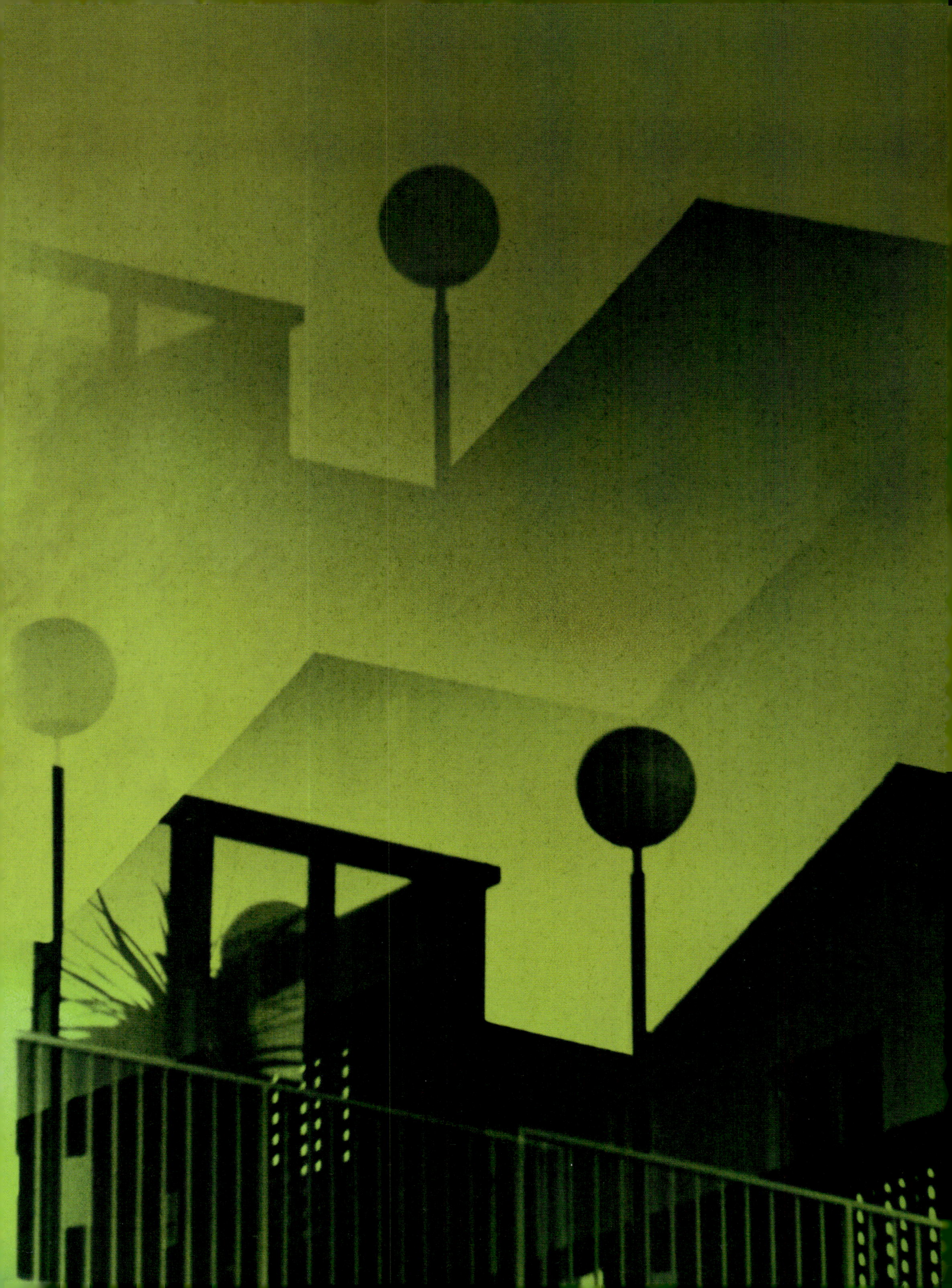

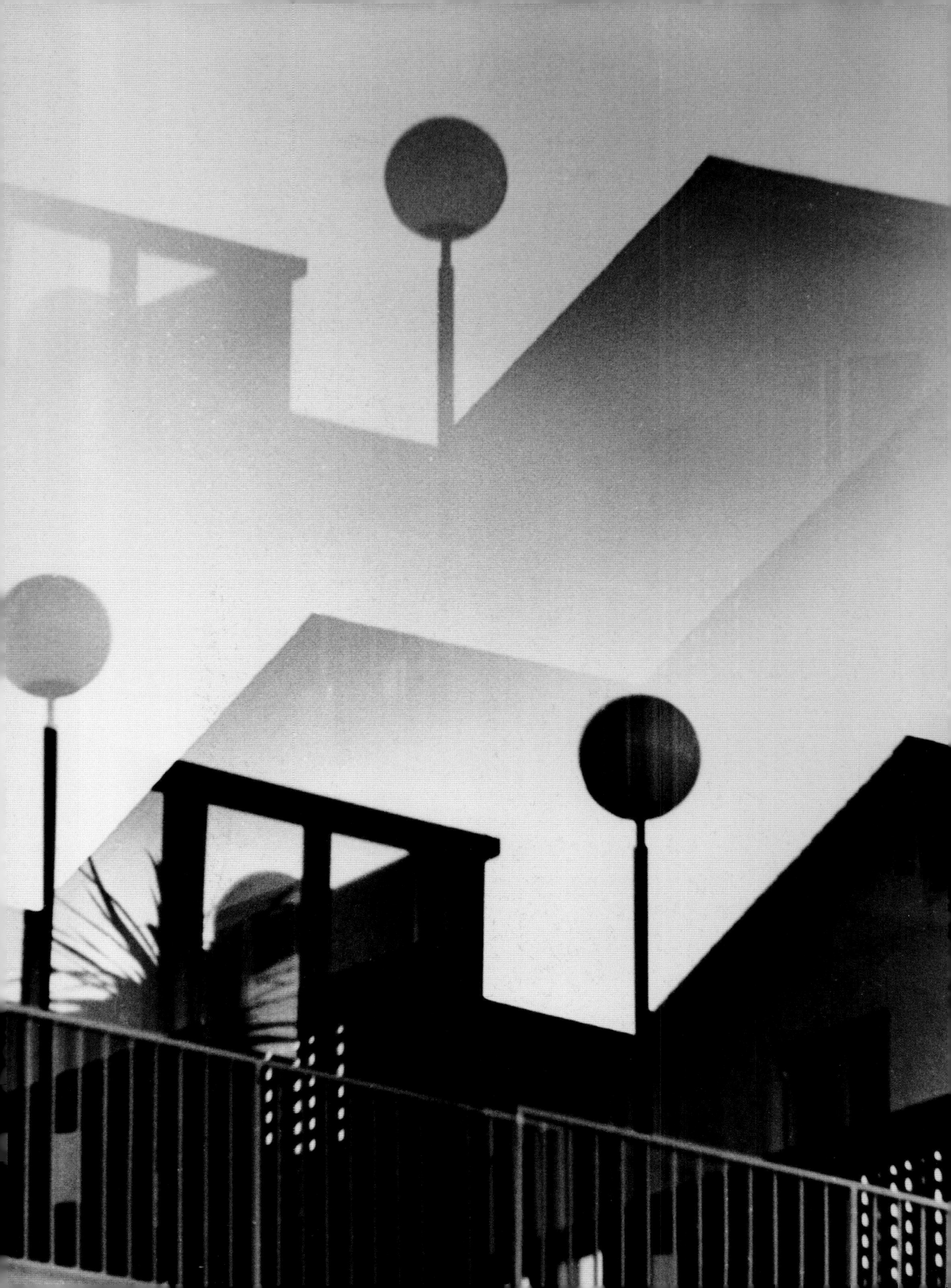

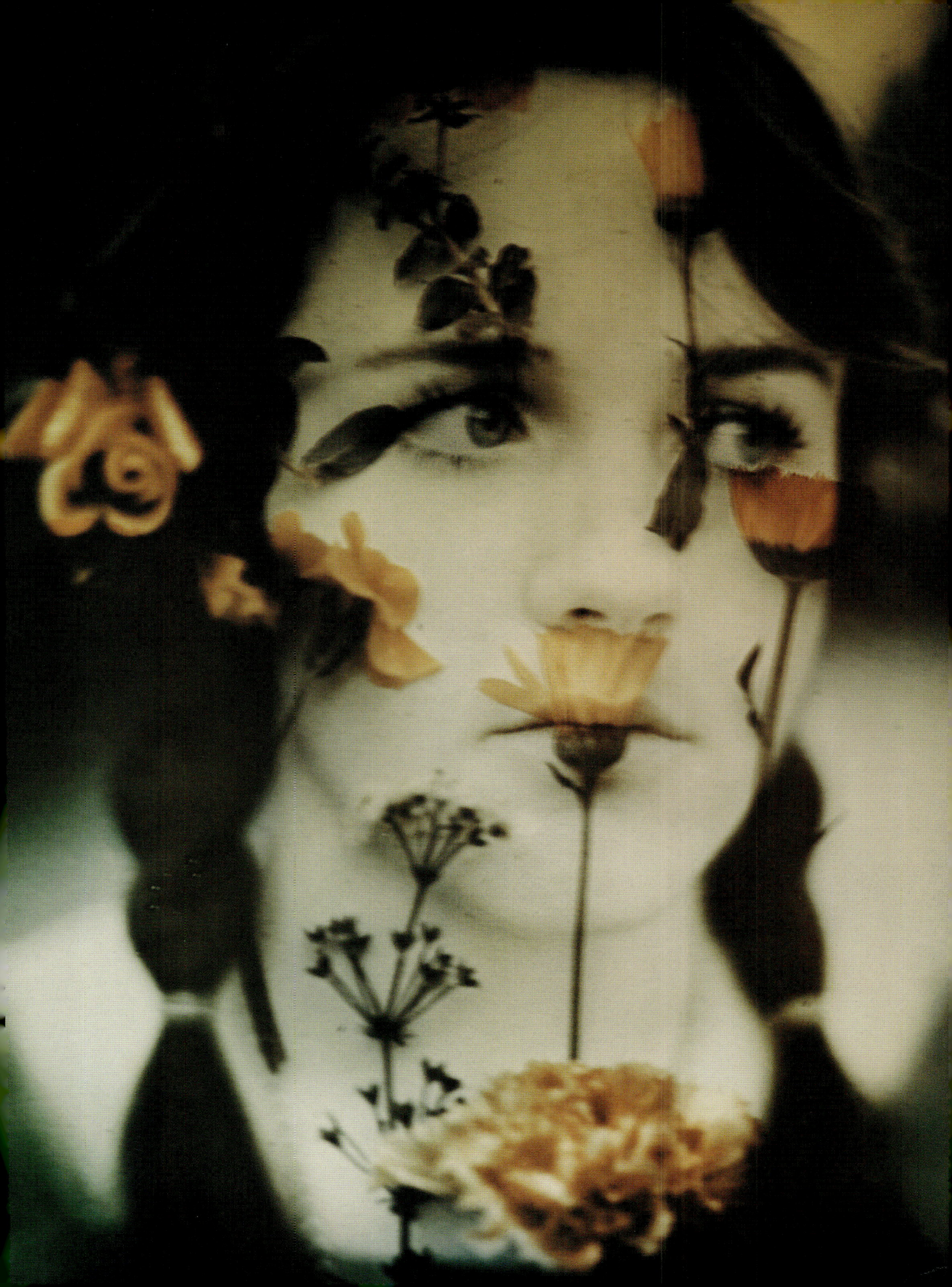

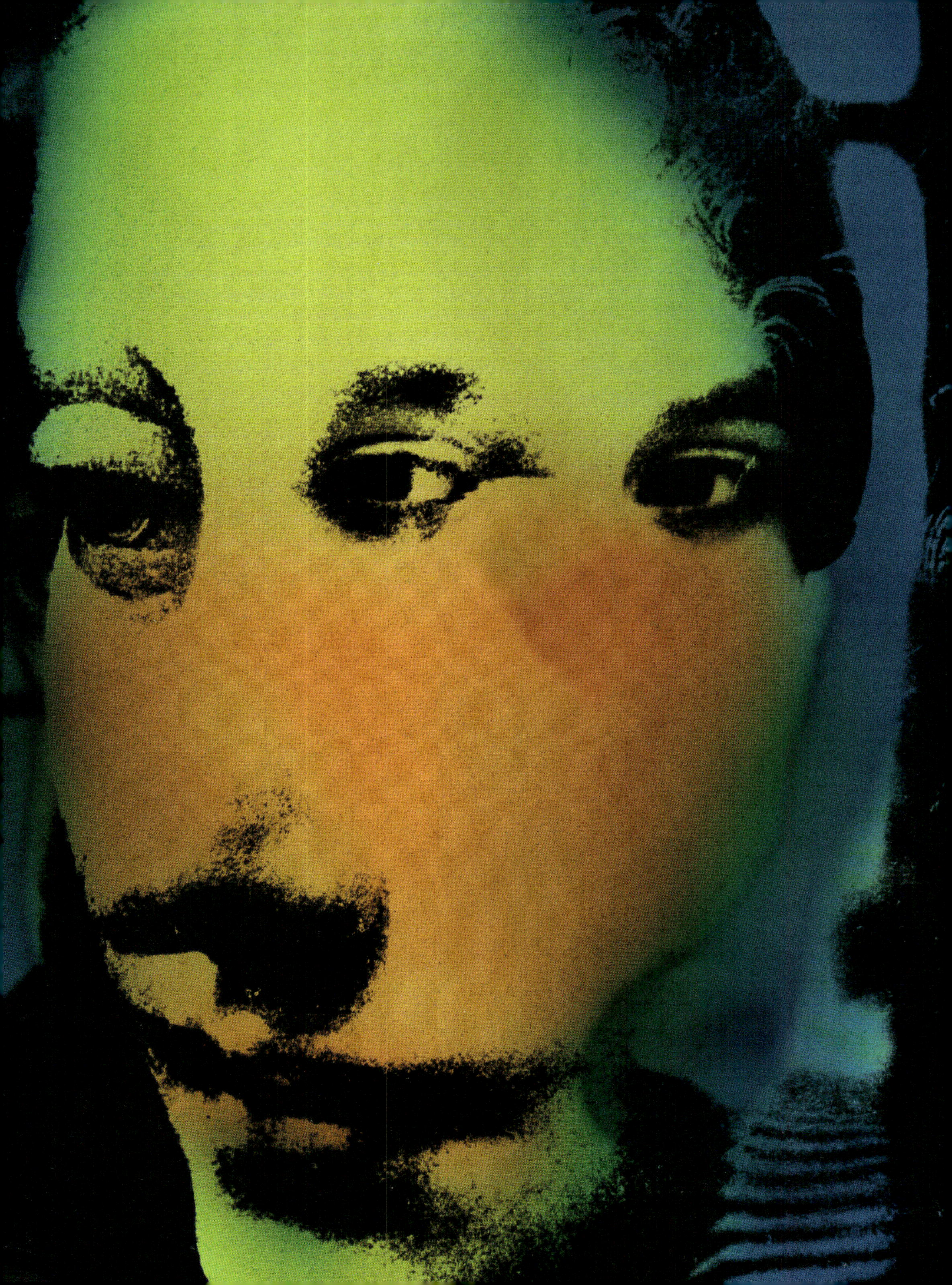

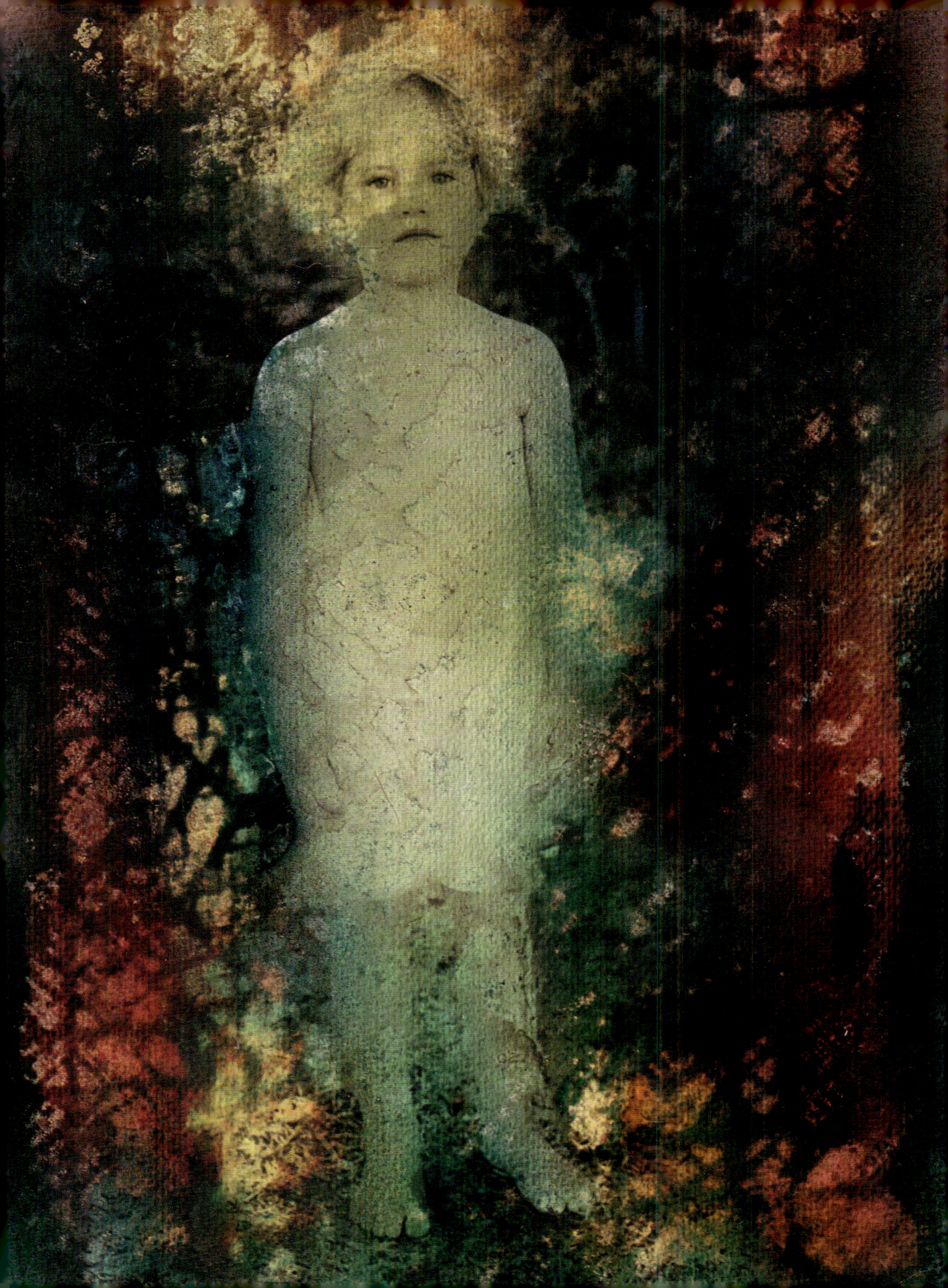

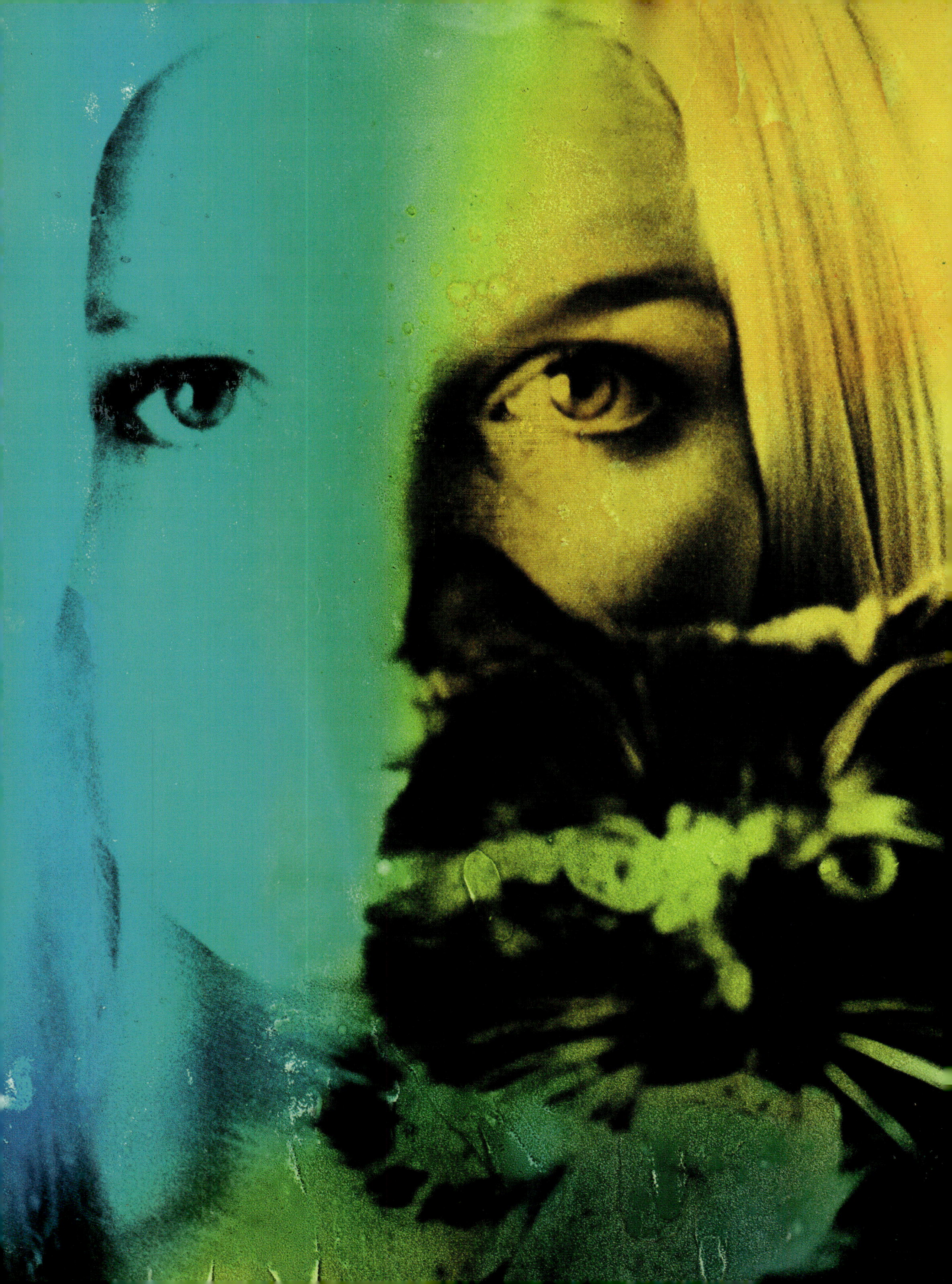

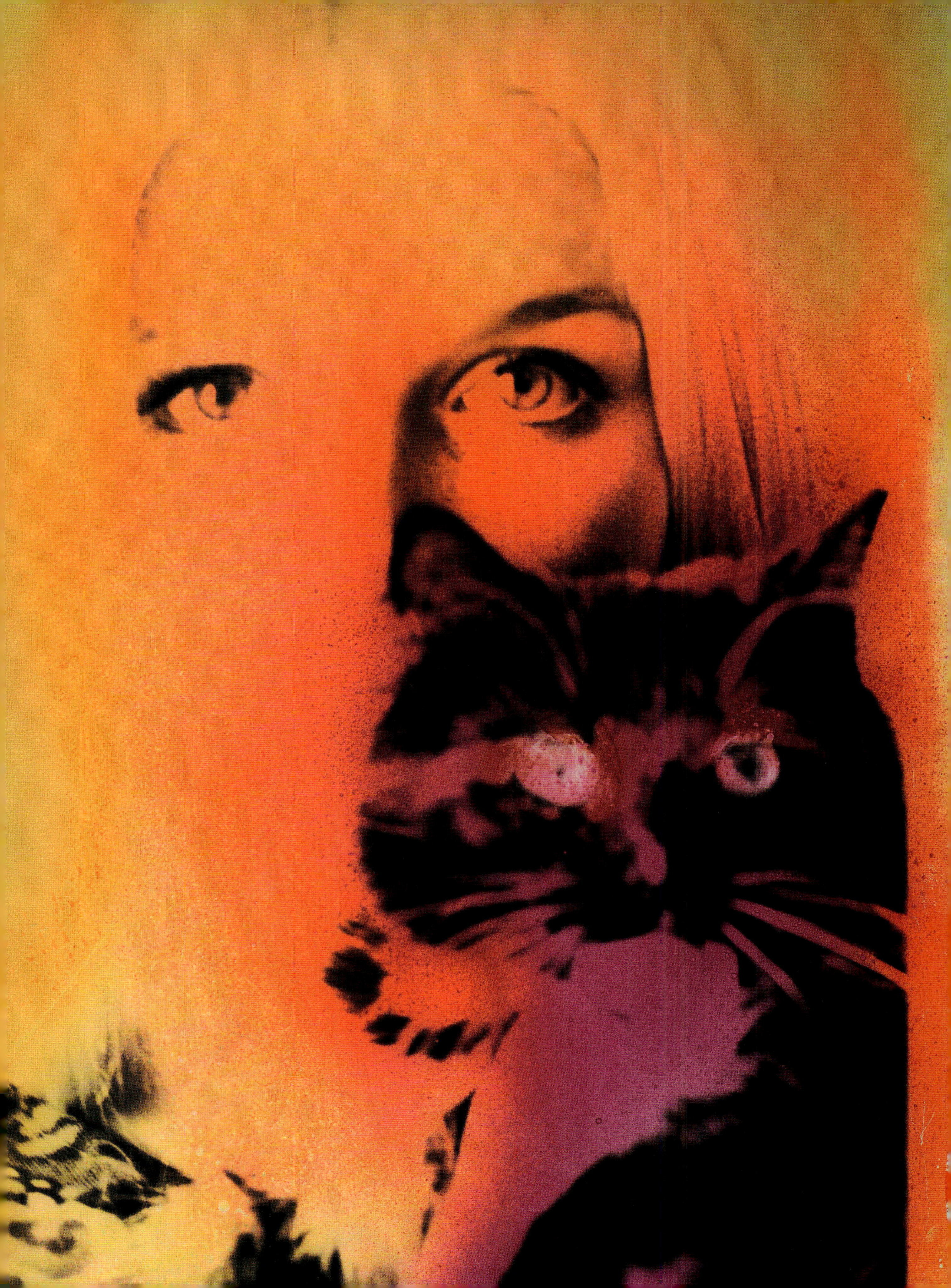

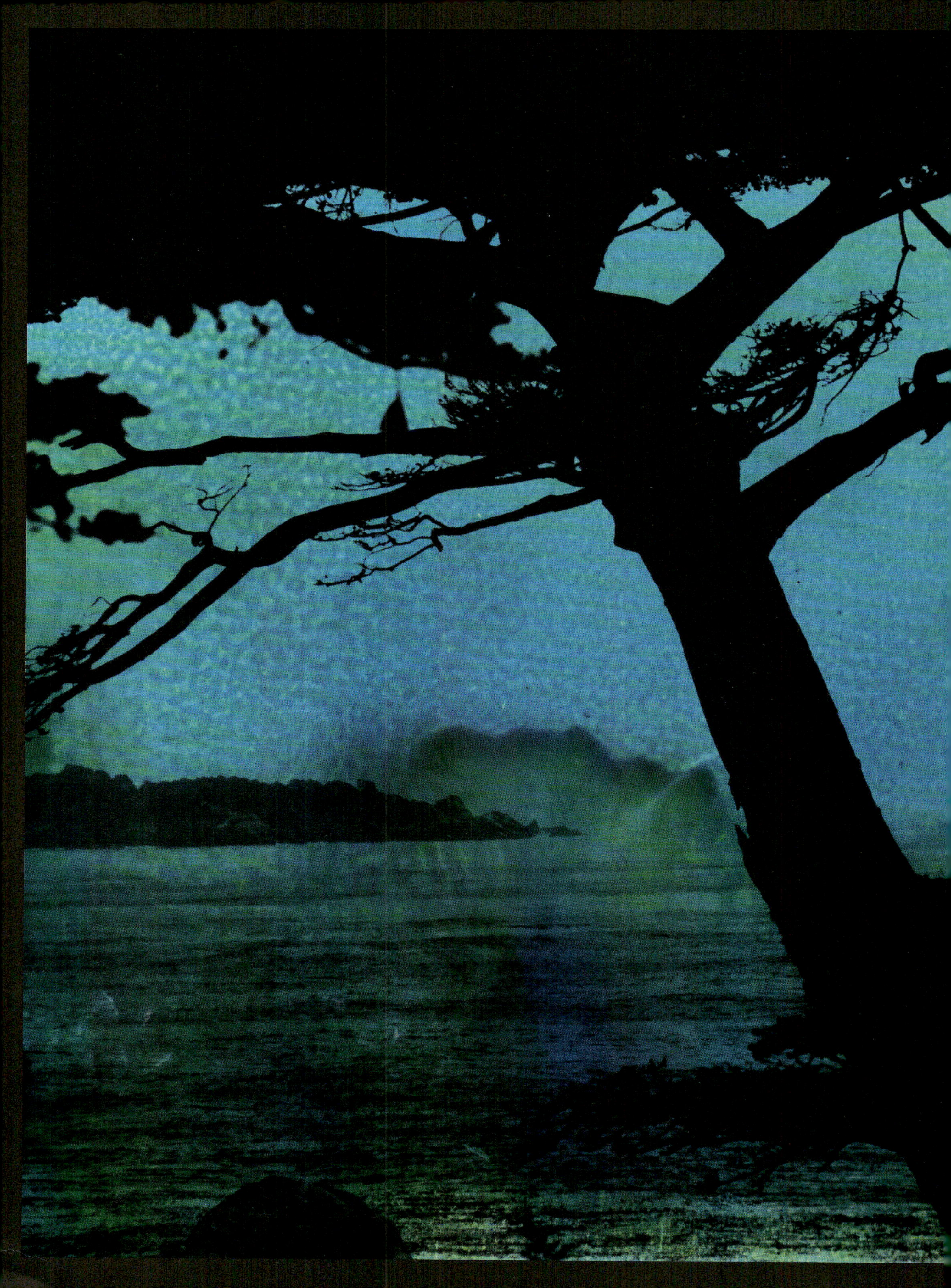

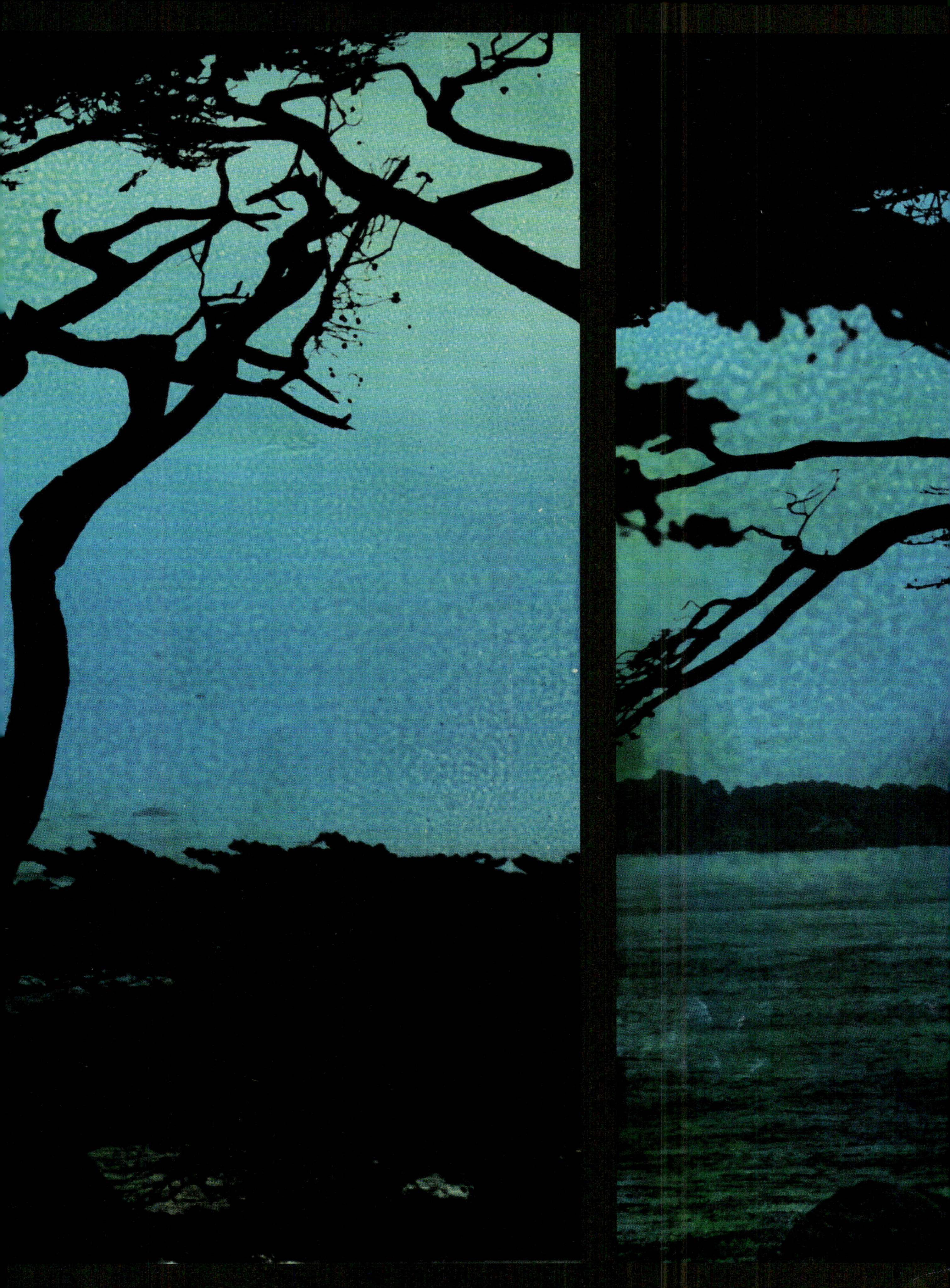

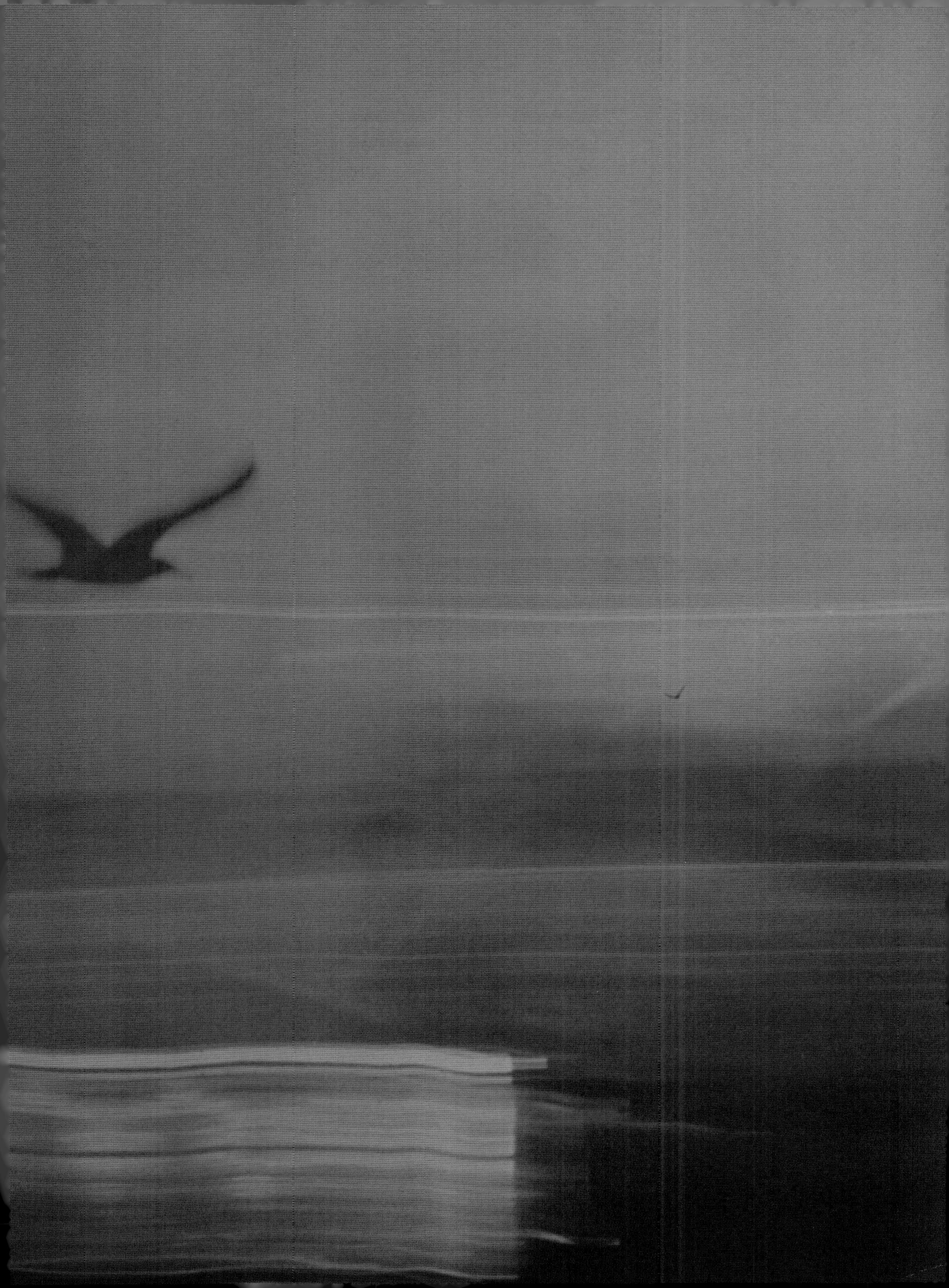

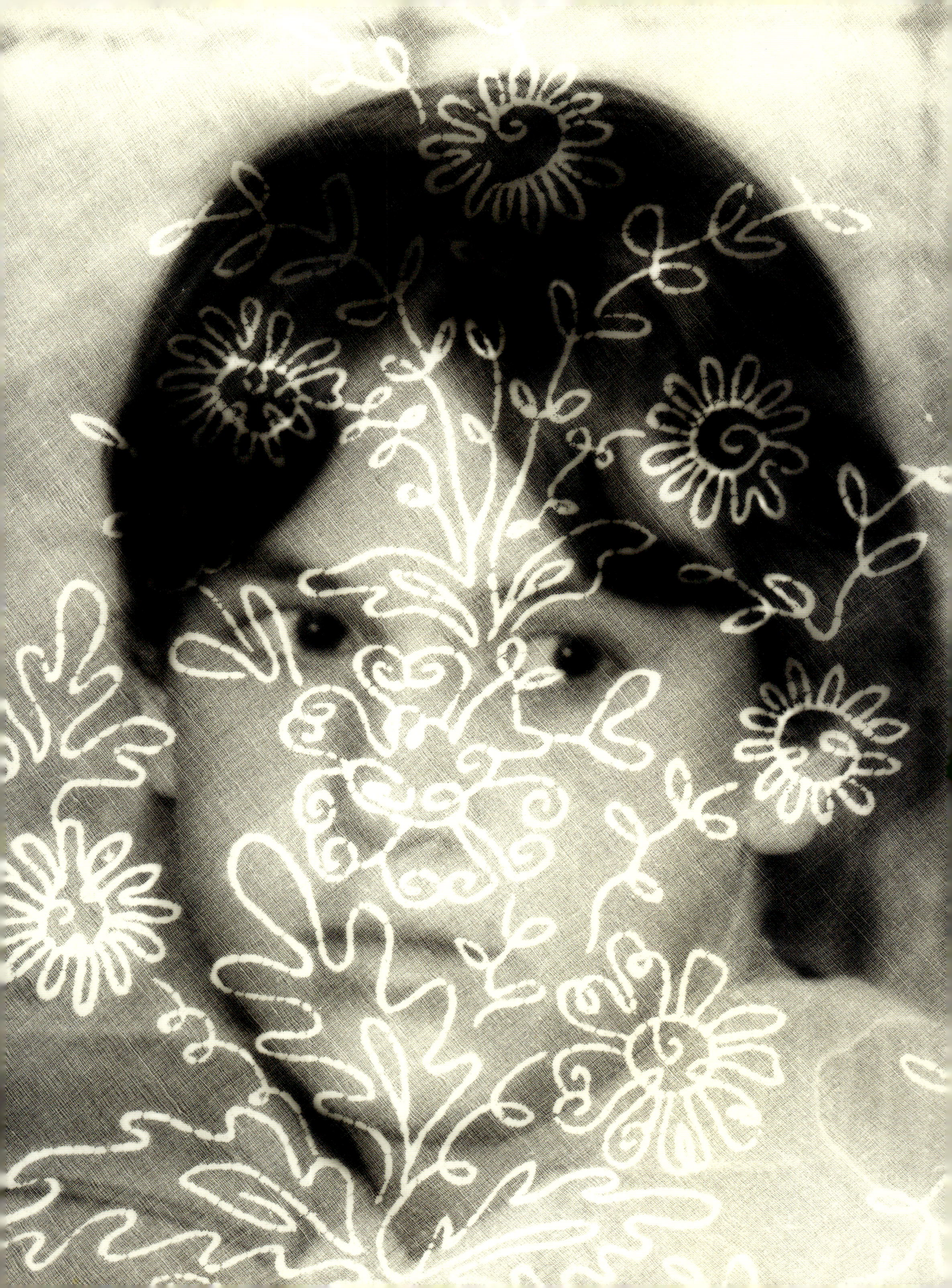

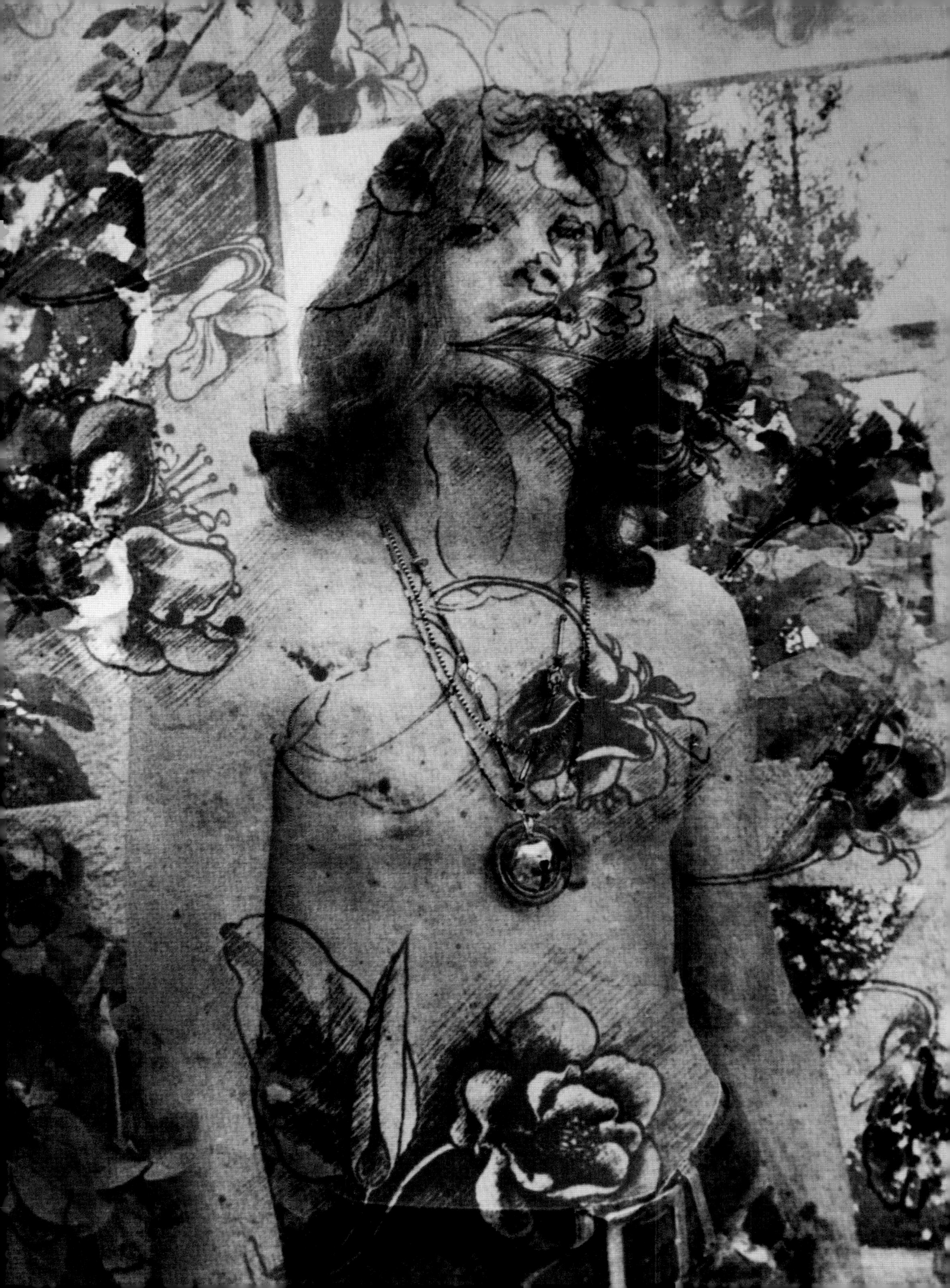

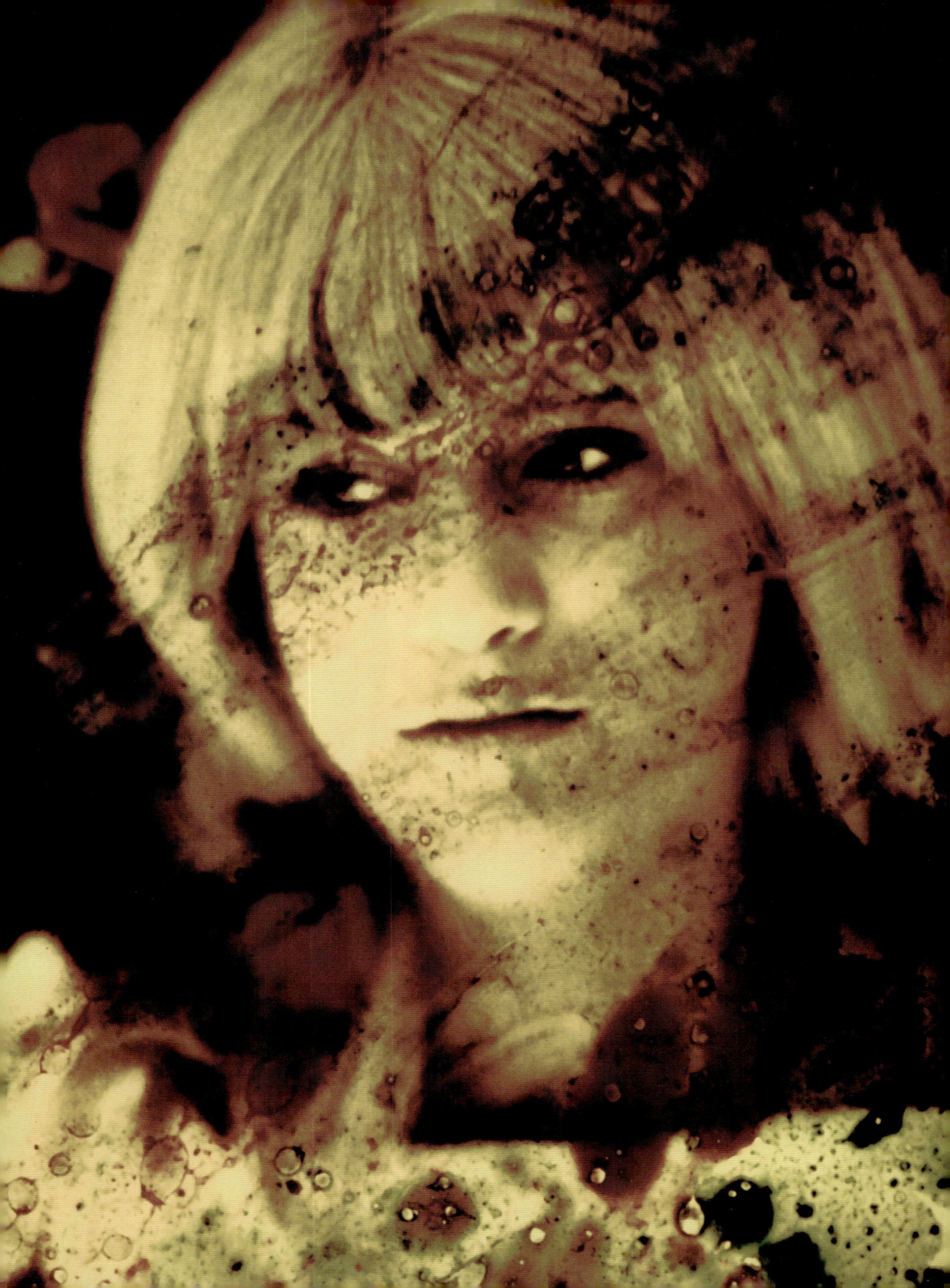

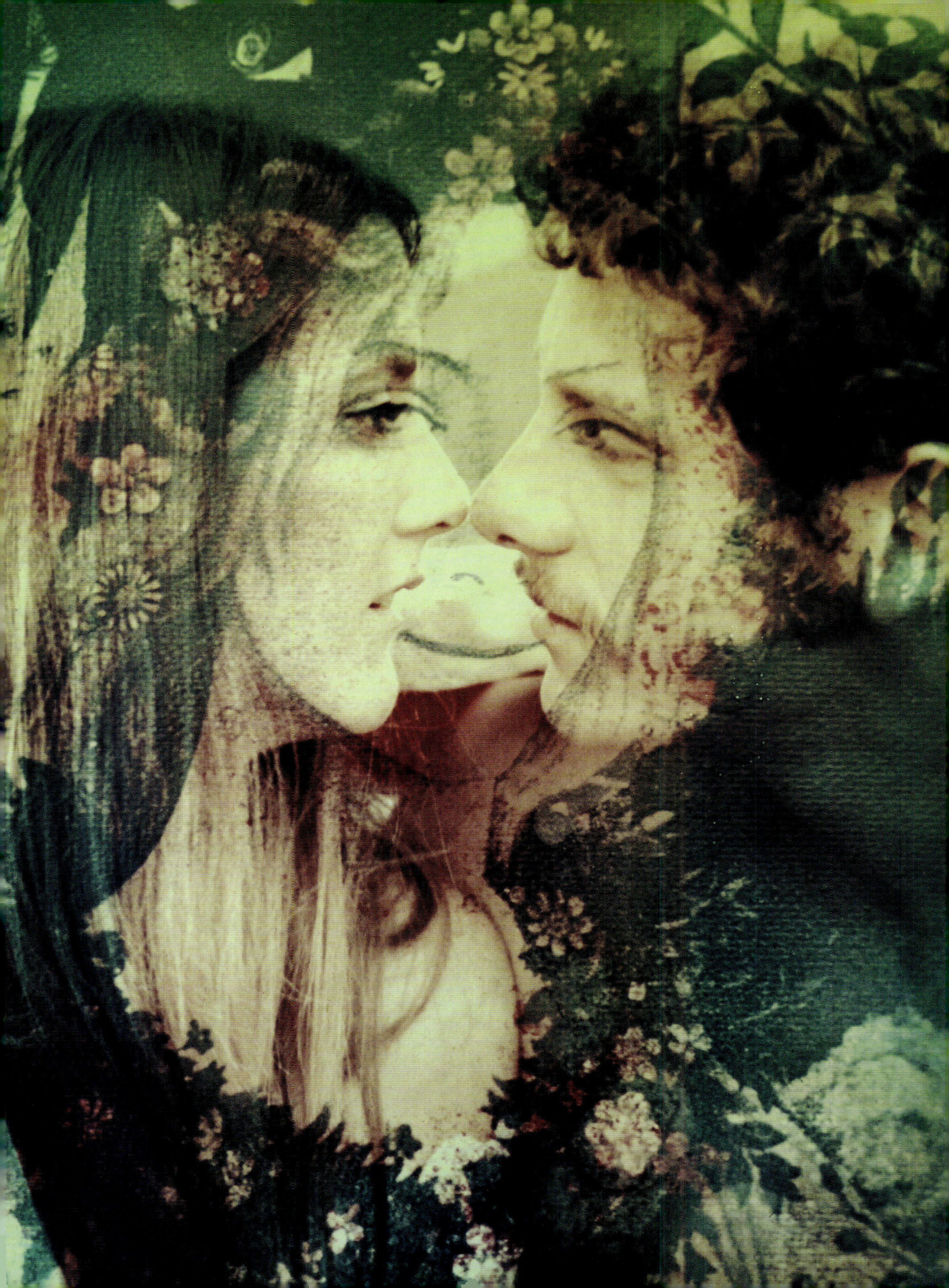

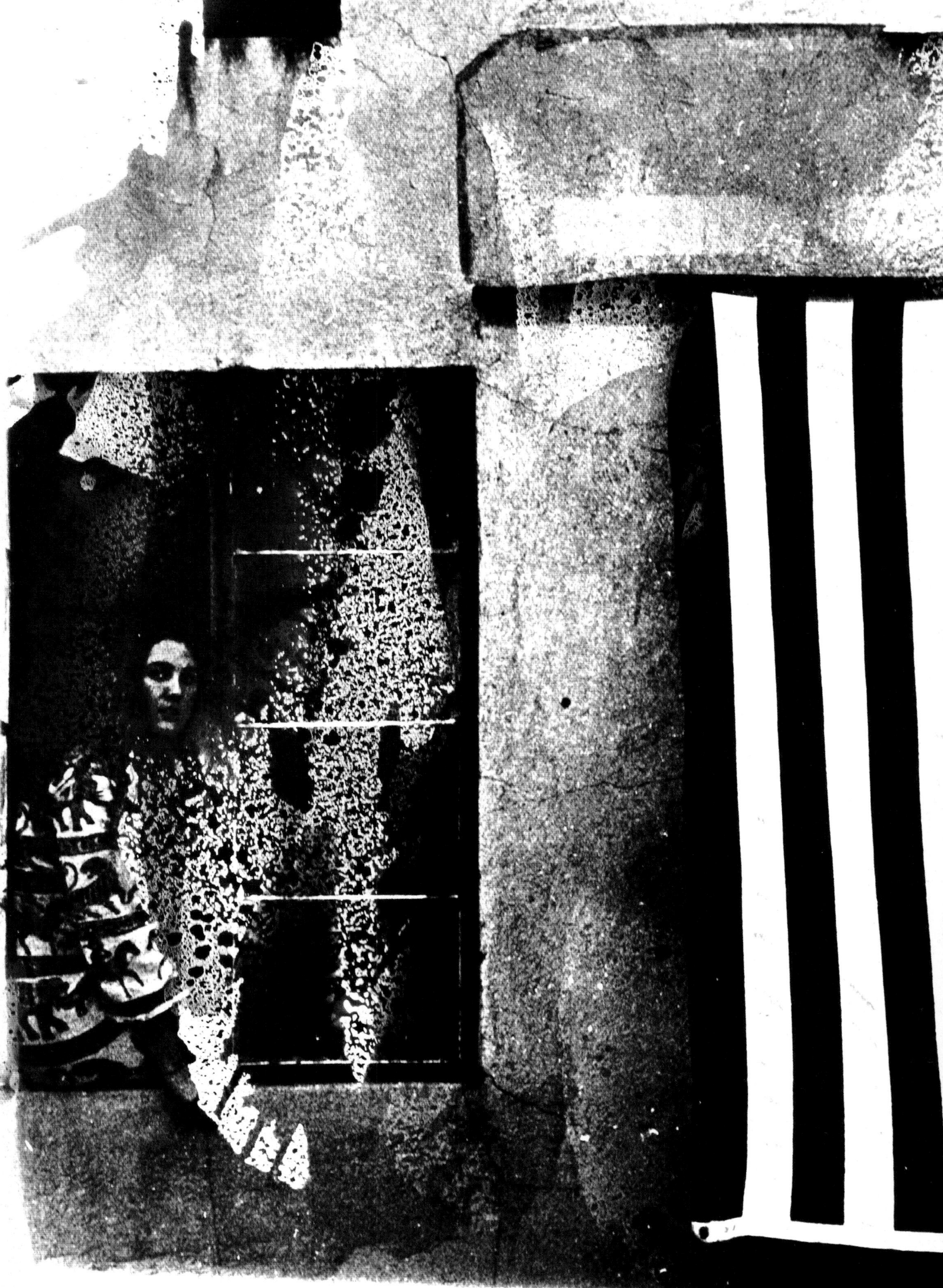

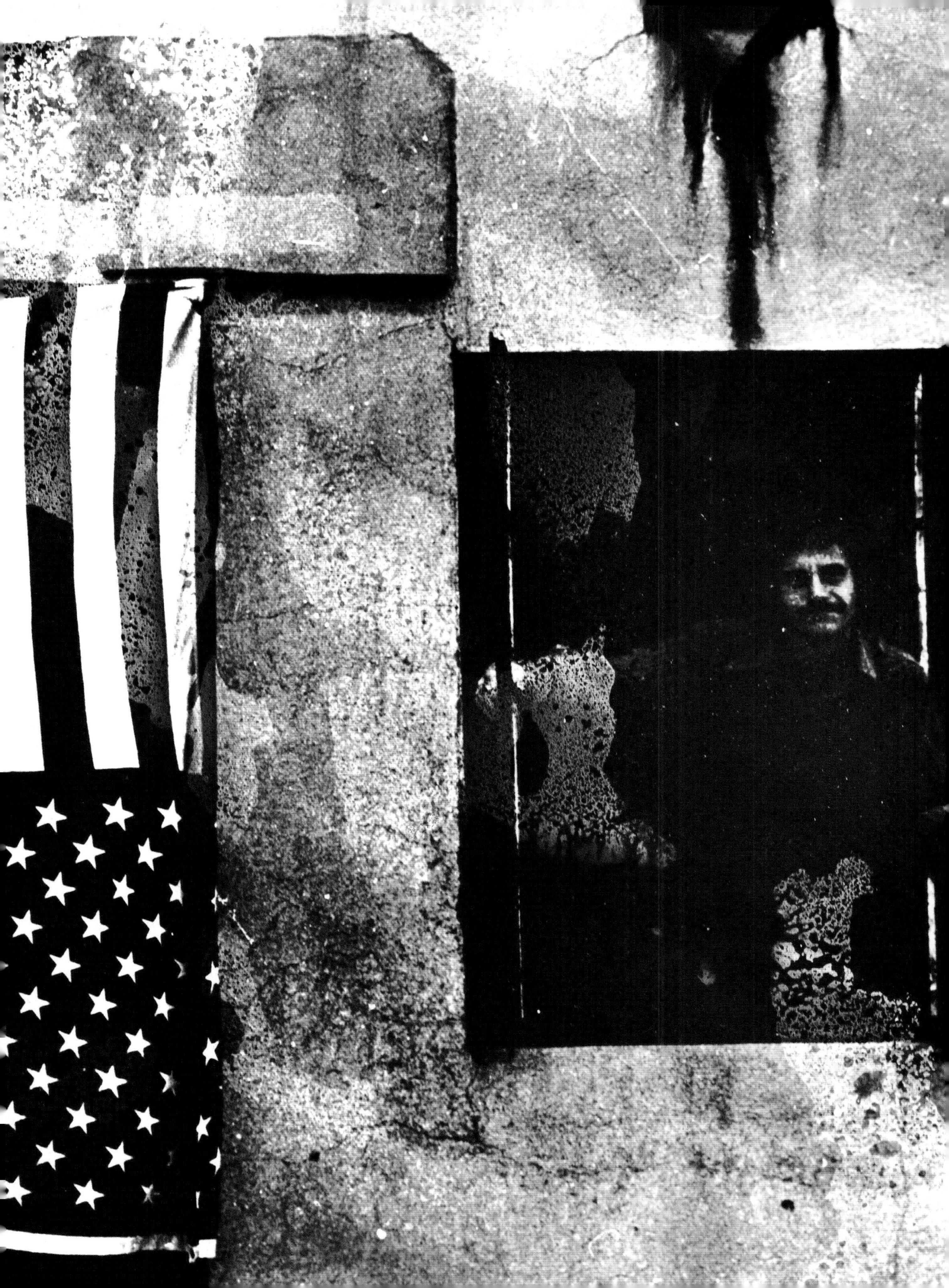

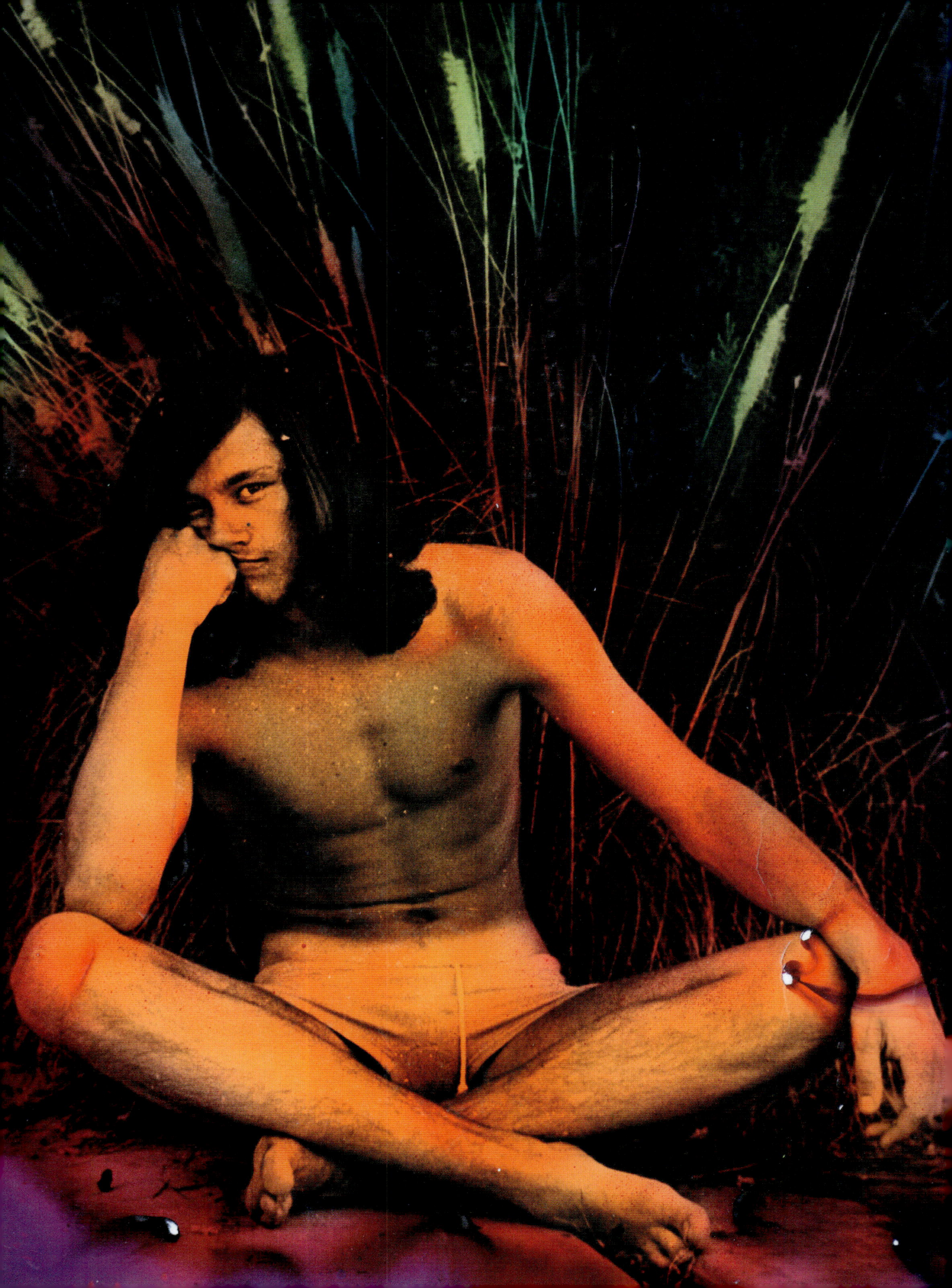

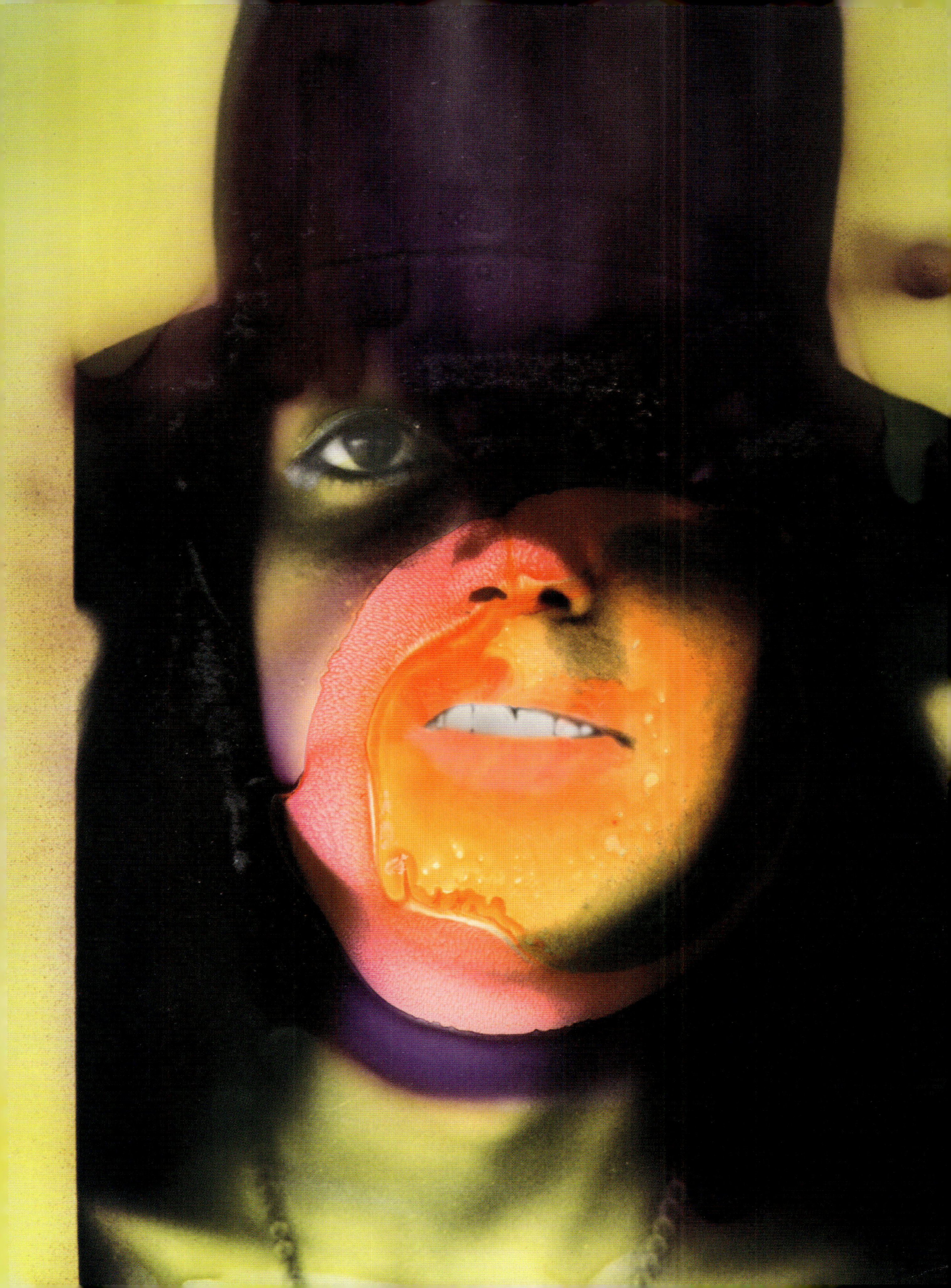

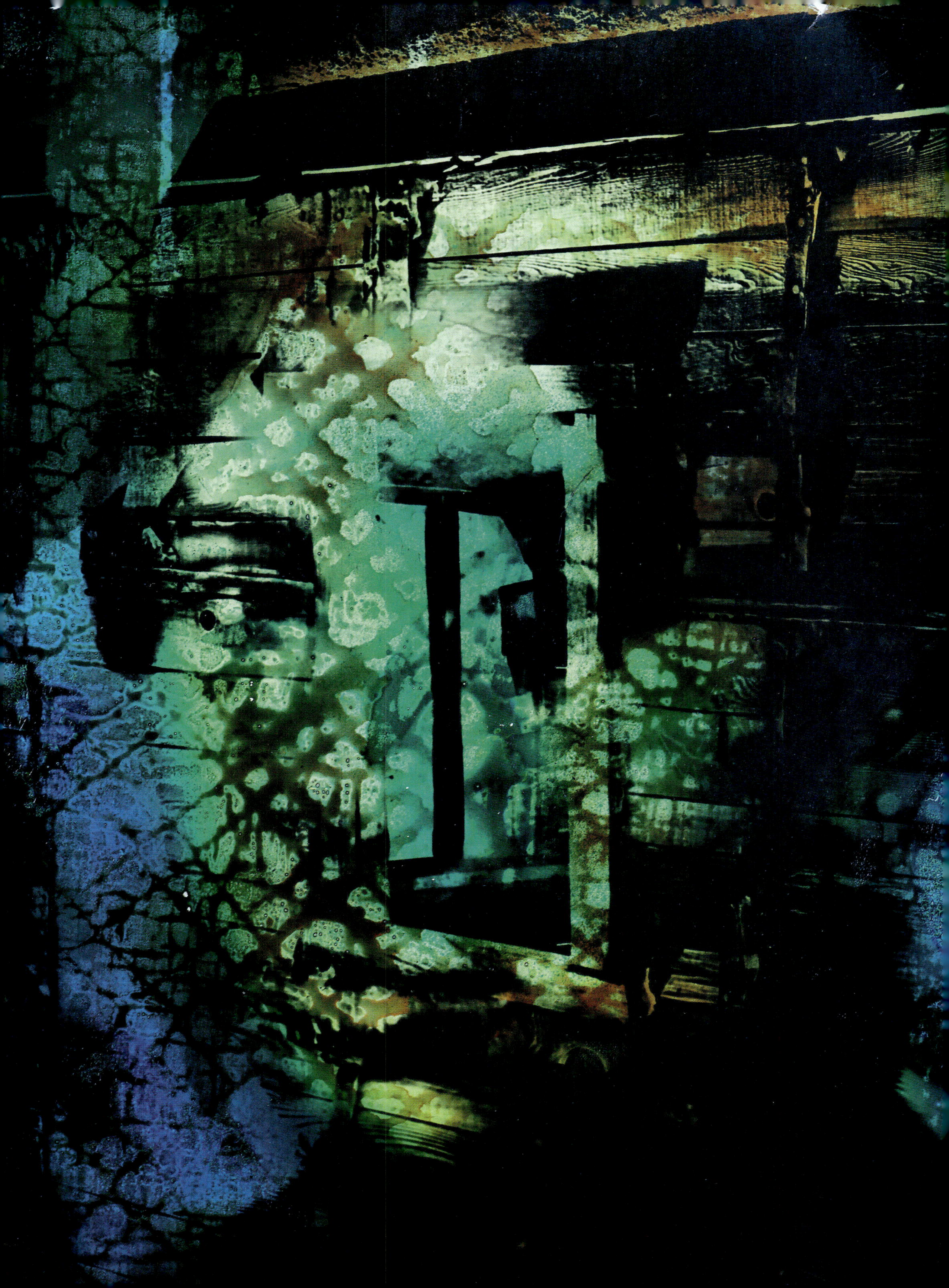

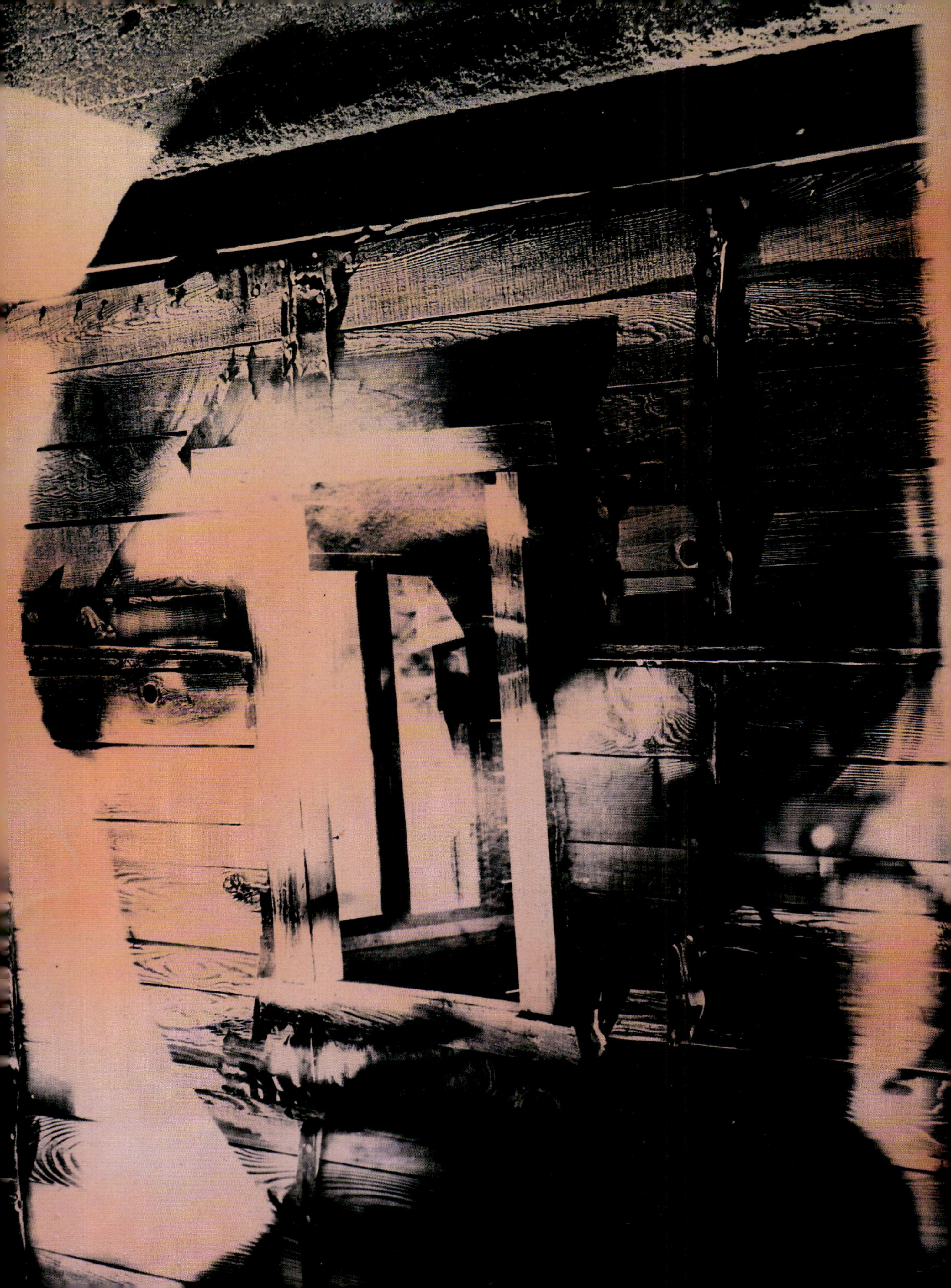

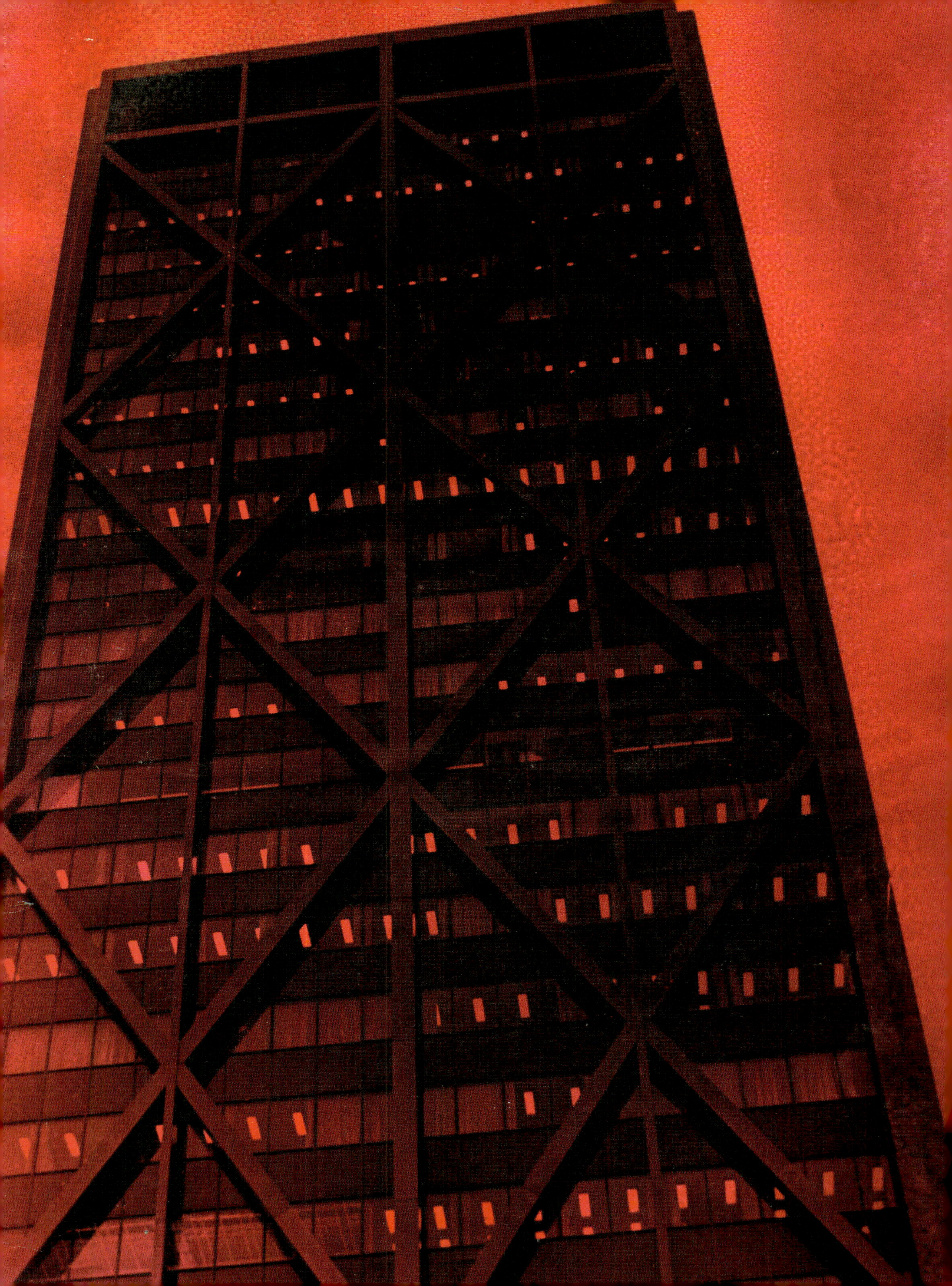

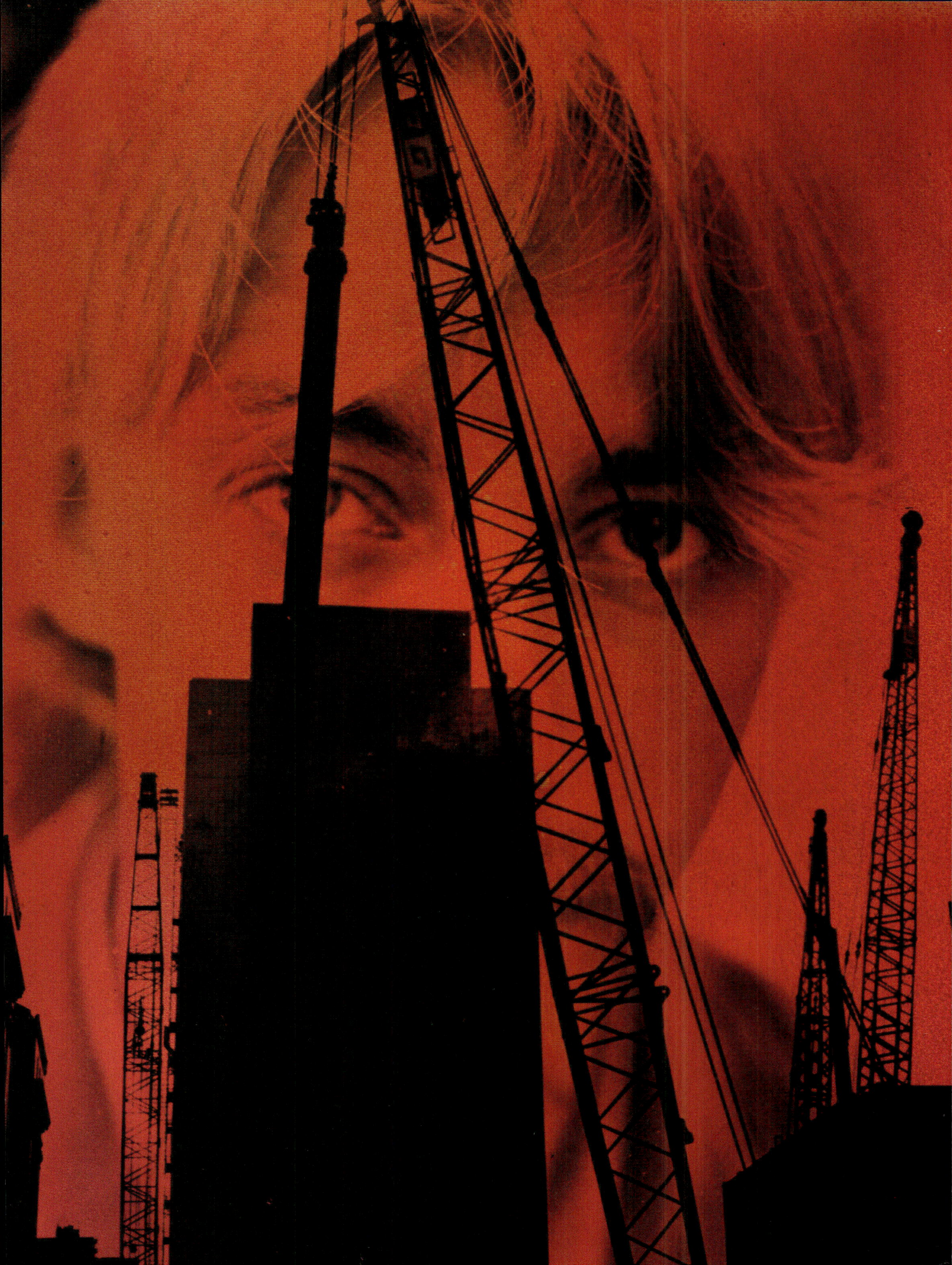

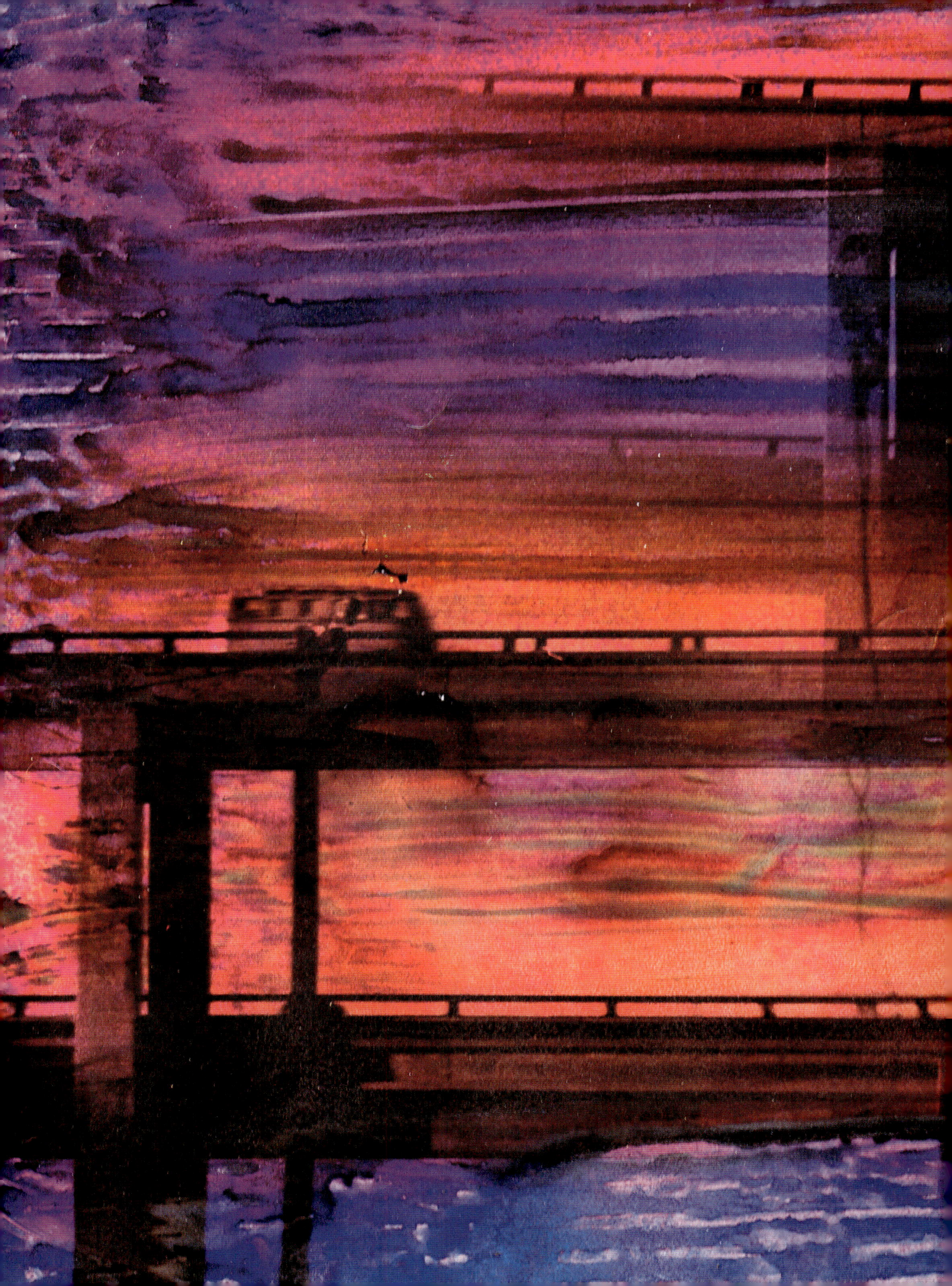

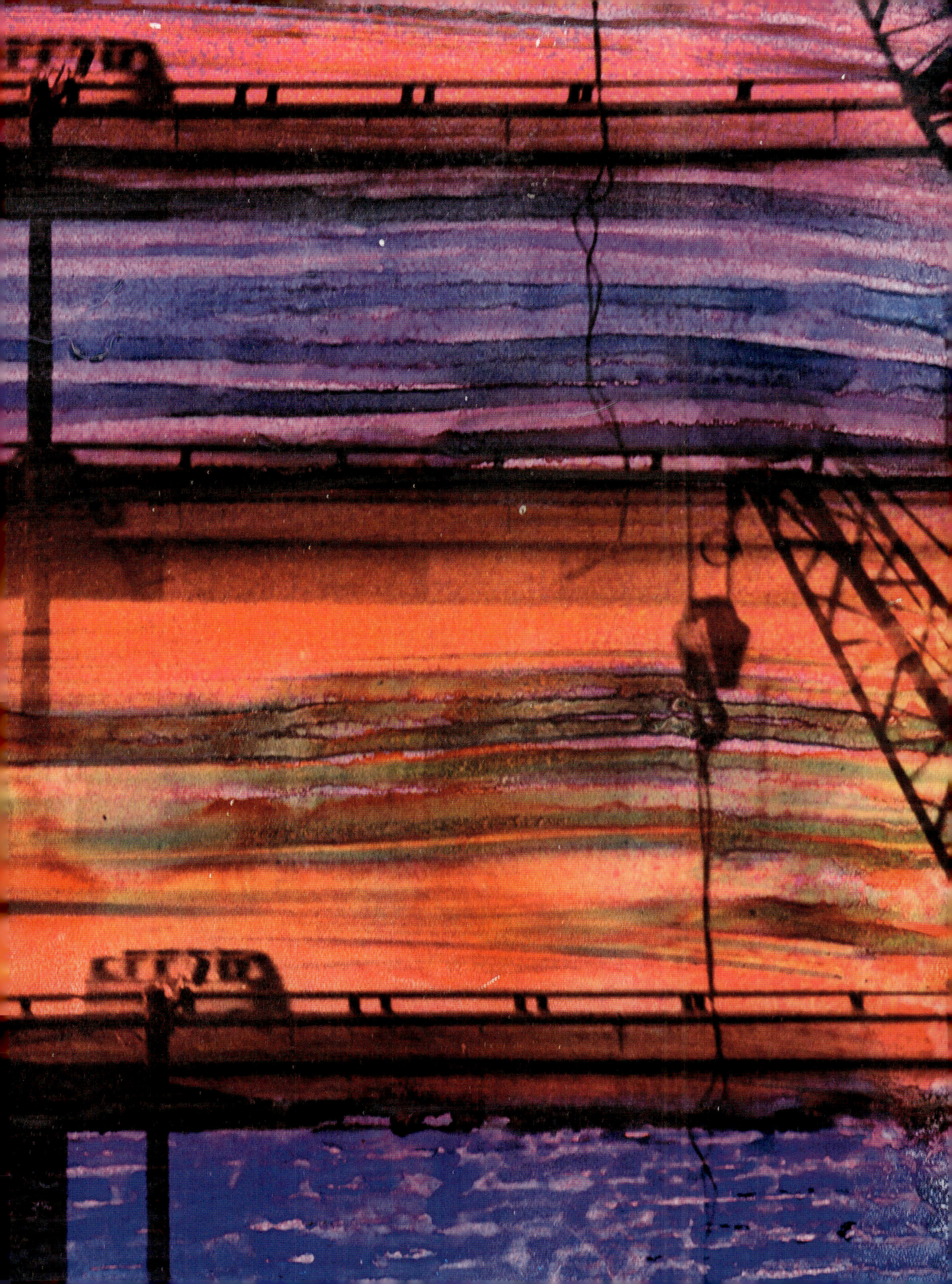

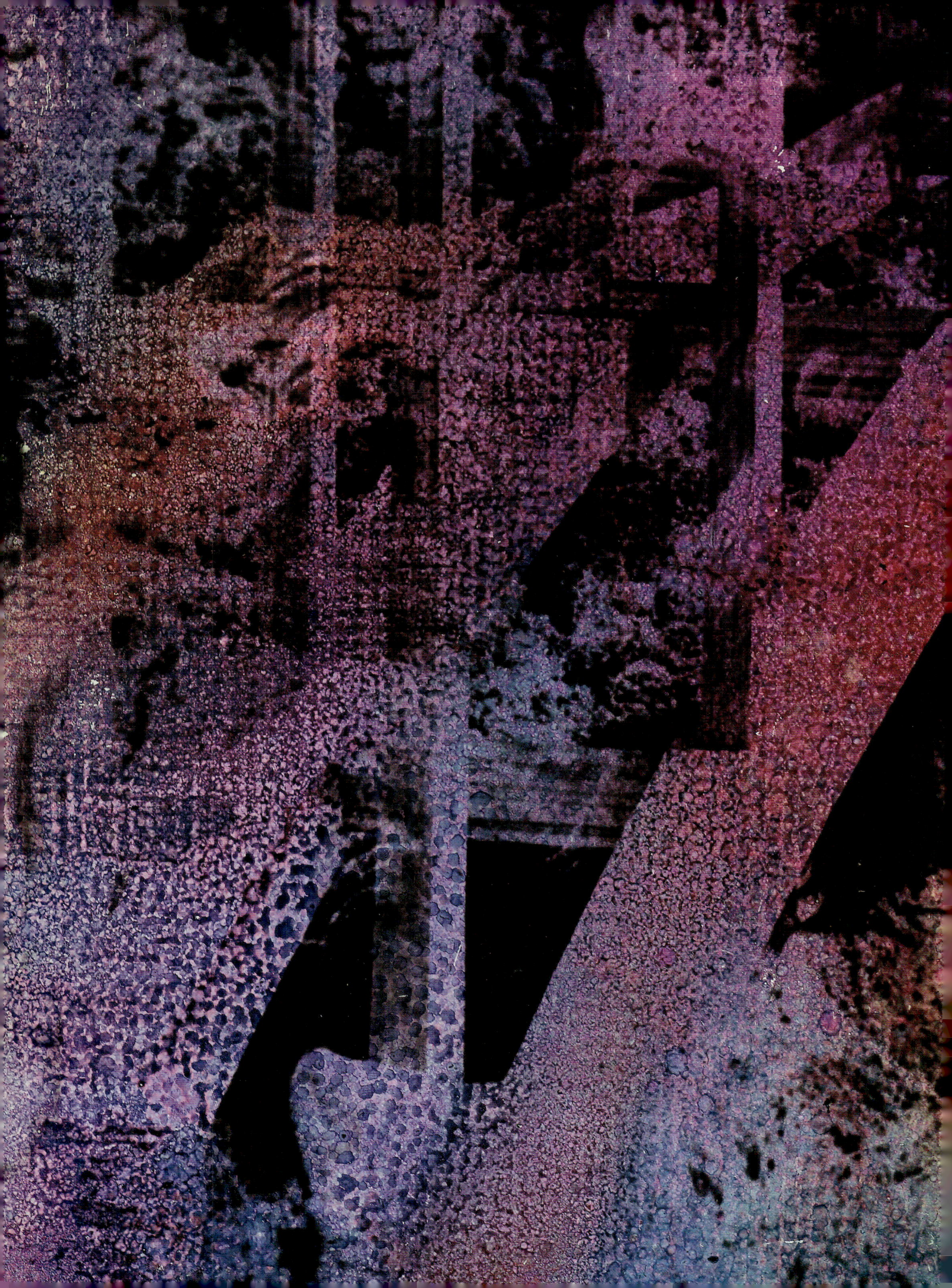

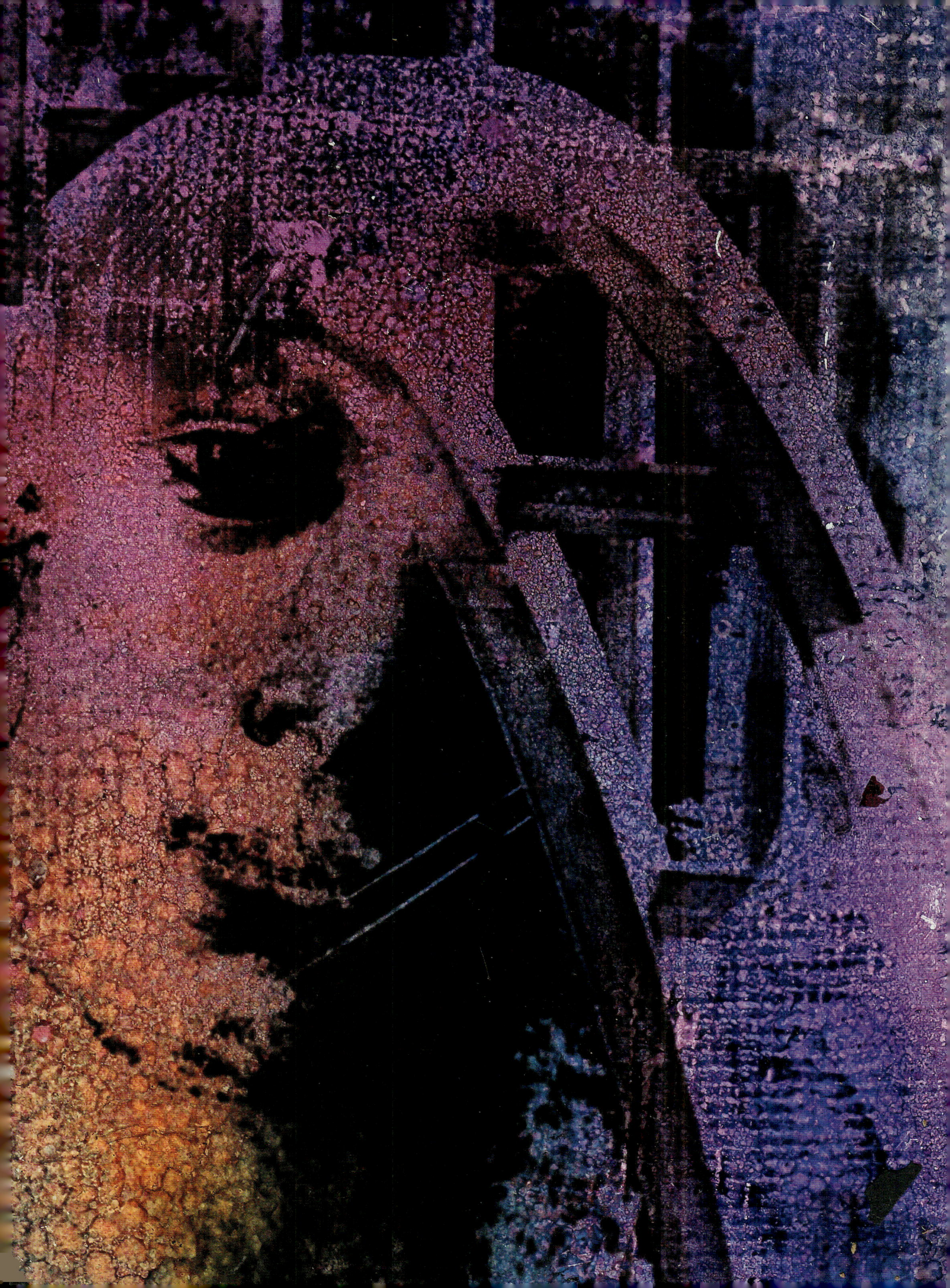

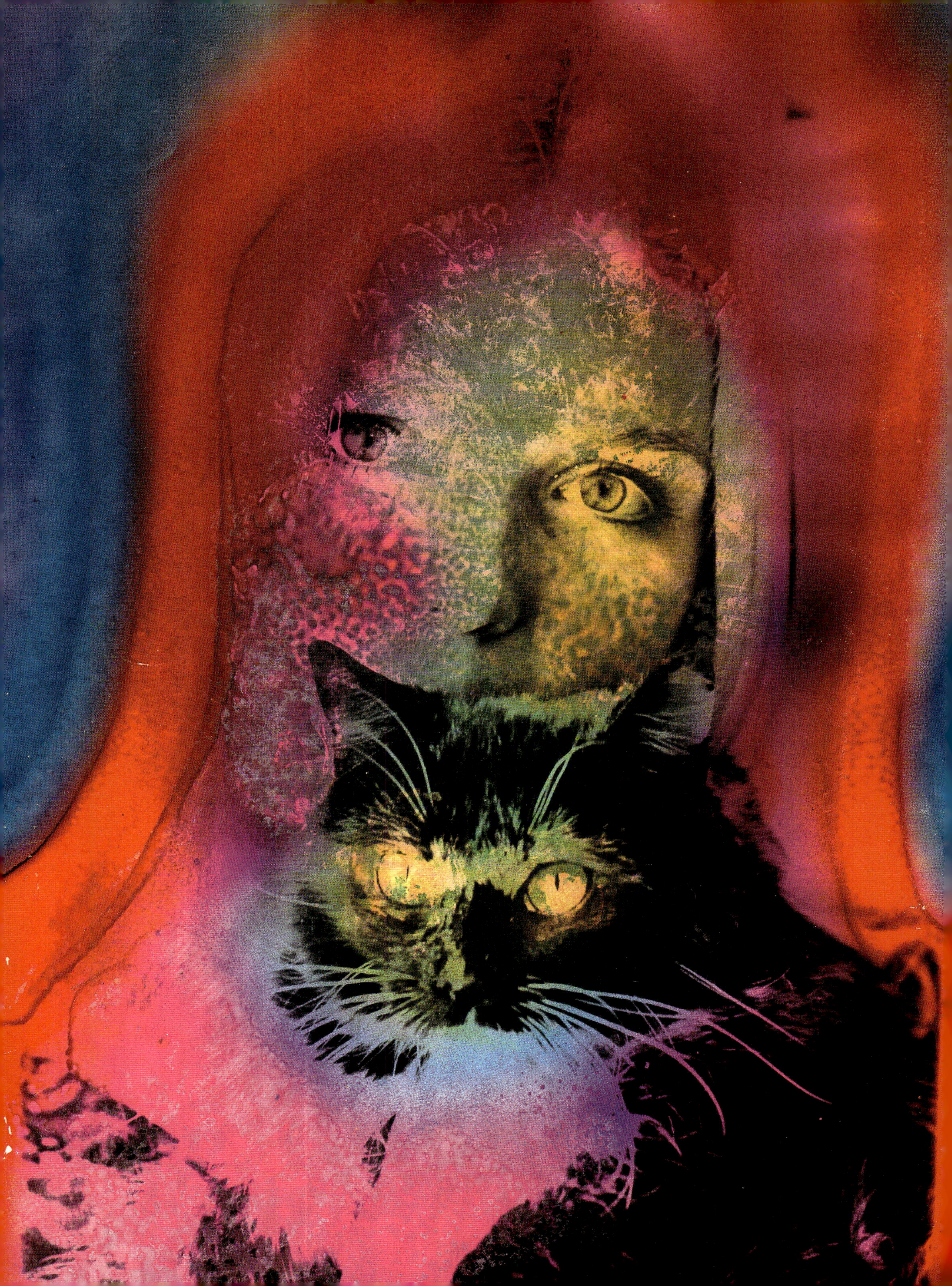

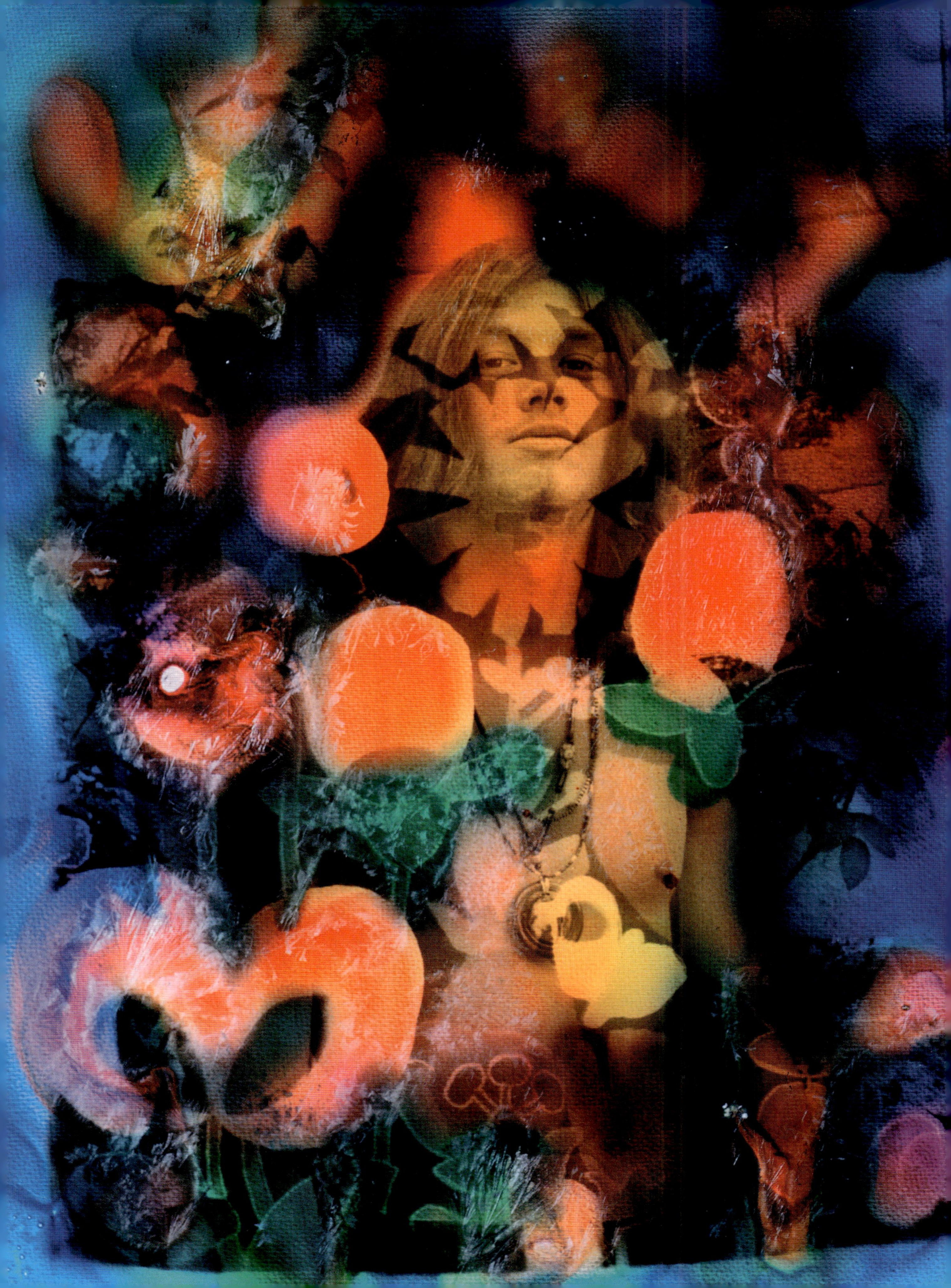

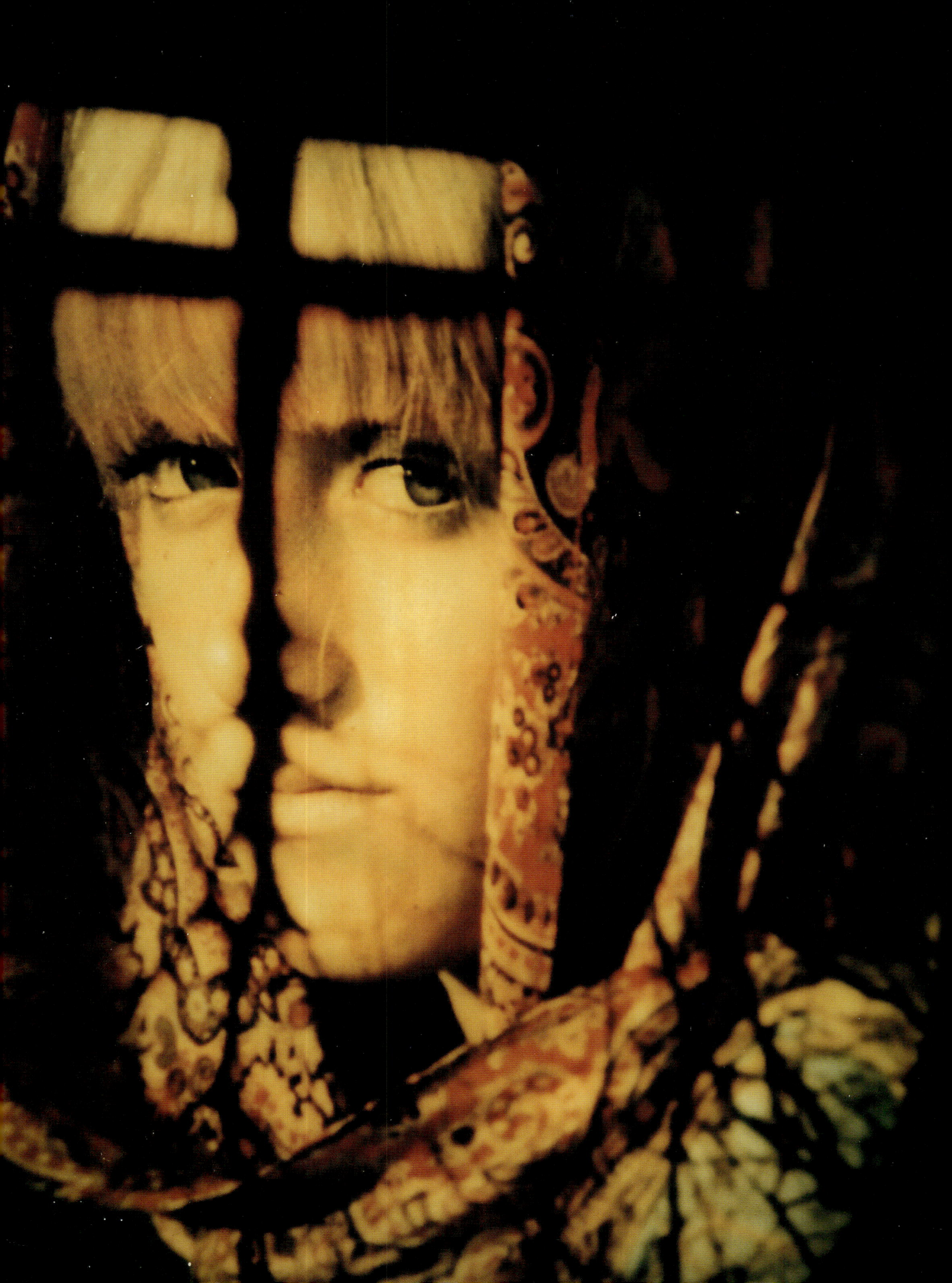

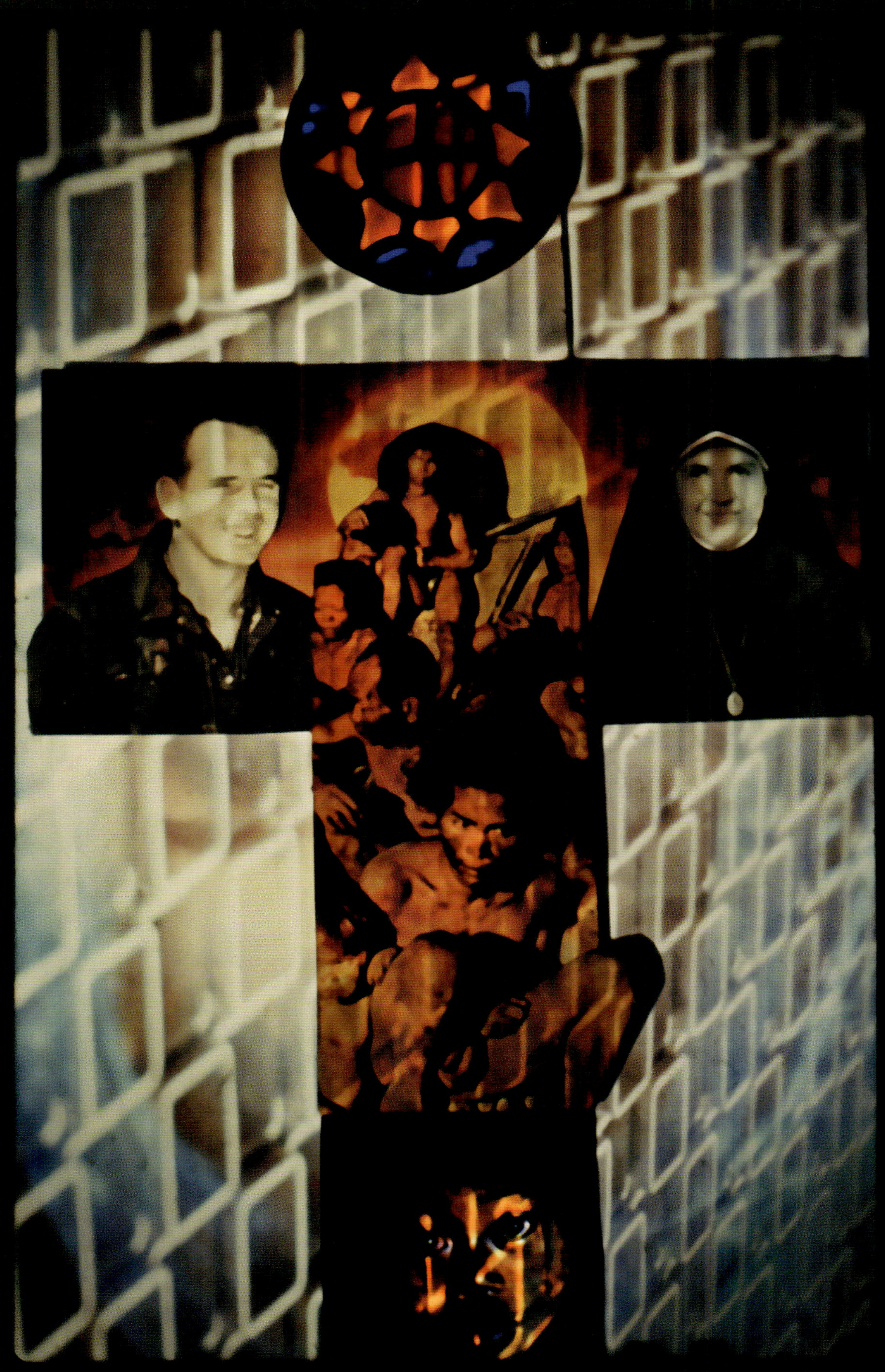

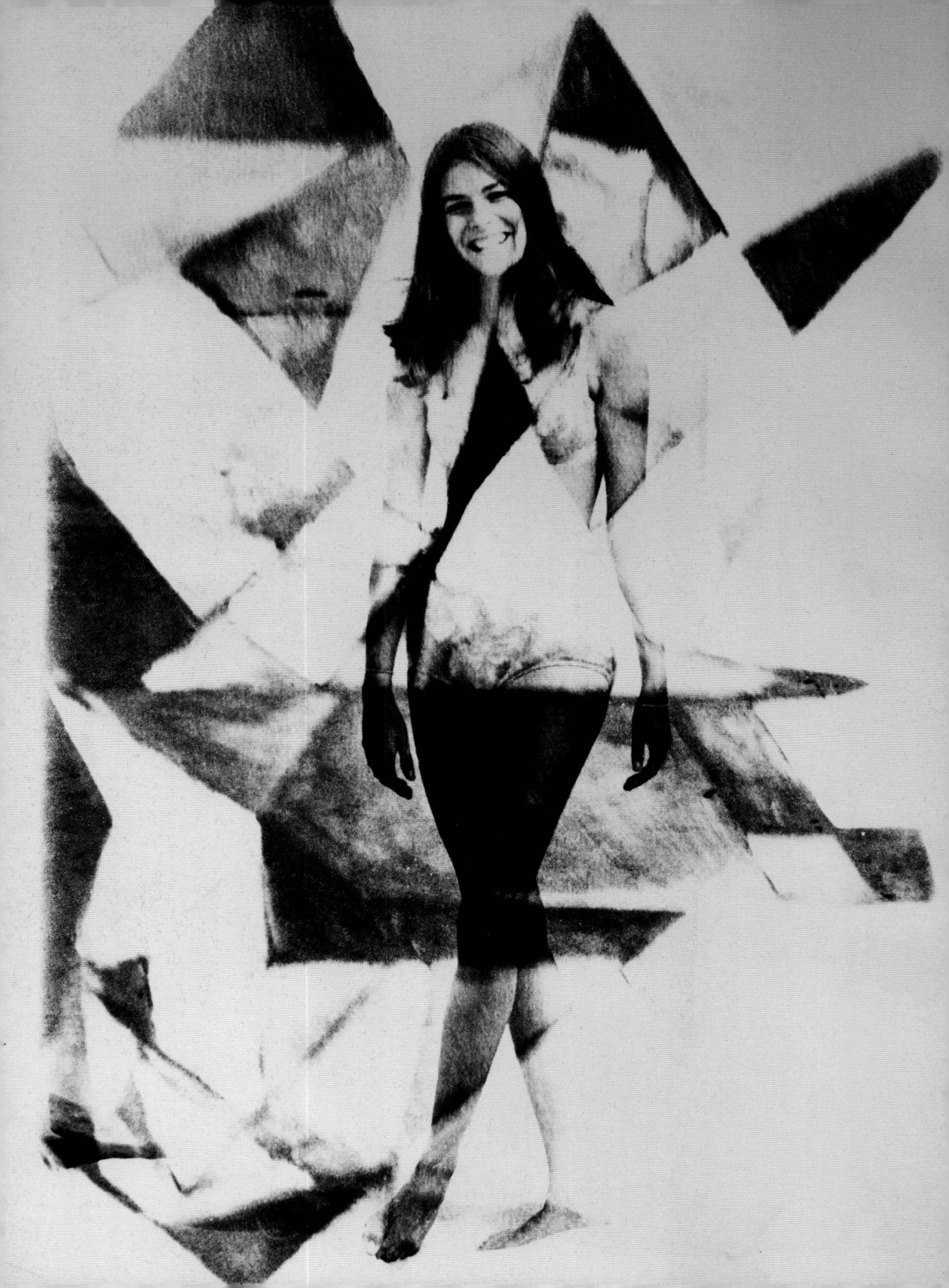

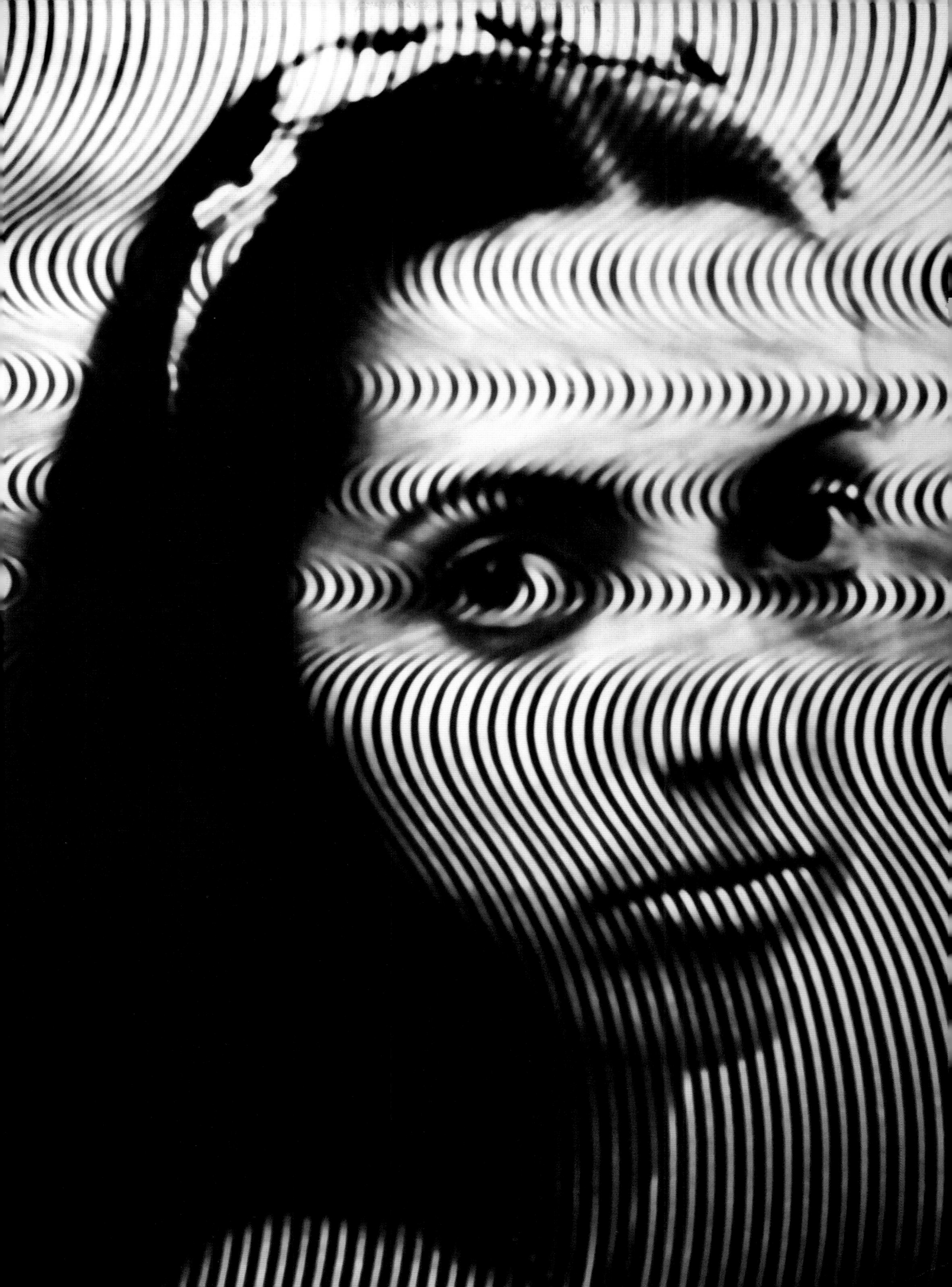

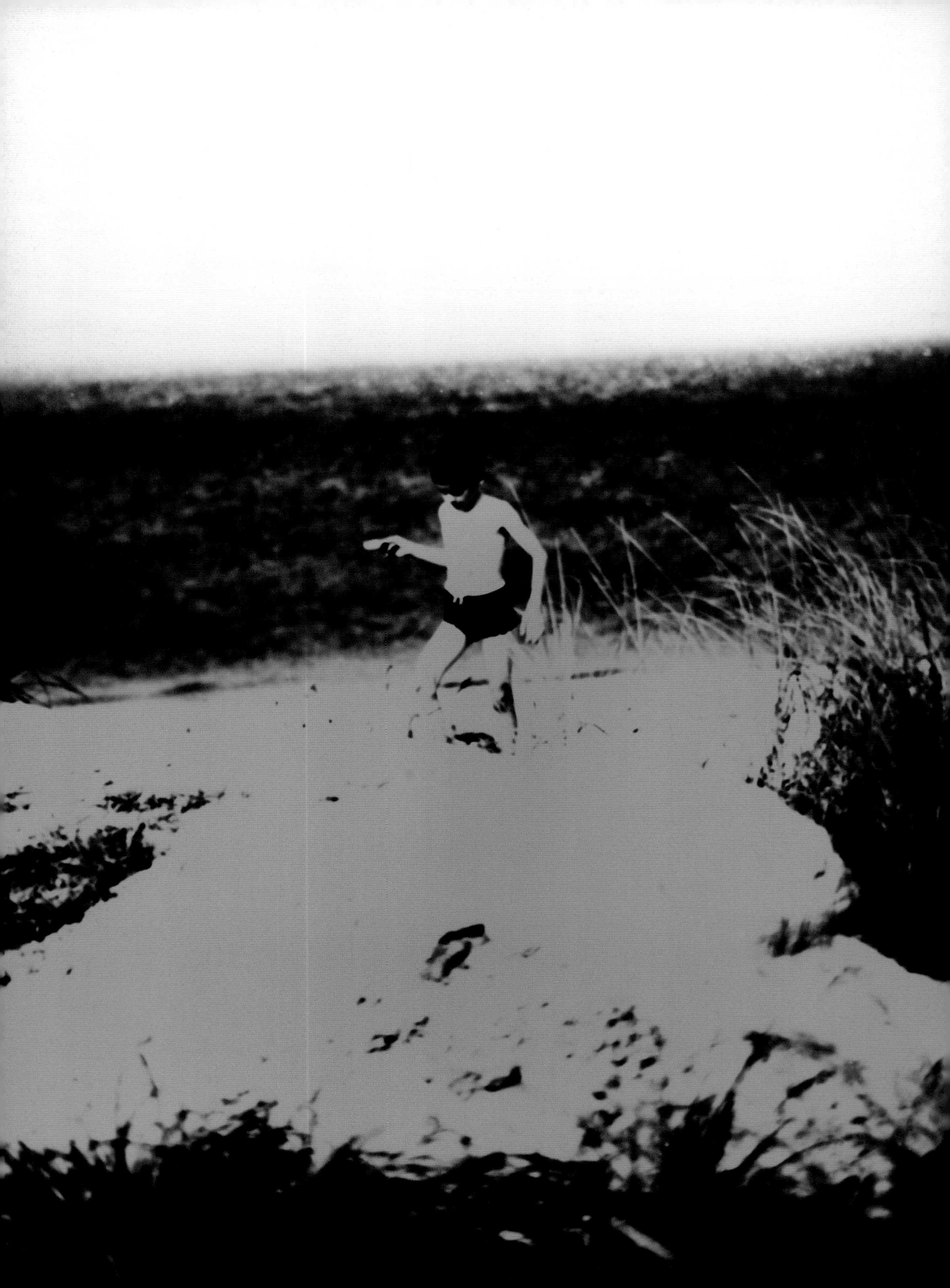

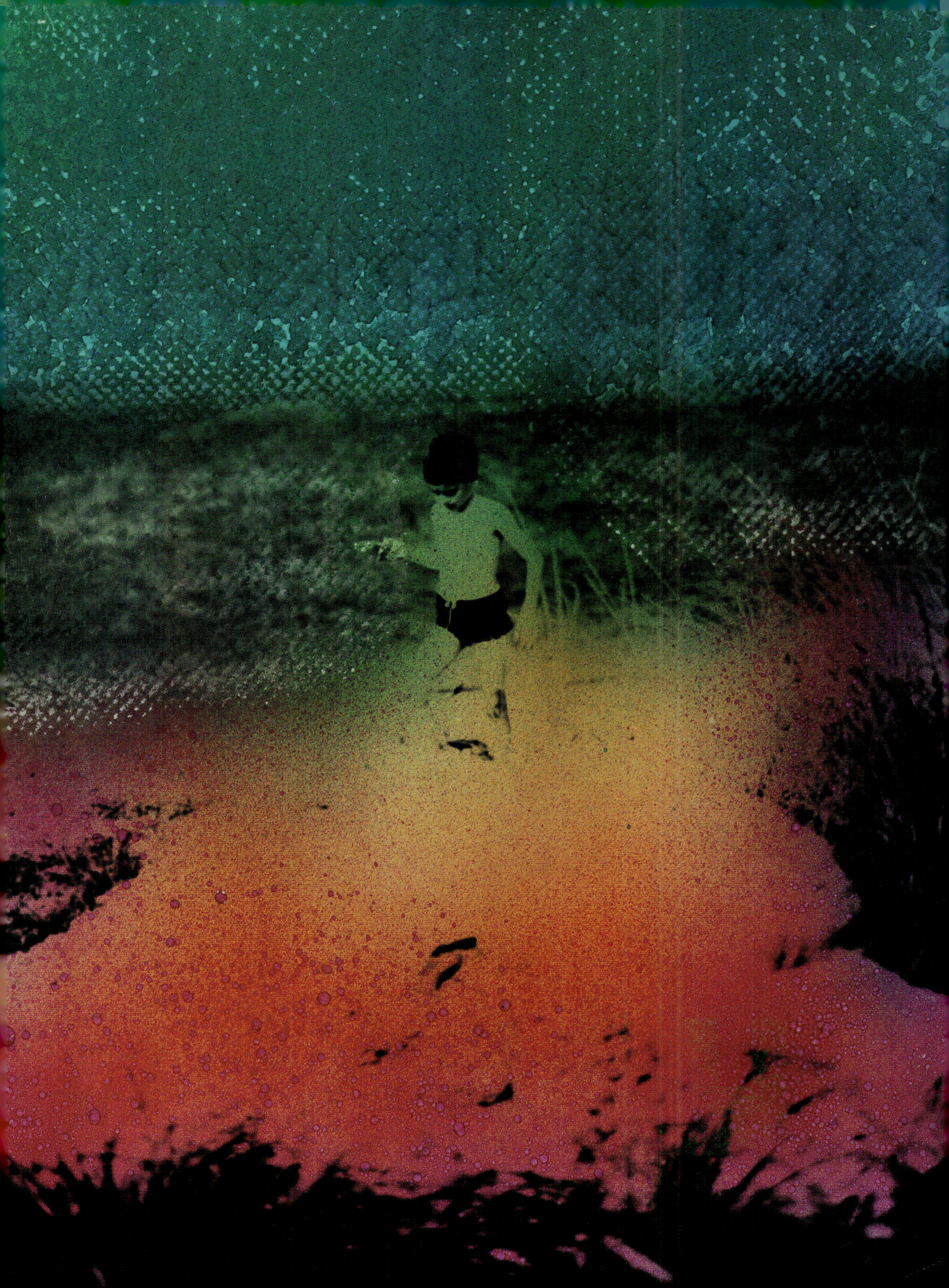

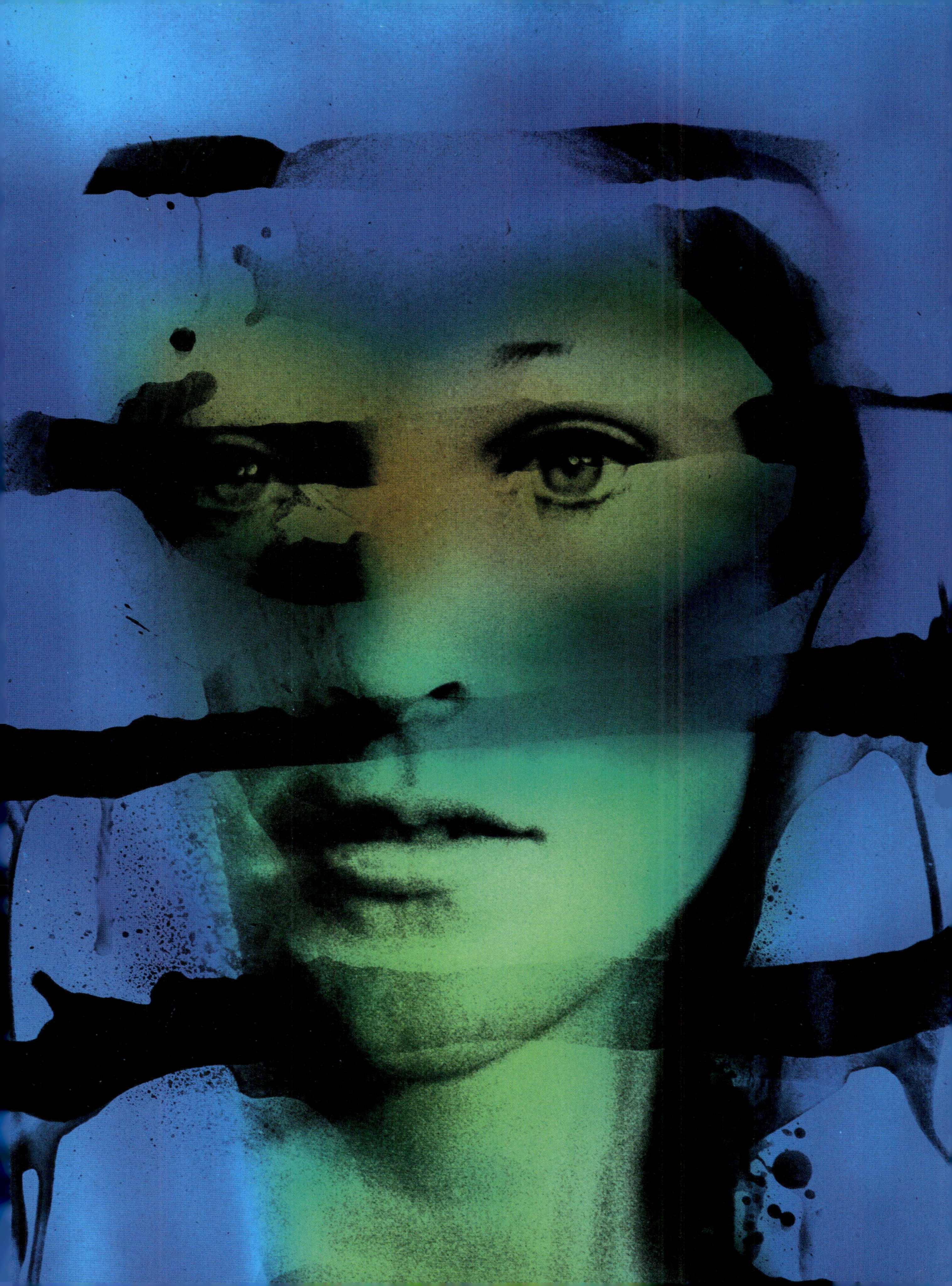

KALI'S SECRET ARCHIVE BY BRIAN WALLIS

During the long decade of social and political turbulence bounded by the Watts riots in 1965 and the end of the Vietnam War in 1975, Los Angeles became a roiling countercultural laboratory of creative experimentation in photography. Amid a freewheeling environment encouraged by the rise of various liberation movements, anti-war protests, psychedelic rock, the New Hollywood, and commercial advertising, and without the constraints of an entrenched museum and gallery system, artists in Southern California were freed to reconsider photography as a found subject matter and as a material object. Exhibitions like *Photography into Sculpture* at the Museum of Modern Art, in New York in 1970, and *California Photographers* 1970, shown at the Oakland Museum in the same year, highlighted this unwieldy new work and demonstrated how thoroughly many California artists had rejected the medium-specific legacy of straight photography handed down by West Coast photographers like Ansel Adams and Edward Weston. Critic Margery Mann wrote at the time that wild, young photographers in the Oakland Museum show were "using reproductive processes such as Xerox and Thermofax as creative tools [and] combining photography with printmaking techniques, including silk screen and lithography, and even with sculpture."[1] She regarded this as a positive development.

Experimentation with what a photograph might be and how its meaning was constructed was for these California artists the name of the game. In Los Angeles, artists like Robert Heinecken, Wallace Berman, Llyn Foulkes, John Baldessari, and Ed Ruscha seemed to regard photography as more of a thing than an image. Playing with the physical form and the visual connotations, artists and photographers in Los Angeles, in particular, treated photographs as found objects, delivered in newspapers and magazines, and malleable in form and material. Heinecken was typical: he described himself as a "para-photographer" because he felt his works that used photo reproductions appropriated from magazines and advertisements were only "beside" or "beyond" photography. He famously titled his 1965 essay, "The Photograph: Not a Picture of, but an Object about Something."[2] Instead of individual framed prints, these artist-photographers often presented their images as books, posters, mailings, magazines, sculptures, slideshows, collages, and assemblages. They were influenced not only by art history but also by mass media, television, magazines, advertising, and the movies. They used, among other things, appropriated imagery, distorted exposures and printings, various reproduction print technologies, hand coloring, and obsolete processes to challenge both the vulnerable materiality of the photographic print and the presumed transparency of the photographic image. By recasting expectations of what photography could be, they played freely with the material forms and real-life sources of the images they used. Given the rampant experimentation of much of this work, viewers for years wondered whether it was even photography at all.

Among the rebellious photographic experimenters active in Los Angeles at this time was a largely unknown artist named Joan Archibald, whose archive was only recently uncovered when her homes were cleaned out shortly before her death in 2019. Archibald was a self-described isolationist and not part of any defined artistic group, in fact, she was so secretive about her work that few outside her family even knew of its existence. Yet dozens of boxes and suitcases filled with her brightly colored prints from the 1960s and 1970s were discovered as well as eighty-three rolls of unprocessed film, salvaged from hundreds, documenting her late-life obsession with UFOs. These photographic artifacts—now preserved at the Stuart A. Rose Manuscript, Archives, and Rare Book Library at Emory University in Atlanta—reveal a diligent and committed photographer whose large rainbow-colored photographic prints of long-haired flower children and California surfers with peace medallions from the 1960s exemplify the era's exuberant artistic practices and its limitations.[3] On a yellowed newspaper clipping from 1970, found among her papers, Archibald boldly declares, "Photography, in my opinion, is the most fascinating progressive art form. Technically, for me, the work is one big experiment. I follow no rules except the very basic ones."[4]

Archibald was born on August 27, 1932, during the Great Depression, in suburban Islip, New York, on Long Island, as Joan Marie Yarusso. While she was still young, her mother split from her father, an electrician and remarried. Under the guidance of a generous stepfather, young Joan was raised in relative affluence attending private schools and taking courses at the Art Students League. In her early twenties, she married an itinerant musician, Robert Archibald, and gave birth to two children. But by 1962, Joan Archibald was fed up with domestic life: she divorced her husband; sent her children to live with her mother who enrolled them in boarding school; and fled to the West Coast. Arriving in California, she first lived in a small Malibu apartment near the beach. By 1964, she had moved into a stylish mid-century modern house in Palm Springs, made the scene in her Studebaker sports car, and adopted the name "Kali," the signature of her new persona.[5] (Though she often went by Kali Archibald, she preferred Kali as a single name, like Twiggy.) It is unclear exactly what Kali was doing in California for the first five or six years, but her snapshots from the time depict hunky surfers in Malibu and Joan herself posing with handsome young actors like Richard Chamberlain, then starring as television's popular Dr. Kildare.

During 1968, Kali began to take her photography seriously, and she enrolled in a night course at the nearby College of the Desert, a junior college in Palm Desert, where she took detailed notes. But mostly she was self-taught, laboring in artistic isolation, seemingly oblivious to the teeming L.A. arts scene, and without the benefit of sharing work or trading tips with fellow photographers. At home, Kali used her daughter, and her daughter's teenage friends as models; developed negatives in her darkroom; and colored the prints by floating them in a dye-filled swimming pool. For an intense five-year period, from about 1968 to 1973, Kali worked feverishly on her photography. There was an ambition and a tenacity to her pursuit, and a deliberate pattern to her photographic experiments. In her surviving archive one can observe clear themes and preoccupations, articulated in both subject matter and in ways of working. Her photographs can be clearly divided into three main projects or phases: an initial burst of experimentation produced between 1968 and 1973, which she named *Artography*, since they were a bona fide combination of art and photography; an overlapping investigation of Polaroid photography from about 1970 to 1973; and a much later obsession with charting UFOs and other paranormal light phenomena from 2003 to 2005.

By far the largest and most deliberate of these series, comprising over seven hundred finished prints, is the collection of hand-dyed photographs that Kali called Artography.[6] These works best exemplify her questing spirit of experimentation. In these photographs, Kali took what otherwise might be regarded as banal hippie imagery—moody sunset landscapes, half-naked surfers, astrological signs, waifish California girls—and made it vibrant through her bold use of color and material transformation. It is what she did after taking the photographs that sets them apart. Typically, she would make individual sixteen-by-twenty-inch black-and-white photographs, often employing innovations in printing, including sandwiching negatives, double and triple exposures, high-contrast developing, and geometric or op art overlays. Then, she would color the prints using a variety of techniques, including, but not limited to, acid-colored dyes, spray paint, and additives like sawdust, iron filings, and sand. Kali claimed to have developed forty-five different techniques for printing and transforming her photographs.[7] Ultimately, each photographic print was different and unique.

Whether she knew it or not, Kali was part of an underground movement throughout the country of artists manipulating photographs in various ways to challenge the entrenched standards of photographic production. Critic Robert Hirsch calls this movement, begun in the 1960s, "handmade photography," and he cites the likes of artist-photographers like Betty Hahn, Bea Nettles, Naomi Savage, and Robert Fichter as "makers"—those who direct and control their images through various interventions and manipulations—rather than "takers" who merely snap photographs of the everyday world.[8] The makers Hirsch identifies created radically different types of photographs by using new materials, like cloth and metal; graphic printing technologies, such as Kwik Print and Kodalith; alternative processes, including gum bichromate and cyanotype; as well as more traditional printmaking techniques, especially silk screen and photoetching. Their goal, like Kali's, was to establish original and dynamic forms of personal expression through hybrid forms of photography.

Kali was principally concerned with effects of light and color in experimenting with alternative approaches to photography. In a 1970 artist's statement, she wrote:

"Currently, I am doing a lot of time-light-space things and am using refracted light through prisms and glass. I do all my own black-and-white processing, followed by the artwork and color, which probably come from a lifelong obsession I have had with color."[9]

Using a little handbook titled *Light and Color* as her guide, Kali created her own method of achieving dynamic color patterns: by juxtaposing contrasting colors of equal value and intensity she was able to create an op art-like vibration effect.[10] In some cases, Kali used a color wash or filter to saturate the image with intense purple, orange, or red. Usually these colors were applied over heavily contrasted and multi-exposed prints. Sometimes, she montaged drawn or photographed elements, such as butterflies, or overlaid the images with graphic screens or transparencies. The results were often startling. Through the application of acidic color and montage overlays, a conventionally sweet picture of a teenage girl is converted into a haunting, even shocking portrait. For one work, titled *Psychedelic Mary* (1971), Kali claimed to have created a hundred different versions from the original black-and-white negative, utilizing over thirty different coloring techniques.[11]

Surprisingly, Kali was able to elicit the same sorts of pictorial effects with various Polaroid cameras, not by manipulating the actual photograph, but rather by using various projections to make new instant images. In a fascinating and occasionally hilarious document from about 1971, entitled "An Experiment by Kali or How to Print Color Slides Instantly,' Kali lists her step-by-step efforts to master the newly released Polaroid Big Shot, an awkward portrait camera with a large attached flash and a fixed focal length.[12] While most photographers dismissed the Polaroid instant cameras as too commercial or amateurish, Kali embraced them enthusiastically. In addition to using the Polaroid for copy work, Kali produced remarkable portraits with the Polaroid Big Shot and, decades later, used the sleek SX-70 for her UFO investigations. Most extraordinary is the protracted series of self-portraits, haunting in their directness, and scrambled with layers of swirling color and lacy overlays. Many of Kali's Polaroids replicate the experiments of her Artography, but they are made more powerful by the miniature format, especially when collected in grids of sixteen, her preferred mode of presentation.

Kali sought commercial application for her Artography, and what is interesting to note is how homegrown photographic surrealism connected to mass-cultural versions of psychedelic and hippie images of the period. While the vernacular psychedelia of the rock-music industry—such as concert posters by Rick Griffin and Victor Moscoso, and album covers by Mati Klarwein and John Van Hamersveld—announced a new graphic style, Madison Avenue advertisers and Hollywood promoters quickly sought to cash in on the scene. High-profile photographers like Richard Avedon and David Bailey made trendy advertising photographs of Cher and groovy posters of the Beatles in Day-Glo colors. This, more than the contemporary art world, was the market Kali sought to conquer. Through the dogged, pavement-pounding efforts of her mother-agent, Betty Dick, Kali gained representation from Globe Photos and Transworld Feature Syndicate Inc., two prominent outlets for commercial photography then. The responses were telling about the commercial application of experimental photography at that time.

One agent from an agency called Photo Researchers showed interest in Kali's work and sent a copy of a catalogue of psychedelic black-light posters from the New York company Gemini Rising. Depicting reigning rock stars like Jimi Hendrix and Bob Dylan, these sources borrowed from and contributed to a stylistic lexicon of psychedelia: high-contrast imagery, rainbow colors, stylized lettering, op art graphics. Another referred her to CRM Publishers, a new firm noted for publishing science textbooks and the magazine *Psychology Today*, known for its radical art director Tom Suzuki and its adventurous illustrators like Karl Nicholason and Phil Kirkland.[13] This intersection of commercial and high-art photography, typical of the medium's boundary transgressions of the time, reveals a far more complex experience of photography in California and its vernacular applications.

Kali's efforts to promote and monetize her work were largely unsuccessful, in the end; despite her boundless creativity, Kali rarely exhibited her art and had little success getting it published. She had a small exhibition of her work at the gallery of the J. Walter Thompson advertising firm, in New York, during August 1970, and a more substantial exhibition at the Pacific Grove Art Center in California, in September of that year.[14] Then in November 1970, her work was featured prominently in the national magazine *Camera 35*, where appeared alongside Ralph Gibson's dreamlike photo essay "The Somnambulist" and David Vestal's review of Minor White's *Mirrors, Messages, and Manifestations*. This was in many ways the high point of Kali's public recognition. The brief, unsigned article accompanied three full-page color reproductions of Kali's work. "There is no way magazine reproduction can do justice to a Kali creation," the author admitted. "They offer physical texture and surface modulations that are beyond the capabilities of mere machines."[15]

Throughout the early 1970s, Kali wrote poems to accompany her photographs; they reflect her mixture of innocence, naivete, and utopian optimism. Despite showing only passing interest in the period's tumultuous political events, many of which had dramatic public manifestations in Los Angeles, her poems and photographs occasionally referenced social trends and upheavals with titles like "Idiot House," "Pollution," "Psychedelic Phenomena," "Hippy, Yippy," "Freedom Marchers," "War." But mainly she concentrated on the upbeat visual talismans of the broader cultural movement, the peace and love generation, what author Charles Reich famously described in his 1970 best seller *The Greening of America* as "the youth revolution." That year, Kali made plans to publish an ambitious monograph of her work, comprising seventy full-color works of Artography and alternating poems, but for some unknown reason, after being announced, this never happened. And by 1973, around the time she married prominent Los Angeles lawyer Karl L. Davis, Jr., and moved to Pacific Palisades, Kali had largely abandoned her Artography experiments.[16]

But there was one final chapter. Perhaps the wildest and most unexpected legacy of Kali Archibald's work is her sudden, intense, and even bizarre engagement with UFOs and extraterrestrials from 2003 to 2005. Following the death of her husband in October 2000, Kali became increasingly paranoid living in a large house alone. She began to closely monitor the numerous infrared security cameras that surrounded her property in Pacific Palisades, and the experience seems to have triggered an earlier obsession with the paranormal. Although there is no previous record, Kali's daughter, Susan Archibald Oddo, recalls her mother's claims of sighting UFOs in the desert and her mother's numerous reports to the authorities in the 1960s; she also believes her mother may have been abducted.[17] Kali might have been influenced by the widespread media coverage of the so-called Phoenix Lights in 1997, in which a large number of Arizona residents, including Governor Fife Symington, witnessed a massive delta-shaped craft cruising silently through the night sky over Squaw Peak, a mountain range in Phoenix. Whatever rekindled her paranormal interest, Kali filled numerous spiral notebooks with wild scribbles and drawings documenting her close scrutiny and repeated reviewing of the security camera videotapes. She was, as she wrote, "Looking for Wows" or "Entities."[18]

Reflecting the growing mass-culture popularity of books and movies on aliens and extraterrestrials, Kali compiled a glossary of words to describe what she saw: "globes," "orbs," "rods," "lites," "rays," "beams," "angels," "aliens," "bio-luminescence." These names were attempts to accommodate her observations of bright video flares or nocturnal light anomalies to the cultural patterns with which she was most familiar, such as spirits ("ghosts") or shapes ("orbs"). She was not so interested in verifying the apparitions or defending herself from them as she was fascinated by describing and classifying them accurately. Her notebooks are filled with scrawled descriptions, precise time codes, and linear outlines of the mysterious lights. Unlike the existing systems for classifying UFOS, such as the Hynek or Vallee typologies, Kali's tabulation was based entirely on the shapes of light formations on her surveillance tapes, which she traced assiduously in her copious notebooks. Many of the drawings she created are themselves quite bold and dramatic, and interesting as speculative visual reconstructions of paranormal light phenomena.

Aside from the outsider art-like drawings in Kali's frenzied records, her worried documentation also resulted in astonishing photographs, which she rephotographed from video cameras and copied with her Polaroid camera and enlarged. These mostly abstract images generally reveal no discernible landmarks of her backyard landscape, but instead show streaks and blobs of light intersected by the flickering transmission lines of the video cameras. The result is a surprising mixture of abstract imagery with occasionally prominent visual phenomena, which Kali then pored over, traced, and interpreted. Her notes are jumbled and even paranoid as she sketches the white blobs and light flares, carefully noting the dates and time codes. "What is it?" she wonders in her notebook. Then she quickly notes, "Someone or something is erasing the images." Whether or not there is a rational explanation for the phenomena Kali witnessed, her engagement with this socially sanctioned mythology, prevalent in both popular culture and tabloid news, was linked to her earlier interests in spiritualism and celestial order, as well as her lifelong passion for light and color.[19]

Photography is such a public and performative medium, it is always surprising when bodies of work appear that were not previously known. The rediscovery of Kali Archibald's secret archive was a revelation to everyone. Despite her earlier ambitiousness, Kali remained tight-lipped about her photography until the day she died. For this reason, it would be easy to dismiss her as an amateur or a dabbler, or even as some kind of outsider artist. But these labels would be misleading. Kali was a maverick. Working at a moment of tremendous social upheaval and artistic creativity, Kali was able to create a brash and unique style by dramatizing the visual culture of hippie modernism. Kali's Artography is a singular vernacular manifestation of the investigations around photography that took place in Los Angeles in the 1960s and 1970s. Today, that artistic intervention has been recognized as a valedictory achievement, a farewell to photography as usual.

NOTES

1 Margery Mann, "Revolutions in Medium—But What About Message?," *Popular Photography* 67, no. 2 (August 1970): 25, 26. See also A. D. Coleman, "California Report: A Break with Tradition," *New York Times*, July 5, 1970, 60; and, for more recent analysis, see Charles Desmarais, *Proof: Los Angeles Art and the Photograph 1960–1980* (Laguna Beach, CA: Laguna Art Museum, 1992); and Erin O'Toole, "Delightful Anxiety: Photography in California circa 1970," in Mary Statzer, ed., *The Photographic Object 1970* (Berkeley: University of California Press, 2016), 93–99.

2 Robert Heinecken, "The Photograph: Not a Picture of, but an Object about Something" (1965), in Eva Respini, ed., *Robert Heinecken: Object Matter* (New York: Museum of Modern Art, 2014), 155.

3 For a summary of these holdings, see the finding aid to the Kali Archibald Papers, Stuart A. Rose Manuscript, Archives, and Rare Book Library, Emory University, Atlanta, GA: https://findingaids.library.emory.edu/documents/archibald1448.

4 Kali Archibald, quoted in "'Kali' Experiments with Time-Space-Prism Photography," *Carmel Pine Cone*, August 6, 1970, 12.

5 Kali is also the name of the Hindu goddess of death, whose iconography is typified by ferocious feminine energy, and who is widely recognized as symbolic of motherly devotion, making her an appropriate avatar for a single mom with two young children.

6 Archibald often claimed to have copyrighted or trademarked the term *Artography* though no evidence exists that she did so. She did, however, incorporate an entity called Kali Kolor, Ltd. in legal documents filed July 31, 1969. Kali Archibald Papers, Rose Library, Emory University, Atlanta, GA (hereafter cited as Kali Archibald Papers, Emory University).

7 At the time, she said, "I have evolved forty-five art techniques that were applied to the black and white prints …I work with a great deal of emphasis on double and triple exposure, sandwiching, double printing, and use refracted light, prisms and glass, and muti-image combinations. I also make my own texture screens." Kali Archibald, letter to Edward Meyers, Executive Editor, *Popular Photography*, April 2, 1973, Kali Archibald Papers, Emory University.

8 Robert Hirsch, "Flexible Images: Handmade American Photography, 1969–2002," *exposure* 36, no. 1 (2003): 23–42; and, more recently, Robert Hirsch, *Transformational Imagemaking: Handmade Photography Since 1960* (New York: Routledge, 2014).

9 Kali Archibald, "Statement," ca. 1970, Kali Archibald Papers, Emory University.

10 Clarence Rainwater, *Light and Color* (New York: Golden Press, Racine, WI: Western Publishing Co., 1971). Kali's copy is in the Kali Archibald Papers, Emory University.

11 Kali's interest in serial imagery and mass reproduction may reflect the widespread popular attention to the pop art of Andy Warhol, whose repetitive thirty-two *Campbell's Soup Cans* (1962) she may have seen at the Ferus Gallery, in Los Angeles, in 1962.

[12] Kali Archibald, "An Experiment by Kali or How to Print Color Slides Instantly," four-page mimeographed document, ca. 1971, Kali Archibald Papers, Emory University.

[13] For a brief history of CRM (Communications Research Machines) textbooks, see Geoff Alexander, *Academic Films for the Classroom: A History* (Jefferson, NC: McFarland & Co., 2010), 82–84. Graphic-design historian Steven Heller profiles CRM art director Tom Suzuki in "Tom Suzuki, 76, a Designer Who Transformed Textbooks, Dies," New York Times, September 12, 2006, https://www.nytimes.com/2006/09/12/books/tom-suzuki-76-a-designer-who-transformed-textbooks-dies.html?searchResultPosition=1. For information on the surrealistic illustrations of Karl Nicholason, see Emily Temple, "Surreal Illustrations from 1970s Psychology Textbooks," *Flavorwire*, January 3, 2013, www.flavorwire.com/360321/surreal-illustrations-from-1970s-psychology-textbooks.

[14] The J. Walter Thompson gallery show was held in New York, August 21–28, 1970, and was noted in *J. Walter Thompson News*, vol. 20 (Aug. 21, 1970). Kali's largest exhibition was presented at the Pacific Grove Center, Pacific Grove, California, September 16–October 18, 1970.

[15] "Eyes by Kali," *Camera 35* 14, no. 6 (November 1970), 48–51.

[16] After 1973, Kali stopped making photographic prints, but she continued her work in slide and Polaroid form. During this period, her creativity apparently never waned, and she continued to experiment with color slides, hundreds of which remain unexamined in her archive.

[17] Susan Archibald Oddo, videotaped interview, May 8, 2018, Kali Archibald Papers, Emory University.

[18] These and subsequent quotations are from Kali Archibald, "UFO notebook, no. 2," 2003, Kali Archibald Papers, Emory University.

[19] Amid the vast literature on UFOs, two useful considerations of the narrative construction of these experiences are William J. Dewan, "A Saucerful of Secrets: An Interdisciplinary Analysis of UFO Experiences," *The Journal of American Folklore* 119, no. 472 (2006): 184–202; and Susan Lepselter, *The Resonance of Unseen Things: Poetics, Power, Captivity, and UFOs in the American Uncanny* (Ann Arbor: University of Michigan Press, 2016).

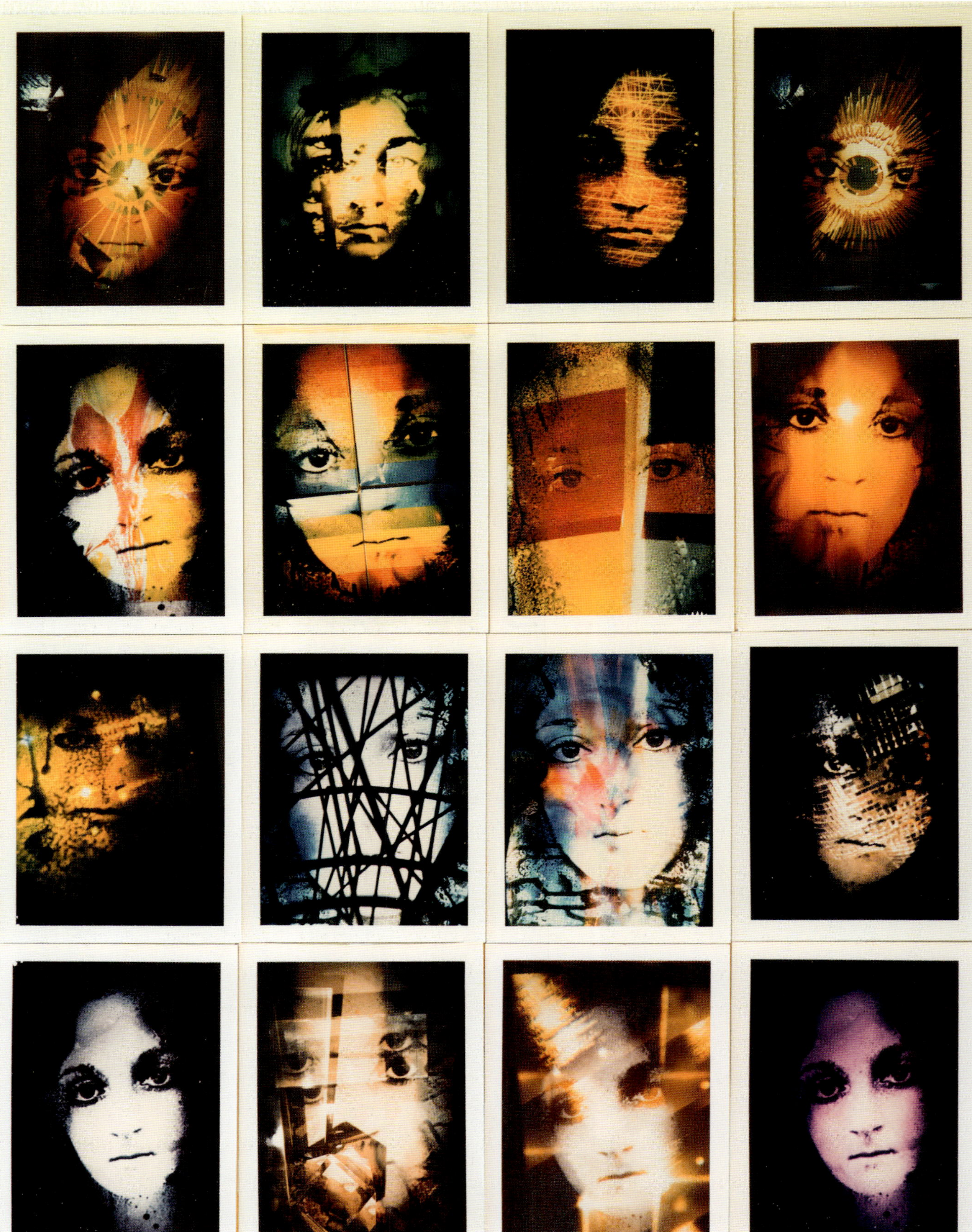

POLAROIDS

Kali began using a Big Shot camera in the 1970s. This particular Polaroid camera took a film pack that had ten exposures and corresponding mounting boards for each print. The camera itself acted as a miniature darkroom; each self-contained film pack was an entire processing chamber. Paper and celluloid would apply together as the photographer pulled the thin white tab out of the camera slot; the stainless-steel rollers worked in unison to squish and mix the built-in pack of processing fluids. Over the course of just sixty seconds, the paper could be peeled off to reveal, bit by bit, as if by magic, the captured print in Kali's hand. This particular camera had the ability to make multiple exposures on one print as well as capture near-perfect color and a professional depth, much like a darkroom print. The ability to develop fast, high-quality Polaroids was a boon for any perfectionist, as a near-instantaneous image meant more chance for added layers, or for a more precise set of eyes at just the right angle.

Kali would then mount the photographs taken with both the Big Shot and other Polaroid cameras onto larger boards; she seemed intrigued with multiplicity of imagery. Her original purpose in this endeavor is unknown to all but herself, but the images from this time period resulted in some of her most iconic work.

A certain time and place resides on these boards and in Kali's archive, from the low desert of Palm Springs to the Santa Monica State Beach of the '60s and '70s. There was a journey to India, remembered in photographs of the Taj Mahal, but the predominant geographical feel of Kali's archive is California. A young mother's own coming of age is documented as she photographs her teenage daughter's youthful eyes as well as those of visiting neighborhood kids—"Psychedelic Mary," Margie, and a mysterious Cindy (Sherman)—layering them on top of the physical landscape.

—A.J.

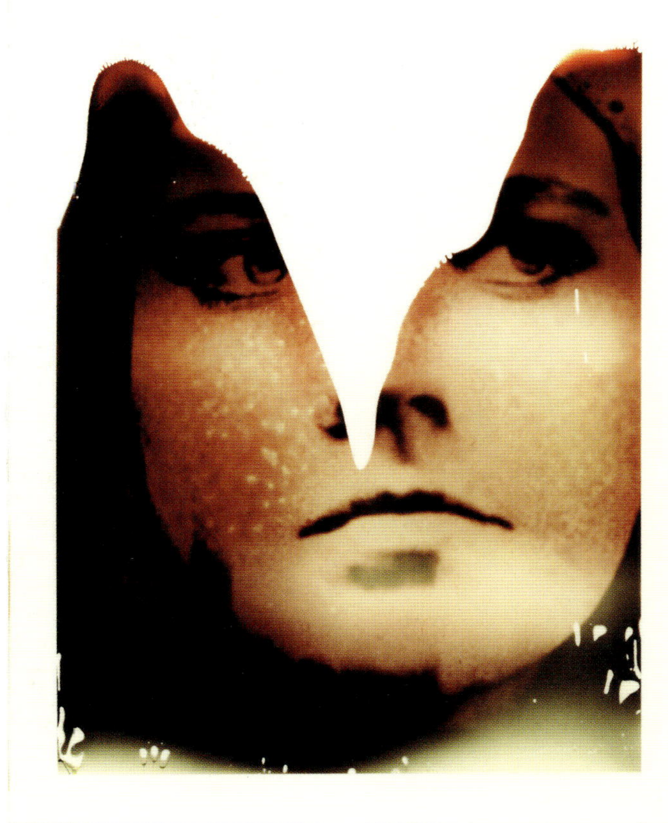

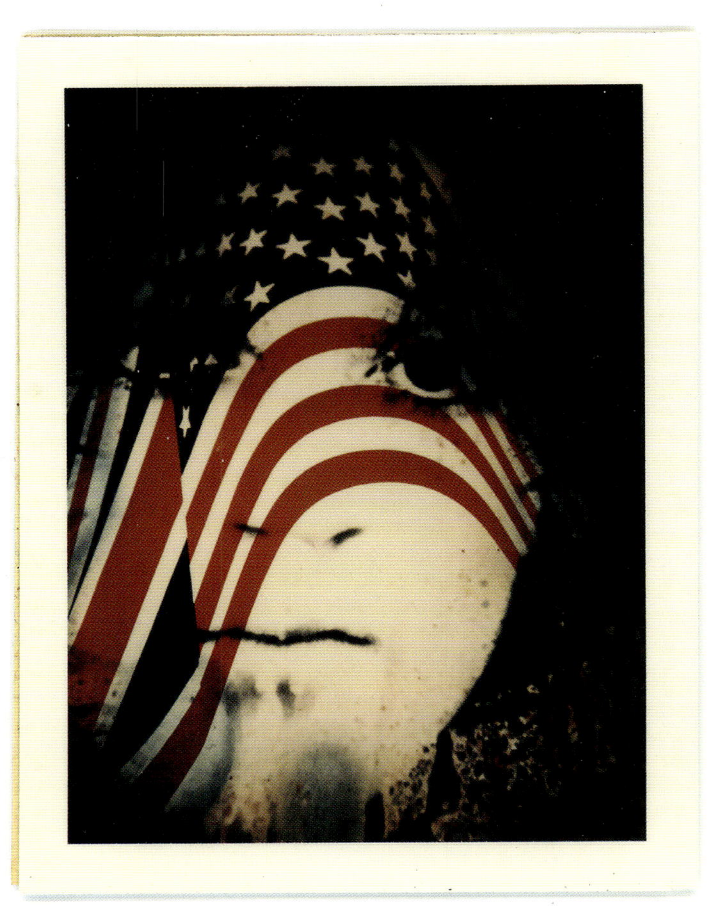

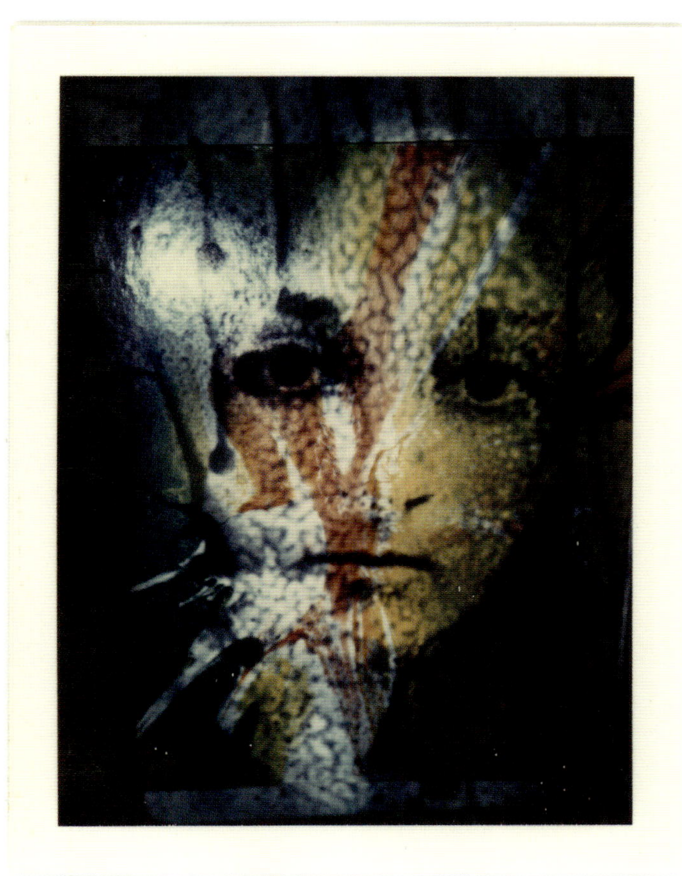

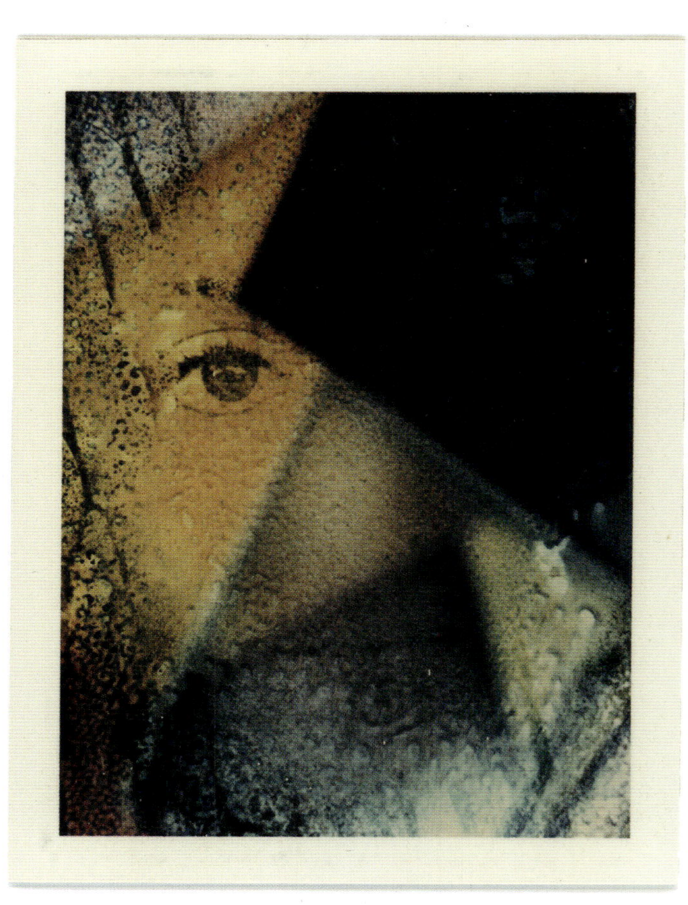

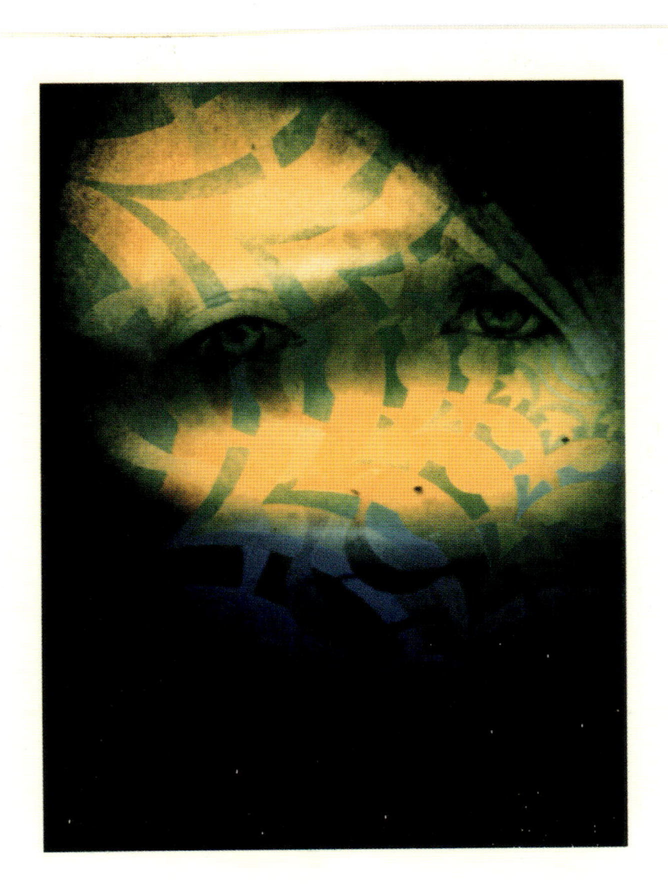

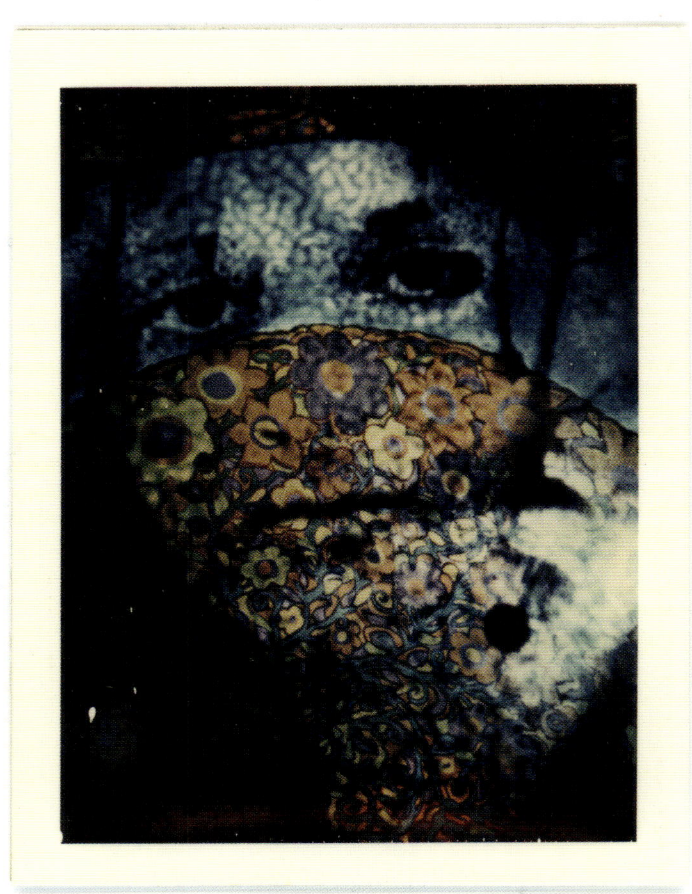

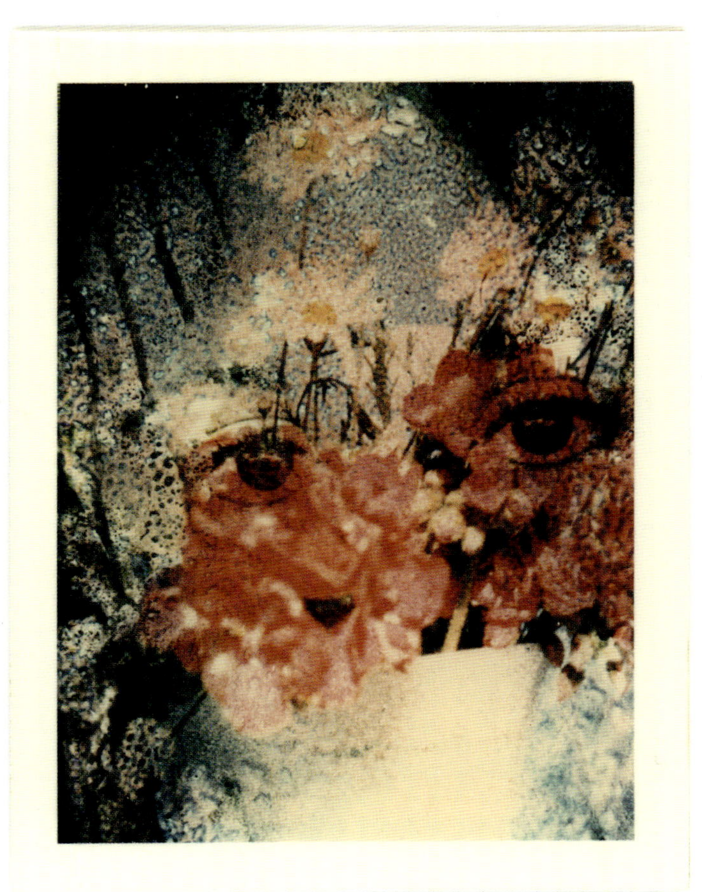

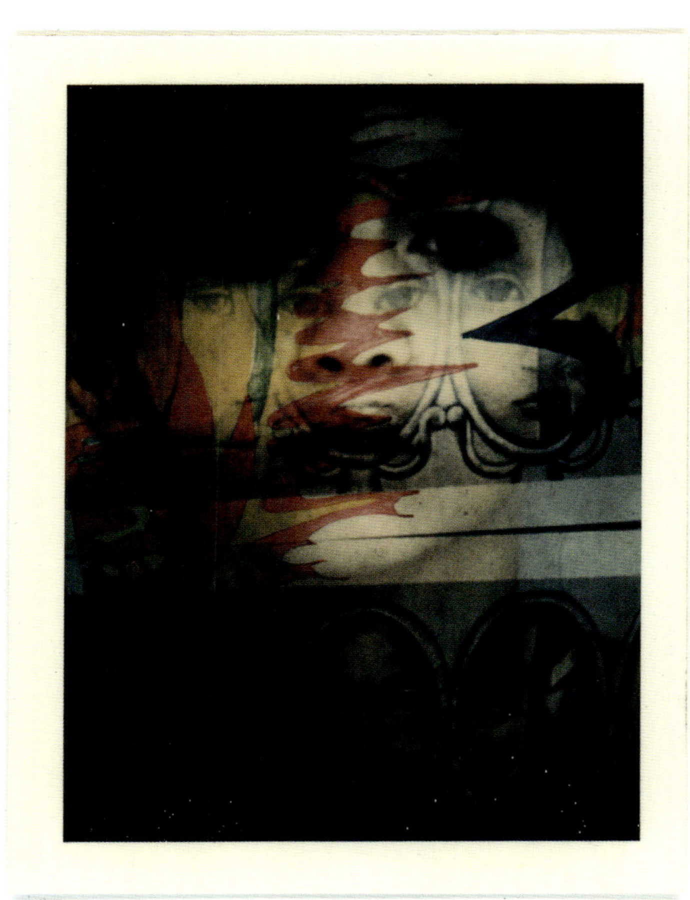

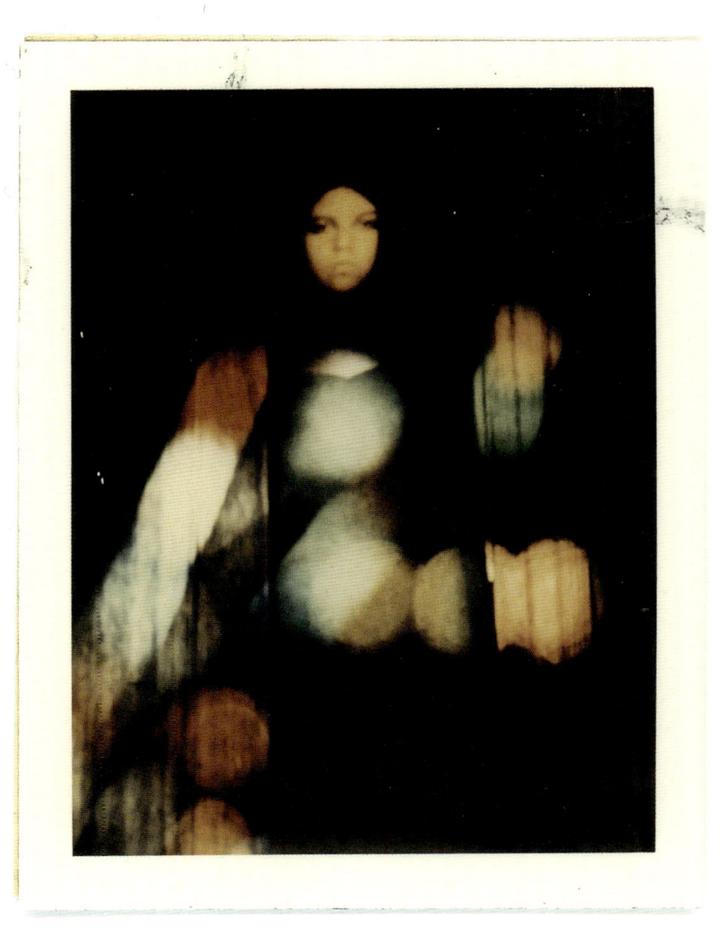

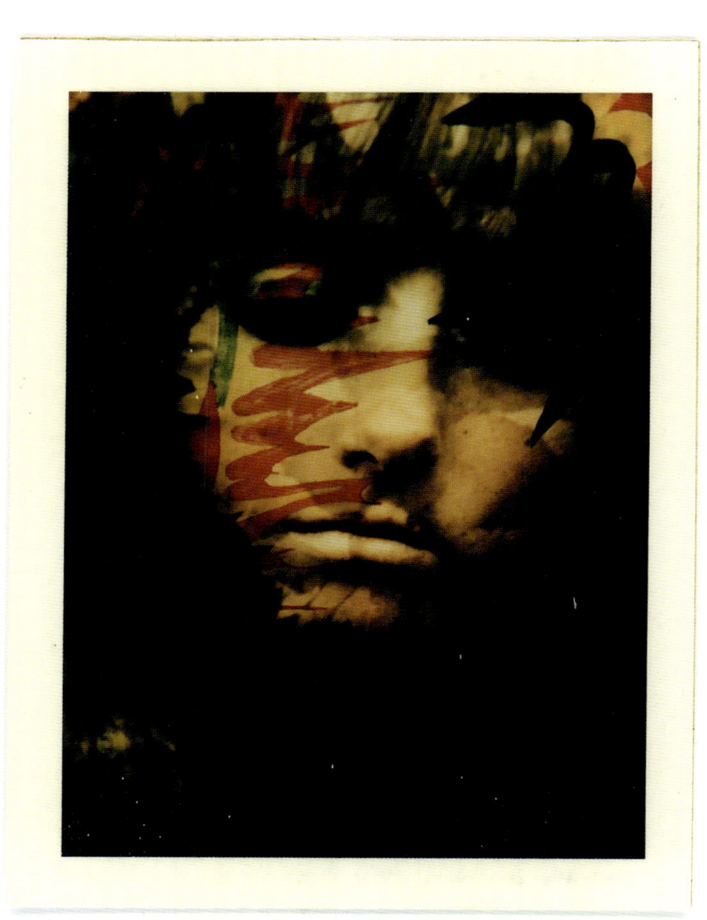

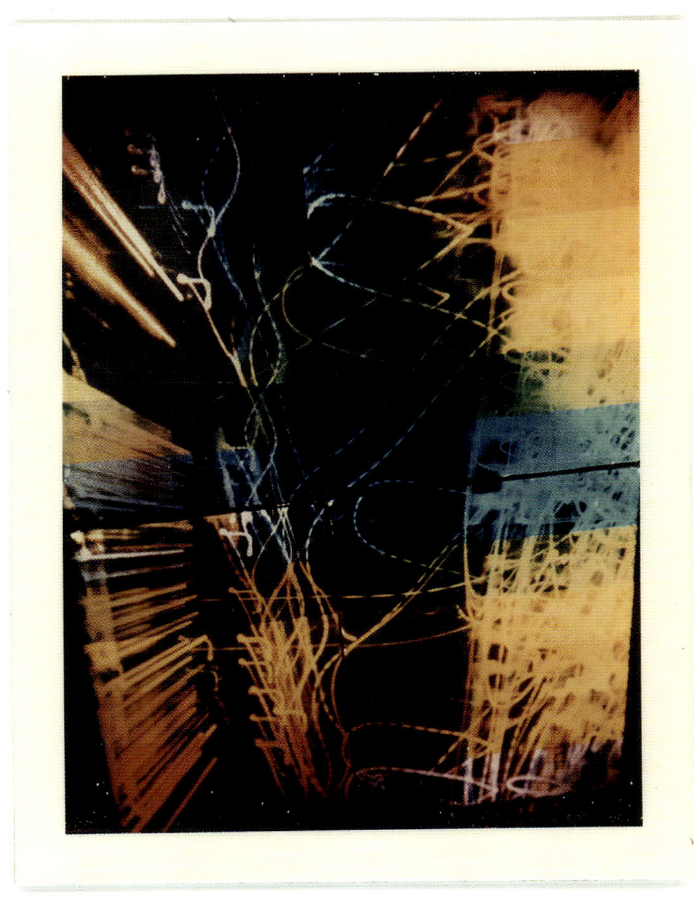

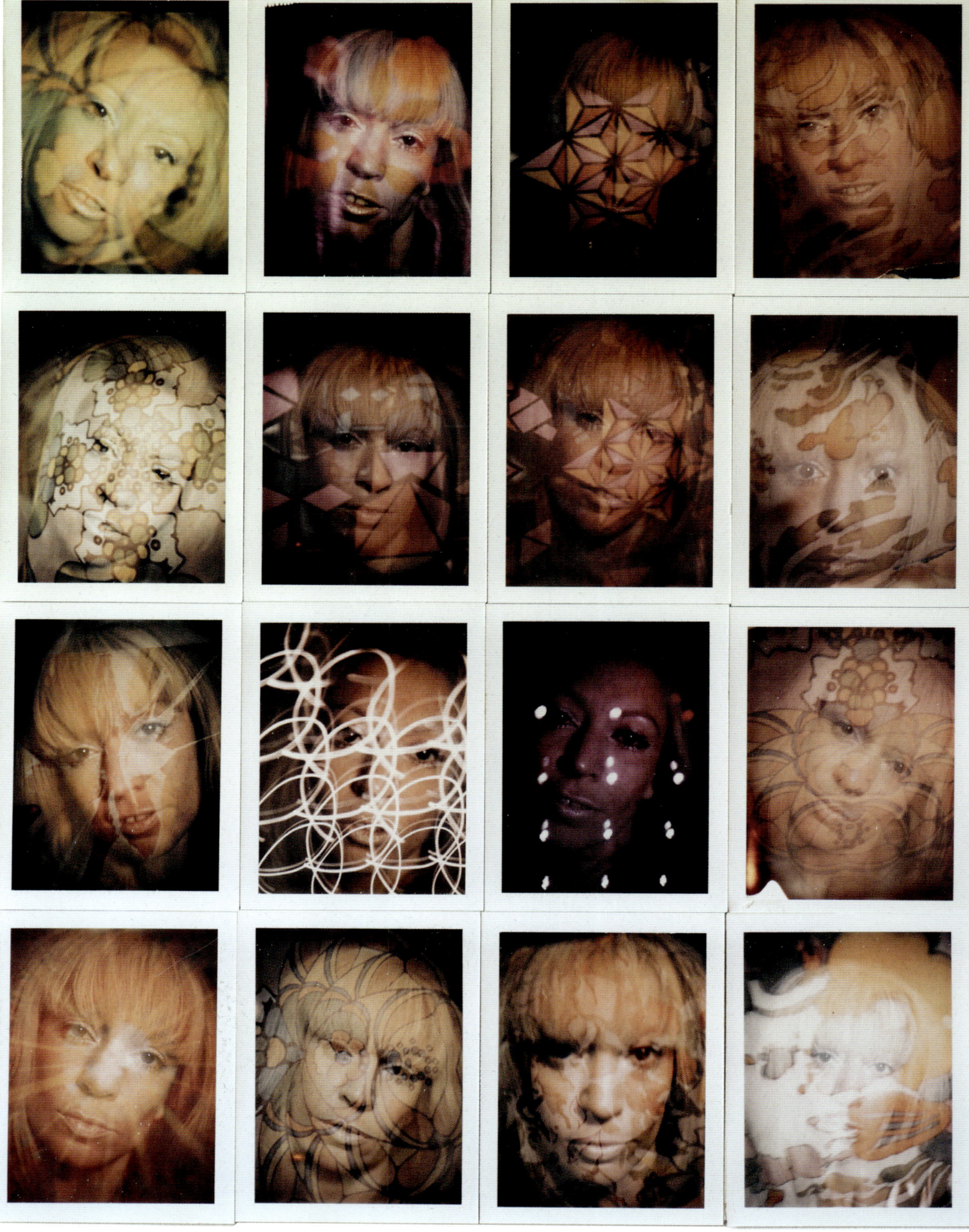

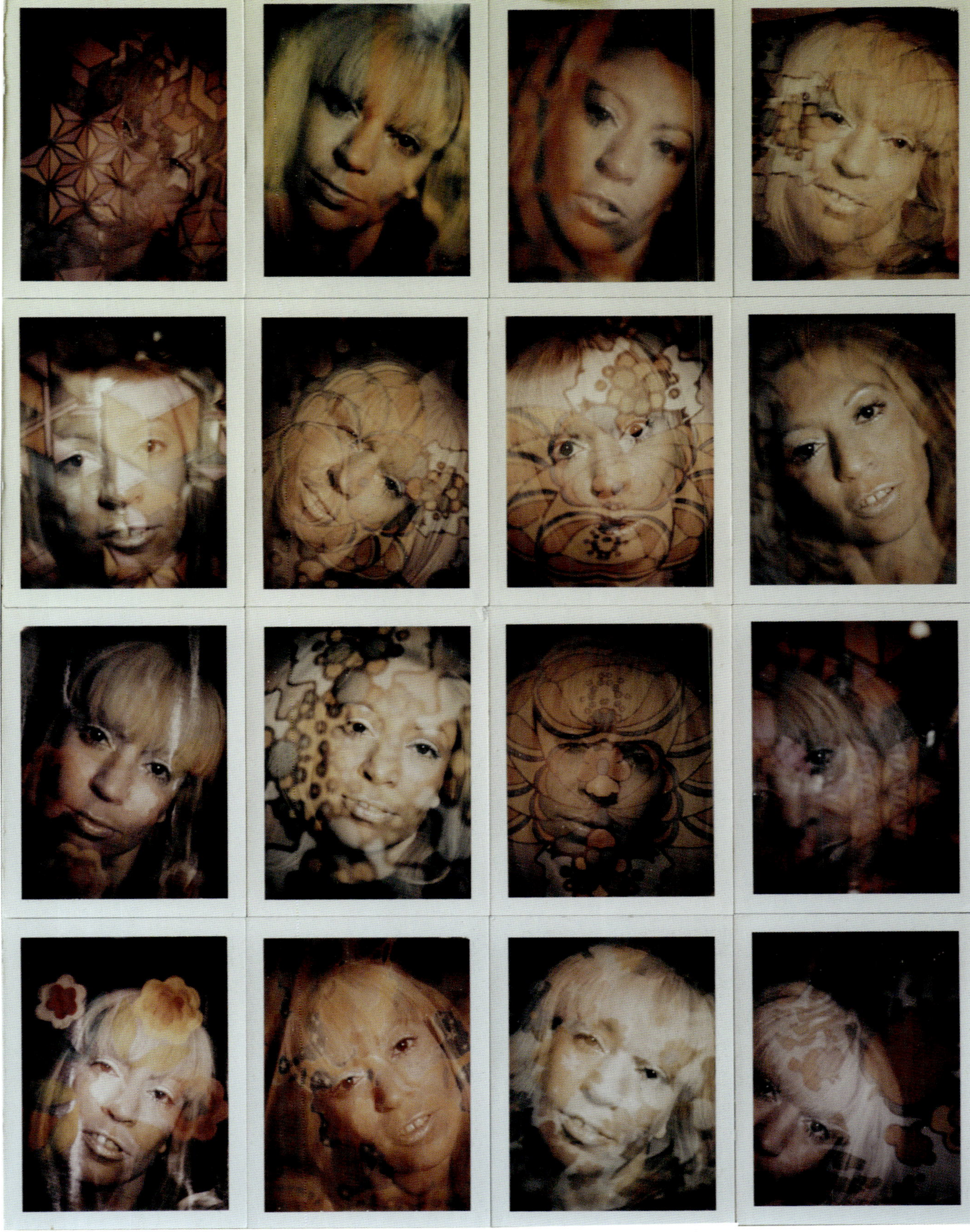

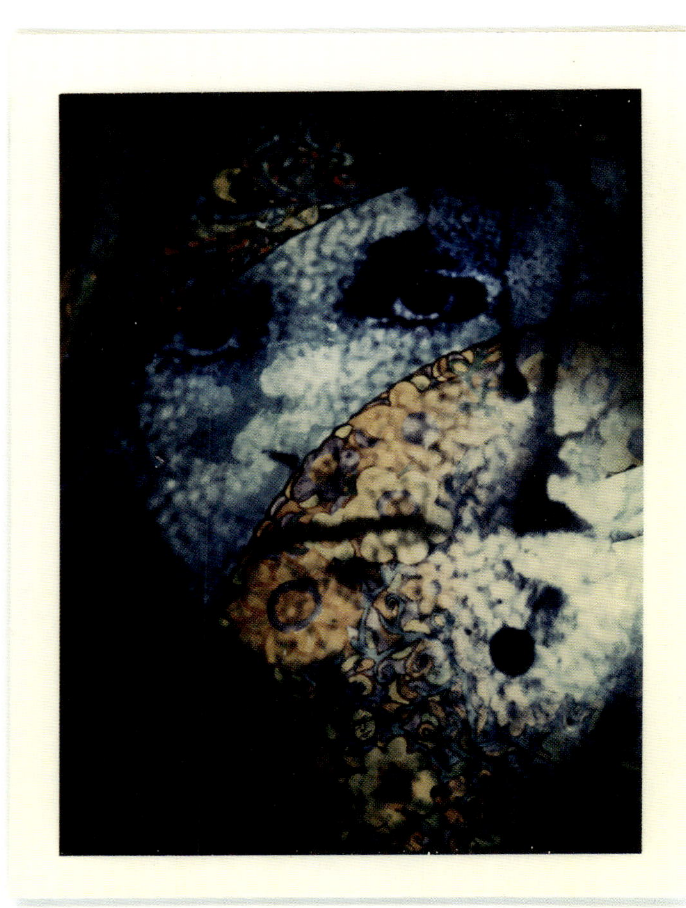

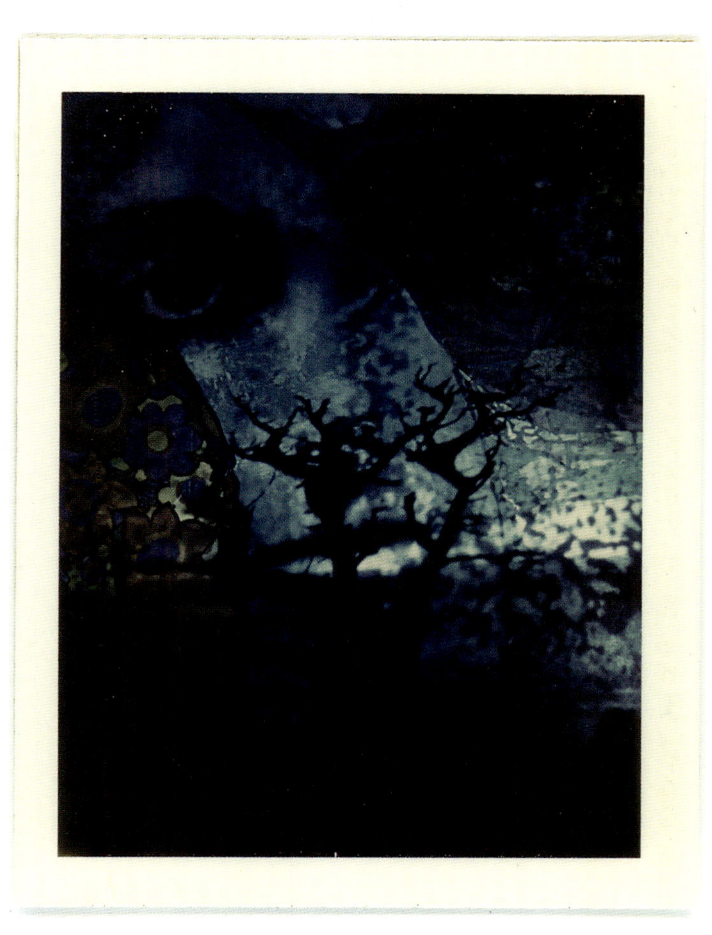

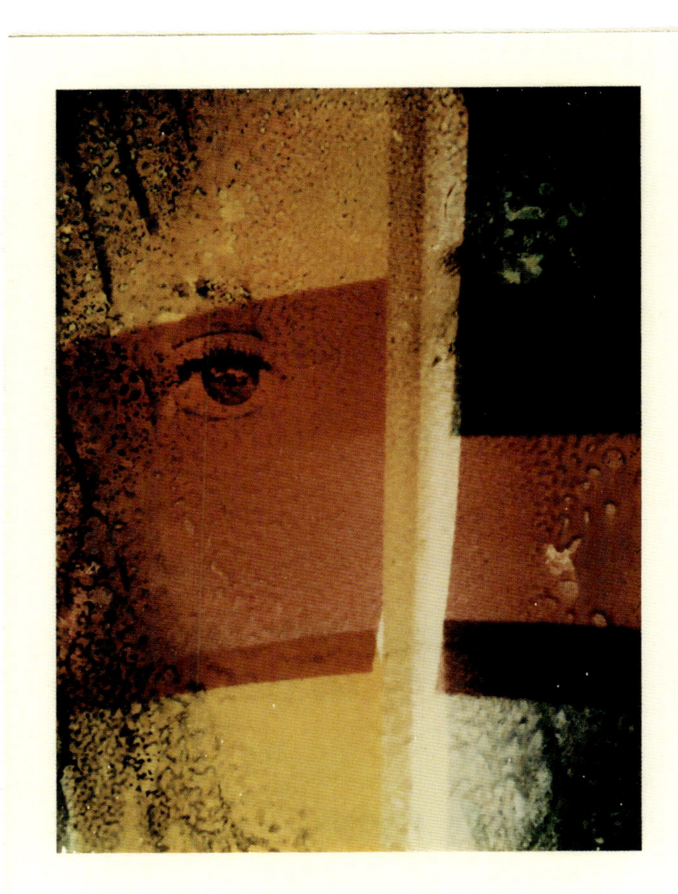

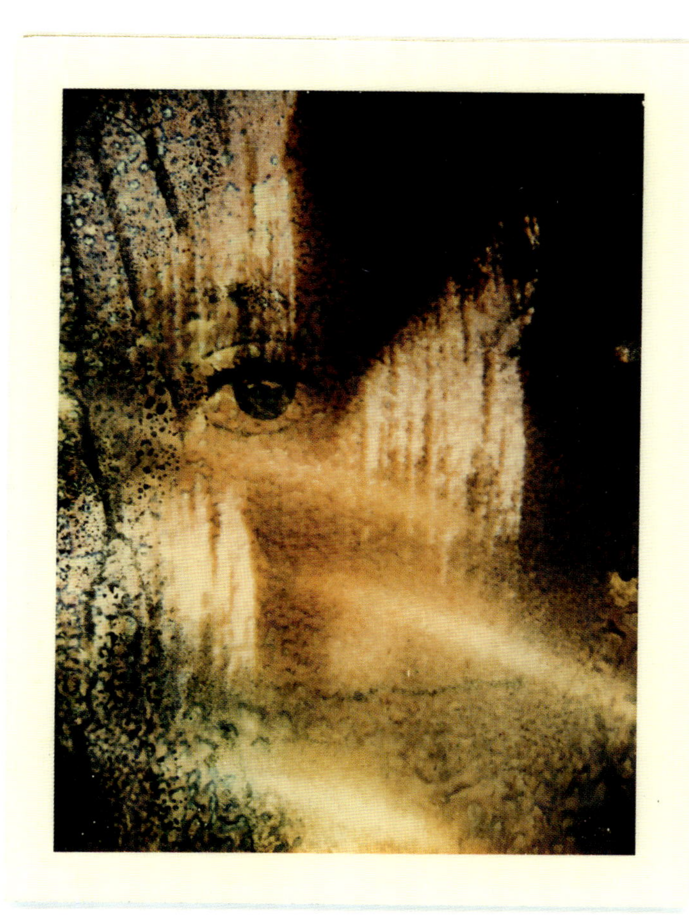

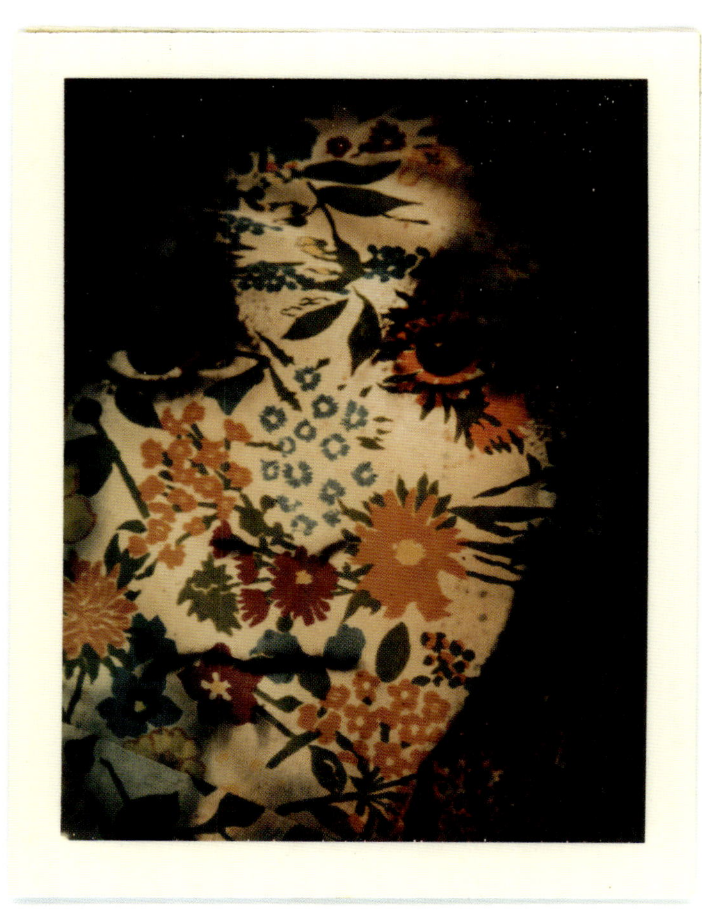

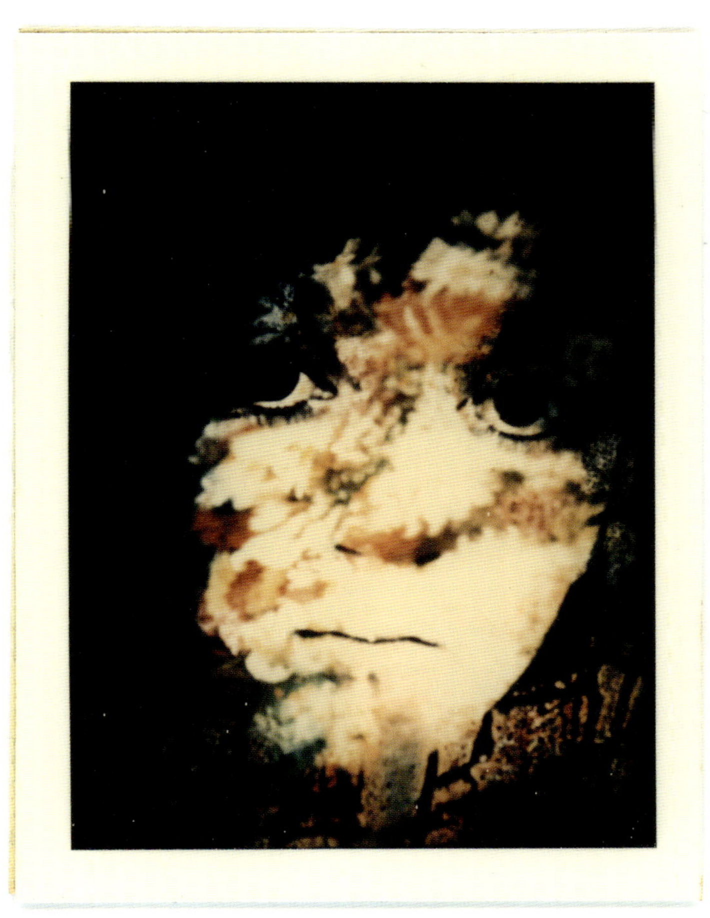

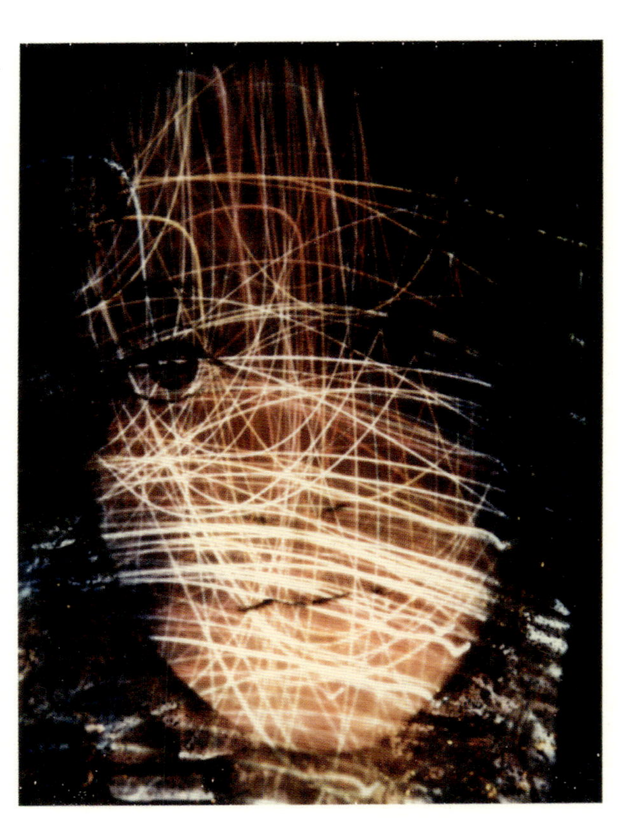

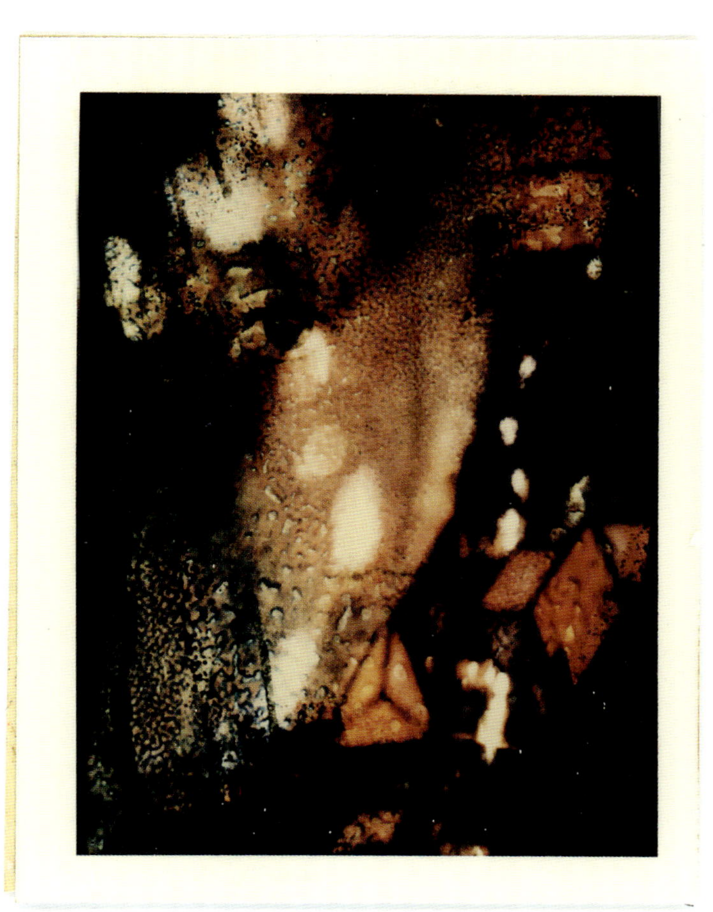

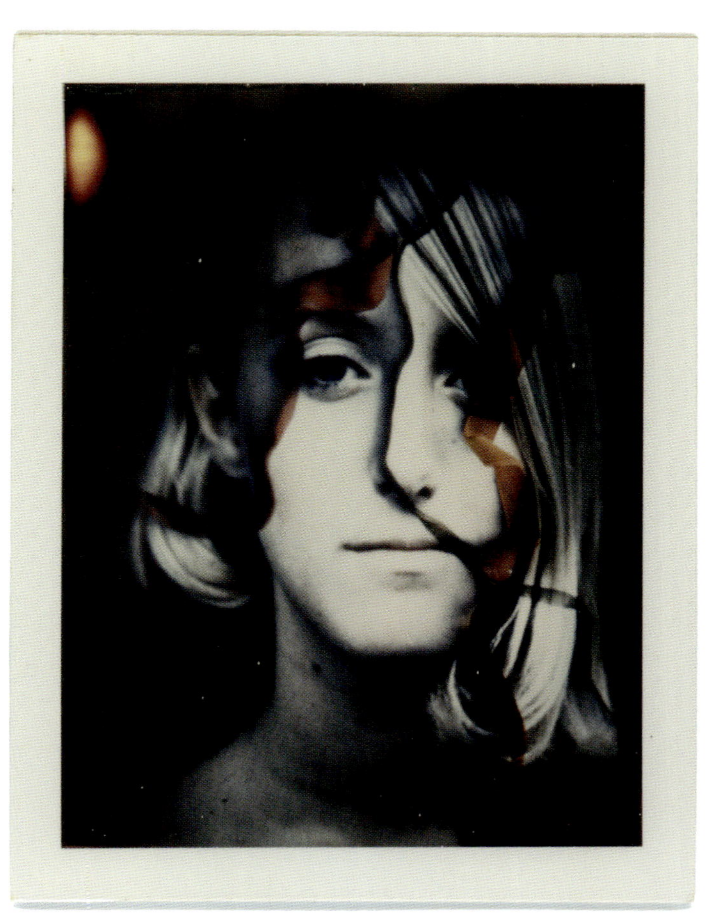

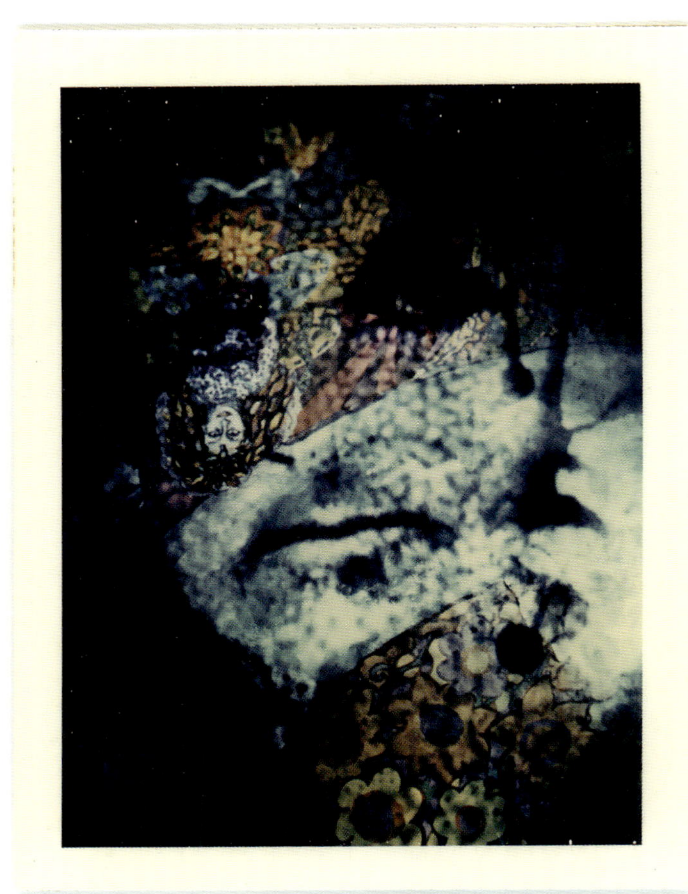

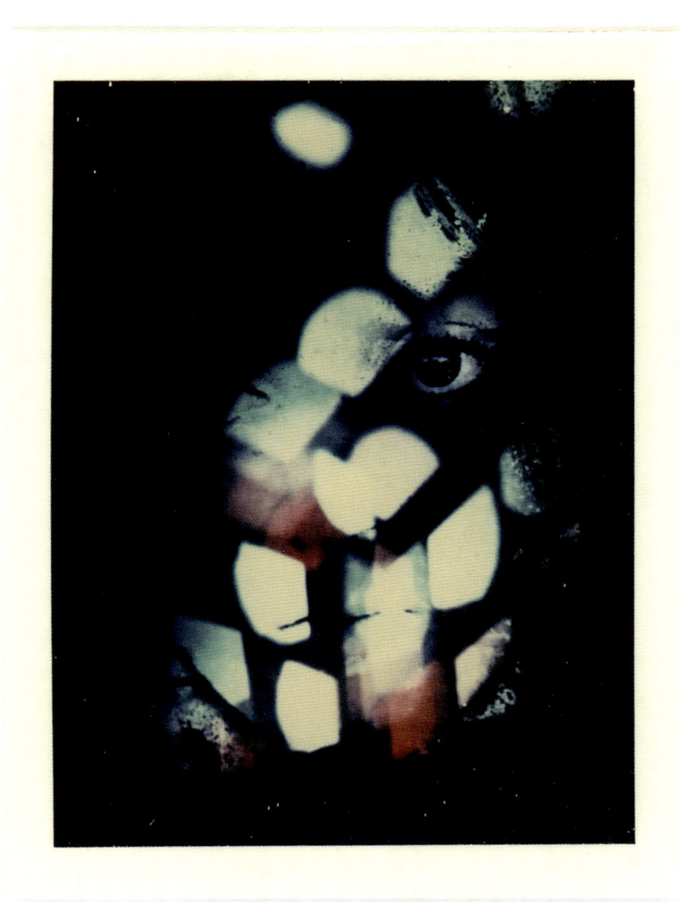

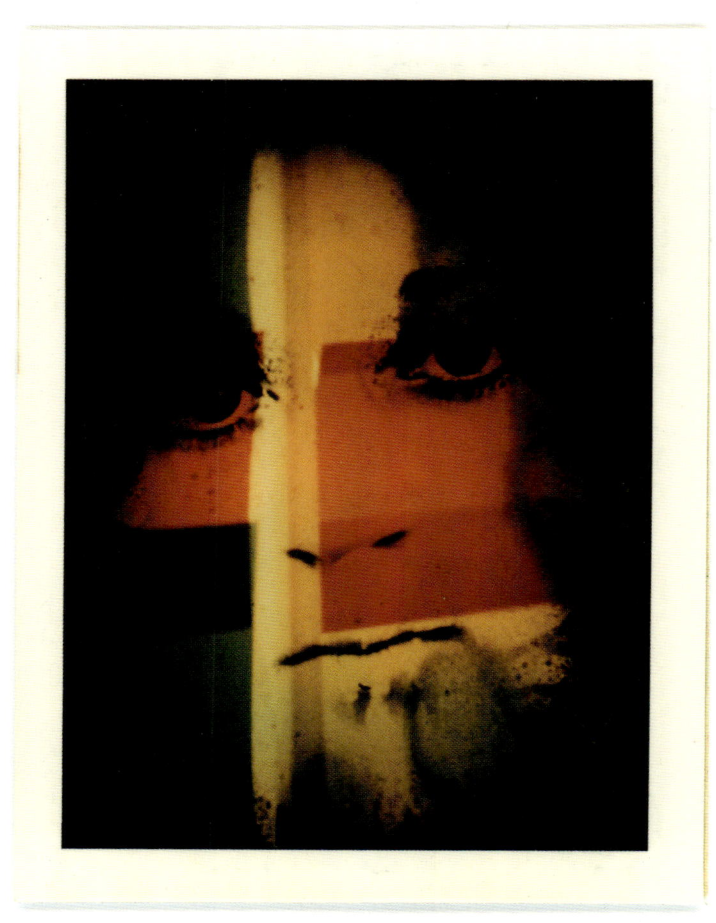

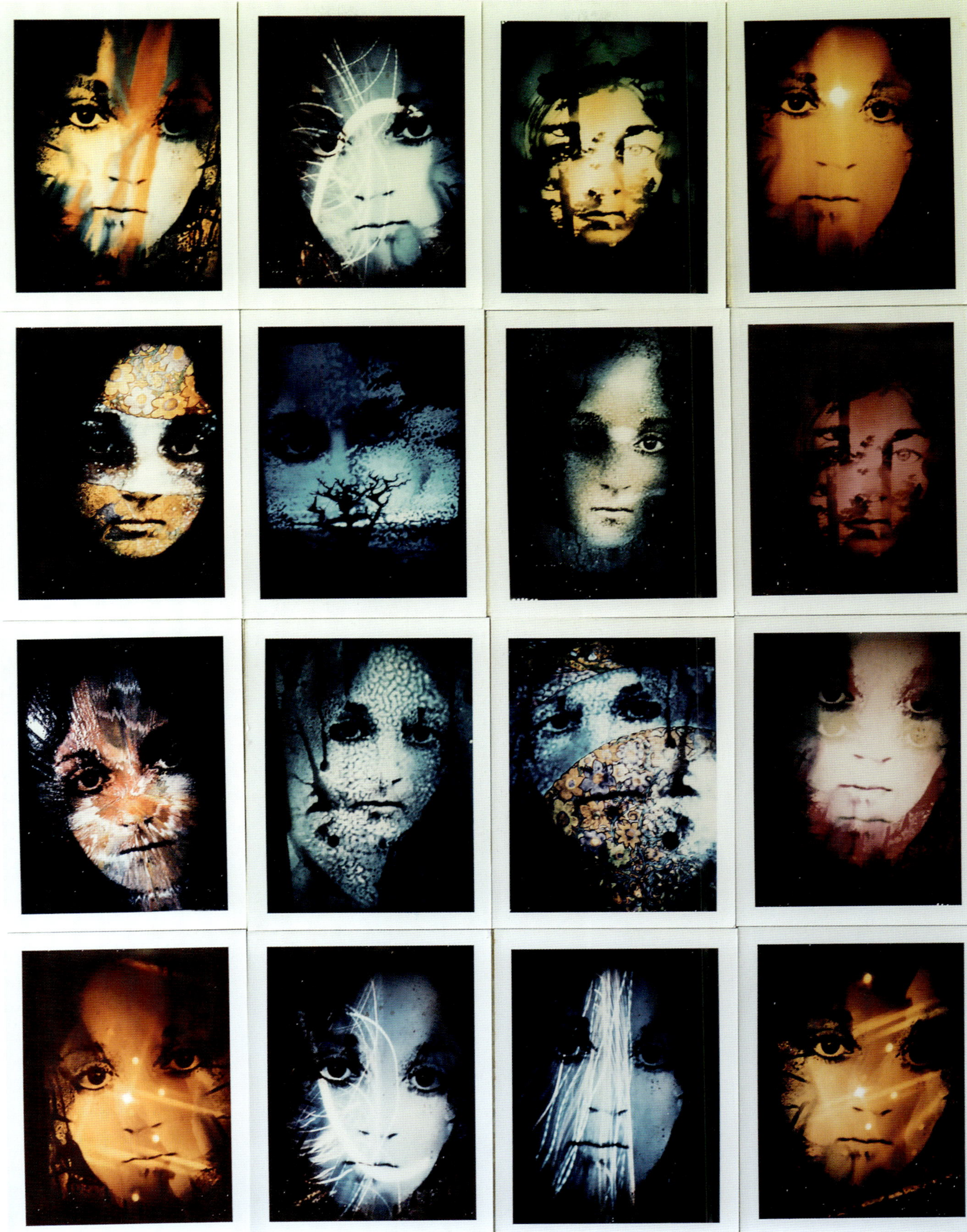

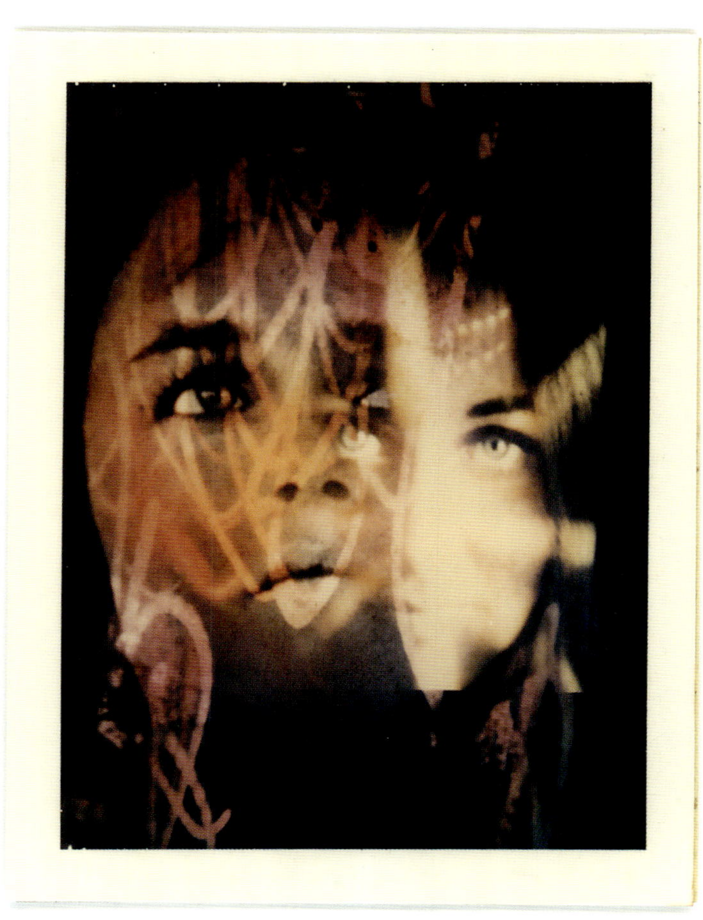

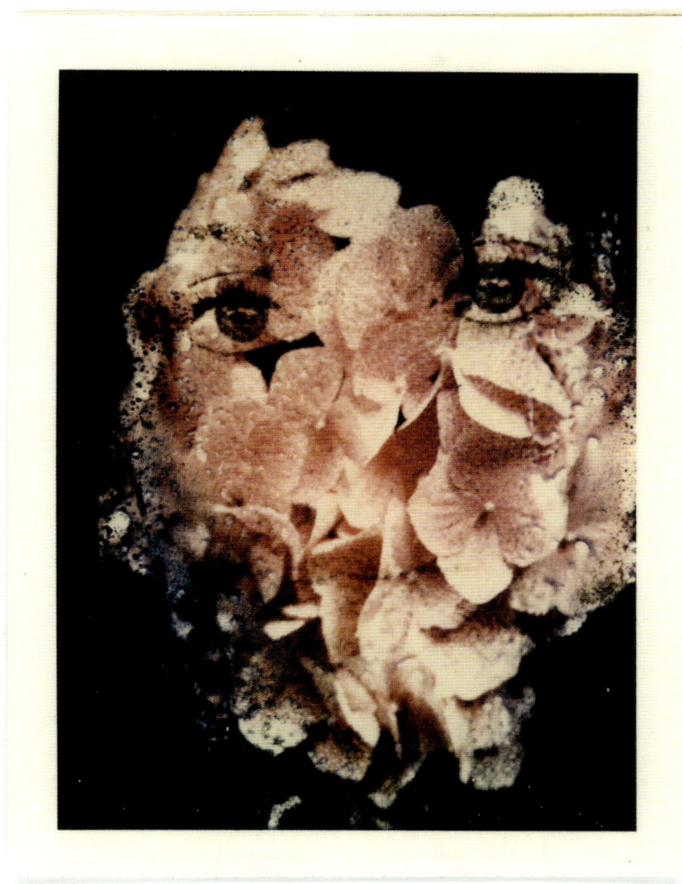

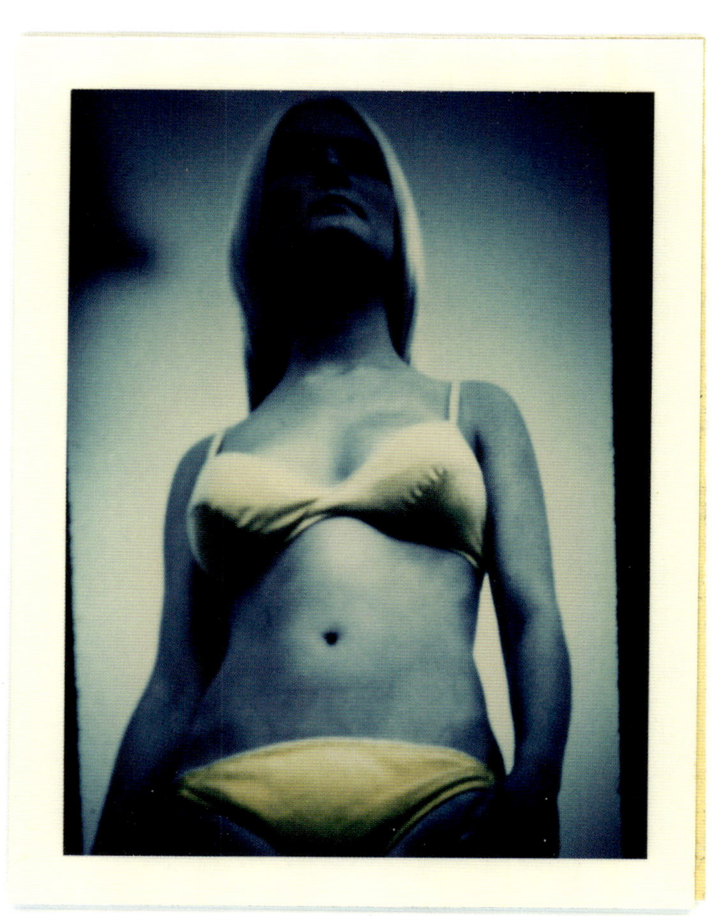

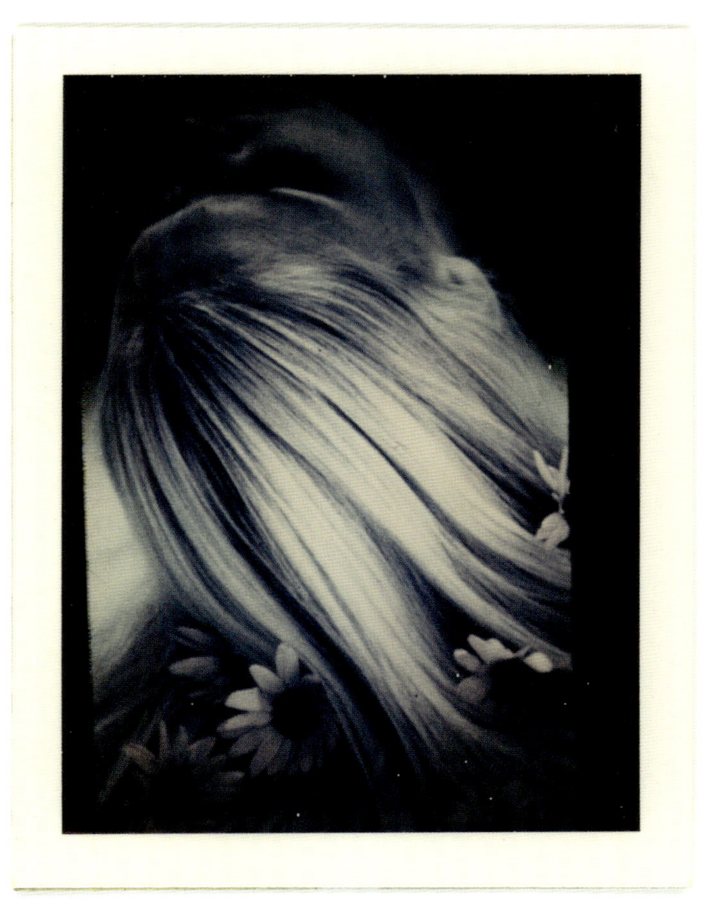

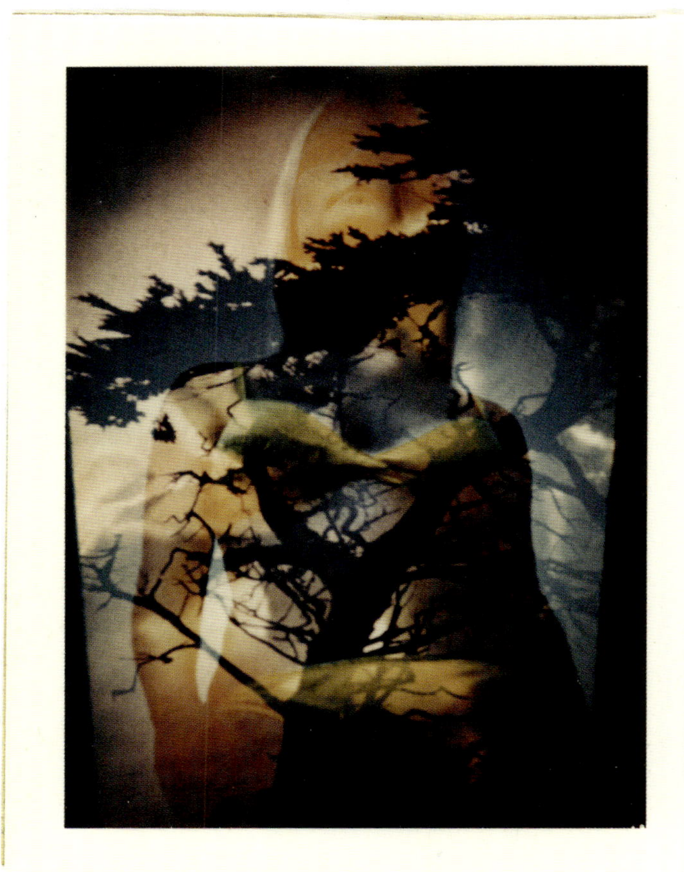

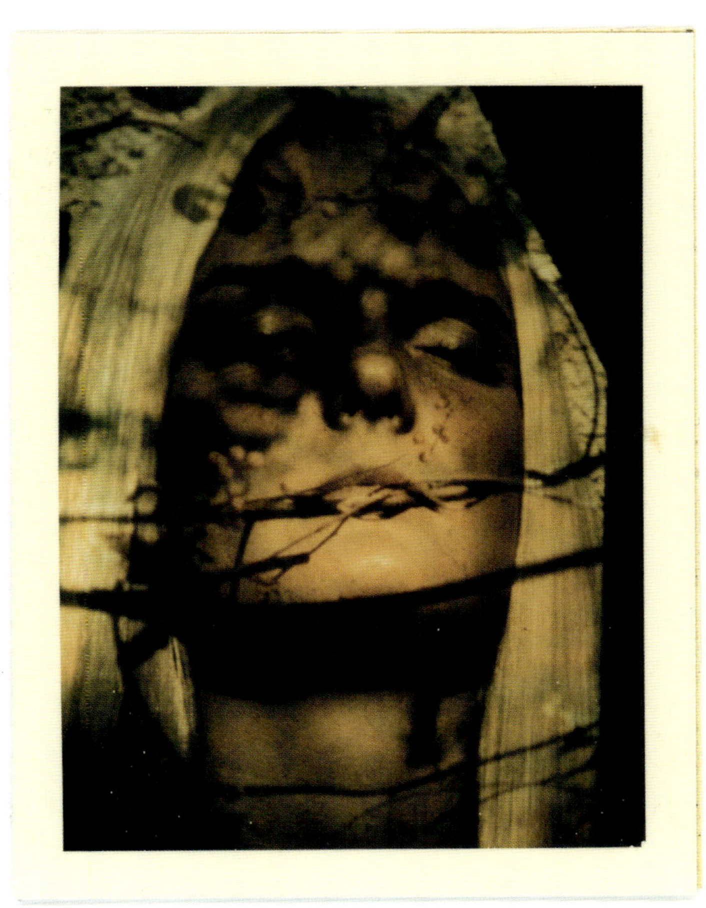

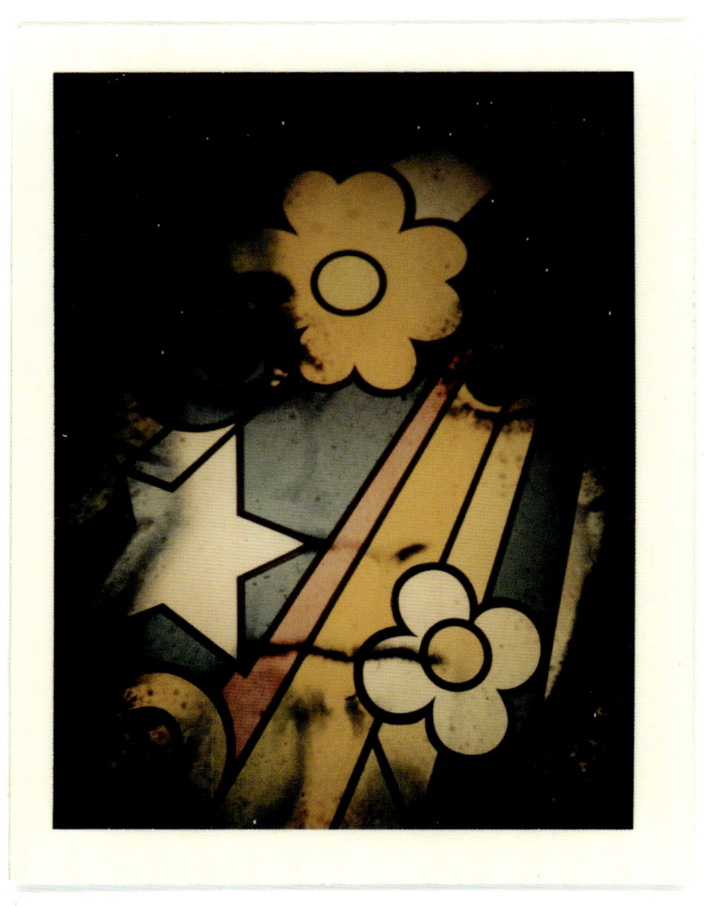

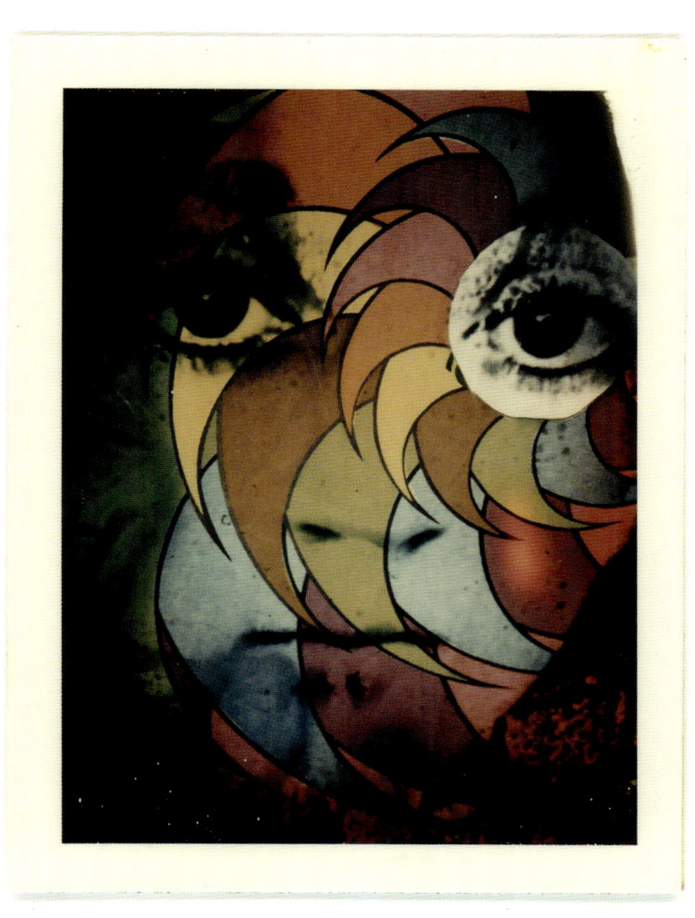

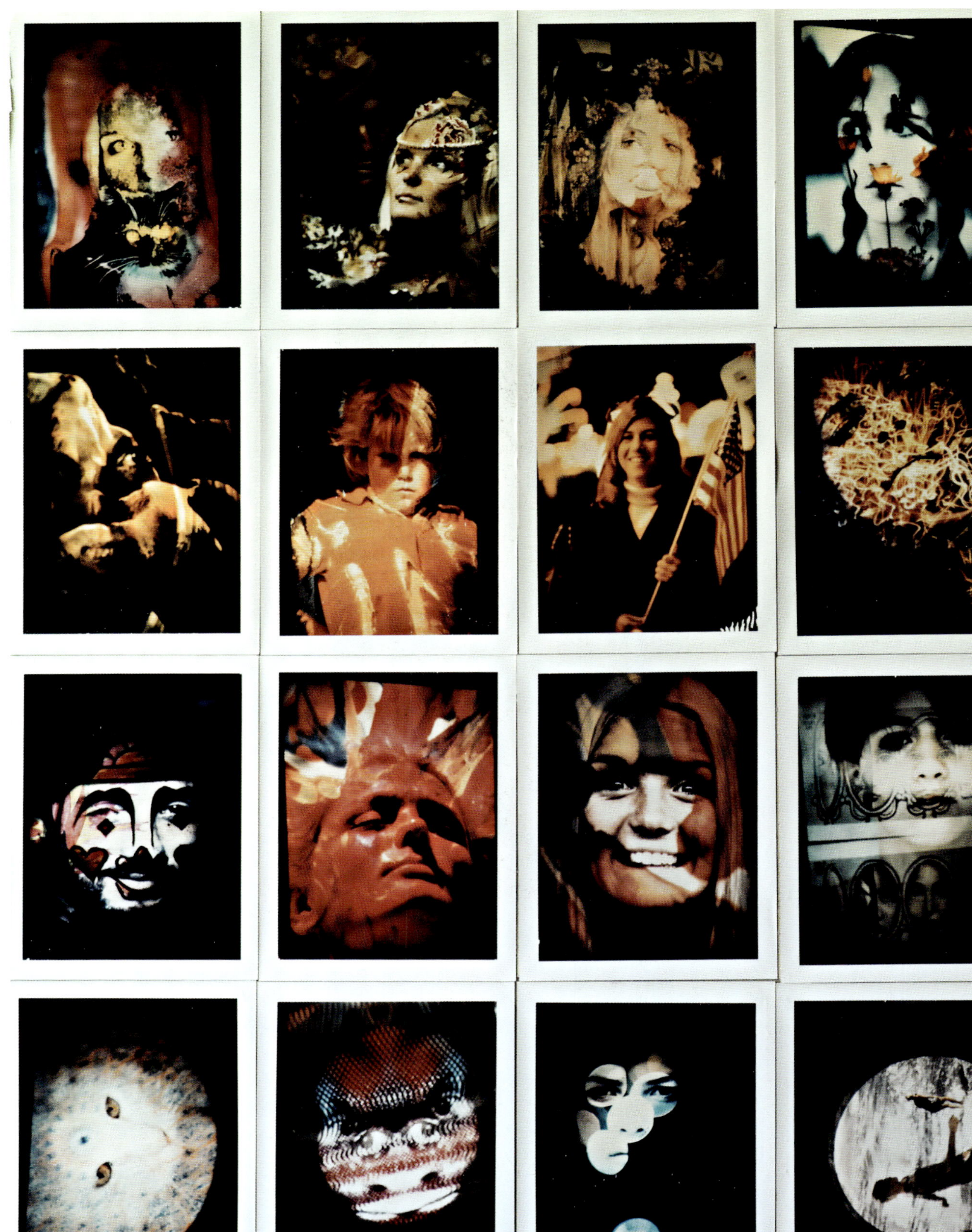

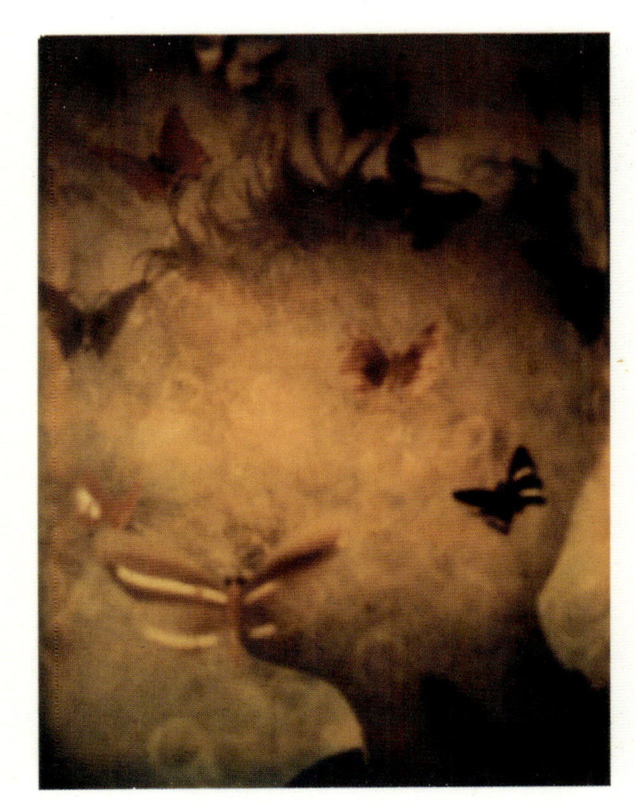

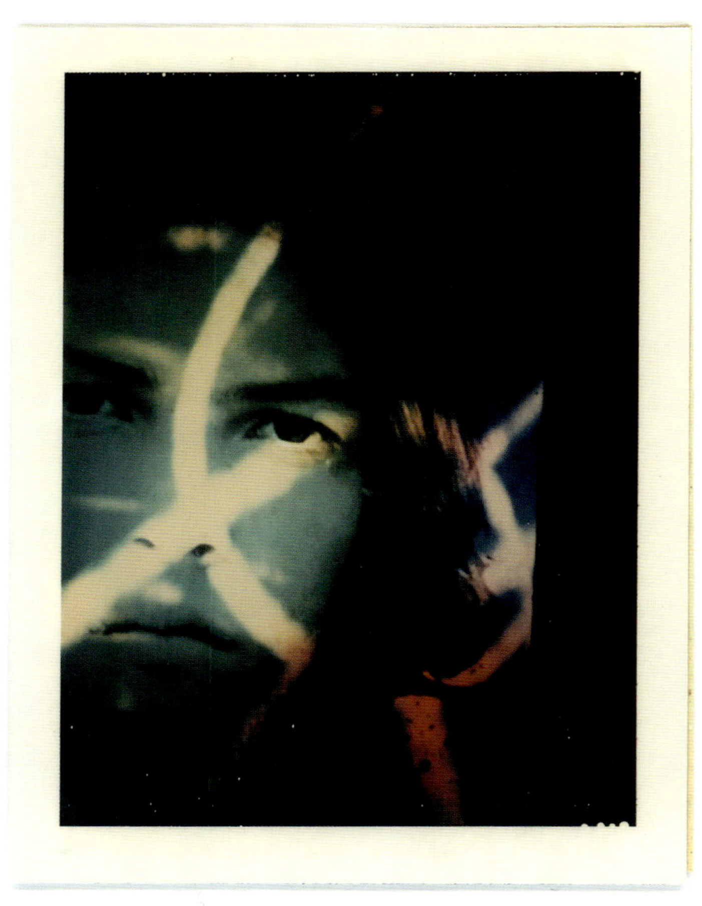

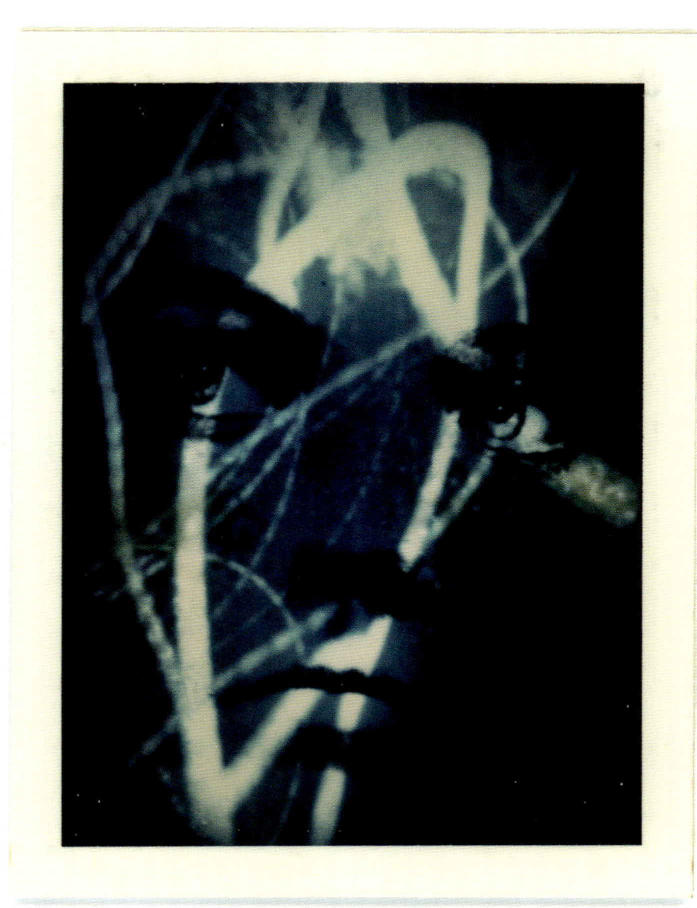

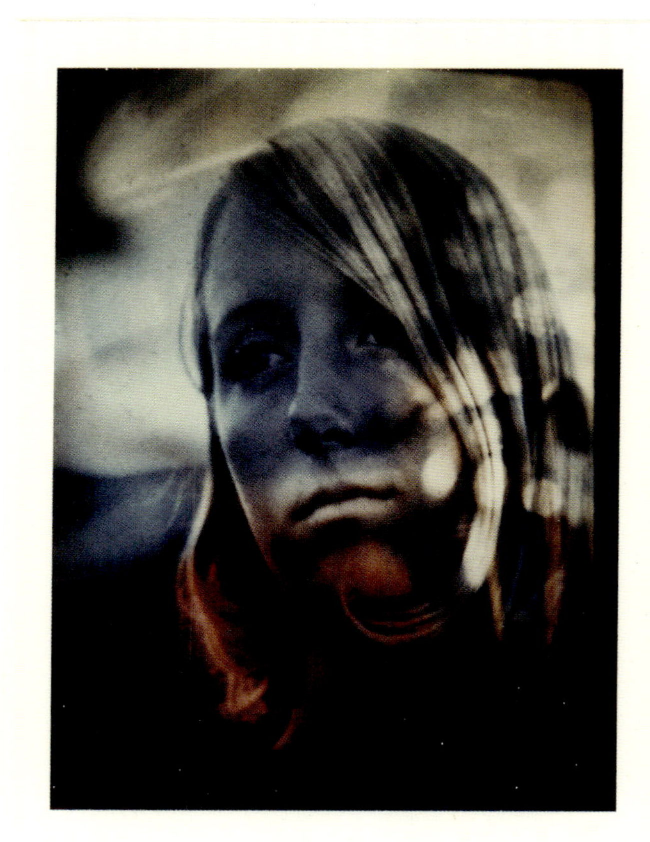

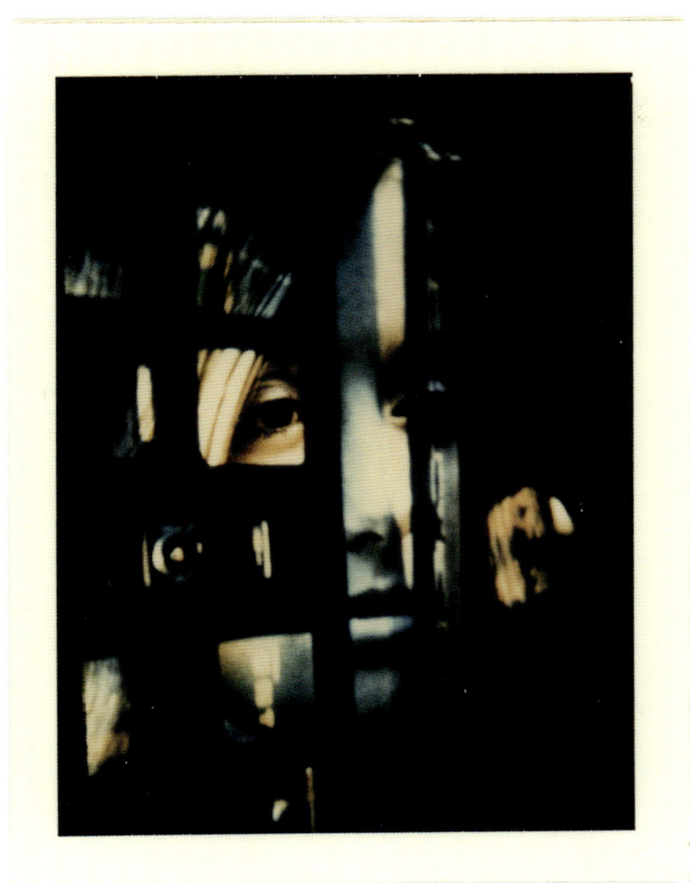

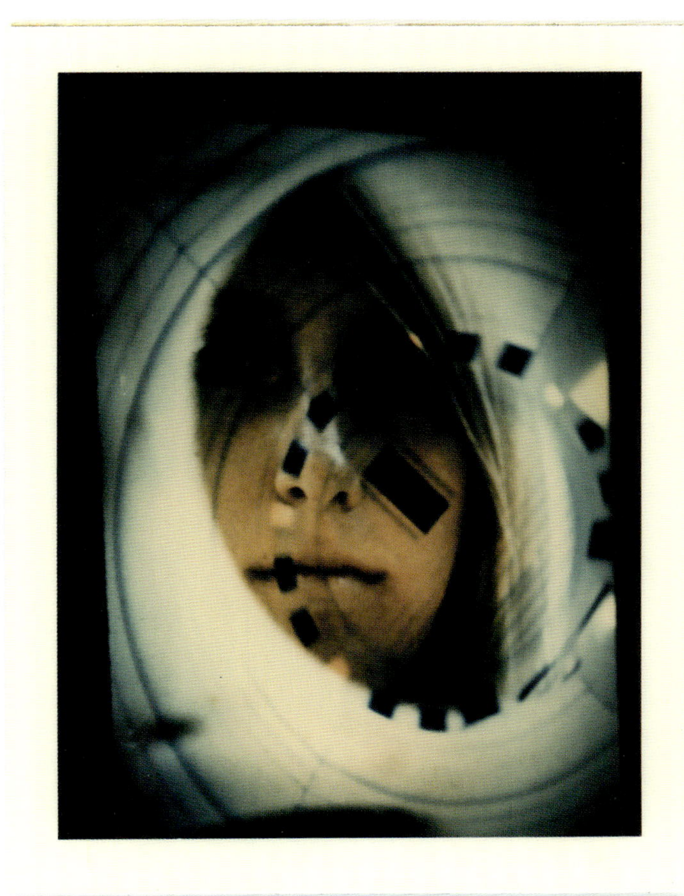

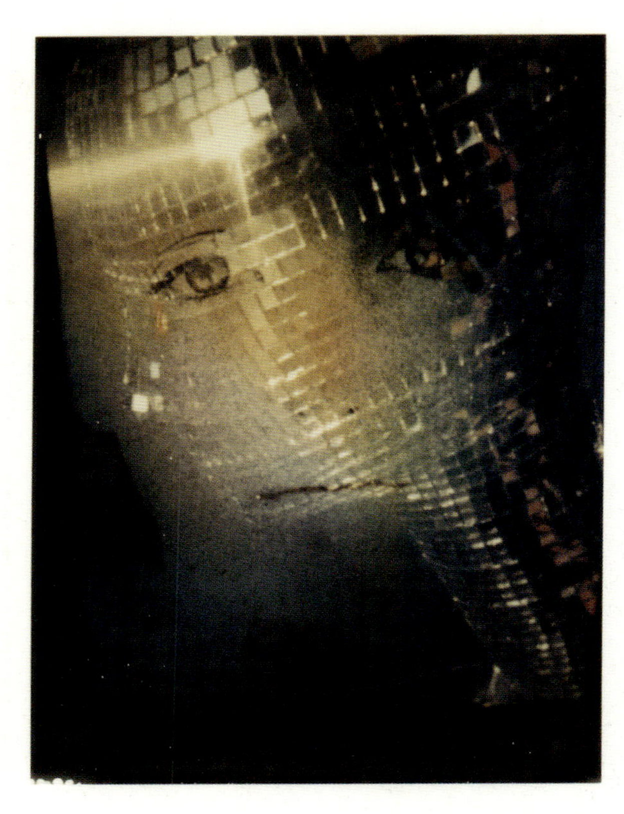

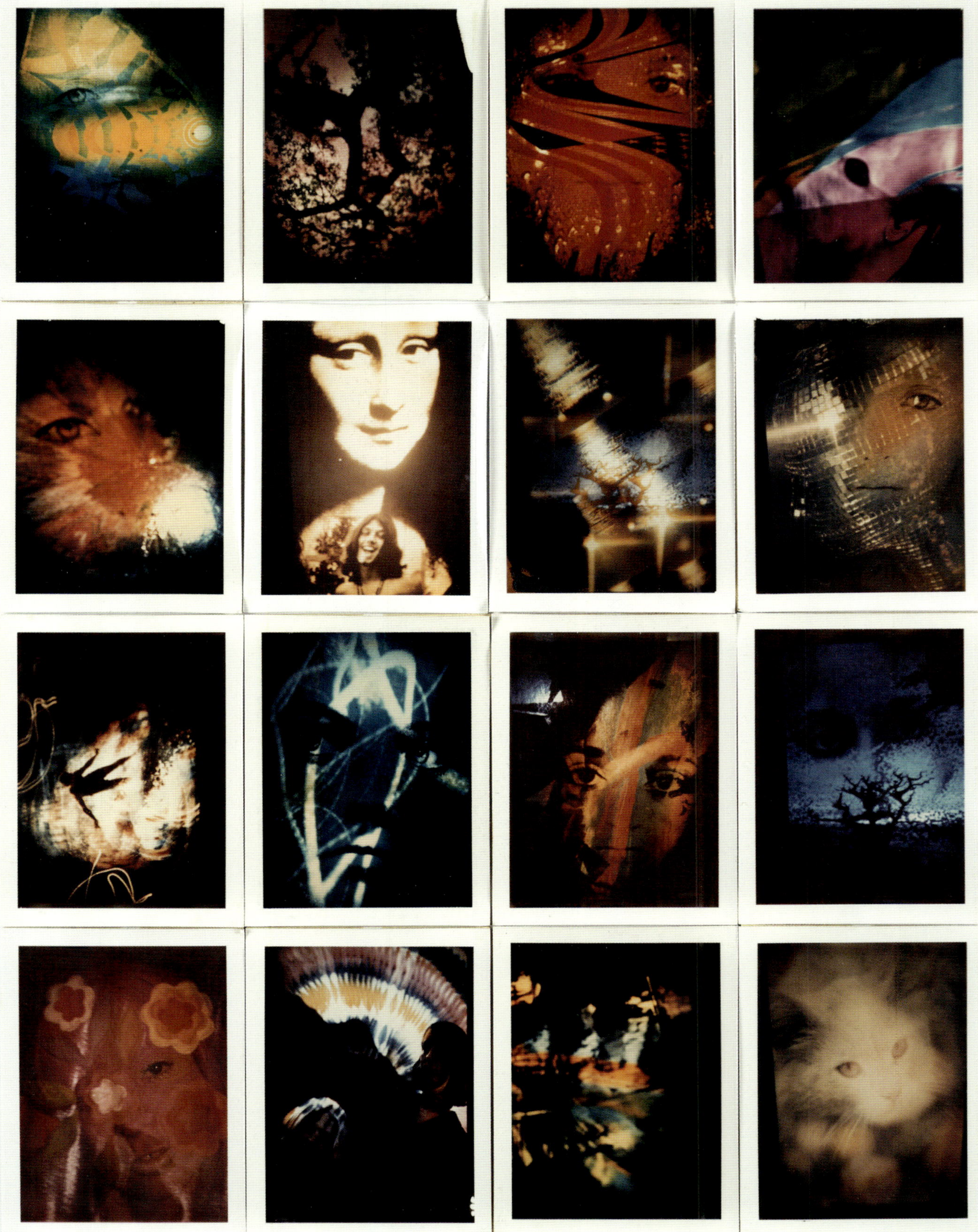

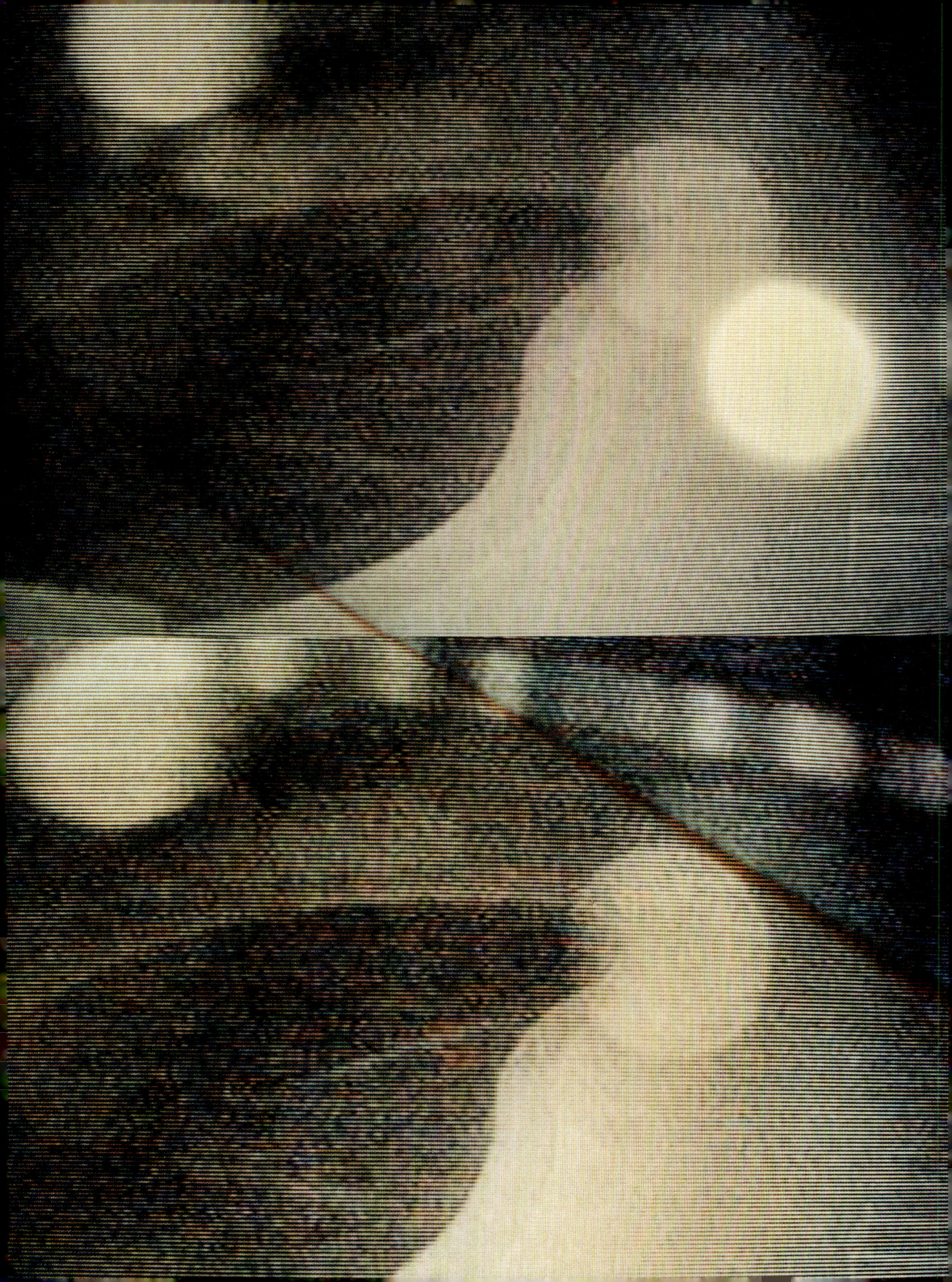

OUTER SPACE

You either do—or do not—believe in the existence of unidentified flying objects. Kali believed. In the 1960s, she set out to document proof of the floating orbs and phenomena she was seeing. These flashes of light would appear on the late-night drives Kali took under the star-filled desert sky that engulfed the area around Palm Springs. She was not alone on these drives, often waking her children in the middle of the night to accompany her. The children's mouths hung open as they strained to see what Kali saw: "Archie! Look at the spaceships!"

Forty years later, a reclusive Kali, now living in the Pacific Palisades, installed a multitude of video cameras around her property after seeing the same unexplained phenomena over her swimming pool and birdbath. The videotape ran twenty-four hours a day, every day, with viewing monitors inside Kali's bedroom-cum-studio. She would spend weeks not leaving her home, poring over the tapes in search of evidence. Kali was a meticulous notetaker, filling notebooks with dates and time codes connecting the footage with film exposures and the Polaroid SX-70 images she took during paused playback of the tapes. There are hundreds of pages of time codes, descriptions, and dates that correspond directly to each still frame taken by Kali. Every photographed frame was accompanied with a sketch.

Inexplicable figures can be seen moving in and out of spheres—legs, wings, and huge ring bars of light. The videotape even catches Kali herself, in a brave moment, walking slowly, meditatively, among the floating orbs as she fades gradually into the distance. In this moment, Kali enters her own art, capturing a realm outside of our own experience, leaving the viewer to decide…can they see it too? —A.J

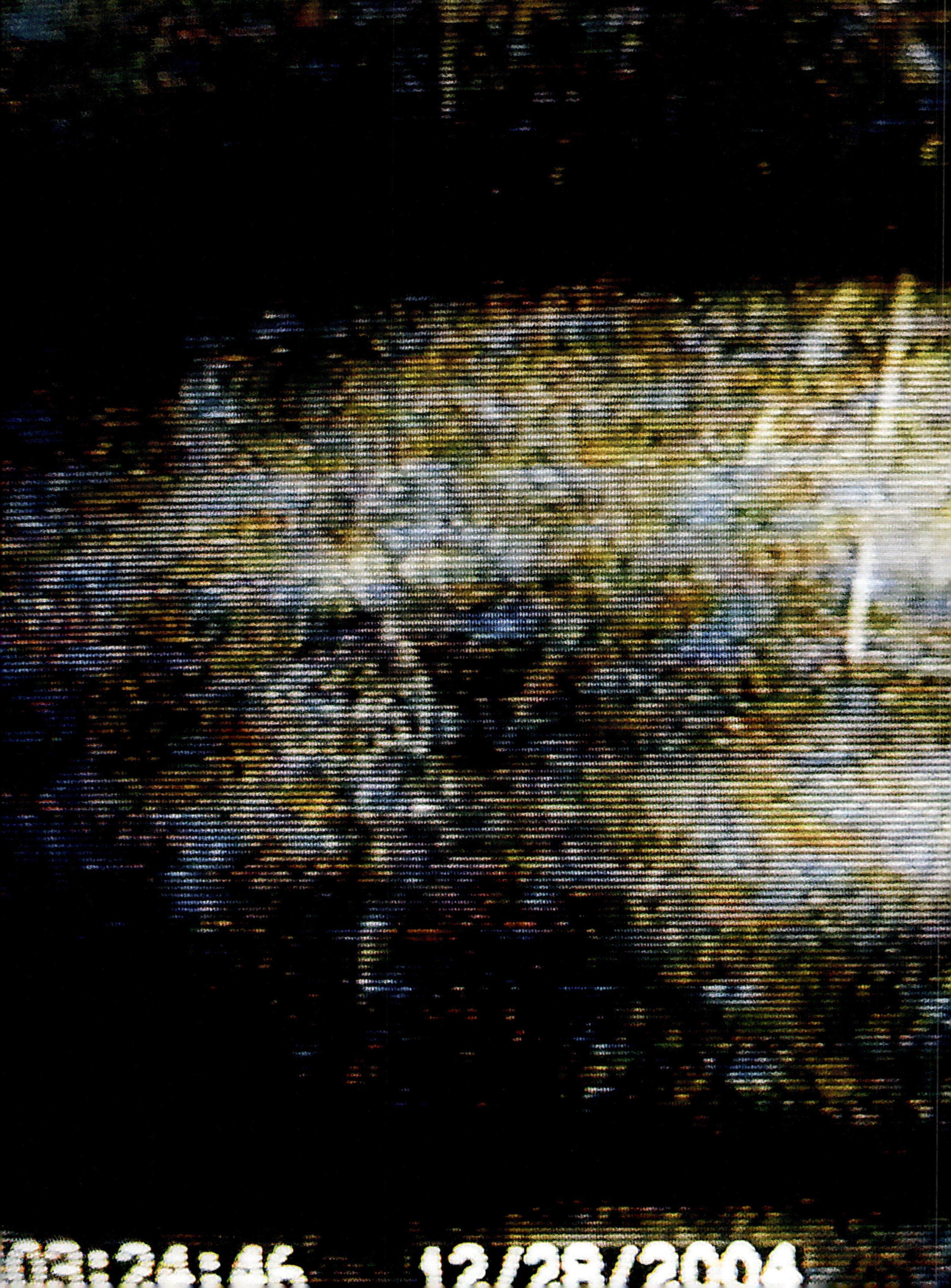

03:24:46   12/28/2006

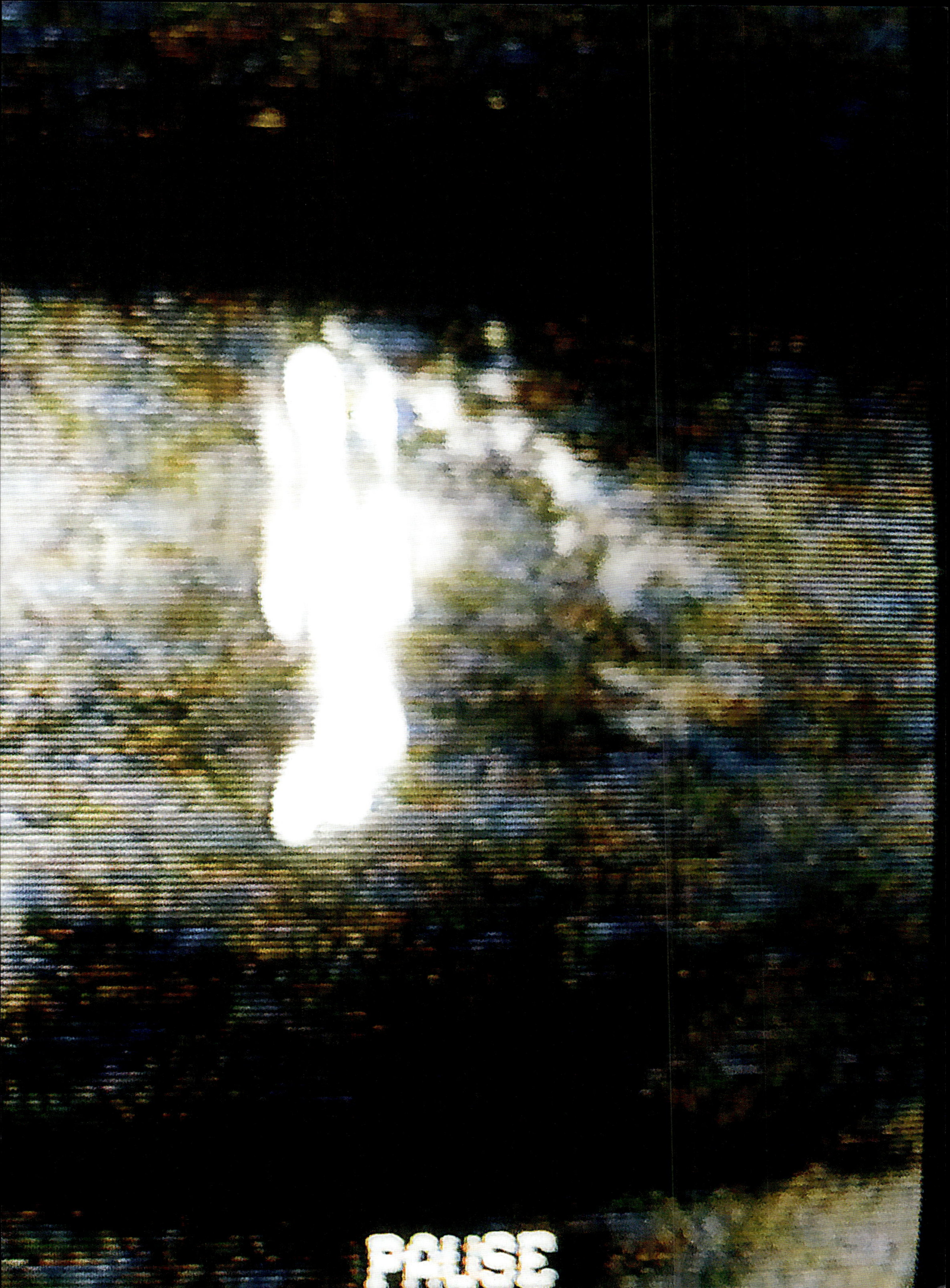

PAUSE

Book 2   "WoWs"

Tape 124   08/02/2003
(1) Overview   Written WoWs
(3) 13:01:20

A WoW!

Com 2
DESIGNS
IN AREA

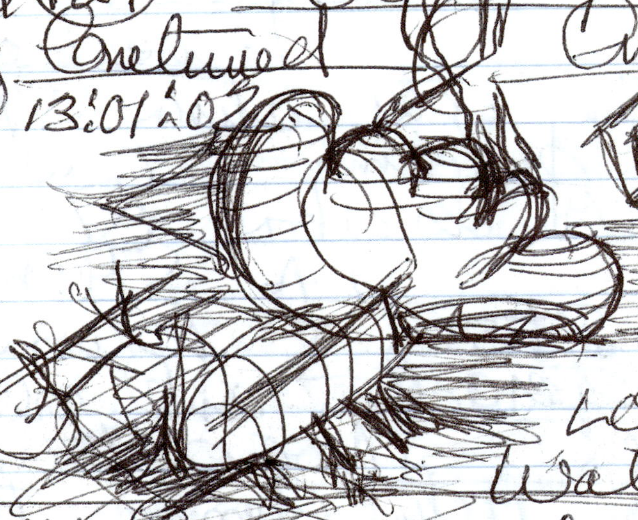

HERE IT
LOOKS LIKE A
Water   LILY
(4) 13:01:04   similar to (3)
(5) 13:01:05

More UFO
SHIP
LIKE

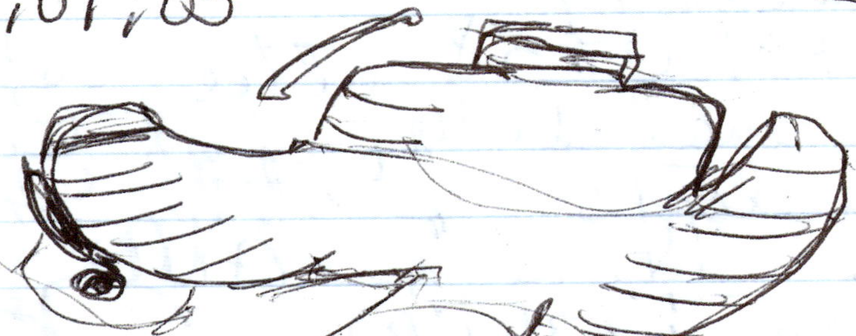

(6) 13:01:06

Morgan

Hayes

2 Exhaust
Look

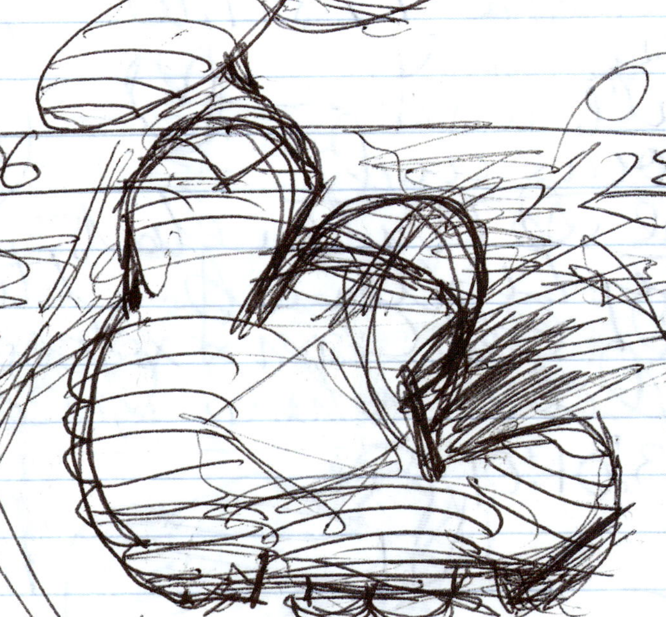

(7) 13:01:08
Similar as
above
(8) 13:01:09   Continued

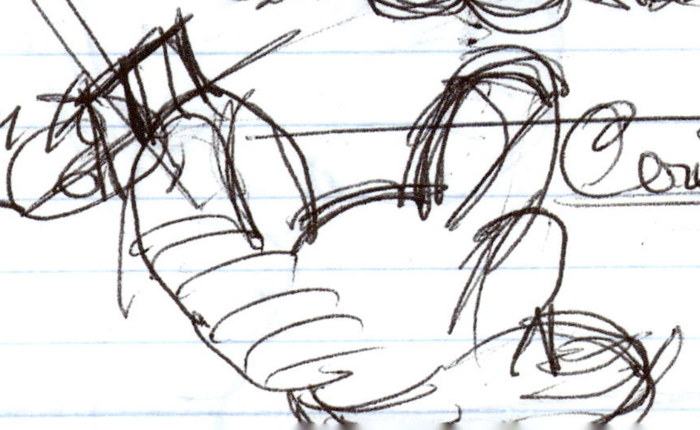

4 POLOROID
18 PHOTOS

10:46:35
08/02/2003
UFO +
AW ORB
CAM 2

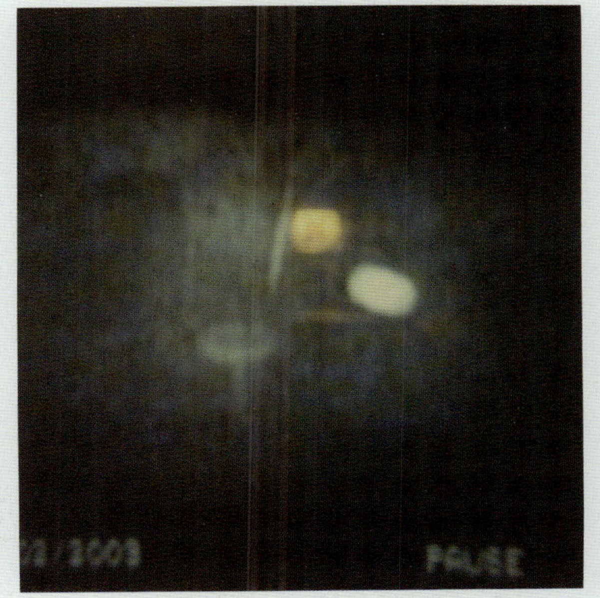

10:43:40
08/02/2003
3 RINGS
TOGETHER
2 pm 4

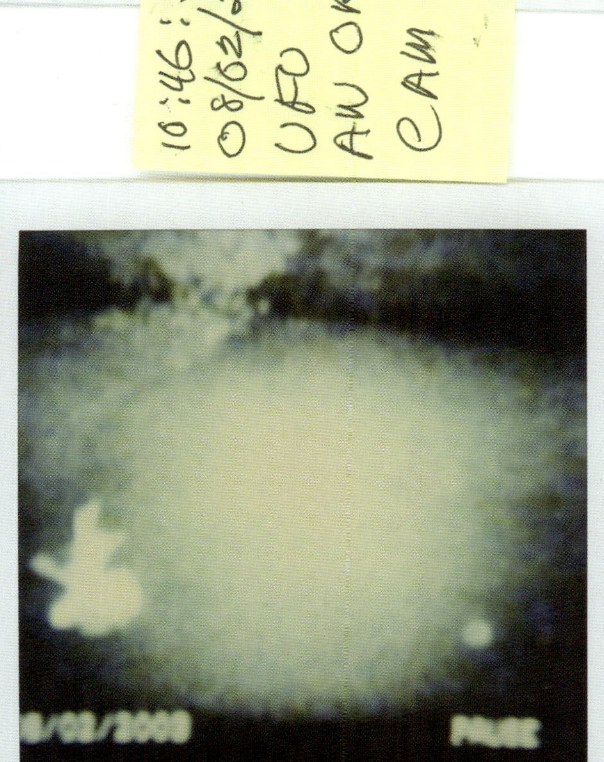

10:16:35
08/02/2003
UFO PLUS
AW ORB
CAM 2

10:46:35
08/02/2003
UFO +
AW ORB
CAM 2

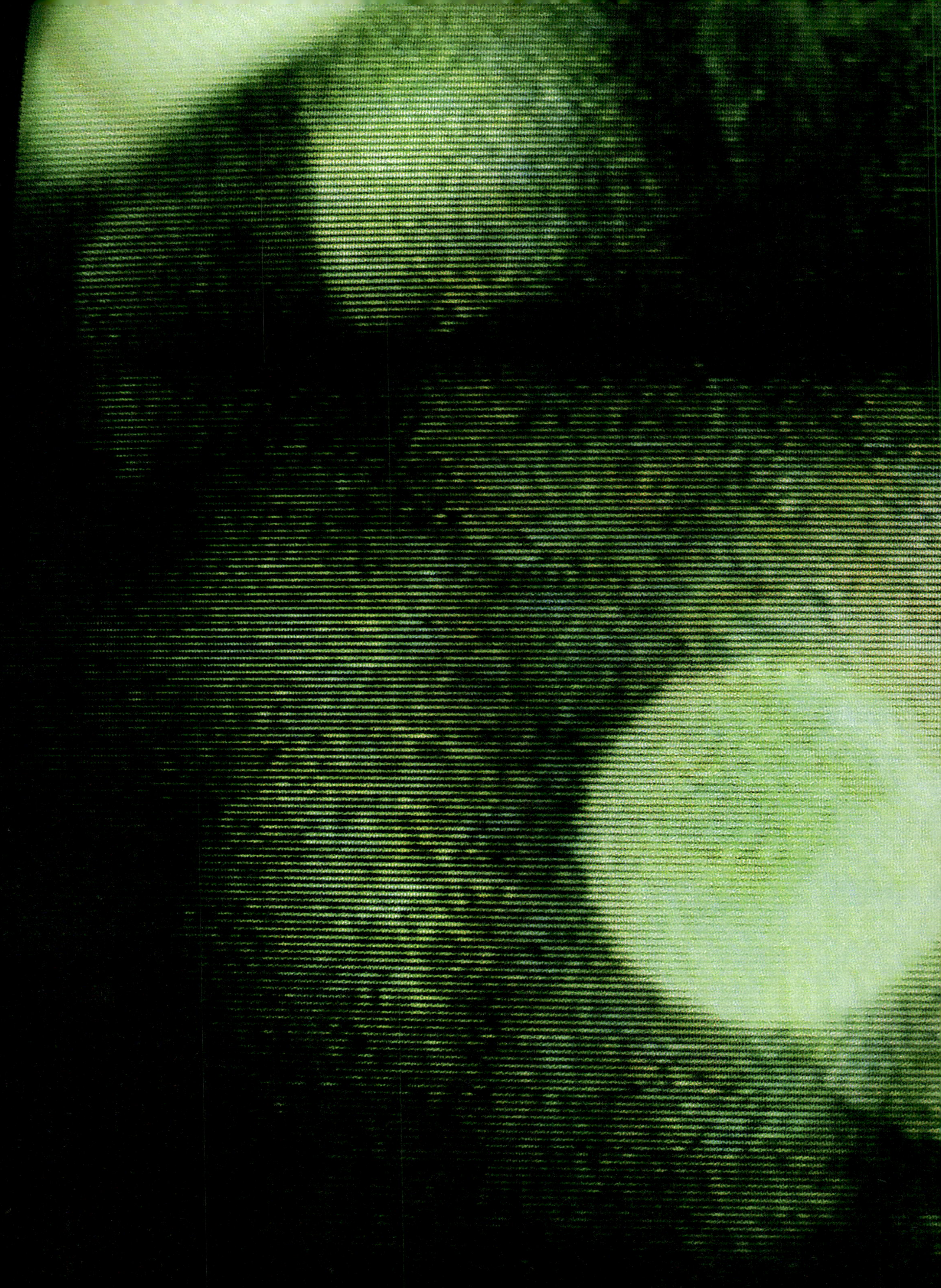

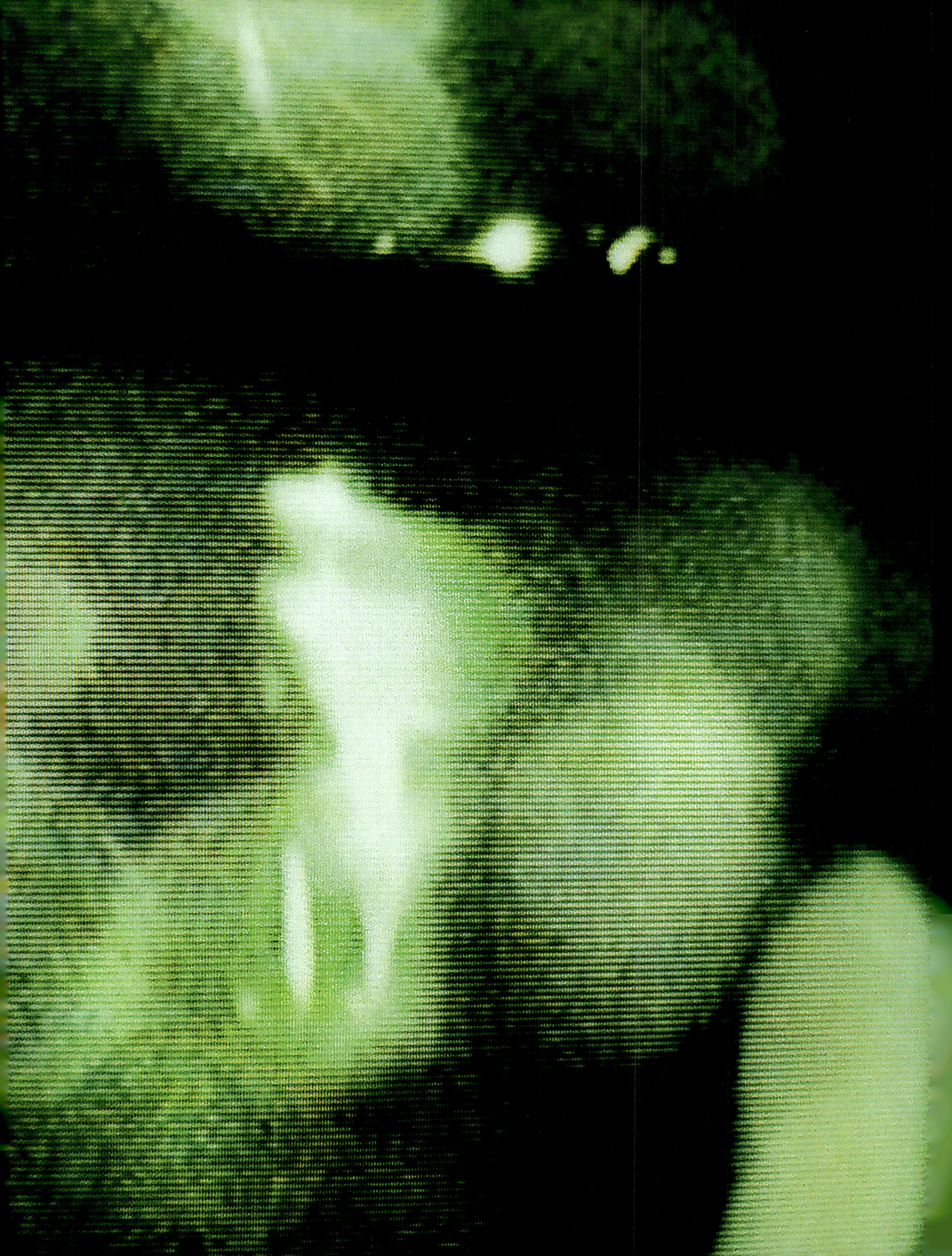

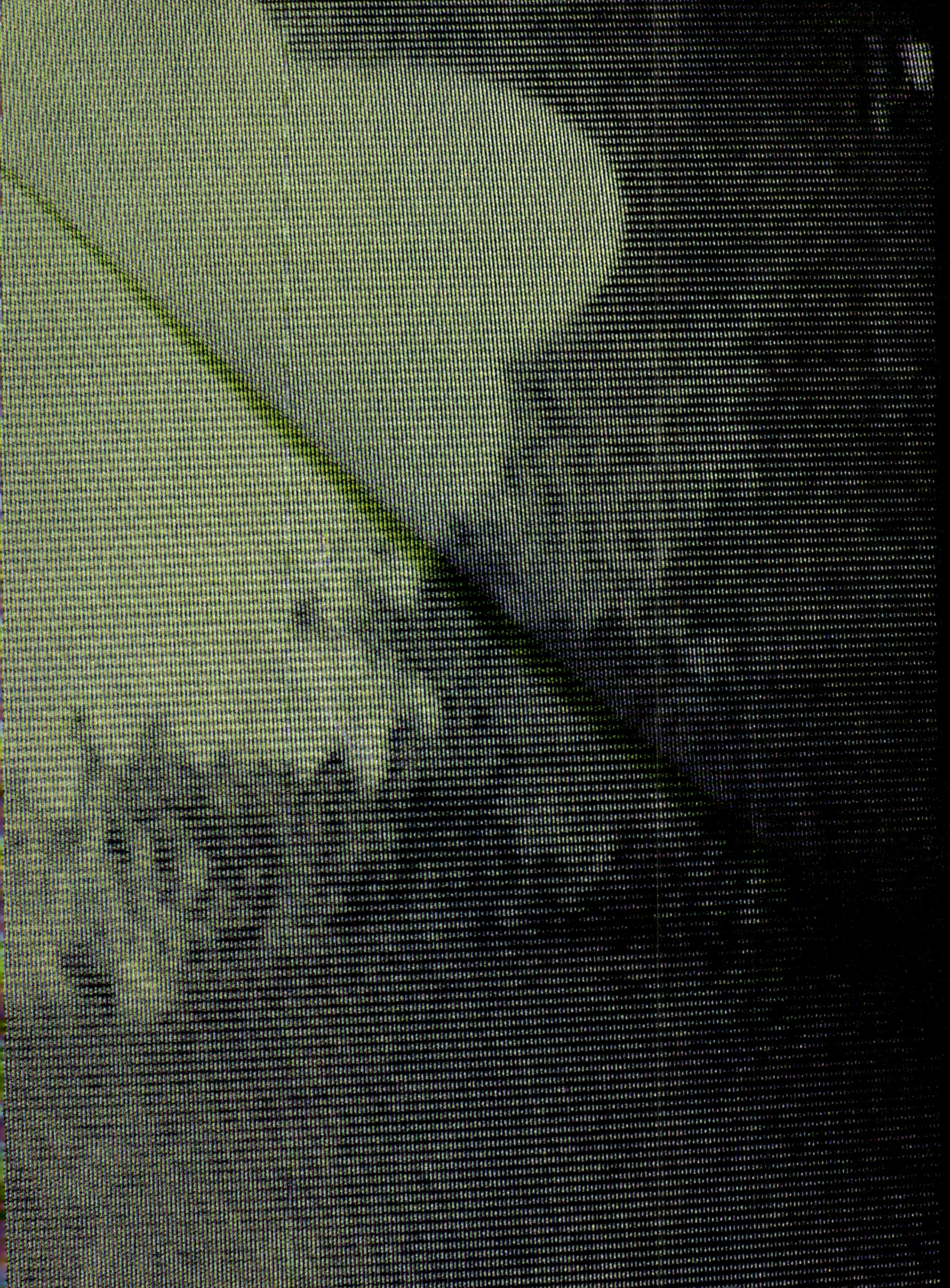

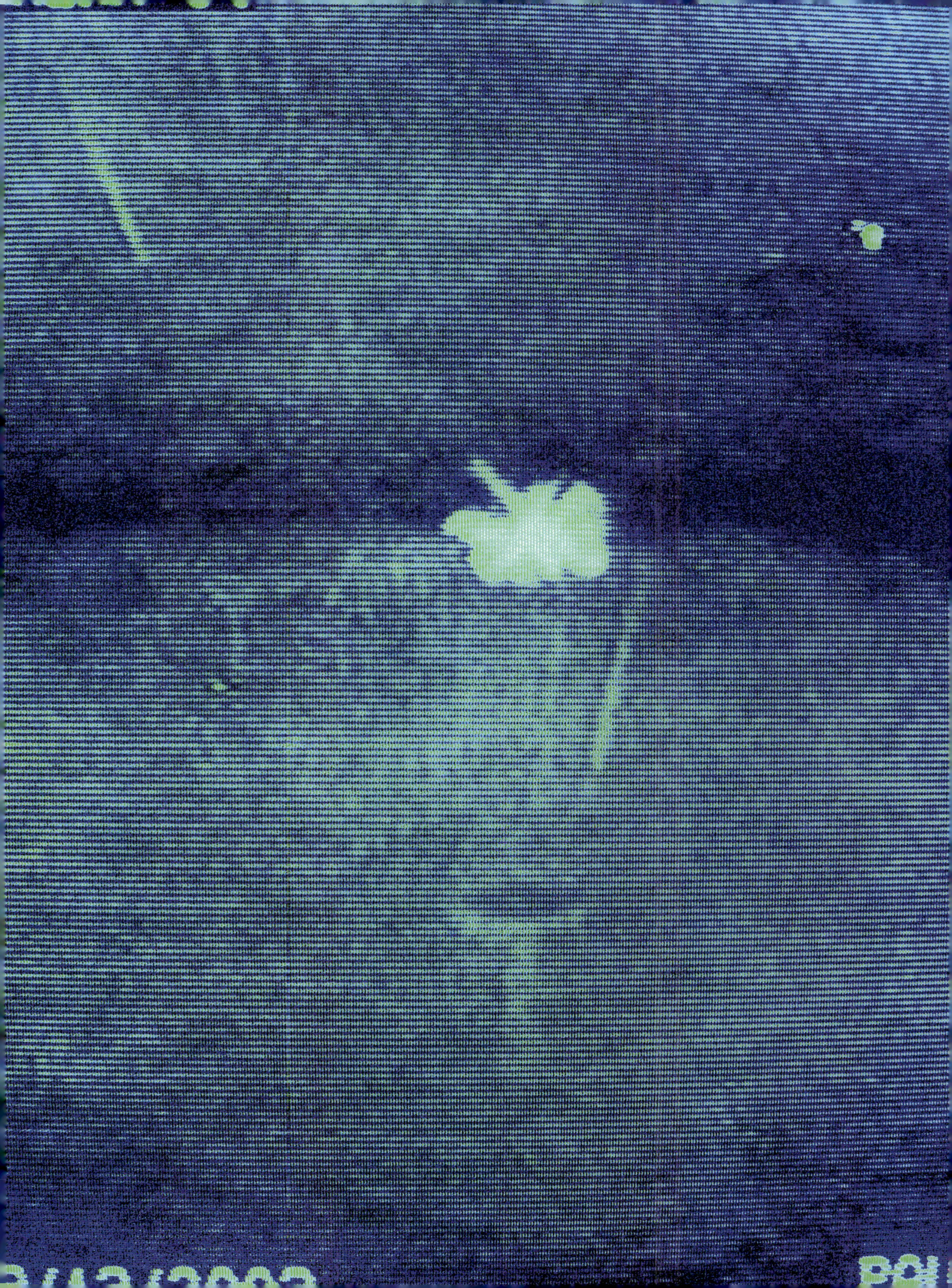

"EPI"
08/22/2003

page 28
4:28:15

[CAM 2]

ORBY

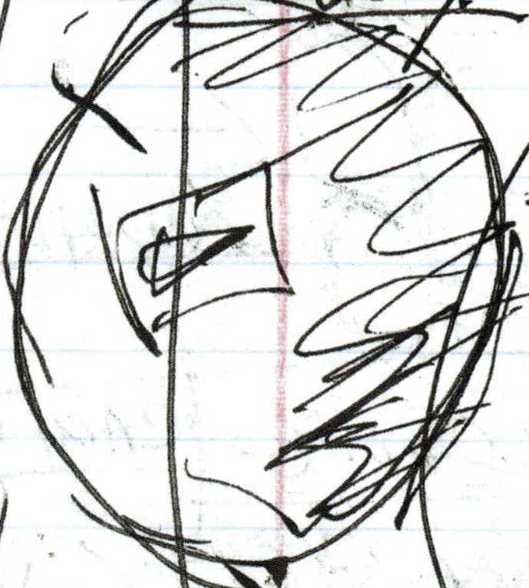

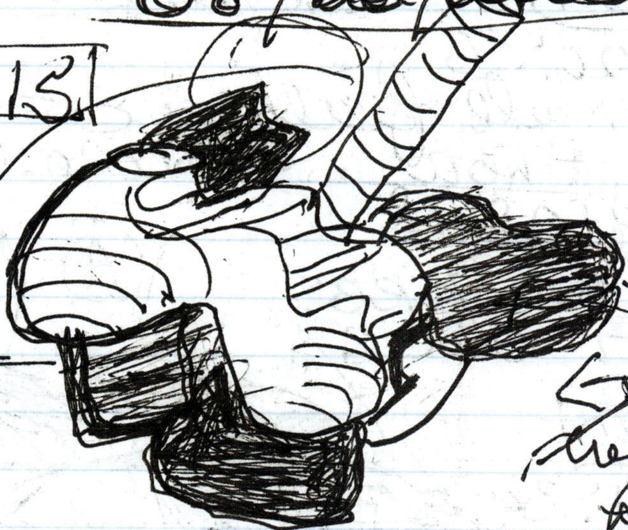

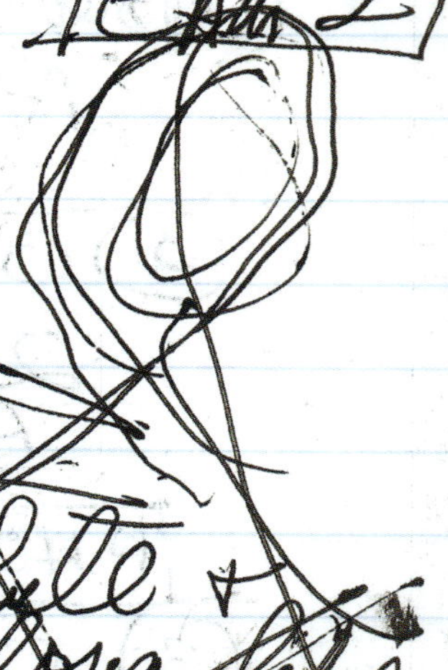

"ORBY HAS A VISITOR" PHOTO POLOROID

TREES

ORBY IS STILL ALIVE   See page 18

08/17/2003 CAM 2

② 18:52; UFO + ORBY

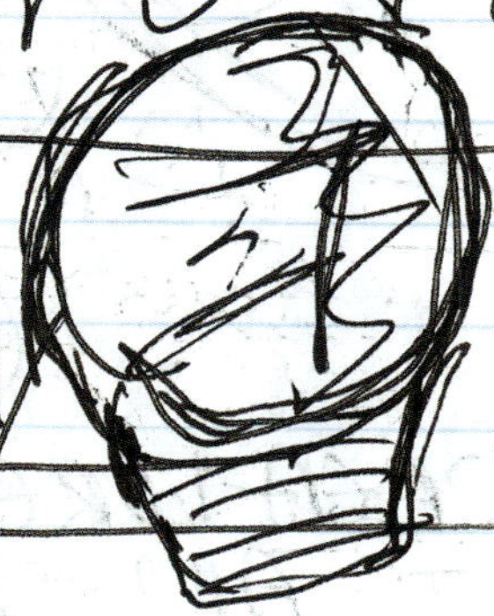

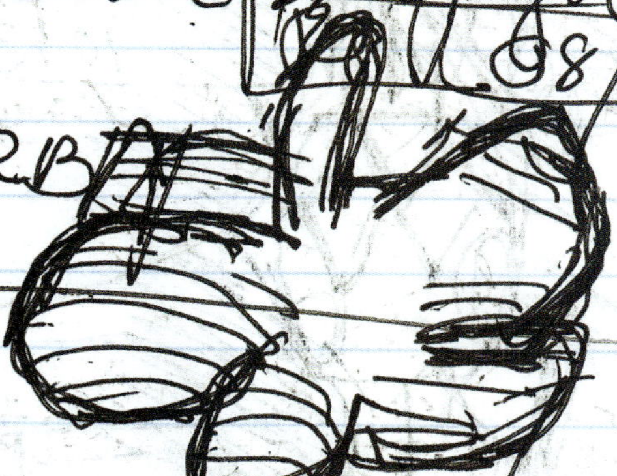

ORBY

1 PHOTO

UFO 1 POLOROID

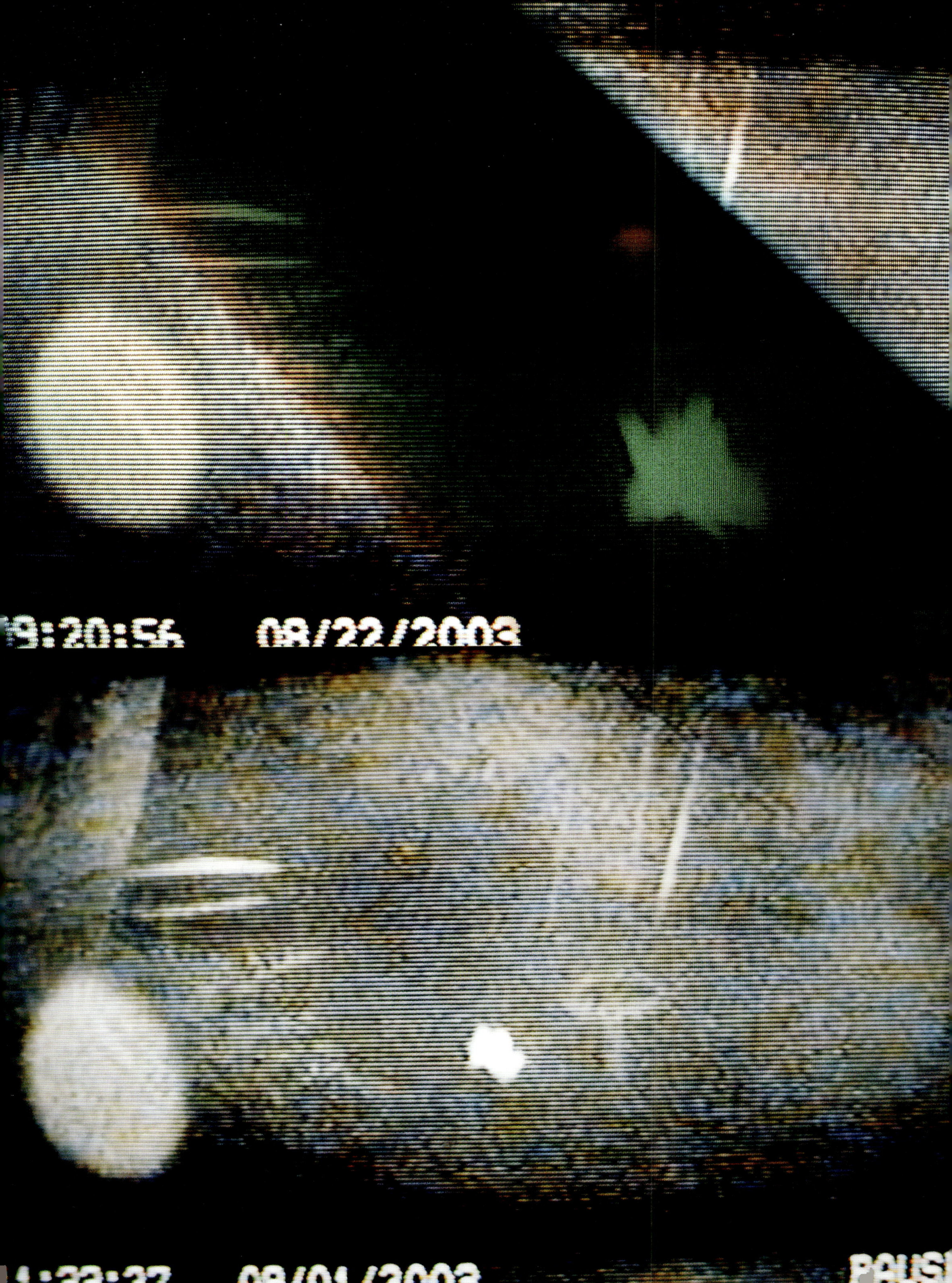
9:20:56   08/22/2003
1:33:27   09/01/2003
PAUS

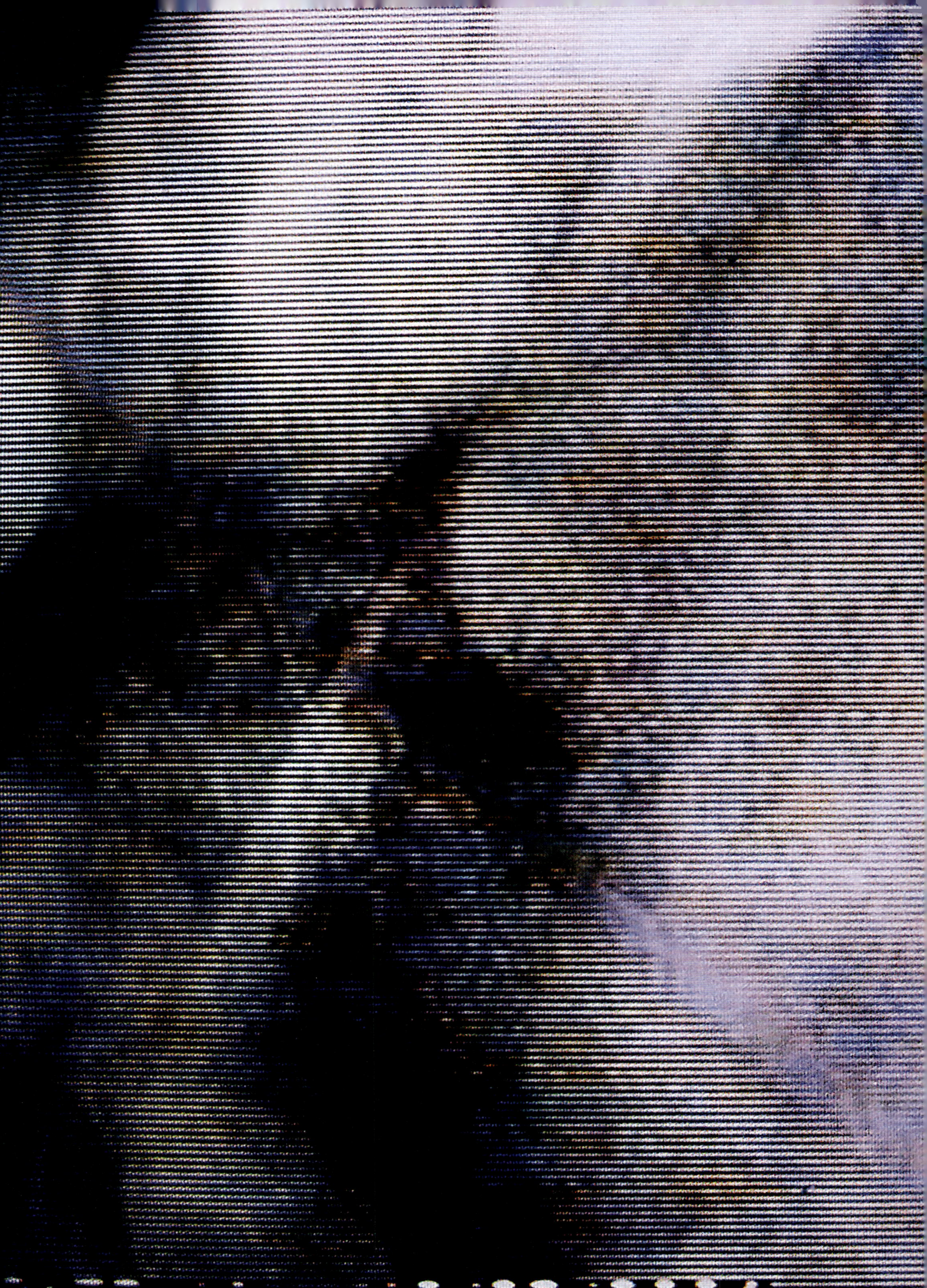

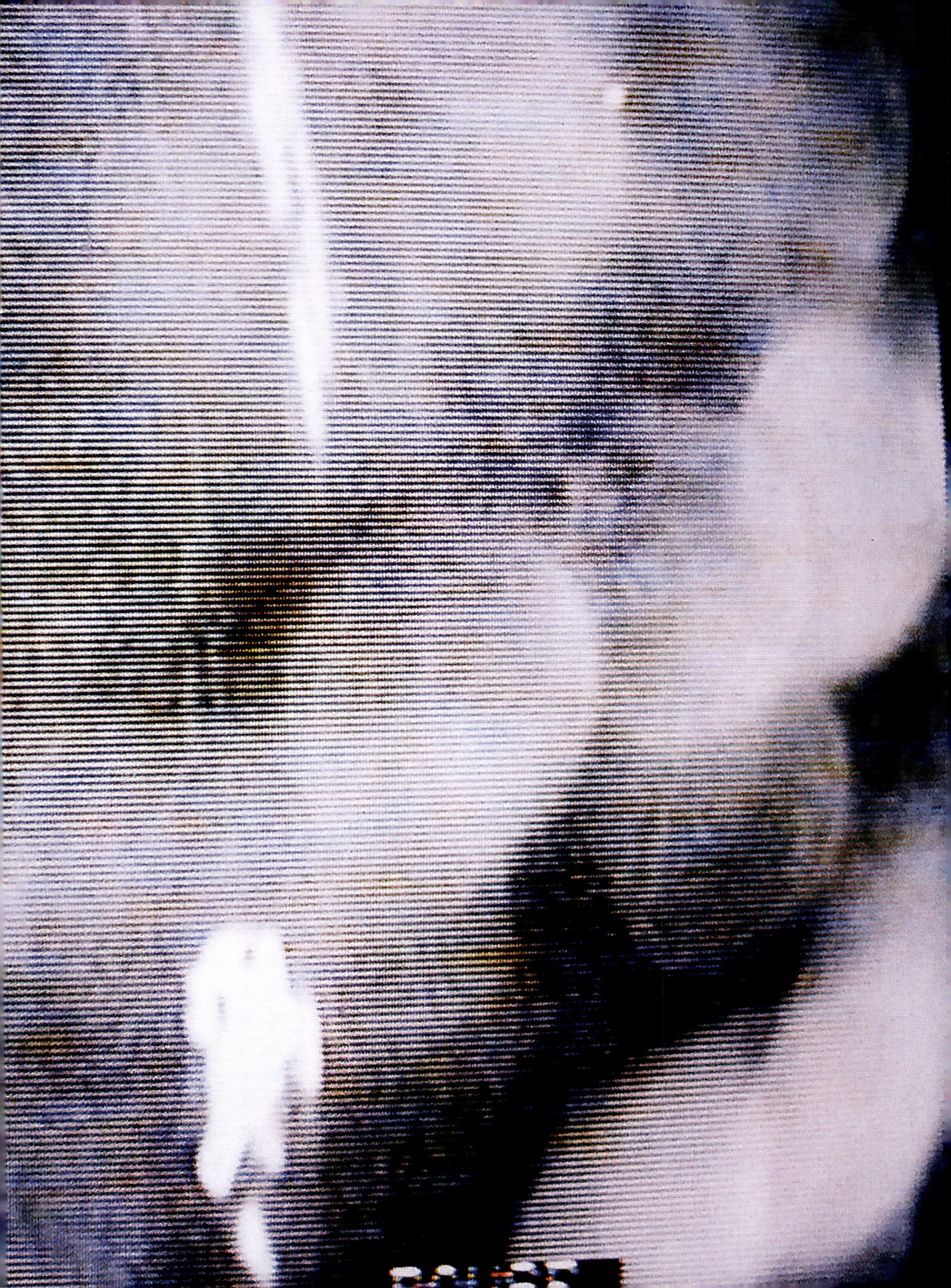

BOOK ②

Page 160 | "WoWS" | LOOKING FOR | Cam2
A | Continued | 08/04/2003 AFLYING W/ WB |
BIG | ① this Creature Looks like |
WOCO! | a beautefull Flyeg Reptile |
GTS !! | white WING too Entity |
Amazing! definitely from Empty |
LOOKING THE thing Scene PLAC 16:55:42 |
ABOUT THE No Exptw Creature THIS! |
PICTORE NOT from our Planet |
OR y'ml Zone! |
FUZZ they are gone on 1/60/ |
OR a baseball or 1/?? Less |

6:53:42

FUZZY
HERE

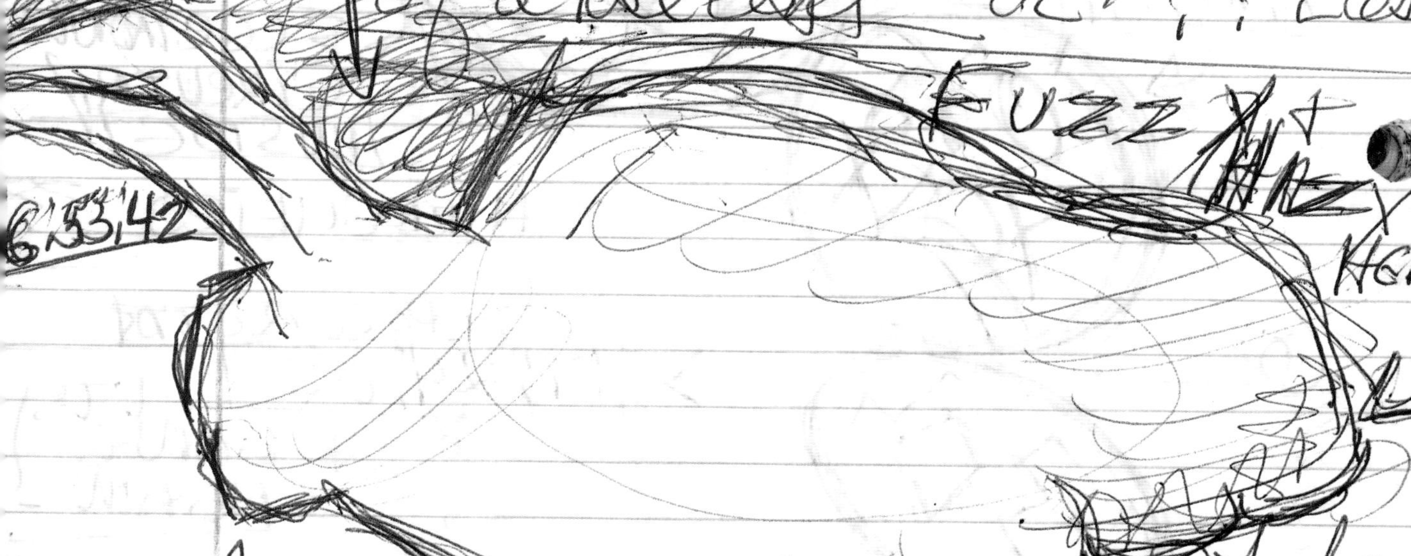

A
SOLID
White GLOWING
WINGED
Flyeg
Creature!
THIS one Looks Like OK WINGS
NO LEGS as on 153 But legs or
Extendes could be pulled inc/for
flight ! DRAWING CAN'T DO IT
JUSTICE

A has
an either
Around it
an AURA
VISIBLE
ALSO

01:11:14 04/23/2004
ET LANDED IN POOL CAM4

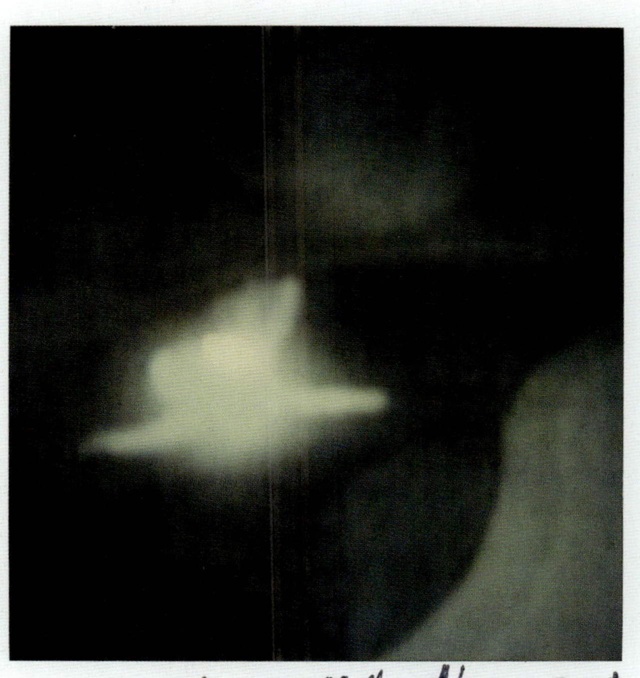

01:11:14 04/23/2004
ET IN POOL CAM4

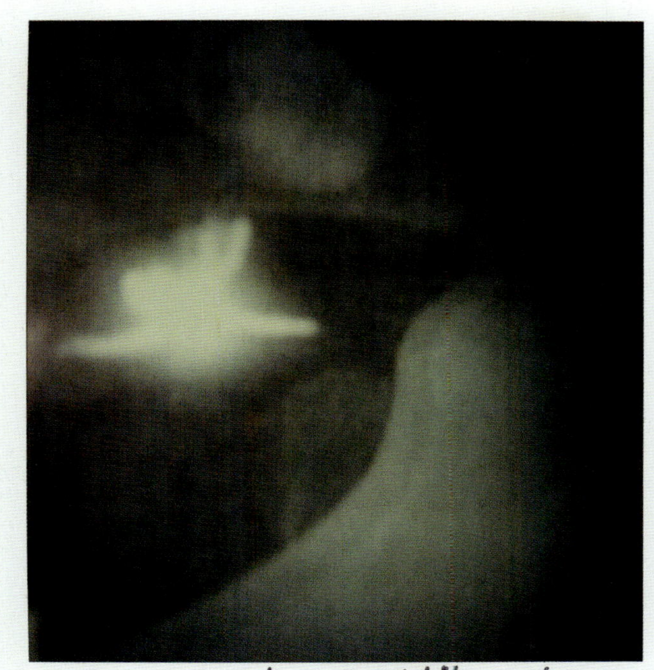

01:11:14 04/23/2004
ET-LANDED-POOL CAM4

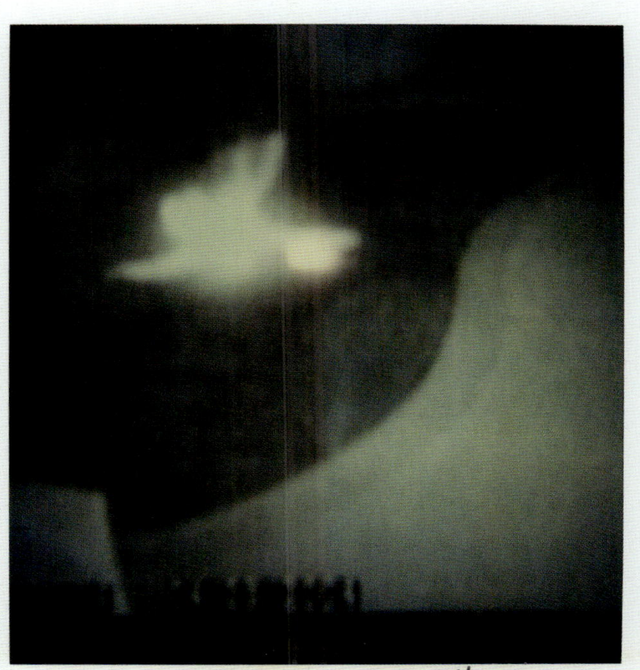

01:11:14 04/23/2004
ET IN POOL CAM4

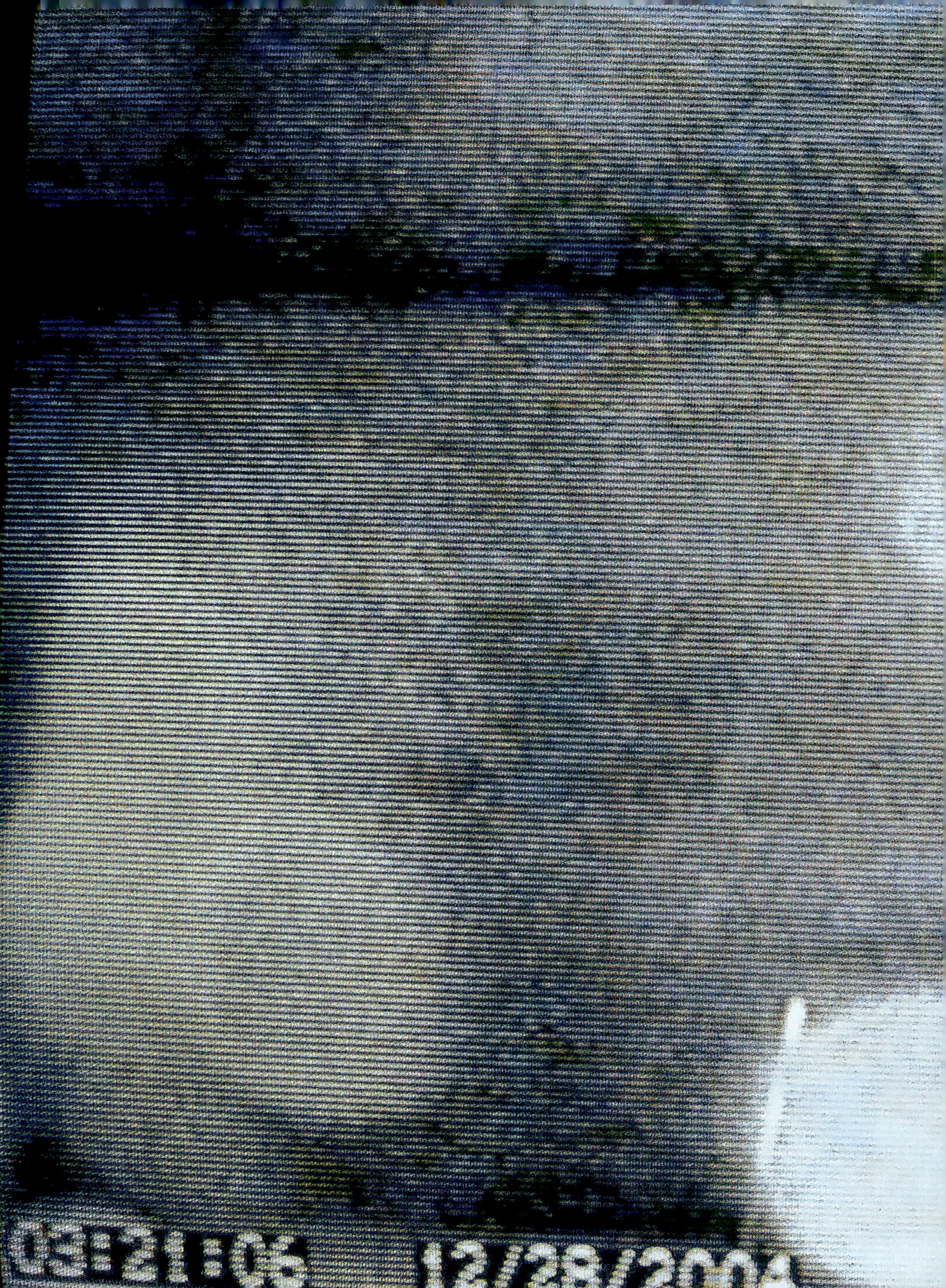

03:21:05   12/28/2002

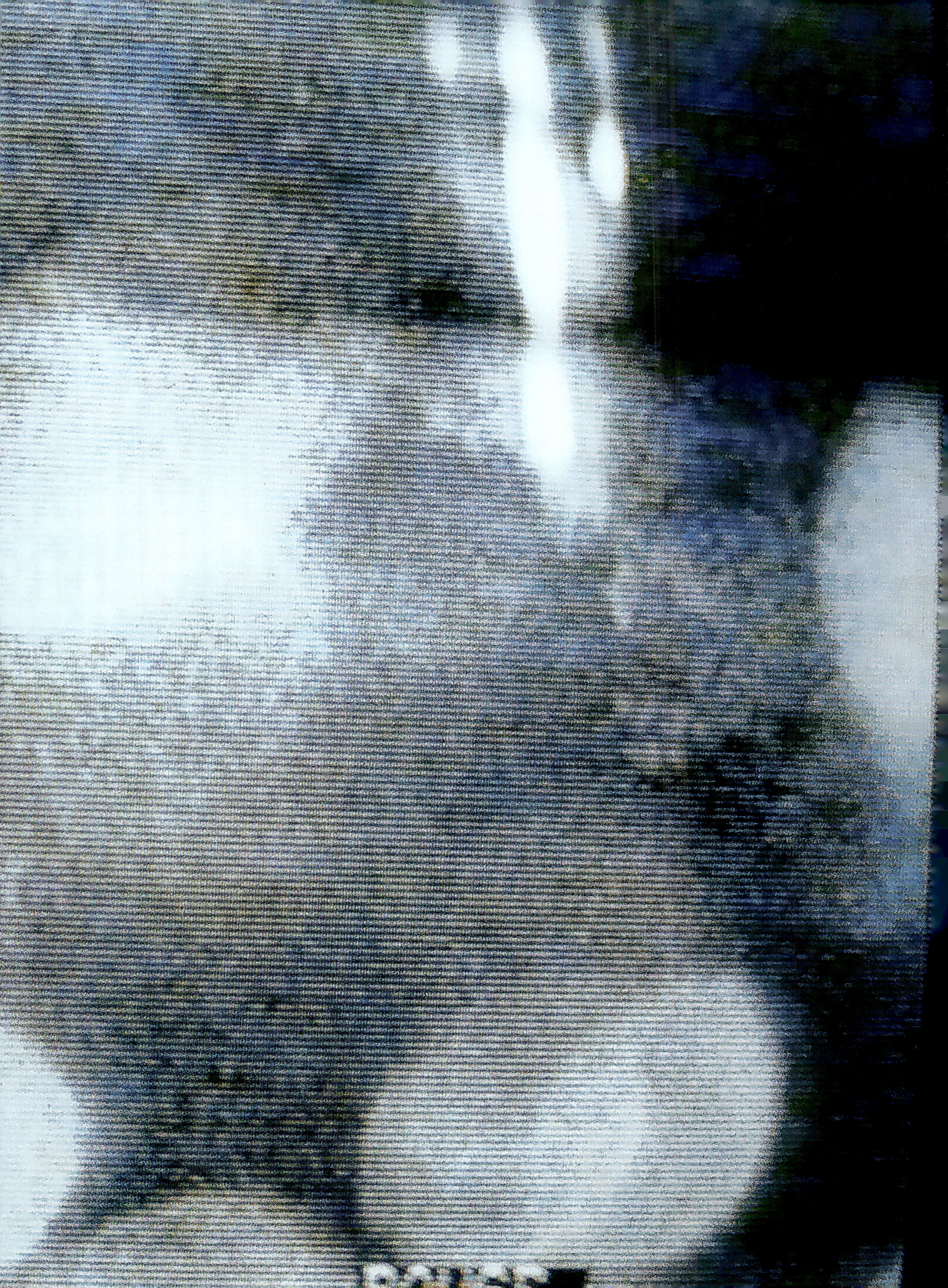

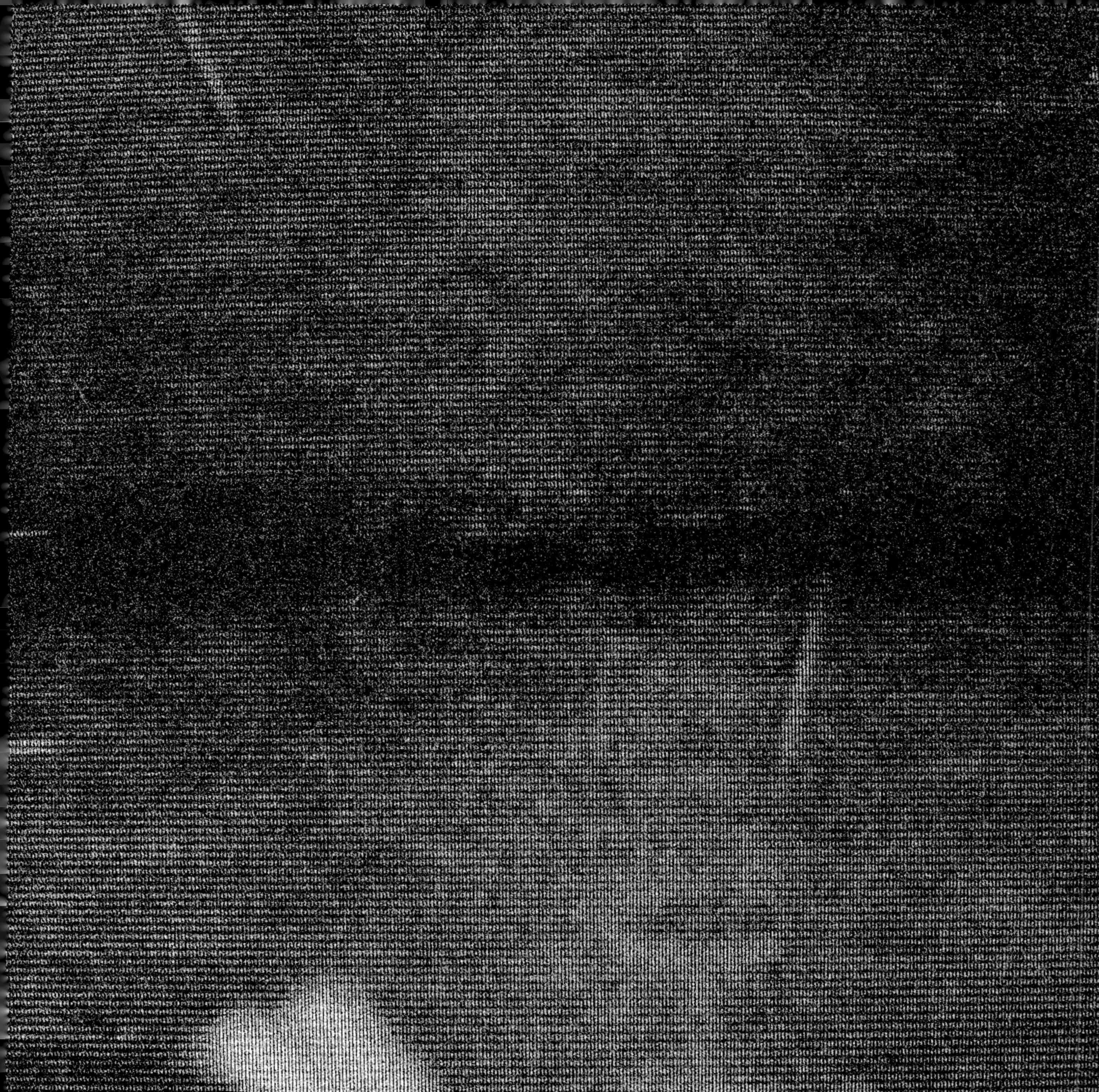

EPT

① Page 1   08/14/2003   CAM 1
① 08:19:11   LETTERS
POLOROID   ← GOLD/LOGOS
PHOTO   RED RIM &D
+ LOGOS   ← BG16G/ LETTER R   CAM 4
② 8:40 → 8:43:06
Cen Aerobat
③ 10:20:49 /TRIPLE ORB/PHOTO   CAM 1
④ 11:04:42 Same as ABOUE
B16d white
        PHOTO/Polaroid   Cam
⑤ 12:15:17
B16 Dragonfly UFO
POLOROID   & PHOTO 4' wing span
         Rainbow   Colors
⑥ 12:48:36 picture/AB16 alien   Cam 2
fluffy Dragonfly UFO
         PHOTO
        POLOROID
⑦ 13:02:28   CAM 2

PHOTO   AN ODD ONE
                                A MULTI
                                shaped ion
                                the ground

2:55 04/27/2004

PAUSE

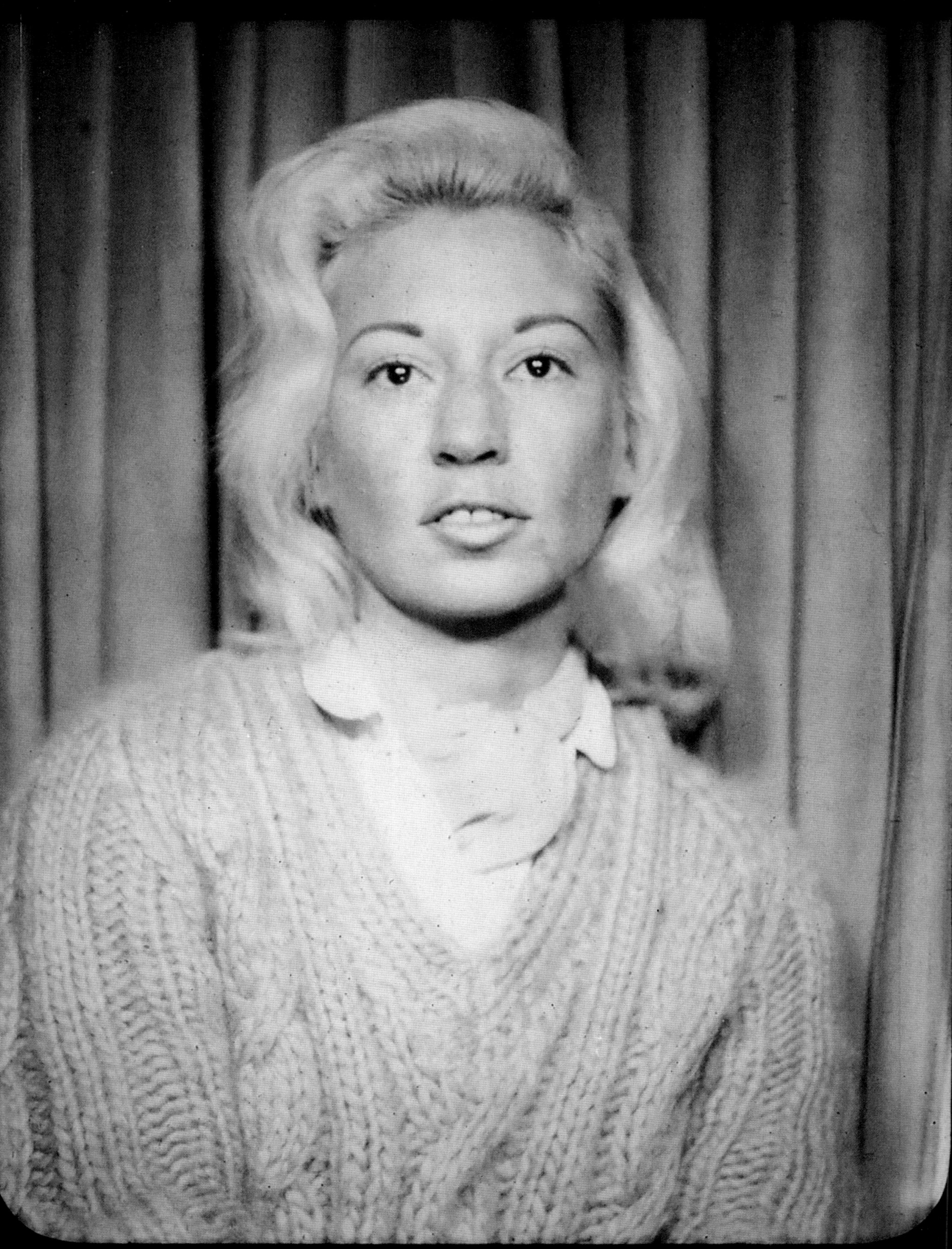

AFTERWORD BY LEN PRINCE

As we complete the delivery of files and writings by various artists in their fields I find myself with a heart full of gratitude, especially while living through a global pandemic that allows me this long break from my usual life. From the moment my dear friend Susan Archibald asked for my help sorting through her mother's photography, boxes showed up at my doorstep. I was whisked away with the jaw-dropping experience of Kali's hidden works of art. And not ten or twenty but thousands of original, unique, multi-layered thick prints piled on top of one another in suitcases, boxes, portfolios, and 83 unprocessed rolls of film along with many other goodies in a flight bag from the '60s. After many deliveries from California to my doorstep up in the North Country of New York my beautiful living room-gallery became a whirring studio of computers, scanners, hard drives, and lots of cables, now called The Kali Room.

Kali's hidden secrets were now mine to sort through. And possibly produce what Kali couldn't: a viewable body of work. I couldn't stop, as I'd never seen anything like this…and this after being married to Susan! All those years I had never been told about this work, much less had a photographer-to-photographer conversation with my mother-in-law. Family secrets run deep; I was never told of my mother's relatives inventing scientic and photographic equipment, and bringing Nikon to America in the '60s and later through Ehrenreich Photo-Optical Industries… is art in the blood? What's the chance of two separate families being so organically intrigued with the camera?

I have so many people to thank on this experience. As usual I may forget a name out of nerves but here we go. Thanks to Randy Gue, the curator of Political, Cultural, and Social Movement Collections at the Stuart A. Rose Manuscript, Archives, and Rare Book Library at Emory University in Atlanta, Georgia. Thanks to Sam Shahid, my Guru Designer and his unflawed conviction, along with his Art Director Matt Kraus…always cool and sending me in the right direction, Daniel Power of powerHouse Books…A huge thanks to Matt Tyrnauer for his brilliant and historical introduction; he really got Kali and Susan. To Brian Wallis for his brilliant essay, which evolved as Kali's work burned in his head…thank you Brian! To Alexandra Jarrell for her writing of the individual book introductions, editing, and suggestions…thanks for the big help my little sister. Thanks to Donna Ghelerter for her precise knowledge and editing of Kali's Index of works 300-plus images, and for the final polish on Brian's piece. A special call out to the woman I still hold the highest regard for in art, Fay Gold, who simply said while looking at Kali's work at my request for input "Len! It's such a shame you didn't take these photographs…they're great!" And last but never least, to my brave tour de force friend, ex-wife, and crusader for her mother Kali's sacrificial life in Art: Susan Archibald, a huge THANK YOU for bringing me along on this unexpected journey.

The experience of archiving someone else's body of work gave me perspective, balance, and a slice of where I came from culturally, which I'd never derive from staying forever in my own shadow. I also believe a journey can come without warning, showing us a new path. After 50 years of my own photography day in, day out, Kali gave me life and clarity. I wish we had talked about f-stops…

After first encountering Kali's work, I found myself searching my bookcases for Germaine Greer's 1979 *The Obstacle Race* and a decades-old photocopy of Linda Nochlin's 1971 *Artnews* article "Why Have There Been No Great Women Artists?". From today's perspective, it is hard to believe that no one had asked that simple question until the 1970s. Why were art books and museum walls filled almost exclusively with the work of only one-half of the human race?

As a woman who has spent her working life in art museums, has long held an abiding interest in photography, and is only one generation younger than Kali, looking at her work plunges me back to that moment of revelation that women artists did indeed exist—moreover, they always had. To me, Kali's story very much belongs to that moment. This is a story that I recognize and understand fully only through the lens of gender.

Historically, women artists most often either were born or married into a family of artists. Kali was neither. She was a young, divorced mother of two who decamped to California and the promise of a new life that place seemed to offer to so many in her generation. This was a tumultuous time in America, characterized by questioning assumptions, upending expectations, distrust of previous generations, endless searches for various truths, and rampant experimentation. For women there were new choices, new freedoms, and widened possibilities that were unimaginable to most of their mothers and grandmothers. What Joan Archibald chose in that moment was to become the artist Kali. To mark this transformation, she adopted an artistic persona and designed her distinctive "Kali" stamp with which to sign her works.

Choosing photography as her medium also resonates with that moment. Unlike today, photography struggled to be accepted by the art world. Like earlier generations of women, Kali found photography an easier medium to take up. No one would have noticed—or cared about—another young woman becoming a photographer. A few classes at local colleges provided Kali with the basics; she then was free to experiment. And experiment she did. Working independently and outside of an established art tradition, Kali developed her own artistic practice— an amazing amalgamation of photography and painting. She christened her creation "Artography." She sustained and expanded the mastery of her practice for several years, creating the large body of alternative photography that we now know. In the context of the early 1970s, one cannot help but be struck by the breadth of Kali's ambition and determination—and all done prior to the advent of digital photography and Photoshop.

As a woman artist, Kali's output and the rhythm of her practice was significantly impacted by her personal life in ways far different from her male counterparts. Kali's mother, Betty Yarusso, believed in her daughter and her talent. Betty supported her in myriad ways, but none more crucial than in helping raise her two children, which provided Kali with the vital creative time that women who are also mothers often have to sacrifice. Betty also campaigned to have her daughter's work recognized in the broader world. Betty was the force behind a November 1970

Camera 35 article—the only article on Kali's work to appear during her lifetime. Unsurprisingly, Kali's practice as an artist slowed during her second marriage when she again took on the responsibilities of a wife. Later as a widow, her artistic activity intensified again, and her work shifted in a new direction, giving us her late UFO pictures.

Most, although certainly not all, artistic practice thrives in the company of other artists and in the immediacy of an audience and the recognition that audience provides. Kali's was an exceedingly private, and highly personal project, almost hermetic in nature. Her work, which captures both the zeitgeist of American pop culture during her productive years and, in retrospect so clearly transcends that time, was nourished and sustained solely by her creative drive. Her intentions about who she imagined her audience was may never be known, but that does not mean that she believed that she did not have an audience. Kali is far from the first artist whose work has been discovered posthumously. Still, such discoveries are rare. There have been others, most notably Henry Darger and Vivian Maier. Most, like Kali, are artists working in the margins of the art world. Each discovery raises its set of unsettling questions, including the nature of audience and the artist's intentions. Each time we are surprised anew that such talent existed unrecognized in our midst.

Three generations of strong women are essential to this story. Kali provided the talent, persistence, vision, and sense of self—all of which and more—were requisite. Her mother, Betty, provided the granite foundation upon which her daughter rested. And Kali's daughter, Susan Archibald, understood the importance of her mother's work when she discovered the trove that she barely knew existed. Like her grandmother, Susan wanted Kali's work to be known to the world, and committed herself to finding an audience. We are that audience.

The discovery of an important artist who was almost unknown during her lifetime is unquestionably exciting. The Columbus Museum of Art is proud to have organized the first museum exhibition of Kali's work, which accompanies this publication by powerHouse Books and designed by Shahid / Kraus & Company. We have many to thank for enabling us to become part of the journey of Kali's work into the world. First and foremost, we thank Len Prince, who was the consulting curator of the exhibition in Columbus, and who we have had the privilege of working with previously. His steadfast belief and persistence that we needed to stop, look at Kali's work, and recognize Kali's unique talent made all of the difference. We also thank Kali's daughter, Susan Archibald, for welcoming Columbus into the project. The Columbus exhibition would also not have been possible without the assistance of our friends at Staley-Wise Gallery in New York. Perhaps most importantly, we extend our profound gratitude to Sally Ross Soter, whose belief in and support of the Columbus Museum of Art's photography program enables exhibitions such as this one to take place. Columbus came to photography late, and Sally's commitment to building a photography collection, establishing an active exhibition program, and endowing our Curator of Photography, has transformed our institution, and will for years to come

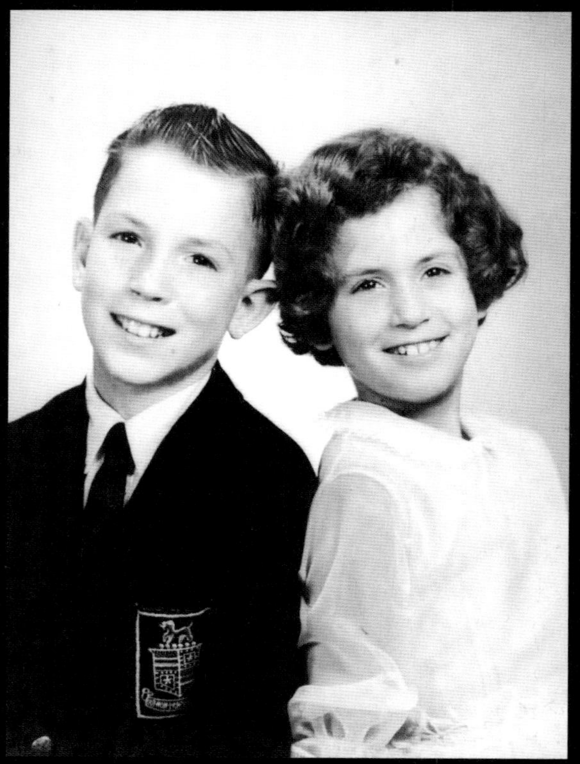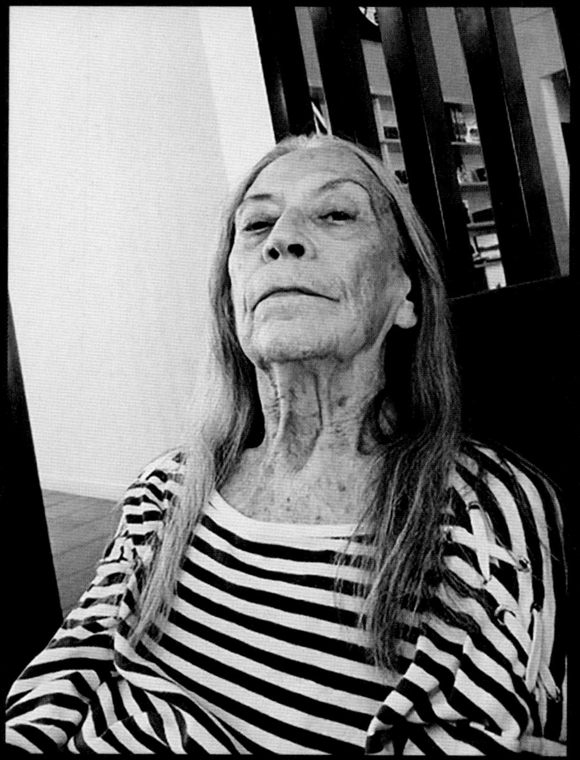

DEDICATION: GRANDMA BETTY, AND TO MY BROTHER ARCHIE

To the woman who watched over us all, while inspiring our life's dreams and independence: Grandma Betty, who looked after me throughout her life with heartfelt guidance. And most of all allowed her daughter, Kali, (my mom), to follow her heart and soul within all realms of her original creativity in art and photography, and in her zest for life. Grandmother, you never wavered in your belief, confidence, and knowledge.

Archie: My big brother, what more can I say…I'm sending the first copy of Len's book to you in heaven for Mom (Kali). Love you forever more…and after that!

IN MEMORY:

Kali (aka Joan Archibald) 1932-2019…Our very own undiscovered genius. Your hidden Artography images are bringing us joy each and every day…How and when you did all these, just simply amazes me. We hope this book is something you can show your friends up there…We still feel your strength!

—SUSAN ARCHIBALD ODDO

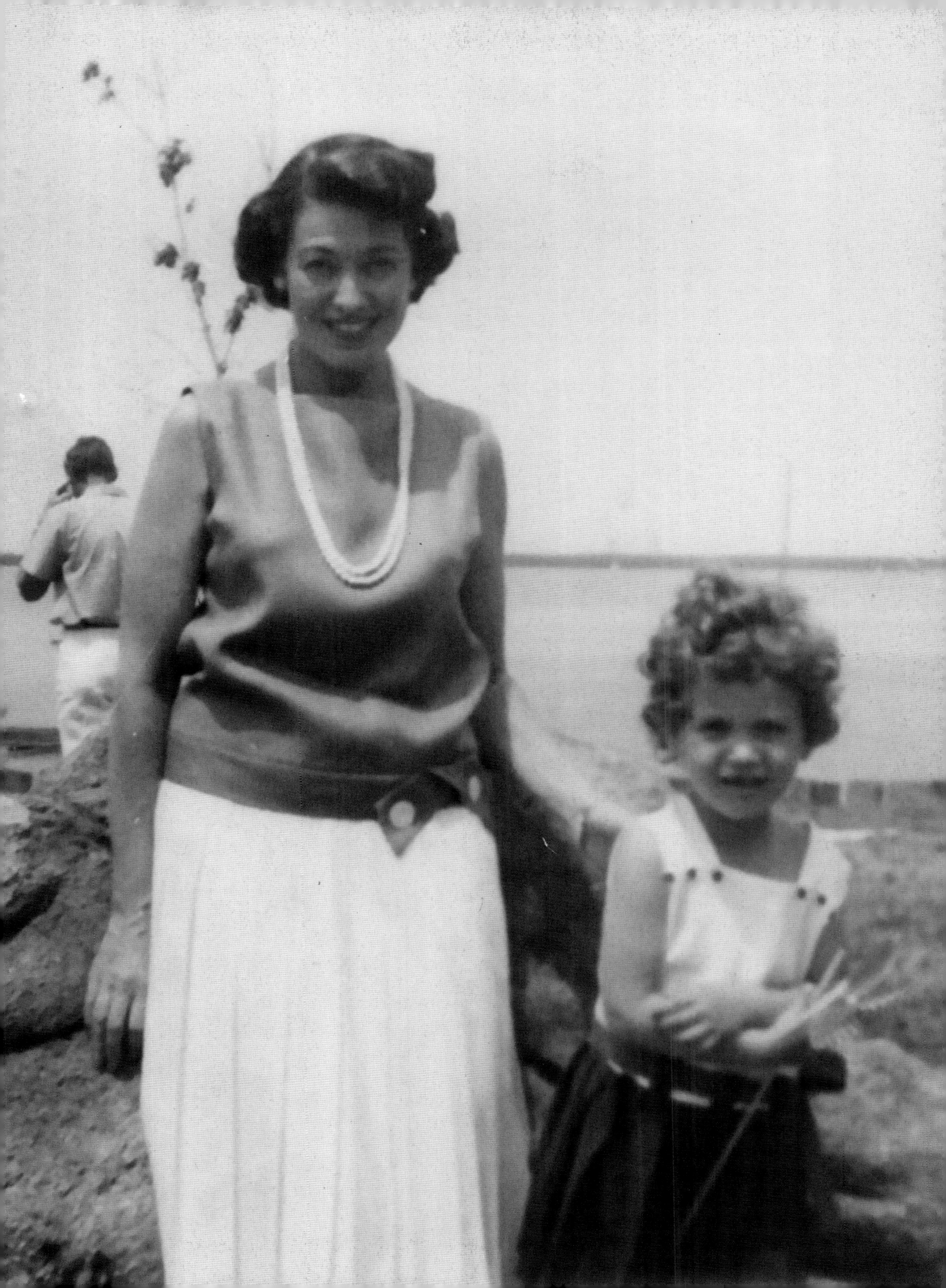

IMAGE INDEX

COVER *Kali Photo Booth Self Portrait,* Los Angeles, CA, 1964 **BACK COVER** *Blue Stripe Face,* Palm Springs, CA, 1967 **CASE COVER (BACK)** *Untitled Polaroid Collage #11,* Palm Springs, CA, 1973 **CASE COVER (FRONT)** *Untitled Polaroid Collage #13,* Palm Springs, CA, 1973 **ENDPAPERS** *Kali's Experiment Notes Page #1,* Palm Springs, CA, 1970 **PAGE 3** *Kali's Experiment Notes Page #2,* Palm Springs, CA, 1970 **PAGES 4–5** *Carousel with Poem,* Santa Monica, CA, 1968 **PAGE 6** *Joan Archibald (aka Kali),* Malibu, CA, 1962 **PAGE 8** *Su in front of family home,* Palm Springs, CA, 1964 **PAGE 8** *Palm Springs Home "renovated,"* 2019 **PAGES 10–11** *Joan, Robert, and Susan, Roslyn,* New York, NY 1960 **PAGE 13** *Camera 35* (3 images) 1970 **PAGES 14–15** *Fall Branches, Yellow,* Great Neck, NY, 1968 **PAGE 16** *Frank Sinatra Blue,* Palm Springs, CA, 1969 **PAGE 19** *Kali's Things To Do Note Pad, Angel,* 2004 **PAGES 20–21** *Kali Bikini with Pillow—Self Portraits,* Palm Springs, CA, 1968 **PAGES 22–23** *Kali's Note to Popular Photography's Head Editor,* 1970 Letter Pages #2 & #3 **PAGE 24** *Debbie and Paul, Bw/Color* (4 images), Malibu, CA, 1967 **PAGE 26** *Wild Horses,* Northern California,1968 **PAGE 27** *Bill Sells* (3 images), Palm Springs, CA, 1968 **PAGES 28–29** *Kathy in The Tower #1 & #2,* Palm Springs, CA, 1968 **PAGE 30** *Computer Match,* Palm Springs, CA, 1968 **PAGES 32–33** *Highway 1 Bridge,* Big Sur, CA, 1966 **PAGE 34** *Paul, Light My Fire,* Palm Springs, CA, 1968 **PAGE 35** *Paul, Light My Fire, B&W,* Palm Springs, CA, 1968 **PAGES 36–37** *Purple Swirl Maine Light House,* Maine, 1966 **PAGES 38–39** *NYC Construction Site,* 1966 **PAGES 40–41** *Light House with Butterflies,* Maine, 1966 **PAGE 42** *TLS Mountains,* Las Vegas, NV, 1967 **PAGE 43** *Highway Lamp Posts,* Los Angeles, CA, 1966; *Marina,* Maine, 1965; *Clock Tower NYC,* 1966 **PAGES 44–45** *Kathy, Taj Mahal,* Palm Springs, CA, 1972 **PAGE 46** *Psychedelic Mary Blue/Green,* Palm Springs, CA, 1968 **PAGE 48** *Nepenthe Dark Angel with Kali's ashes #1,* Big Sur, CA, 1967 **PAGE 49** *Brunette Model #2,* Carmel, CA, 1970 **PAGE 50** *Paul with Mosquito,* Palm Springs, CA, 1968 **PAGE 51** *Devendorf Park Hippy Model,* Carmel, CA, 1967 **PAGE 52** *Untitled Close-up #1,* Palm Springs, CA, 1967 **PAGE 53** *Untitled Close-up #2,* Palm Springs, CA, 1967 **PAGES 54–55** *Male Surfers,* Carmel, CA, 1967 **PAGE 56** *Mary Carmel,* Carmel, CA, 1968 **PAGE 57** *Dylan, Galaxy Violet,* Palm Springs, CA, 1968 **PAGE 59** *Untitled Orange Angel,* Palm Springs, CA, 1968 **PAGE 60** *Red Su, Astrology Series Virgo,* Palm Springs, CA, 1970's **PAGE 61** *Blue Aquarius 83,* Palm Springs, CA, 1970s; *Pink Gemini 84,* Palm Springs, CA, 1970s; *Multi Su Virgo 85,* Palm Springs, CA, 1970s; *Margie Yellow Scorpio 86,* Palm Springs, CA, 1970s; *Peach Cindy Libra 87,* Palm Springs, CA, 1970s; *Purple Su Virgo 88,* Palm Springs, CA, 1970's; *Blue Mary Capricorn 89,* Palm Springs, CA, 1970s; *Pink Susan Sagittarius 90,* Palm Springs, CA, 1970s **PAGE 62** *Madonna and Child by Lippi,* Great Master Series, Palm Springs, CA, 1972 **PAGE 63** *Primavera by Botticelli, Red-Green,* Palm Springs, CA, 1971 **PAGE 64** *Amber Self Portrait with Kali Cat,* Palm Springs, CA, 1968 **PAGE 66** *Close-up Sleeping Beauty, Blue,* Palm Springs, CA, 1968 **PAGE 67** *Close-up Sleeping Beauty, Flame,* Palm Springs, CA, 1968 **PAGE 68** *Face Puppet,* Palm Springs, CA, 1969 **PAGE 69** *Margie with Space Bubbles,* Palm Springs, CA, 1968 **PAGE 70** *Mona Lisa 2nd Eye,* Palm Springs, CA, 1968 **PAGE 71** *Flipped Botticelli,* Palm Springs, CA, 1971 **PAGE 73** *Margie 1-Eye,* Palm Springs, CA, 1969 **PAGE 74** *Psychedelic Kitty-Orange,* Palm Springs, CA, 1967 **PAGE 75** *Pink Dylan Smokin,* Palm Springs, CA, 1968 **PAGES 76-77** *Nepenth Cat,* Big Sur, CA, 1968-9 **PAGE 78** *Mary-Multi Plaid,* Palm Springs, CA, 1968 **PAGE 81** *Henna Mask,* Palm Springs, CA, 1968 **PAGE 82** *Colorful Paul-Peach,* Palm Springs, CA, 1968 **PAGE 83** *Crystal Face,* Palm Springs, CA, 1968 **PAGE 84** *Masks,* Palm Springs, CA, 1970 **PAGE 85** *Madonna with Child by Lippi,* Great Masters Series, Palm Springs, CA, 1971 **PAGE 86** *Impish Paul,* Palm Springs, CA, 1968 **PAGE 87** *Woven Su,* Palm Springs, CA, 1968 **PAGE 88** *Margie's Eyes,* Palm Springs, CA, 1968 **PAGE 89** *Botticelli in Pink Lace,* Palm Springs, CA, 1971 **PAGE 90** *Sleeping Beauty, Red,* Palm Springs, CA, 1968 **PAGE 91** *Sleeping Beauty, Black & White,* Palm Springs, CA, 1968 **PAGES 92–93** *The Birth Of Venus, Blue, Botticelli,* Great Masters Series, Palm Springs, CA, 1970 **PAGE 94** *Tahoe Blue,* Lake Tahoe, CA, 1970 **PAGE 95** *Young Boy Construction,* Palm Springs, CA, 1968 **PAGE 96** *Green Globe Architecture,* Palm Springs, CA, 1970 **PAGE 97** *Black & White Globe Architecture,* Palm Springs, CA, 1970 **PAGE 99** *Margie under Flowers,* Palm Springs, CA, 1968 **PAGE 100** *Mona 3 Eyes,* Palm Springs, CA, 1967 **PAGE 101** *Young Girl,* Palm Springs, CA, 1966 **PAGE 102** *Debbie with Kali Cat-Green #1,* Palm Springs, CA, 1969 **PAGE 103** *Debbie with Kali Cat, Pink #2,* Palm Springs, CA,1969 **PAGES 104–105** *Lone Cypress,* Carmel, CA, 1967 **PAGES 106–107** *T.L.S. Seagull,* Carmel, CA, 1970 **PAGE 108** *Susan + Lace,* Palm Springs, CA, 1967 **PAGE 109** *Paul with Roses,* Palm Springs, CA, 1970

PAGE 110 *Blonde Wig*, Palm Springs, CA, 1966 **PAGE 111** *Adam and Eve*, Palm Springs, CA, 1969 **PAGES 112–113** *Mary and Josh, AMERICA*, Indo, CA, 1969 **PAGE 114** *Paul in Bikini #1*, Palm Springs, CA, 1968 **PAGE 115** *Rose Hat #2*, Palm Springs, CA, 1966 **PAGE 116** *Unlocked Eyes, Green*, Palm Springs, CA, 1967 **PAGE 117** *Unlocked Eyes, Pink*, Palm Springs, CA, 1967 **PAGE 118** *Red Windows*, New York C ty, NY, 1970 **PAGE 119** *Christopher*, Los Angeles, CA, 1968 **PAGES 120–121** *Mini Bus, L.A. Highway*, Los Angeles, CA, 1970 **PAGES 122–123** *Face under The Bridge, Botticelli*, Big Sur, CA, 1970 **PAGE 124** *Red Debbie with Kali Cat*, Palm Springs, CA, 1968 **PAGE 125** *Paul with Yellow Butterfly*, Palm Springs, CA, 1968 **PAGE 126** *Cindy Windowpane*, Palm Springs, CA, 1970 **PAGE 127** *Hope*, Pacific Palisades, CA, 2005 **PAGE 128** *Geometric Smile*, Malibu, CA, 1968 **PAGE 129** *Rose Marie Swirl*, Palm Springs, CA, 1966 **PAGE 130** *Beach Boy #1 bw*, Carmel, CA, 1971 **PAGE 131** *Beach Boy #2 Rainbow*, Carmel, CA, 1971 **PAGE 133** *Blue/Green Stripe Face*, Palm Springs, CA, 1968 **POLAROIDS PAGE 142** *#1 Untitled Artography Polaroid Collage*, Palm Springs, CA, 1973 **PAGE 145** *Kathy Process*, Palm Springs, CA, 1968 **PAGE 146** *Mary U.S.A.*, Pa m Springs, CA, 1970 **PAGE 147** *Untitled Face*, Palm Springs, CA, 1970 **PAGE 148** *Half Face 3*, Palm Springs, CA, 1969 **PAGE 149** *Cindy Pattern Face*, Palm Springs, CA, 1970 **PAGE 150** *Mary Mary*, Palm Springs, CA, 1968 **PAGE 151** *Ruby Eyes*, Palm Springs, CA, 1968 **PAGE 152** *Little Budha*, Palm Springs, CA, 1967 **PAGE 153** *Kathy #3*, Palm Springs, CA, 1968 **PAGE 154** *Cindy Painted*, Palm Springs, CA, 1970 **PAGE 155** *T.L.S. Lights*, Palm Springs, CA, 1970 **PAGE 156** *Untitled Artography Collage #4, KALI*, Palm Springs, CA, 1973 **PAGE 157** *Untitled Artography Collaage #5, Kali*, Palm Springs, CA, 1973 **PAGE 158** *Mary #3*, Palm Springs, CA, 1968 **PAGE 159** *Blue Cypress*, Palm Springs, CA, 1969 **PAGE 160** *Half Face #1*, Palm Springs, CA, 1969 **PAGE 161** *Half Face #2*, Palm Springs, CA, 1969 **PAGE 162** *Fabric Mary*, Palm Springs, CA, 1968; **PAGE 163** *Moody Mary*, Palm Springs, CA, 1969 **PAGE 164** *T.L.S. Mary #7*, Palm Springs, CA, 1970 **PAGE 165** *Painted Mary #5*, Palm Springs, CA, 1970 **PAGE 167** *Split Cindy*, Palm Springs, CA, 1970 **PAGE 168** *Lips and Texture*, Palm Springs, CA, 1969 **PAGE 169** *Refracted Face*, Palm Springs, CA, 1969 **PAGE 170** *Red Multi Mary*, Palm Springs, CA, 1970 **PAGE 171** *Untitled Artography Collage #8*, Palm Springs, CA, 1973 **PAGE 172** *Margie & Mary*, Palm Springs, CA, 1969 **PAGE 173** *Pedals*, Palm Springs, CA, 1969 **PAGE 174** *Blue Bikini*, Malibu, CA, 1969 **PAGE 175** *Daisy Hair*, Malibu, CA, 1969 **PAGE 176** *Bikini Cypress*, Palm Springs, CA, 1970 **PAGE 177** *Barbed Wire*, Palm Springs, CA, 1970 **PAGE 178** *Pop Art Mary #1*, Palm Springs, CA, 1970 **PAGE 179** *Pop Art Mary #2*, Palm Springs, CA, 1970 **PAGE 180** *Untitled Artography Collage #18*, Palm Springs, CA, 1973 **PAGE 181** *Butterfly's Imagination*, Palm Springs, CA, 1970 **PAGE 182** *Blue Dreams*, Palm Springs, CA, 1969 **PAGE 183** *T.L.S. Blue Kathy*, Palm Springs, CA, 1969 **PAGE 184** *Cindy Pose*, Palm Spr ngs, CA, 1970 **PAGE 185** *Cindy Keyhole*, Palm Springs, CA, 1970 **PAGE 187** *SiFi Cindy*, Palm Springs, CA, 1970 **PAGE 188** *Disco Cindy*, Palm Springs, CA, 1970 **PAGE 189** *Untitled Artography Collage #11*, Palm Springs, CA, 1973 **OUTER SPACE PAGE 190** *Pool Orbs #1*, Pacific Palisades, CA, 2004; *Pool Orbs #2*, Pacific Palisades, CA, 2004 **PAGES 192–193** *Kali Being Taken*, Pacific Palisades, CA, 2004 **PAGES 194–195** *Untitled Figure #1*, Pacific Palisades, CA, 2004 **PAGE 196** *Note Book #2 WOWS*, Pacific Palisades, CA, 08/02/2003 **PAGE 197** *UFO and Orb #1*, Pacific Palisades, CA, 08/02/2003; *Three Rings Together #2*, Pacific Palisades, CA, 08/02/2003; *UFO and Orb #3* Pacific Palisades, CA, 08/02/2003; *UFO and Orb #4*, Pacific Palisades, CA, 08/02/2003 **PAGES 198–199** *Untitled Figure #2*, Pacific Palisaces, CA, 2004 **PAGES 200–201** *A WOW 10 Foot Globe*, Pacific Palisades, CA, 2003 **PAGE 203** *Butterfly Entity over the fountain*, 15 18 39, Pacific Palisades, CA, 2003 **PAGE 204** *Note Book #2 EPI* 08/23/2003, Pacific Palisades, CA, 2003 **PAGE 205** *Orby Has A Visitor*, Pacific Palisades, CA, 2003; *Orby Is Still Here*, Pacific Palisades, CA, 2003 **PAGES 206–207** *Purple Orbs with Figure*, Pacific Palisades, CA, 2004 **PAGE 208** *Note Book #2 Looking For WOWS*, Pacific Palisades, CA, 2003 **PAGE 209** *#1 E.T. Landed In Pool*, Pacific Palisades, CA, 2004; *#2 E.T. In Pool*, Pacific Palisades, CA, 2004; *#3 E.T. Landed In Pool*, Pacific Palisades, CA, 2004; *#4 E.T. In Pool*, Pacific Palisades, CA, 2004 **PAGES 210–211** *Untitled Orbs and Figure*, Pacific Palisades, CA, 12/28/2004 **PAGE 212** *EPI Dragon Fly UFO*, Pacific Palisades, CA, 08/14/2003 **PAGE 213** *Note Book #2 Page 11*, Pacific Palisades, CA, 08/14/2003 **PAGES 214–215** *The Entity*, Pacific Palisades, CA, 04/27/2004 **PAGE 220** Robert (Archie) Archibald with Susan Archibald, 1964; Kali in Los Angeles, CA, 2018 **PAGE 221** Grancma Betty Yarusso, Long Island, NY, Late 50's **PAGES 226–227** Kali's Experiment's, Manual Pages 3 and 4. Palm Springs, CA, 1966.

Kali: Artography

Artwork © 2022 Len Prince
Introduction © 2022 Matt Tyrnauer
Essay © 2022 Brian Wallis
Prefaces © 2022 Alexandra Jarrell
Afterscript © 2022 Nannette Maciejunes

Published in the United States by powerHouse Books,
a division of powerHouse Cultural Entertainment, Inc.
32 Adams Street, Brooklyn, NY 11201

website: www.powerHouseBooks.com

First edition, 2022

Library of Congress Control Number: 2022935370

ISBN 978-1-64823-021-9

Designed by Sam Shahid and Matthew Kraus, Shahid / Kraus & Company

Printing and binding by GPS / Oddi

10 9 8 7 6 5 4 3 2 1

Printed in Slovenia

Now, you can put the room lights on and operate the developing, as usual. Pull the white tab, the green tab, and the film out. Turn on the 60 second timer (Yes, it even has one), and presto -- one minute later -- a _color print_ from a _slide_, with no muss, no fuss, no watery chemicals, filters, or special color head enlarger.

Well, as you can see, my first print was a very faint ghost image, but by now, I understood that in doing **Polaroid**, too light a print mean't **too much time** or light, while too dark a print, not enough. So I decided to try filters _to cut down on light_.

Experiment 2. F8 - 2 sec. exposure, Unicolor red filter, dev. 60 sec. (I tried the Unicolor because they are easy to use with a Bessler enlarger. - Result--- better--I had much more hope, but still too light!

Experiment 3. F 16 - ½ sec. Unicolor green - dev. 1 minute. Here I got some better results.

Experiment 4. F16 - ½ sec. (yellow and orange gels for filters) dev. 1½ min. Result - Image still too faint.

Experiment 5. F16 - dark purple gel - ½ sec. Image getting better. dev. 1½ min.

Experiment 6. F16 - dark purple, plus a red gel. dev. 1½ min. Image quite good.

Experiment 7. F16 - ½ sec. Dark blue filter, dev. 2 min.--Best results so far.

Nxperiment 8. F16 - ½ sec. - (multi-filter) dev. 2 min. Here, I used a home made multi filter, with not good results, but see _No. 14._

Experiment 9. I tried my Cromega Color-head enlarger this time, at exp. F 16 - 2 sec. dialed in 60 magenta and 50 yellow, developed 1½ min. for an interesting color variation.

Experiment 10. F16 - 1 sec., dev. 1 min., _no filter_. Result-- A color print from a color slide, done in approximately 1 min. 1 sec1, with a minimum of effort. It was badly cropped, and too light, but I was quite pleased with the convenience and speed of the process. Having done color printing before, and knowing the work and time consuming elements involved, this was quite a break through for me. And for me, the experiment proved to be a success. I went on to perfect this technique, plus shooting the slides from projection, but more about this later!

Experiment 11. F22 - ½ sec. Dev. 1 min. 20 sec. As you can see, better color saturation, but could be better.